The Knight, the Cross, and the Song

THE MIDDLE AGES SERIES

RUTH MAZO KARRAS, *SERIES EDITOR*
EDWARD PETERS, *FOUNDING EDITOR*

A complete list of books in the series is available from the publisher.

The Knight, the Cross, and the Song

CRUSADE PROPAGANDA AND
CHIVALRIC LITERATURE, 1100–1400

Stefan Vander Elst

PENN

UNIVERSITY OF PENNSYLVANIA PRESS *Philadelphia*

THIS BOOK IS MADE POSSIBLE BY A COLLABORATIVE GRANT
FROM THE ANDREW W. MELLON FOUNDATION.

Published by
University of Pennsylvania Press
Philadelphia, Pennsylvania 19104-4112
www.upenn.edu/pennpress

Printed in the United States of America
on acid-free paper

10 9 8 7 6 5 4 3 2 1

A catalogue record for this book is available from the
Library of Congress.

ISBN 978-0-8122-4896-8

For Cynthia and Leo

CONTENTS

BB   Cook, Robert Francis, ed. *Le Bâtard de Bouillon: Chanson de geste.* Geneva: Librairie Droz, 1972. Translation mine.

BS   Boca, Louis N., ed. *Li Romans de Bauduin de Sebourc, IIIe roy de Jhérusalem: Poème du XIVe siècle publié pour la première fois d'après les manuscrits de la Bibliothèque Nationale.* 2 vols. Valenciennes: B. Henry, 1841. Translation mine.

C   Myers, Geoffrey M., ed. *The Old French Crusade Cycle. Vol. 5, Les Chétifs.* University: University of Alabama Press, 1981. Translation mine.

CA   Nelson, Jan A., ed. *The Old French Crusade Cycle. Vol. 4, La Chanson d'Antioche.* Tuscaloosa: University of Alabama Press, 2003. Translation taken from Susan B. Edgington and Carol Sweetenham, trans. and eds. *The Chanson d'Antioche: An Old French Account of the First Crusade.* Farnham: Ashgate, 2011.

CCGB   Hippeau, C., ed. *La Chanson du Chevalier au Cygne et de Godefroid de Bouillon.* Paris: A. Aubry, 1874–1877.

CJ   Thorp, Nigel R., ed. *The Old French Crusade Cycle. Vol. 6, La Chanson de Jérusalem.* Tuscaloosa: University of Alabama Press, 1992. Translation mine.

CR   Bédier, Joseph, ed. *La Chanson de Roland.* Paris: L'édition d'Art H. Piazza, 1960. Translation taken from Glyn S. Burgess, trans. and ed. *The Song of Roland.* London: Penguin, 1990.

CTP   Peter of Duisburg. *Chronica Terre Prussie.* In *Scriptores rerum Prussicarum: Die Geschichtsquellen der preussischen*

Vorzeit bis zum Untergange der Ordensherrschaft, ed. Theodor Hirsch, Max Töppen, and Ernst Strehlke, 1:21–219. Leipzig: S. Hirzel, 1861. Translation mine.

GDC   Gautier de Tournay. *L'histoire de Gille de Chyn by Gautier de Tournay*. Ed. Edwin B. Place. New York: AMS Press, 1970. Translation mine.

GF   Hill, Rosalind, trans. and ed. *Gesta Francorum et aliorum Hierosolimitanorum*. Edinburgh: Thomas Nelson and Sons, 1962.

HFC   Robert of Reims. *Robert the Monk's History of the First Crusade: Historia Iherosolimitana*. Trans. and ed. Carol Sweetenham. Aldershot: Ashgate, 2005.

HI   Robert of Reims. *The Historia Iherosolimitana of Robert the Monk*. Ed. D. Kempf and M. G. Bull. Woodbridge: Boydell Press, 2013.

KVP   Nicolaus von Jeroschin. *Di Krônike von Prûzinlant*. In *Scriptores rerum Prussicarum: Die Geschichtsquellen der preussischen Vorzeit bis zum Untergange der Ordensherrschaft*, ed. Theodor Hirsch, Max Töppen, and Ernst Strehlke, 1:303–624. Leipzig: S. Hirzel, 1861. Unless otherwise stated, translation taken from Nicolaus von Jeroschin. *The Chronicle of Prussia by Nicolaus von Jeroschin: A History of the Teutonic Knights in Prussia, 1190–1331*. Trans. and ed. Mary Fischer. Farnham: Ashgate, 2010.

PA   Guillaume de Machaut. *La Prise d'Alixandre*. Trans. and ed. R. Barton Palmer. New York: Routledge, 2002.

S   *Saladin.*

Throughout this book, I have Anglicized geographical cognomina, except where the original is commonly used in historical and literary criticism. I will therefore refer to, for example, Robert of Reims and Graindor of Douai, but to Chrétien de Troyes and Guillaume de Machaut.

The Knight, the Cross, and the Song

Introduction

Toward the end of the fourteenth century, the English polemicist John Gower turned his attention to the Crusade, which was approaching its three-hundredth anniversary. Although he was not altogether opposed to the holy war,[1] Gower argued that in his day the practice of crusading had fallen into disrepute because its supporters and participants no longer had the right motivations. The prelates who urged their flock to take the cross, he said, often merely sought to further their own worldly goals.[2] Furthermore, those who took up arms against the unbeliever were rarely driven by noble aspirations. In the *Mirour de l'Omme* of ca. 1376–1379, Gower enumerated the reasons for which his contemporaries set out on Crusade, two of which he found especially reprehensible:

> The first is (so to speak) pride in one's own prowess—"I will go in order to win praise." Or also, "It is for my beloved, so that I may have her affection—for this I will work." . . . If you will work in pride for worldly vainglory, whereby you may be superior to the others, then you must give your garments and your wealth to the heralds, so that they may proclaim with great clamor your valor and largess. . . . On the other hand, if it be that you go over the sea because of a woman of whom your heart is enamored, hoping that on your return the girl or lady for whom you have labored may deign to have pity on you, then you are lacking the right medicine.[3]

Rather than to serve God, which alone made Crusade worthwhile by Gower's standards, his contemporaries were fighting out of a desire for worldly renown or to win the favor of women. Although Gower may not have liked it, the first of these motivations is perhaps not surprising. He specifically talks about the chivalric class, the knights who for many years had carried most of the burden of crusading, and as early as the eleventh century chivalry had found common ground between the desire to achieve glory through deeds of prowess and the wish to serve God.[4] The Crusaders of Gower's time certainly were not the first to set out hoping to save their souls and win renown in the process, or vice versa. The second of Gower's concerns, however, was less evident in military history. To brave faraway dangers to win the love of a lady demonstrates another kind of idealism, one whereby service to God is complemented or even replaced by the service to women; it is to be expected from the heroes of chivalric romance—a Lancelot or a Tristan—but not of those risking life, limb, and fortune to fight the pagan on the frontiers of Christendom. If we believe Gower, then some of the Crusaders of the later Middle Ages were guided by motives reminiscent of imaginative literature.[5]

An important body of Crusade scholarship has examined what motivated those who first left to fight for the cross. Although some have proposed socioeconomic and political motivations,[6] more recent work has highlighted the role of lay piety in the decision to participate in Crusade.[7] Scholars such as Jonathan Riley-Smith and Marcus Bull have argued that individual devotion, often grounded in local religious practice, was what propelled those who set out for the frontiers of Christianity.[8] Turning from the motivations of individual participants to the arguments used to convince them to take the cross, Bull has also emphasized the preeminence of piety in the call to Crusade. He has claimed that, although some Crusaders may also have been motivated by other factors, such as patriotic pride, the desire for personal glory, and family honor, these issues were never part of the Crusade appeal itself: "Patriotic and militaristic enthusiasms might have influenced the way in which an arms-bearer interpreted the crusade appeal: they cannot adequately explain why he should have been thinking about it in the first place. At the heart of the crusade message lay an appeal to piety."[9] Although individual piety undoubtedly played an important role, the critical preoccupation with religious motivations has obscured crucial aspects of Crusade propaganda, which exhibits far more breadth and complexity. This book examines how, from the very beginning of the Crusade in the last years of the eleventh century, historiographical works that propagated the holy war appropriated the formal and thematic characteristics of chivalric literary genres to appeal specifically to aristocratic interests that ranged *beyond* religious devotion. These genres—the chanson de geste and chivalric romance—were popular with the fighting class that was most often called upon to participate in the Crusade, and throughout their history they served to bring issues important to this class into public consciousness. By using the commonplaces of chivalric literature to shape their writings, the lay and clerical Crusade propagandists discussed in this book actively sought to associate the holy war with other, more secular matters to which arms bearers were drawn—from the loyalty and mutual obligation between lord and vassal, to family honor, the thirst for adventure, and the desire for women—and to invoke these as parallel or complementary motivations for participating in the Crusade. As the following chapters explore, exactly how they utilized the characteristics of chivalric literature depended on the religious, sociopolitical, and military concerns they addressed with their works, whether the precarious position of the Christian principalities in the Levant, the ambitions of powerful men, or the need for recruits in an era of Christian defeat and disillusionment.

Ever since Louis Bréhier wrote, more than a century ago, that "dans la Chanson de Roland . . . apparaît l'idée de la guerre sainte contre l'Islam,"[10] scholars have argued that chivalric literature could propagate interreligious conflict in the Middle Ages. As Simon Lloyd says when speaking of thirteenth- and early fourteenth-century knighthood: "A significant proportion of the literature composed for their entertainment was concerned with the deeds of knights confronting the infidel. The struggle lay at the heart of the Charlemagne cycle and provided the crucial focus of the *chansons de croisade* and compositions which celebrated later crusading heroes such as Richard I. Arthurian romance held up the ideal in somewhat different fashion, but works such as *Perlesvaus* and the *Queste del Saint Graal* served equally to instil the notion that the knight should wield his sword in a sacred cause."[11] Chansons de geste and romances could therefore serve as "edificatory tales, with a strong exemplary content."[12] As this book will show, however, the import of the chansons de geste and chivalric romances for medieval Crusade propaganda extended far beyond the salubrious messages contained within the texts themselves. In fact, from the very beginning of the Crusade, both lay and clerical authors imported the formal and thematic characteristics of chivalric literature into—generically often very different—historiographical writings in order to motivate their audience to participate in the Crusade. Furthermore, in line with the recent critical focus on piety in Crusade motivation, most of those who have investigated the role of chansons and romances as Crusade propaganda have argued that they served to incite especially religious sentiments.[13] In contrast, this book examines how Crusade propaganda utilized aspects of the chanson de geste and chivalric romance to appeal to specifically secular motivations to take the cross; accordingly, it will show not only that chivalric literature was used far more widely in Crusade propaganda than has been assumed but also that it served very different purposes.

Crusade propaganda—the formal and informal ways used to further the cause of the holy war and to convince fighting men to risk all on the far reaches of Christianity—came in many forms, from papal encyclical and clerical sermon to lay narrative and song, and much of this has been the subject of study in recent years.[14] However, historiographical writings on the Crusade that functioned as exhortatory constructs have on the whole received less scholarly attention. This is unwarranted; as Gabrielle Spiegel has observed, medieval historiographical writings provide rich soil for the study of techniques of exhortation and propaganda: "Historiography, as the medieval genre par excellence devoted to a 'realistic' representation of the social and political world, is at the same time a genre thoroughly saturated with ideological goals. Especially in the Middle Ages, historical writing, precisely to the degree that it claimed to be free of imaginative elaboration, served as a vehicle of ideological elaboration."[15] The ensuing chapters discuss a broad range of historiographical writings, from narrative history to aristocratic biography, chronicle, and what is usually referred to as "popular history"; these date from the twelfth century to the fourteenth, and were written in Latin and the vernacular, by both clergymen and laymen, in places ranging from the Near East to northern France to the Baltic. While they exhibit great variety, the works analyzed in this book are tied together by several factors. First, they all purport to narrate the history of the Crusade or the deeds of individual Crusaders;[16] although some, notably the works of the First and Second Old French Crusade Cycles, are very imaginative, even these were considered truthful accounts of events in the Middle Ages.[17] Second, they all serve to propagate the holy war and to motivate their audience to aid the *cause d'Outremer*. Third, they unrelentingly appropriate the conventions of chivalric literature to fulfill that purpose.

The book consists of two parts, the first of which examines the use of the formal and thematic commonplaces of the chansons de geste in Crusade propaganda over roughly the first century after the First Crusade. Chapter 1 describes the continuing need for manpower in the Crusader states in the aftermath of the First Crusade, outlines the origin and genre characteristics of the chansons, and examines their usefulness for Crusade propaganda. The *excitatoria* I discuss in chapters 2 to 4—the anonymous *Gesta Francorum et aliorum Hiero-solimitanorum* (completed by early 1101), Robert of Reims's *Historia Iherosolimitana* (ca. 1106–1107), and the three texts of the so-called historical cycle of the First Old French Crusade Cycle (*La Chanson d'Antioche*, *Les Chétifs*, and *La Chanson de Jérusalem*, redacted in the late twelfth or early thirteenth century)—describe similar subjects, all narrating the remarkable events of the First Crusade. Insofar as Robert of Reims drew extensively on the *Gesta Francorum* when writing his work, and the Old French Crusade Cycle in turn was heavily influenced by the *Historia Iherosolimitana*, the texts provide excellent ground for comparative study. These works furthermore illustrate the role of the successful First Crusade in later Crusade propaganda and show the importance of Jerusalem in early Crusade ideology.[18] I will demonstrate how their authors turned to the chansons to address the requirements of the nascent Crusader states, the expansionist aspirations of Bohemond of Taranto, and the need for manpower after the Battle of Hattin in 1187, respectively.

The second part explores how chivalric romance, which gained in popularity from the last quarter of the twelfth century onward, affected the propagation of the Crusade until the end of the fourteenth century. Chapter 5 demonstrates that romance, with its heavy emphasis on secular and often illicit love, was at first thought antithetical to the goals of Crusade, and that its commonplaces were consequently used sparingly in propaganda. Chapters 6 to 8, however, show how excitatoria increasingly looked toward romance to shore up support for the holy war, especially after the collapse of the Crusader states in 1291. The works examined in these chapters illustrate the expansion of the Crusade beyond the Holy Places: Nicolaus of Jeroschin's Middle High German *Krônike von Prûzinlant* (ca. 1331–1344) describes the subjugation of much of the Baltic by the Teutonic or German Order; the works of the Second Old French Crusade Cycle (in particular *Le Bâtard de Bouillon* and *Baudouin de Sébourc*, ca. 1350–1370) see Christians ranging as far as Baghdad and assaulting

Mecca; while *La Prise d'Alixandre*, written by Guillaume de Machaut in the early 1370s, narrates the conquest of the Egyptian port of
Alexandria by Peter I of Cyprus in 1365. Beyond highlighting the
spreading reach of the holy war in the centuries following the First
Crusade, to include population groups and target areas farther afield,
the works I analyze in the second part of the book have in common
the virtue of demonstrating a different awareness and interpretation
of geographical space. They show remarkable interaction between
Christian heartland and non-Christian frontier; as they appropriate
the characteristics of chivalric romance to suit their purpose as Crusade excitatoria, they turn this frontier into a world of courtly love
and adventure.

A study of the rhetoric and the strategies of persuasion in Crusade excitatoria cannot explain why those who chose to take up
arms throughout the many centuries of Crusade did so. Nevertheless, the old dictum that propaganda has a target audience that, it is
hoped, will respond positively to it suggests that the authors I discuss
expected their approach to have such an effect. Although we cannot
know what Crusaders thought when deciding to take the cross, the
repeated use by Crusade excitatoria of the tropes of vernacular chivalric literature over the better part of three centuries suggests an audience receptive to the portrayal of the Crusade in terms reminiscent
of the chansons de geste and chivalric romance, and perhaps equally
willing to think of the Crusade in those terms. Those knights who,
under the critical gaze of John Gower, set out on Crusade to win the
favor of their ladies did so after many years of the rhetoric of Crusade
associating it with the extraneous, chivalric concerns embodied in
vernacular literature. If propaganda for the Crusade affected its audience as it intended to, then what horrified Gower may have had deep
roots that extended back as early as the First Crusade.

The notion that chivalric literature affected how the Crusade
was presented in excitatoria, and so may have influenced how it was
understood by an audience of the Western aristocracy, adds a further
dimension to an important stream of recent criticism. The past few
decades have seen scholars consider imaginative literature such as the
chansons de geste and romance not only as entertainments with the
power to incite their audience to action but also as a reflection of aristocratic attitudes, including attitudes toward the Crusade.[19] Chivalric
literature has come to be regarded as a storehouse of arms bearers'
memory of and concern for the holy war to which so much of their

effort was devoted. This approach is, however, decidedly unidirectional; in seeing literature as a reflection of historical understandings of and opinions on the Crusade, it mostly ignores how imaginative literature in turn shaped these understandings and opinions. This book therefore argues for a bilateral consideration of the relationship between perceptions of the Crusade and lay literature. Across the three most important centuries of Crusade, those propagating it continually appropriated literature, and reacted to literary developments, in order to mold Western understanding of the nature and purpose of holy war.[20] Just as chivalric literature reflected aristocratic attitudes toward the Crusade, it contributed perhaps in equal measure to their formation.

PART I

The Chanson de Geste in Crusade Propaganda

CHAPTER I

Pilgrims and Settlers

THE AFTERMATH OF THE FIRST CRUSADE

When the dust settled on the battlefield of Ascalon on 12 August 1099, the "will of God" had been fulfilled. Under cries of "Deus lo vult" a disparate Latin army,[1] made leaner and more effective by three years of almost continuous struggle, its identity having coalesced into novel but tenuous form as "crucesignati," "Iherosolimitani," or "Franci," had conquered the Holy Places and the city of Jerusalem. In doing so it laid the foundations of a new kingdom that, through increase and decline, would help shape the political landscape for the next two centuries. Furthermore, in its wake it had secured a number of other cities and towns that now formed the nuclei of several Christian principalities: to the north, on the Syrian coast, Bohemond of Taranto ruled over Antioch and the surrounding territories, while to the far northeast Baldwin of Boulogne had made himself master of a county ranging from Edessa to Turbessel. In light of a degree of success that was perhaps undreamed of by any but the very devout, a great number of those who had enthusiastically followed Urban II's call considered their vows fulfilled and returned home.[2]

To those who remained in the East, however, the following years were almost as challenging as the previous ones had been. Some, like Raymond of Saint-Gilles, the count of Toulouse who had led the Provençal contingent, had been left without territorial holdings of their own and sought to remedy this by aggressively expanding Christian dominion to the nearby regions that had as of yet avoided conquest.[3]

The three established principalities of Jerusalem, Antioch, and Edessa had to stabilize their frontiers against repeated attacks from their Turkish and Arab neighbors,[4] as well as build up the machinery of a functioning state: fiefs had to be divided, obligations formalized, and systems of administration and collection established.[5] A clerical hierarchy had also to be put in place; in the kingdom of Jerusalem, first under the rule of Godfrey of Bouillon (1099–1100) and then under that of his brother Baldwin I (1100–1118), this proved especially problematic, as the successive appointments to patriarch of Arnulf of Chocques in 1099 and of Daimbert of Pisa later that same year were disputed[6] and led to conflict both within the clergy and between the clergy and the monarchy. Finally, disparate groups of Norman, Flemish, Italian, French, and Provençal settlers had to find common cause, and common identity, as subjects of new rulers who were often alien to them.[7]

The demands of state formation were made all the more difficult by a chronic shortage of settlers in the new principalities. The need for more men to cross the sea to help with the tasks of settlement, fight the battles, man the ramparts, work the land, and trade its products was a concern to the leaders of the Crusade army even before the final victory at Ascalon. Raymond of Aguilers, a priest of Provençe who traveled to the East in the retinue of Raymond of Toulouse, and who chronicled the Crusaders' slow advance toward Jerusalem, described how the need for additional manpower affected the thinking of the army's leaders. When discussing how to progress after the fall of Antioch in 1098, they wondered: "Will Christians from the West come if they hear of the fall of Antioch, Gibellum, and other Islamic towns? No, but let us march to Jerusalem, the city of our quest, and surely God will deliver it to us; and only then will cities on our route, Gibellum, Tripoli, Tyre, and Acre be evacuated by their inhabitants out of fear of the new wave of crusaders from Christendom."[8] The return home of much of the army after the conquest of the Holy Places furthermore removed the cutting edge that had carved out the principalities. The almost constant conflict of the ensuing years, coupled with high mortality among the Latins adapting to their new surroundings,[9] compounded the demographic pressure on the nascent states. If they were to survive and flourish, the flow of motivated men, money, and material from West to East had to continue.[10]

In the West, the desire to sustain the Crusade enterprise was equally resilient. Popular interest was understandably strong—returning Crusaders, coming home with news of their spectacular victories, fired the imagination. Large new groups of Crusaders, joined by men who had not yet fulfilled the Crusade vows they had made in 1096, set out for the East, where, in the late summer of 1101, at Mersivan and Heraclea, they were defeated and scattered by Seljuq and Danishmend Turks.[11] The extent to which the Western clergy, with the papacy at its heart, supported continued military expeditions to the lands beyond the sea is instanced by the vigor with which it encouraged—pursued, even—the Crusaders of 1101. Even though the liberation of the Holy Places, the professed goal of the Crusade as Urban II had presented it at Clermont and beyond, had been achieved, some of the underlying motives for his call to arms were rather more open ended. The spiritual revival of the Latin West, the moral reform of Latin chivalry, and the clerical control of lay violence—all of which the Crusade was intended to advance—were hardly completed when the Crusaders scaled the ladders at Jerusalem.[12] Although the Crusaders had come to the aid of the Eastern Christians, there were now even more Christians in the Levant that needed protection against the threat of Islam; and if Urban had ever been concerned about the overpopulation of Western Europe, as Robert the Monk claims, that problem was not likely to be solved by the events of 1096–1099.[13] There was still much work to be done, and church authorities were steadfast in their encouragement of the expeditions to the lands beyond the sea.

The First Crusade, however, had resulted from a more or less impromptu outpouring of popular enthusiasm, strongly tied up with the indelible image of a threatened Jerusalem. To guide the spiritual and martial energies that had driven the First Crusaders to the East into something enduring and continuing, now that the city was under Christian control, required some intellectual reorientation. Even though the campaign itself had on the whole been extremely successful, the status of the Crusader, or even the very meaning of Crusade, had been remarkably undefined.[14] Although many considered participation a form of pilgrimage,[15] there was no one notion of what it meant to go on Crusade, what should motivate those taking the cross, how it might benefit them, or what place Crusading occupied within the greater framework of Christian history. The job of convincing others to tread on the path laid by the First Crusaders therefore apparently depended, to a significant extent, on clarifying and interpreting what those First Crusaders had actually achieved.

The task of retelling the events of the First Crusade, and of placing them in an interpretative matrix that would encourage continued lay enthusiasm, fell to a number of writers who wrote about their experiences or adapted those of others in the years following the conquest of Jerusalem. Several of the earliest chroniclers, such as the anonymous author of the work known as the *Gesta Francorum et aliorum Hierosolimitanorum*,[16] Peter Tudebode,[17] Raymond of Aguilers, and Fulcher of Chartres, had themselves participated in the Crusade. Others, such as Albert of Aachen and Ralph of Caen, relied on the eyewitness testimony of those who had.[18] A third group of writers with less direct access, such as Robert of Reims, Guibert of Nogent, and Baldric of Bourgueil, reworked earlier writings to suit their purposes.[19] Their writings looked forward as well as back; they narrated the remarkable successes as well as the setbacks of the First Crusade, highlighting their moral or historical justice and their value as indications of God's approval or disapproval while encouraging their audience to emulate the work so promisingly begun. It is, however, important to realize that there were multiple pressures at work on them. On the one hand, members of the clergy understandably were most interested in interpreting the events spiritually, seeking to read them morally or typologically so as to clearly show the path God laid out for the righteous. To them, the Crusade had been a pilgrimage to the heavenly Jerusalem as well as to the earthly place, a journey during which sins could be shed and the West purified under the auspices of the church.[20] Indeed, far from their families and under constant duress from the elements, starvation, and enemy attack, the First Crusaders had sought salvation, in life or death, almost as if they had been monks. As most of these writers, with the possible exception of the author of the *Gesta Francorum*, were churchmen of varying degrees of importance, it is not surprising to see these concerns weigh heavily in how they represent the events of 1096–1099. Ranging from Raymond of Aguilers's enthusiastic recognition of miracles throughout the campaign[21] and Robert of Reims's comparison of the Crusaders to the Israelites of the book of Exodus,[22] to Guibert of Nogent's description of Crusade as a divine answer to the internecine wars of the West,[23] they expanded upon the place of the Crusade and the Crusader within providential history and church reform.

The writers of the early histories were, however, often also aware that the First Crusade had resulted in three (later four) incipient and very isolated Christian states, and that, rhetoric notwithstanding, the priorities of these were not always identical to those of the Latin Church. Pilgrims from the West could help conquer a city or keep the enemy tide at bay, but they would eventually return home just as so many of the First Crusaders had done. The settlements in these early years needed a continuous stream of financial and human reinforcement—the money to build up their structures and defenses, and the people to populate the newly Christian territories—that exceeded what a periodic expiation of individual sins could provide. The nascent Crusader states had, furthermore, to compete for such resources with other areas that saw Latin Christian expansion at the time, such as Spain and the lands east of the Elbe, a struggle in which their location on the far end of the Mediterranean put them at a disadvantage.[24] They therefore required as many as possible of their Western coreligionists—including those who, for some reason or other, had led perfectly saintly lives—to be engaged in their survival. To do this they had to appeal broadly, and to emphasize the justice of their cause as well as the personal connection of the West to the newly conquered lands and their populations.

Some of the early histories therefore accommodate approaches to the Crusade that range beyond the religious, and speak of them as more than divinely inspired journeys toward individual spiritual salvation. Sometimes they called upon less lofty emotions, and these were often quite incongruous. Ironically, the priest Albert of Aachen played upon a deep-rooted desire for retribution. Vengeance in his writings is not the Lord's but the force that drives much of the Crusade forward—each outrage perpetrated upon the Christians, sometimes by other Christians, must be answered in kind.[25] Robert, the monk of Reims, gleefully narrates how those who conquered Jerusalem "per vicos et plateas discurrentes, quicquid invenerunt rapuerunt, et quod quisque rapuit suum fuit. Erat autem Ierusalem tunc referta temporalibus bonis. . . . Tunc quippe filios suos de longe ad se venientes ita ditavit, quia nullus in ea pauper remansit" [HI 100; HFC 201: "ran through streets and squares, plundering whatever they found; and each kept what he plundered. Jerusalem was full of earthly good things. . . . She made her sons, come from afar, so rich that none remained poor in her"].[26] Undoubtedly some of the First Crusaders had had less elevated motives[27]—Baldwin of Boulogne and Bohemond of Taranto had even abandoned the Crusader army to take up temporal lordship—and the door had to be kept open even for these. Beyond these straightforward appeals to the darker side of human nature, however, another very useful way to appeal to the tastes and enthusiasm of the Western laity were the popular songs of war and

conquest known as the chansons de geste. The early writers on the
Crusade took to them immediately, infusing their works with the
themes, commonplaces, and style of the chansons, and even casting
them into chanson form.

THE CHANSONS DE GESTE

By the time the First Crusaders set out for the East in 1096, the chansons de geste, vernacular songs about the heroic acts of the ancestors,
had existed for several decades. Although the earliest manuscript versions of the chansons date from the twelfth century, the genre had
originated in France in the middle of the eleventh.[28] Its exact begin-
nings have been the subject of intense debate. A "traditionalist"
approach follows Gaston Paris in seeing the chansons as the result of
a collective process of composition and oral transmission connecting
them to the events they purport to describe; according to this interpretation, they were cast into the shape in which they have come down
to us by the itinerant performers known as jongleurs, who expanded
upon a tradition of oral poetry decades or even centuries old.[29] A second approach, first voiced by Joseph Bédier, has been termed "individualist" and considers the chansons not as the end point in a long
sequence of oral performance, transmission, and development but as
original creations of talented poets who may have drawn on older
legends.[30] Recent scholarship has further developed this individualist
interpretation of the chansons de geste: Simon Gaunt has argued that
the stylistic characteristics suggesting an oral antecedent to extant
works such as the *Chanson de Roland* may have been poetic artifice
aimed at producing a "fiction of orality," and that these may therefore not have had oral precursors at all,[31] whereas Paula Leverage has
applied the principles of cognitive science to the chansons and has
concluded that their "oral style" is "a sophisticated aesthetic, which
manipulates active, creative audience engagement" rather than an
indicator of their origin.[32]

Whether the result of oral transmission or auctorial strategy, the
form of the chansons was suited to sung or spoken performance, with
a stanzaic structure that was easily expandable, a regular rhythm, frequent use of direct speech, and much repetition of phrases, formulae,
and sounds. They were constructed of sequences of stanzas or *laisses*
of irregular length, which could range from a handful to hundreds or
thousands of verses each.[33] Although eventually rhyme also became

common to the form, chanson de geste verses were originally united within the laisse through assonance, each verse ending with the same sound, either in "masculine" assonance with stressed final syllables (e.g., *CR* ll. 244–45: "Seignurs baruns, qui i enveieruns, / En Sarraguce, al rei Marsiliuns?" ["My lord barons, whom shall we send / To King Marsile in Saragossa?"]); or in "feminine" assonance with stressed syllables followed by unstressed ones (e.g., *CR* ll. 22–23: "N'i ad paien ki un sul mot respundet, / Fors Blancandrins de Castel de Valfunde" ["There is no pagan who utters a single word in reply, / Except for Blancandrin from Castel de Valfunde"]).[34] The verses themselves were usually decasyllabic, although occasionally octosyllabic and, from the thirteenth century onward, alexandrine verses were also used.[35]

The chansons de geste narrated the deeds of the Franks, mostly during the reigns of Charlemagne and his son Louis the Pious, occasionally during those of Clovis and Charles Martel.[36] They spoke of their struggle with the pagan forces threatening them from outside (e.g., the *Chanson de Roland* and the *Chanson de Guillaume*), and of the dynastic, generational, and personal conflicts pitting them against each other (e.g., *Raoul de Cambrai* and *Les Quatre Fils Aymon*). Some of these chansons drew on the memory of historical events: the destruction of Charlemagne's rear guard at Roncesvalles in 778 inspired the *Chanson de Roland*, and the murder of the son of Raoul de Gouy by the sons of Herbert of Vermandois in 943 provided the foundation for *Raoul de Cambrai*.[37] Others, such as *Huon de Bordeaux* and *La Chevalerie Ogier de Danemarche*, have no clear historical basis and may have drawn mostly on folklore. As they composed, performed, and reworked these songs about historical or pseudo-historical conflicts, the jongleurs included within them many ideas about and interactions between the Christian and Islamic worlds. They spoke of the ideal Christian warrior, of the ties of family, friendship, and love that connected him to others, and of the responsibilities upon which the relationship between lord and vassal was built. They expanded upon what they knew and thought of the character and religion of the Muslim adversary[38] and imagined contacts between Frank and Saracen through words and warfare.

These ideas, replete with ideal and prejudice, found their way into a number of themes, commonplaces, and stereotypes that became characteristic of the chansons de geste. The Frankish heroes of the chansons are usually strong adherents to the Christian faith.[39] Their

relationship with God is one of mutual support: they serve God loyally and defend his people against the physical and religious threat
of the unbeliever, while God in return helps them when needed, and
welcomes them into heaven upon the completion of their labor.[40] As
Turpin says before the Battle of Roncesvalles:

> "Crestientet aidez a sustenir!
> Bataille avrez, vos en estes tuz fiz,
> Kar a voz oilz veez les Sarrazins.
> Clamez voz culpes, si preiez Deu mercit;
> Asoldrai vos pur vos anmes guarir.
> Se vos murez, esterez seinz martirs,
> Sieges avrez el greignor pareïs."
> Franceis descendent, a tere se sunt mis,
> E l'arcevesque de Deu les beneïst:
> Par penitence les cumandet a ferir.

> [CR ll. 1129–35: "Help us now to sustain the Christian faith. / You
> will have to engage in battle, as you well know; / For you see the Sar-
> acens with your own eyes. / Confess your sins, pray for the grace of
> God; / To save your souls I shall absolve you all. / If you die, you will
> be blessed martyrs / And take your place in paradise on high." / The
> Franks dismount and kneel upon the ground; / In God's name the
> archbishop blessed them. / As penance he orders them to strike.]

Reciprocal bonds that are very similar to those that tie the Christian
to his God tie the vassal to his secular lord. Here too there must be
a relationship of mutual loyalty and benefit. It is the vassal's duty to
fight his lord's wars and to uphold or expand the latter's dominion.
He must redress the wrongs done to his lord and be willing to suffer and die for him: "Pur sun seignor deit hom susfrir destreiz / E
endurer e granz chalz e grans freiz, / Sin deit hom perdre e del quir e
del peil" [CR ll. 1010–12: "For his lord a vassal must suffer hardships
/ And endure great heat and great cold; / And he must lose both hair
and hide"]. The vassal serves his lord in all, and to a large extent his
lord's success rests upon his shoulders.[41] The lord, whose very word
is the law by which his vassal lives, in turn must respect his rights,
support him militarily and financially, and avenge him if necessary.[42]
The importance of the vassal–lord relationship to the chansons de
geste is further demonstrated by the fact that some chansons, such
as Gormond et Isembart and Les Quatre Fils Aymon, speak of the
disastrous consequences of its breakdown. Treason is the worst possible transgression: the sociopolitical order of the chansons de geste

stands and falls with the adherence of both parties to their respective sides of the arrangement.[43]

These two relations of mutual loyalty, based on an elaborate system of gift and obligation most often thought to reflect the organizational principles of feudal society,[44] are proven in battle. Here the hero displays his prowess, which wins him glory and demonstrates his value to his earthly and heavenly lords. The battlefield therefore takes a central place in the chansons de geste. The authors of the chansons typically go to great lengths to provide their audience with detailed accounts of the sights and sounds of battle, to make them experience warfare as directly as possible, seeing the sun glint off the weaponry and hearing the shattering of the trumpets in their minds:[45]

> Clers fut li jurz e bels fut li soleilz:
> N'unt guarnement que tut ne reflambeit.
> Sunent mil grailles por ço que plus bel seit:
> Granz est la noise, si l'oïrent Franceis.

> [CR ll. 1002–5: The day was fine and the sun bright; / They have no equipment which does not gleam in the light. / They sound a thousand trumpets to enhance the effect. / The noise is great and the Franks heard it.]

> Luisent cil elme as perres d'or gemmees,
> E cil escuz e cez bronies sasfrees;
> .VII. milie graisles i sunent la menee:
> Grant est la noise par tute la contree.

> [CR ll. 1452–55: Their helmets, studded with gold and gems, shine bright, / And so do their shields and their saffron byrnies. / Seven thousand bugles sound the charge; / Great is the noise for miles around.]

Within the sensory maelstrom of the battlefield, the hero proves his worth. Uniquely skilled at warfare, he fights as a knight—heavily armored, on horseback, with lance and sword.[46] The nature of combat in the chansons, of horseman against horseman, frequently turns the description of battle into a sequence of individual duels, a catalogue of notable Franks falling upon Saracen counterparts and killing them, or—rather less frequently—vice versa.[47] This formulaic display of skill at arms is interspersed with vivid description of the ultimate show of prowess—the "epic strike" by which the enemy is split in half:

La bataille est merveilluse e cumune.
Li quens Rollant mie ne s'asoüret,
Fiert de l'espiet tant cume hanste li duret;
A .XV. cols l'ad fraite e perdue;
Trait Durendal, sa bone espee, nue,
Sun cheval brochet, si va ferir Chernuble.
L'elme li freint u li carbuncle luisent,
Trenchet le cors e la cheveleüre,
Si li trenchat les oilz e la faiture,
Le blanc osberc, dunt la maile est menue,
E tut le cors tresqu'en la furcheüre.
Enz en la sele, ki est a or batue,
El cheval est l'espee aresteüe.

[*CR* ll. 1320–32: The battle is terrible and now joined by all. / Count Roland is no laggard; / He strikes with his spear, while the shaft still lasts. / With fifteen blows he has broken and destroyed it; / He draws forth Durendal, his fine, naked sword, / And spurs on his horse to strike at Chernubles. / He breaks his helmet with its gleaming carbuncles, / Slices off his coif and his scalp, / As well as slicing through his eyes and his face, / His shining hauberk with its close-meshed mail / And right into his saddle which is of beaten gold; / His sword came to rest in the horse itself.]

Opposing the Franks, on the battlefield and within the wider universe of the chansons de geste, are the Saracens. To a large extent the Saracen, or the non-Christian in general, is constructed as a mirror image of the Frank. At the heart of the Saracen world as well lies a relationship of mutual obligation between lord and vassal as an organizing principle. The Saracen too is wise in counsel and brave in war, a consummate fighter who fights very much as the Frank does. Indeed, it is rather a platitude of the chansons to say that had they only been Christians there would have been no better knights:

Uns amurafles i ad de Balaguez;
Cors ad mult gent e le vis fier et cler;
Puis que il est sur sun cheval muntet,
Mult se fait fiers de ses armes porter;
De vasselage est il ben alosez;
Fust chrestiens, asez oüst barnet.

[*CR* ll. 894–99: An emir is there from Balaguer. / His body is very handsome and his face fierce and fair. / When he is mounted on his horse, / He bears his arms with great ferocity. / He is well known for his courage; / Had he been a Christian, he would have been a worthy baron.]

De vasselage est suvent esprovet;
Deus! quel baron, s'oüst chrestientet!

[CR ll. 3163–64: His courage has often been tested in battle. / O God,
what a noble baron, if only he were a Christian!][48]

Despite the apparent similarity between them, the Franks and Saracens are separated in the chansons by many qualities. Compared with
the ascetic and virtuous Frank, the Saracen lives in wealth and abun-
dance and is morally permissive to the point of debauchery.[49] Whereas
the Frankish world is one of simplicity, the Saracen's is one of opulence and multiplicity. While the Franks constitute a single political
entity, are subjects of a single hegemonic empire composed of several
dependencies, such as Flanders, Maine, and Anjou, the Saracens are
a vastly diverse group of people, united only by their perceived non-
Christian religion and their geographic origin beyond the Frankish
borders. The ethnic makeup of the Saracens in the chansons is therefore wildly imaginative. Included among them are wholly fantastical
peoples, as well as ones that were not historically Muslim: opposed
to Charlemagne at Roncesvalles are Armenians, Moors, Pechenegs,
Persians, Turks, Huns, Hungarians, and a whole host of others, such
as the "Micenes as chefs gros; / Sur les eschines qu'il unt en mi les dos
/ Cil sunt seiet ensement cume porc" [CR ll. 3221–23: "large-headed
Milceni; / On their spines, along the middle of their backs, / They are
as bristly as pigs"].[50]

A similar opposition between unity and diversity also applies to
the religion and religious attitudes of the adversaries. The Franks
worship one God; the Saracens are polytheist and worship a number
of gods, usually Tervagant, Apollion, and Mahomet, whose images
they venerate in "mahomeries."[51] Whereas the Franks are stalwart
in their faith even in—especially in—the direst of circumstances, the
bond between pagan and pagan gods is far more fragile. The Saracen
relationship with the divine, too, is a reciprocal one—they worship
their gods in return for support. But of course here one party cannot deliver on its promise: in the crucible of battle, Tervagant, Apollion, and Mahomet cannot bring victory; this is where the God of the
Franks proves them right and the pagans wrong. Consequently the
Saracens often turn on their gods violently:[52]

Ad Apolin en curent en un crute,
Tencent a lui, laidement le despersunent:
"E! malvais deus, por quei nus fais tel hunte?

Cest nostre rei por quei lessas cunfundre?
Ki mult te sert, malvais luer l'en dunes!"
Puis si li tolent sun sceptre e sa curune,
Par les mains le pendent sur une culumbe,
Entre lur piez a tere le tresturnent,
A granz bastuns le batent e defruisent;
E Tervagan tolent sun escarbuncle
E Mahumet enz en un fosset butent
E porc et chen le mordent e defulent.

[CR ll. 2580–91: They rush off to Apollo in a crypt, / Rail against
him and hurl abuse at him: / "O, wretched god, why do you cause us
such shame? / Why did you permit our king to be destroyed? / Anyone who serves you well receives a poor reward." / Then they grab
his scepter and his crown / And hang him by his hands from a pillar;
/ Then they send him flying to the ground at their feet / And beat him
and smash him to pieces with huge sticks. / They seize Tervagant's
carbuncle / And fling Muhammad into a ditch / Where pigs and dogs
bite and trample on him.]

The Christians are therefore constant in their faith, the pagans erratic.
Both habitually attempt to draw the other toward their own religion,
offering unimaginable riches if Frank would take on the worship
of the pagan gods or if Saracen would become Christian; however,
the inconstancy of the pagans makes them far more likely to switch
sides.[53]

The opposition between Frank and Saracen, between Christian
and non-Christian, as we find it in the chansons de geste is to a large
extent based on the way the jongleurs and their audiences imagined alterity. On a human level Franks and Saracens are remarkably
similar—both can be brave, wise, treacherous, or cowardly, and the
epic epithets used to describe them as such are the same. Beyond that,
the difference is one between unity against multiplicity, order against
licentiousness. The Franks are one people obeying one king, obeying
one law, worshipping one God; the Saracens, on the other hand, are
disunited, serving many kings and many gods to whom their loyalty
is suspect, reveling in opulence and dissipation.

In the years before the First Crusade, the chansons therefore spoke
of the heroic deeds of the ancestors in a time awash with conflict
between Christian Franks and pagan Saracens. The earliest extant representatives of the genre characteristically describe a world in which
the Christian frontier, political as well as psychological, is threatened
by a religious outsider and is eventually enlarged at his expense. The

chansons de geste were popular and reached a wide audience;[54] this popularity quickly extended beyond the French-speaking areas, and within a century of their origins chansons had been composed in, or translated into, Provençal and Middle High German.[55] The chansons' particular representation of the opposition between Christian and non-Christian reached far and wide. The chroniclers of the First Crusade therefore wrote for an audience well aware of the form, themes, and socioreligious prejudices of the chansons, and they relied upon these to present the Crusades in a way that suited their purposes. As I will show below, writers used the conventions of the chansons de geste in a variety of ways, depending to a large extent on the circumstances in which they wrote their works. However, they turned to the chansons in the first place for a shared purpose: to instruct, motivate, and control the forces needed to maintain and support the Christian presence in the Holy Land.

If the chansons were popular, they appealed especially to the very people whose political, social, and military concerns and practices they reflected: knights. From the beginning of the Crusades, knights had been vital to their success.[56] Urban II, in a letter to the monks of Vallombrosa of October 1096, identified them especially as the audience of the sermon at Clermont: "We were stimulating the minds of knights to go on this expedition, since they might be able to restrain the savagery of the Saracens by their arms and restore the Christians to their former freedom."[57] The next few years showed his farsightedness, as the participation of others in the Crusade proved disastrous; the popular campaigns of the early years led only to unrestrained violence and eventual annihilation, from the cities of the Rhineland to Xerigordon and Civetot.[58] Conversely, the army that conquered Jerusalem was built around knights and their retainers. The experiences of the First Crusade amply demonstrated that only trained and disciplined fighters with the financial wherewithal to maintain themselves on campaign could successfully contribute to Christian progress in the East. Were the Crusades to continue, and the Christian principalities in the Levant to survive, the unrelenting enthusiasm and participation of knights was absolutely necessary.

Crusade appeals therefore had to address and convince knights to join the fray. There were many benefits of using the chansons in excitatoria aimed especially at knights. In the years following the First Crusade, when the theological and legal framework of Crusading was still under development, the chansons approached the holy war with a certain moral clarity, as a conflict between resolute, Christian Frank and dissolute, pagan Saracen, in which the former must eventually be victorious because of the superiority of his deity. They put a religious premium on the display of prowess in chivalric warfare, where the duty owed to God was repaid through blows of the sword.[59] They played upon their audience's pride of ancestry, sense of continuity, and desire to emulate; Urban, or Robert, recognized these emotions as important early on:

> Moveant vos et incitent animos vestros ad virilitatem gesta predecessorum vestrorum, probitas et magnitudo Karoli Magni regis et Ludovici filii eius aliorumque regum vestrorum, qui regna paganorum destruxerunt, et in eis fines sancte ecclesie dilataverunt. . . . O fortissimi milites et invictorum propago parentum, nolite degenerari, sed virtutis priorum vestrorum reminiscimini.

> [HI 6; HFC 80: May the deeds of your ancestors move you and spur your souls to manly courage—the worth and greatness of Charlemagne, his son Louis and your other kings who destroyed the pagan kingdoms and brought them within the bounds of Christendom. . . . Oh most valiant soldiers and descendants of victorious ancestors, do not fall short of, but be inspired by, the courage of your forefathers.][60]

Finally, the chansons put front and center the ties of loyalty and support between vassal and overlord, as well as the bonds of kinship between knight, peers, and family. These relationships, as recent historical criticism has shown, were of great importance in the recruitment of early Crusaders and motivated many to take the cross.[61]

The advantages of using the conventions of the chanson de geste— its form, its themes, and its commonplaces—to present the Crusade were therefore many. Writers could connect the events of 1096–1099 to an extensive, popular body of works that presented religious war in a way that knights especially would understand and find attractive. Beyond informing and motivating knights, however, the use of the chansons also perhaps made it possible to control them. To those who saw a central role for the papacy in the Crusade, or believed in the *militia Sancti Petri*, the chansons' foregrounding of the relationship between overlord and vassal offered a way to bind knighthood to the church with ties of obedience.[62] In a campaign against God's enemies, fought over Christ's inheritance, at his request ("Deus lo vult"), God was both spiritual and temporal overlord of the *cruces-ignati*; even more than to any prince, the knights' duty was above all to him, or his representatives on earth. Beyond the individual fight for salvation, Crusade was therefore also armed service owed to God. Conversely, laymen keen to continue the Crusades, such as the settlers of Outremer, could also find benefit from associating these to the works of the jongleurs, for it allowed them to stimulate the influx of desperately needed fighters independently of clerical sanction. Relying on papal proclamation of a Crusade to motivate knights to take the cross left support of the Holy Land beyond the control of its inhabitants; the settlements in their infancy needed help rather more frequently than that. The chansons, by highlighting reasons to fight the Saracen other than the indulgence—to demonstrate prowess, for vengeance, out of loyalty, or to defend and retake Christian land—took the explanation of what constituted Crusade out of the domain of the clergy and allowed laymen too to define and therefore to a certain extent control it.[63] After all, if a *preudomme* could get remission of his sins only on campaigns sanctioned by the church, he could fight the Saracen as duty owed to a divine overlord, or to demonstrate his skills as a knight, whenever he wanted.

CHAPTER 2

The *Gesta Francorum*

Given the potential advantages the forms and conventions of the chansons offered for propagandizing the Crusade to Western audiences, it is not surprising that they began to be used almost immediately after the conquest of Jerusalem. The first known work to advocate for continued Latin commitment to the Crusade, the *Gesta Francorum et aliorum Hierosolimitanorum*, depends heavily on the stylistic and thematic tropes of the chansons to make its case. Rather than relying on his own experiences or observations, its anonymous author consistently turns to literary commonplaces to describe the Crusaders, their Muslim opponents, and their interactions on and off the battlefield, turning the First Crusade into the continuation of a far older conflict and giving Western Christians additional justification to appropriate much of the Middle East.

Among the first group of narratives of the First Crusade, those written by eyewitnesses and participants, the *Gesta Francorum* stands out not only as the oldest but also as the most popular and influential.[1] Completed no later than the beginning of 1101 by a south Italian Norman who traveled to the East in the contingent of Bohemond of Taranto,[2] its ten books tell the story of the Crusade from the crossing of the Balkans by the Crusader armies in 1096 to the conclusion of the campaign three years later. The first nine books, which discuss the Crusaders' progress until the Battle of Antioch on 28 June 1098, show the author, who is commonly known as "the Anonymous," to have been strongly partisan toward Bohemond, to whom he repeatedly refers as "dominus" ["lord"][3] and describes with such grandiose epithets as "bellipotens Boamundus" [*GF* 7: "Bohemond, that great warrior"], "sapiens uir Boamundus" [*GF* 18: "the valiant Bohemond"], and "uir uenerabilis Boamundus" [*GF* 61: "the honoured Bohemond"]. The Anonymous clearly supports Bohemond's ambitions and shares his antagonism toward the Byzantine Empire.[4] After the fall of Antioch and Bohemond's defection from the Crusader army, the Anonymous left his service for that of Raymond of Toulouse, and the relatively short tenth book discusses the march to Jerusalem, its investment and conquest, and the defeat of the Egyptian army at Ascalon.

Very little is known of the Anonymous beyond what he reveals of himself in his writings, and even that has been the subject of some dispute. That he was an Italian Norman with a close association with Bohemond of Taranto is not doubted, but the capacity in which he served Bohemond, and in which he traveled to the East, is unclear. Ever since Hagenmeyer first edited the *Gesta Francorum* in 1890,[5] the Anonymous has been thought to have been a fighter: his extensive descriptions of battle—especially when compared with those of a cleric such as Raymond of Aguilers, for whom a battle is never worth more than an offhand remark[6]—suggests he was repeatedly in the thick of it.[7] Furthermore, his knowledge of Bohemond's military contingent and his clear interest in the concerns of the *milites* as opposed to those of the *pauperes* on Crusade may also indicate that the Anonymous was a knight,[8] perhaps one of Bohemond's Apulian vassals, whose family therefore may have had a longstanding allegiance to the house of Hauteville.[9] However, the Anonymous's learning, the quality of his Latin, and the skill with which he includes alliteration, assonance, and rhyme in his work all suggest that he had a clerical education, and Colin Morris argues that he may even have been a clerk and not a fighter at all.[10]

Whether written by an educated knight or by a clerk with an overpowering interest in the clash of arms, the *Gesta Francorum* is a sophisticated work, and the thought the Anonymous put into its composition elevates it above the simple "war diary" that Hagenmeyer saw in it.[11] Although the Anonymous most likely died shortly after completing his work, the *Gesta* had an extraordinarily long afterlife. Its impact on the historiography of the First Crusade was immediate and far-reaching. Within a few years another eyewitness to the Crusade, the Poitevin priest Peter Tudebode, wrote an account of the campaign, *Historia de Hierosolymitano Itinere*, that drew so closely on the *Gesta* as to render problematic for more than a century the question of which came first.[12] Within a decade, copies of the *Gesta* circulated widely in the West, and writers who had not participated in the Crusade based their own histories on the work of the Anonymous: especially noteworthy here are the three French Benedictines, Baldric of Bourgueil (*Historia Ierosolimitana*, ca. 1107–1108), Robert of Reims (*Historia Iherosolimitana*, ca. 1106–1107), and Guibert of Nogent (*Gesta Dei per Francos*, ca. 1108–1109). The dissemination of the *Gesta Francorum* into Europe was helped by Bohemond of Taranto himself, who took copies of the work with him when in late 1104 he set out to recruit for his unsuccessful campaign against Byzantium of 1106–1108.[13]

That Bohemond would like the *Gesta*, and would use it as a tool to convince fresh forces to side with him, is understandable—the Anonymous was one of his followers, perhaps even a vassal, and the first nine books read very much like a paean extolling the virtues of the prince of Antioch. However, the wide and enduring popularity of the *Gesta* among those not directly associated with Bohemond is less obvious. That it was an eyewitness report, and an early one, undoubtedly contributed to its appeal, but the relative lack of success of other early eyewitness testimonies, such as that of Raymond of Aguilers, shows that this was hardly enough.[14] Its style, which modern critics have grown to appreciate as subtle and sometimes even playful, was vilified by the Anonymous's contemporaries.[15] Furthermore, its virulent partisanship would be counterproductive to those whose political aspirations differed from those of Bohemond, and not many in the twelfth century shared Bohemond's aspirations. To put it in simple terms, the success of the *Gesta*—among so many different groups, regions, and also generations—was due to its telling the story of the First Crusade in a way that people actually wanted to hear. For all of Raymond of Aguilers's qualities, his obsession with religious dispute and with the divine revelations at work during the Crusade make his work less interesting to those without an enduring interest in theology. The *Gesta*, on the other hand, spoke of the events of 1096–1099 in a way that laymen could understand and relate to, and that fired their imaginations.

From the very beginning of his work, the Anonymous set out not merely to tell the story of the First Crusade but to tell it in a way that would appeal to a wide audience. This teleology has, however, rarely been recognized, and much of the Anonymous's intent has been read as merely indicative of his personality or style. Regarding the Anonymous's knowledge of religion, for instance, critical opinion has often been contradictory: on the one hand, some praise his extensive knowledge and subtle use of scripture in his work, and see this as evidence of a thorough clerical education;[16] others see it as ham-fisted, showing the Anonymous to have been a knight of limited sophistication.[17] Both ignore the possibility that the Anonymous, who throughout the *Gesta* maintains a very simple approach to religion and avoids entangling his account with theological disputes, *chose* to do so— that he was an educated Latinate writer who did his best to appeal to laymen with little theological knowledge.[18] Thus the understanding of the purpose of the *Gesta* and the reasons for its contemporary success may have fallen victim to the urge to identify its author.

More important, another way by which the Anonymous set out to make the Crusade understandable and appealing to his audience— his extensive use of the conventions and obsessions of the chanson de geste—has also been most often thought to demonstrate little more than the author's style or personal background. A number of critics have pointed out that the *Gesta* displays some of the characteristics of the chansons. Rosalind Hill has identified the *Gesta*'s use of epic epithets—"acerrimus Boamundus" [*GF* 46: "the hero Bohemond"], "infelix imperator" [*GF* 10: "the wretched emperor"], "prudens Tancredus" [*GF* 20: "the gallant Tancred"]—and stock phrases to describe the spoils of war, as well as its use of simple doxologies at the end of each of its ten books, as reminiscent of the chansons.[19] Matthew Bennett has noted a number of verbal and thematic parallels between the chansons de geste and the *Gesta*, especially in their depiction of the Muslim adversary,[20] while Morris has suggested that the work's use of alliteration, rhyme, and assonance, repetitive portrayals of landscapes, predilection for direct speech, description of Bohemond as an epic hero, and structure may have been influenced by the chansons.[21] These approaches have on the whole limited the impact of the chansons de geste on the *Gesta* to its aesthetic properties—although it may serve as an indication of the Anonymous's literate background, it is thought to reveal little else.[22] However, both the extent and intent of the Anonymous's use of the conventions of the chansons go far farther than this. Beyond poetic artifice, the Anonymous used the chansons throughout the *Gesta* to create—or recreate—a wholly recognizable image of the conflict between Christian and Muslim, within which he defined the enemy, the Crusaders themselves, the reasons for Crusade, and the justifications for conquest in terms that his audience could understand and embrace, and upon which they could act with full confidence in the historical justice of their deeds.

ENEMIES OF GOD

Perhaps the most remarkable aspect of the *Gesta Francorum* is the way in which the Anonymous describes the peoples the Crusaders encountered in the East. When in early 1097 the armies of the princes left Constantinople and crossed the Bosporus, they entered the territories of the Seljuq Turks, who in the immediately preceding decades had subjected most of the Anatolian plateau and the Levant to their rule. As they moved south toward the Holy Places, the Crusaders fought the Seljuq of Rum at Nicaea and Dorylaeum, captured Antioch from its Turkish governor Yaghi-Siyan despite the efforts of Ridwan of Aleppo and Duqaq of Damascus, and defeated a Seljuq relief army under Kerbogha, the atabeg of Mosul. Yet when the Crusaders reached Jerusalem in June 1099 they were met not by the Seljuq but by the Fatimid Egyptians, who had recaptured the city in the previous year, and it was the Egyptians whom the Crusaders routed at Ascalon in August of that year. Interspersed with these populations, the Crusaders also found Christian Syrians, Greeks, and Armenians.

The Anonymous displays a certain degree of perceptiveness regarding the differences between the peoples of the East. When describing those on the European side of the Bosporus, he differentiates Greeks, Byzantine Turcopoles, and Pecheneg mercenaries.[23] On the Asian side, he separates Syrian and Armenian Christians from Muslim Turks and Arabs, and seems sensitive to the political developments of the recent past.[24] He knows the names of individual army commanders, such as Kilij Arslan I, the sultan of Rum and son of Suleiman ("Solimanus . . . filius Solimani ueteris" [*GF* 22: "Suleiman . . . son of old Suleiman"]), Yaghi-Siyan ("Cassianus" on *GF* 47) and his son Shams ad-Daula ("Sensadolus" on *GF* 50), and Kerbogha ("Curbaram" on *GF* 49);[25] he furthermore refers to others by their cities of provenance, as in "Hierosolimitanus ammiralius" [*GF* 49: "the amir of Jerusalem," Soqman ibn Ortoq] and "Rex Damasci" [*GF* 49: "the king of Damascus," Abu Nasr Shams al-Muluk Duqaq]. Given his subtlety in describing Easterners even through the fog of war, it is all the more remarkable that the Anonymous should be so wildly inaccurate when describing the enemies the Crusaders faced in battle. Although he appears very much aware in books 1–9 that the Crusaders' antagonists are Turks and in book 10 that they are Arabs or Saracens, he is surprisingly imaginative when describing the ranks of the enemy. At the Battle of Dorylaeum, the Crusaders are fighting not only the Seljuq Turks but a wide variety of peoples:

Mirabantur ergo nostri ualde unde esset extorta tanta multitudo Turcorum, et Arabum et Saracenorum, et aliorum quos enumerare ignoro; quia pene omnes montes et colles et ualles et omnia plana loca intus et extra undique erant cooperta de illa excommunicata generatione. . . . Statim autem uenientibus militibus nostris, Turci et Arabes, et Saraceni et Agulani omnesque barbarae nationes dederunt uelociter fugam, per compendia montium et per plana loca. Erat autem numerus Turcorum, Persarum, Publicanorum, Saracenorum, Agulanorum, aliorumque paganorum trecenta sexaginta milia extra Arabes, quorum numerum nemo scit nisi solus Deus.

[*GF* 19–20: Our men could not understand whence could have come such a great multitude of Turks, Arabs, Saracens and other peoples whose names I do not know, for nearly all the mountains and hills and valleys, and all the flat country within and without the hills, were covered with this accursed folk. . . . As soon as our knights charged, the Turks, Arabs, Saracens, Agulani and all the rest of the barbarians took to their heels and fled through the mountain passes and across the plains. There were three hundred and sixty thousand Turks, Persians, Paulicians, Saracens and Agulani, with other pagans, not counting the Arabs, for God alone knows how many there were of them.]

The Christians' victory at Dorylaeum is therefore one over a great many Eastern peoples, some real, some imagined, some as yet unknown. Similarly, the army that confronts the Crusaders at Antioch is a very diverse one:

Non multo post audiuimus nuntios de exercitu hostium nostrorum, Turcorum, Publicanorum, Agulanorum, Azimitarum, et aliarum plurimarum nationum.

[*GF* 45: Not long afterwards we heard news of an army of our enemies, drawn from the Turks, Paulicians, Agulani, Azymites and many other peoples.]

Hierosolimitanus ammiralius in adiutorum cum suo exercitu uenit. Rex Damasci illuc uenit, cum maxima gente. Idem uero Curbaram congregauit innumeras gentes paganorum, uidelicet Turcos, Arabas, Saracenos, Publicanos, Azimitas, Curtos, Persas, Agulanos, et alias multas gentes innumerabiles. Et Agulani fuerunt numero tria milia;

qui neque lanceas neque sagittas neque ulla arma timebant, quia omnes erant undique cooperti ferro et equi eorum, ipsique nolebant in bellum ferre arma nisi solummodo gladios.

[*GF* 49: The amir of Jerusalem came to his help with an army, and the king of Damascus brought a great number of men. So Karbuqa collected an immense force of pagans—Turks, Arabs, Saracens, Paulicians, Azymites, Kurds, Persians, Agulani and many other people who could not be counted. The Agulani numbered three thousand; they fear neither spears nor arrows nor any other weapon, for they and their horses are covered all over with plates of iron. They will not use any weapons except swords when they are fighting.]

The enemy the Crusaders meet in battle is therefore not one people but many—varied, distinct, and if not imaginary then historically out of place. The Anonymous's inaccuracy here is remarkable. It is possible to consider it hyperbole aimed at making the victories seem even more impressive; however, for this one really needs only numbers, not diversity.[26] One can, as Hill does, ascribe it to the Crusaders' ignorance of their enemies,[27] but the Anonymous is otherwise knowledgeable about the peoples of the East, and other eyewitness accounts of the battles display a correct understanding of those against whom the Crusaders were fighting.[28] Rather, the intent with which the Anonymous chose to portray the Muslims as such a varied lot can be seen in the strong resemblance of his descriptions to those of the pagan enemies in the chansons de geste. Note, for instance, how the Anonymous's words compare to the following lines from the *Chanson de Roland*:

Dis escheles establisent après.
La premere est des Canelius les laiz:
De Val Fuit sun venuz en traver;
L'altre est de Turcs e la terce de Pers,
E la quarte est de Pinceneis e de Pers,
E la quinte est de Solteras e d'Avers,
E la siste est d'Ormaleus e d'Eugiez,
E la sedme est de la gent Samuel,
L'oidme est de Bruise e la noefme de Clavers,
E la disme est d'Occian le desert:
Ço est une gent ki Damnedeu ne sert;
De plus feluns n'orrez parler jamais;
Durs unt les quirs ensement cume fer;
Pur ço n'unt soign d'elme ne d'osberc;
En la bataille sunt felun e engrès.

[*CR* ll. 3237–51: Then they draw up ten more divisions. / The first is of ugly Canaanites; / They came across from Val Fuit. / The next is of Turks and the third of Persians, / The fourth of the fiery Petchenegs [*sic*], / the fifth of Soltras and Avars, / the sixth of Ormaleus and Eugies, / The seventh of the people of Samuel, / The eighth of Bruise, the ninth of Clavers / And the tenth of people from Occian the Desert; / They are a race which does not serve the Lord God. / You could never hear of more villainous men, / Their skins are hard as iron. / For this reason they scorn helmets and hauberks; / In battle they are treacherous and fiery.]

As indicated above, the chansons too embraced the historically incorrect and the imagined in their depiction of the pagan enemy, an enemy portrayed as diverse and disparate, creating a frenzy of whatever "others" their authors could imagine.[29] The Anonymous is less imaginative than the jongleurs, but he retains hints of the marvelous: his Agulani, covered head to toe in iron, are perhaps as remarkable as the *Chanson de Roland*'s warriors of Occian, whose very skin is as hard as metal. In their variety and wondrousness, the Muslims of the *Gesta Francorum* are direct descendants of the Saracens of the chansons.

Within the *Gesta*'s invocation of the chansons in its depiction of the enemy we find a first indication of the Anonymous's goal for the work—to apply to the First Crusade an older, literary image of the conflict between Christian and Muslim. Further characterization of the Muslim in the *Gesta*, in descriptions of Muslim martial qualities, social habits, and religious practice, echoes what we find in the chansons. For example, the clichéd chanson description of the Muslim as only a baptism away from being among the finest knights in the world, equal if not superior to the Westerner, is reflected in the Anonymous's account of the Turks:

Quis unquam tam sapiens aut doctus audebit describere prudentiam militiamque et fortitudinem Turcorum? . . . Verumtamen dicunt se esse de Francorum generatione, et quia nullus homo naturaliter debet esse miles nisi Franci et illi. Veritatem dicam quam nemo audebit prohibere. Certe si in fide Christi et Christianitate sancta semper firmi fuissent, et unum Deum in trinitate confiteri uoluissent Deique Filium natum de Virgine matre, passum, et resurrexisse a mortuis et in caelum ascendisse suis cernentibus discipulis, consolationemque Sancti Spiritus perfecte misisse; et eum in caelo et in terra regnantem recta mente et fide credidissent, ipsis potentiores uel fortiores uel bellorum ingeniosissimos nullus inuenire potuisset.

[*GF* 21: What man, however experienced and learned, would dare to write of the skill and prowess and courage of the Turks? . . . They have a saying that they are of common stock with the Franks, and that no men, except the Franks and themselves, are naturally born to be knights. This is true, and nobody can deny it, that if only they had stood firm in the faith of Christ and holy Christendom, and had been willing to accept One God in Three Persons, and had believed rightly and faithfully that the Son of God was born of a virgin mother, that he suffered, and rose from the dead and ascended in the sight of his disciples into Heaven, and sent them in full measure the comfort of the Holy Ghost, and that he reigns in Heaven and earth, you could not find stronger or braver or more skilful soldiers.][30]

There is therefore an essential similarity between Frank and Turk in the *Gesta*: both are outstanding fighters, which, in the eyes of the Turks, is a result of a shared heritage. Nevertheless, this similarity goes hand in hand with an essential difference: the Turks do not believe in the "One God in Three Persons." Although some of the Anonymous's fellow travelers show a relatively sophisticated understanding of the monotheism at the heart of Islam,[31] he himself describes the Muslim as a polytheist. Kerbogha swears "per Machomet et per omnia deorum nomina" [*GF* 52: "by Mohammed and by all the names of our gods"] and his mother "per omnium deorum nomina" [*GF* 53: "by the names of all the Gods"]. The Egyptians are no different from the Turks, and after the Battle of Ascalon the Fatimid emir exclaims: "O deorum spiritus, quis unquam uidit uel audiuit talia? . . . Iuro per Machumet et per omnia deorum numina, quod ulterius non retinebo milites conuentione aliqua" [*GF* 96: "O spirits of the gods! Who has ever seen or heard such things as these? . . . I swear by Mohammed and by the glory of all the gods that I will never raise another army"]. The Anonymous therefore continues to ascribe to Muslims the polytheism that characterizes them in the chansons. He also echoes the jongleurs' suggestion of what happens to those who believe in this multiplicity of gods after death. Just as lines 1265–68 of the *Chanson de Roland* have Gerin strike the Saracen Malpramis, and "L'osberc li rumpt entresque a la charn, / Sun bon espiet enz el cors li enbat; / Li paiens chet cuntreval a un quat. / L'anme de lui en portet Sathanas" ["He rends his hauberk right down to his flesh / And plunges his fine spear deep into his body. / The pagan falls to the ground in a heap; / His soul is carried off by Satan"], so the Anonymous shows the downward trajectory reserved for the Muslim dead: "Illi qui uiui nequiuerunt transire pontem pre nimia multitudine gentium et caballorum, ibi receperunt sempiternum interitum cum diabolo et angelis suis" [*GF* 41: "Those who did not succeed in crossing the bridge alive, because of the great press of men and horses, suffered there everlasting death with the devil and his imps"].

In the eyes of the Anonymous, even though their polytheist religion can lead only to an eternity in hell, the pagans of the *Gesta* are nevertheless quite keen to convert the Christians, and here as in the chansons the rewards for changing sides are impressive (if of course never acted upon). When, before the Battle of Antioch, Peter the Hermit is sent to Kerbogha to negotiate, the Turkish commander sends him back to the Christian army with the following words:

> Vultis namque scire quid uobis dicimus? Reuertimini ergo quantocius, et dicite uestris senioribus, quia si per omnia cupiunt effici Turci, et deum uestrum quem uos inclini colitis abnegare uolunt et leges uestras spernere, nos illis hanc et satis plus dabimus de terra, et ciuitates et castella adhuc autem quod nemo uestrorum remanebit pedes, sed erunt omnes milites sicut et nos sumus; et habebimus semper eos in summa amicitia.

> [*GF* 67: Do you want to know our answer? Then go back as fast as you can, and tell your leaders that if they will all become Turks, and renounce the god whom you worship on bended knee, and cast off your laws, we will give them this land and more besides, with cities and castles, so that none of you shall remain a foot-soldier, but you shall all be knights as we are: and tell them that we will count them always among our dearest friends.][32]

The pagans' apparent generosity, promising to turn every poor foot soldier rich, is rooted in an assumption of Eastern affluence. Throughout the *Gesta*, the armies of the enemy are said to travel with a wealth of provisions that become the Christians' through conquest. As Hill has pointed out, there is something strongly formulaic in the description of the plunder the Crusaders find after every battle. After the Battle of Antioch, for instance, "Illi uero dimiserunt ibi papiliones suos, et aurum, et argentum, multaque ornamenta; oues quoque et boues, equos et mulos, camelos et asinos, frumentum et uinum, farinam et alia multa quae nobis erant necessaria" [*GF* 70: "The enemy left his pavilions, with gold and silver and many furnishings, as well as sheep, oxen, horses, mules, camels and asses, corn, wine, flour and many other things of which we were badly in need"]. Similarly, after the Battle of Ascalon, "Reuersi sunt nostri ad tentoria eorum, acceperuntque innumera spolia auri, argenti, omniumque bonorum;

omniumque animalium genera, ac omnium armorum instrumenta"
[*GF* 97: "Our men went back to the enemy camp and found innumerable spoils of gold and silver, piles of riches, and all kinds of animals,
weapons and tools"]. What here echoes the chansons, however, is not
just the repetitive wording, the structuring of the spoils from pre-
cious metals to valuables to animals and necessary goods, but also
the emphasis on the Easterner as opulent. Everywhere the value of the
Muslims' trappings is shown, such as Yaghi-Siyan's ("Balteum quoque
eius et uaginam appretiauerunt sexaginta bizanteis" [*GF* 48: "His belt
and scabbard were worth sixty bezants"]) and the Egyptian emir's
("Ensem uero emit quidam sexaginta bisanteis" [*GF* 97: "The amir's
sword was bought for sixty bezants"]); even the dead are buried with
"pallia, bisanteos aureos, arcus, sagittas, et alia plurima instrumenta,
quae nominare nequimus" [*GF* 42: "cloaks, gold bezants, bows and
arrows, and other tools the names of which we do not know"].

Furthermore, Muslims in the *Gesta* are not just religiously misguided and opulent, they are also morally decadent: luxurious, pro-
miscuous, and at the same time to a certain extent emasculated.
These characteristics are introduced into the *Gesta* by and through
Kerbogha, the best-described Muslim in the work. Shortly after arriving at Antioch with an enormous army, he finds the Franks in dreadful shape. Buoyed by this, the Anonymous says, he sends a letter to his
coreligionists in Khorasan. In this wholly imaginary missive the atabeg of Mosul elevates entertainment and lust almost to patriotic duty:

> Caliphae nostro apostolico, ac nostri regi domino Soldano militi for-
> tissimo, atque omnibus prudentissimis Corrozanae militibus, salus et
> immensus honor. Satis sint leti et gauisi iocunda concordia, et satis-
> faciant uentribus, imperent et sermocinent per uniuersam regionem
> illam, ut omnino dent sese ad petulantiam et luxuriam, multosque
> filios patrare congaudeant, qui contra Christianos fortiter pugnare
> preualeant.

> [*GF* 52: To the khalif our pope and the lord sultan our king, that
> most valiant warrior, and to all the most gallant knights of Khorasan,
> greeting and boundless honour! Enjoy yourselves, rejoicing with one
> accord, and fill your bellies, and let commands and injunctions be
> sent throughout the whole country that all men shall give themselves
> up to wantonness and lust, and take their pleasure in getting many
> sons who shall fight bravely against the Christians and defeat them.]

What better way to oppose the isolated, starving Franks than to eat,
drink, and rampantly procreate? Interestingly, this passage, which

shows Kerbogha at his most ebullient, confidently urging the Muslims on to debauchery, is followed immediately by another that shows him in a very different light. The passage in which Kerbogha's mother approaches her son and advises him not to fight the Franks has garnered some critical attention; while some have discussed the veracity of the episode and its possible origin as "camp gossip," others, notably Natasha Hodgson, have focused on the remarkable qualities ascribed to Kerbogha's mother and on the implications of her words, which suggest the superiority of the Christian religion.[33] However, even though the episode presents Kerbogha's mother as caring and learned, the Anonymous's intent is not so much to describe Muslim women as it is to cast a shadow over Kerbogha. Although he is depicted as the apex of Turkish power in the text, the one to whom the unfortunate Sensadolus cannot but subject himself and who confidently urges his coreligionists on to enjoy themselves in the expectation of victory, the passage shows Kerbogha struggling to get out from under his mother's wings. It presents him as not only debauched but also immature and perhaps weak—an unheroic foil to the Franks, whose women are mostly limited to serving refreshments to the men on the battlefield.[34]

KNIGHTS OF CHRIST

The Muslim opponents as we find them in the *Gesta* therefore closely resemble the Saracens in the chansons de geste. They are ethnically diverse, wealthy, and polytheist, which makes them less worthy as knights than the Christians. As suggested by the depictions of Kerbogha, the best-described Muslim in the work, we also find them to be both morally dissolute and unduly influenced by women. Confronting the Muslims on the battlefield are the Christians, who are very much the opposite: united, morally just, and of course relentlessly poor and miserable. The Anonymous's description of the Christian army, too, is deeply rooted in the chansons: he relies on them to define the Crusaders' reasons for taking the cross and their relation to the divine, their military qualities and accomplishments, as well as their ethnic makeup. Furthermore, as he bases his definition of Crusade and what it entails to a large extent on his portrayal of the motivations and achievements of the Christians, this also markedly affects his Crusade ideology.

At the very beginning of his work the Anonymous outlines what led so many Christians, among whom he includes himself, to take up arms and set out for the East:

Cum iam appropinquasset ille terminus quem dominus Iesus cotidie
suis demonstrat fidelibus, specialiter in euangelio dicens: "Si quis uult
post me uenire, abneget semetipsum et tollat crucem suam et sequatur
me," facta est igitur motio ualida per uniuersas Galliarum regiones,
ut si aliquis Deum studiose puroque corde et mente sequi desideraret,
atque post ipsum crucem fideliter baiulare uellet, non pigritaretur
Sancti Sepulchri uiam celerius arripere.

[*GF* 1: When that time had already come, of which the Lord Jesus
warns his faithful people every day, especially in the Gospel where
he says, "If any man will come after me, let him deny himself, and
take up his cross, and follow me," there was a great stirring of heart
throughout all the Frankish lands, so that if any man, with all his
heart and all his mind, really wanted to follow God and faithfully to
bear the cross after him, he could make no delay in taking the road to
the Holy Sepulchre as quickly as possible.]

The above, with its heavy reliance on Matthew 16:24, has led Kenneth Baxter Wolf to argue that the Anonymous considered and consequently described the Crusade as nothing more than a pilgrimage:
"The language is exclusively that of a pilgrimage, where the whole
point is to walk in Christ's footsteps and to experience the sufferings of his passion . . . it is the pilgrimage aspect of the crusade, not
the conquests per se, that dominate the account."[35] This, however, is
only half of the explanation offered in the early pages of the *Gesta* of
why Christians set out, and were obligated to set out, for Jerusalem.
Immediately after the Anonymous speaks of the need for the faithful
to take up their crosses, he adds the following:

Ait namque domnus apostolicus "Fratres, uos oportet multa pati pro
nomine Christi, uidelicet miserias, paupertates, nuditates, persecu-
tiones, egestates, infirmitates, fames, sites et alia huiusmodi, sicuti
Dominus ait suis discipulis: 'Oportet uos pati multa pro nomine
meo.'"

[*GF* 1–2: The lord pope said also, "Brothers, you must suffer for the
name of Christ many things, wretchedness, poverty, nakedness, persecution, need, sickness, hunger, thirst and other such troubles, for
the Lord says to his disciples, 'You must suffer many things for my
name.'"]

The Anonymous's quotation of Acts 9:16 here ("I will show him how
much he must suffer for my name") is inaccurate, and Hill has found
in this yet more evidence that he was a layman, if a devout one.[36]
What is remarkable here is, however, not the inaccuracy—the Anonymous quoted the rather longer passage from Matthew correctly—but

the fact that with this modification the passage echoes the famous words of Roland: "Pur sun seignor deit hom susfrir destreiz / E endurer e granz chalz e grans freiz, / Sin deit hom perdre e del quir e del peil" [*CR* ll. 1010–12: "For his lord a vassal must suffer hardships / And endure great heat and great cold; / And he must lose both hair and hide"]. The Christian duty to take up one's cross and follow Christ is therefore closely followed by a reference to a very lay notion found in the chansons, that of a contract of mutual obligation between the Crusaders and God. The Christians must suffer for God and fight the "inimici Dei" [*GF* 40: "God's enemies"];[37] by doing so they become "Christi militia" [*GF* 14: "Christ's army"], "fortissimi milites Christi" [*GF* 18: "most valiant soldiers of Christ"], and "milites . . . ueri Dei" [*GF* 40: "knights of the True God"]. In turn, God's commitment to the Crusaders as defined in the *Gesta* is threefold: he will assist them in the struggle against his enemies and will give them earthly as well as heavenly rewards, thereby combining the duties of secular and spiritual lord.

God in the *Gesta* often helps the Christians, and much agency in the success of the Crusade is ascribed to him. He acts almost as a field commander at Dorylaeum: "Et nisi Dominus fuisset nobiscum in bello, et aliam cito nobis misisset aciem, nullus nostrorum euasisset. . . . Sed omnipotens Deus pius et misericors qui non permisit suos milites perire, nec in manibus inimicorum incidere, festine nobis adiutorium misit" [*GF* 20–21: "If God had not been with us in this battle and sent us the other army quickly, none of us would have escaped . . . but Almighty God, who is gracious and merciful, delivered his knights from death and from falling into the hands of the enemy and sent us help speedily"]. He outflanks the Saracens at Antioch, when "Stabant uero inimici Dei et nostri undique iam stupefacti et uehementer perterriti, putantes nostros se deuincere et occidere. . . . Sed Deus omnipotens hoc illis non permisit" [*GF* 40: "God's enemies and ours were standing about, amazed and terrified, for they thought that they could defeat and kill us . . . but Almighty God did not allow them to do so"].[38] Finally, at Ascalon, he is with the Christians in the front lines: "Bella uero erant immensa; sed uirtus divina comitabatur nobiscum tam magna, tam fortis, quod statim superauimus illos" [*GF* 96: "The battle was terrible, but the power of God was with us, so mighty and so strong that we gained the victory at once"]. God here is not a distant judge of the moral perfection of his followers but an active participant who aids the Christians in their war against his enemies.

Furthermore, he rewards them for their efforts. This is made clear from the very beginning of the work: the Anonymous follows up on the Christians' obligation to suffer with "ac deinceps: 'Persequetur uos larga retributio'" [GF 2: "and afterwards 'Great will be your reward'"]. This reward, intriguingly, is both spiritual and material. For one, if death meant an eternity with the devil to the Muslim, to die in the service of God gave the Christian access to heaven. This applies even to those who did not die in battle; to die while fulfilling one's duty to suffer is sufficient. As the Anonymous says about the very first action of the army of the princes, the siege of Nicaea:

> Fuimusque in obsidione illa per septem ebdomadas et tres dies, et multi ex nostris illic receperunt martyrium, et letantes gaudentesque reddiderunt felices animas Deo; et ex pauperrima gente multi mortui sunt fame pro Christi nomine. Qui in caelum triumphantes portarunt stolam recepti martyrii, una uoce dicentes: "Vindica Domine sanguinem nostrum, qui pro te effusus est."

> [GF 17: We besieged this city for seven weeks and three days, and many of our men suffered martyrdom there and gave up their blessed souls to God with joy and gladness, and many of the poor starved to death for the Name of Christ. All these entered Heaven in triumph, wearing the robe of martyrdom which they have received, saying with one voice, "Avenge, O Lord, our blood which was shed for thee."][39]

Bypassing the absolution of sin, the Christians' suffering "in the Name of Christ" means that God will welcome them to heaven. Furthermore, their death serves as a call for God to avenge them upon the Muslims, as it was Charlemagne's obligation to avenge Roland, Oliver, and the other douzepeers.

God's obligation to the Christian, however, is not only one of spiritual salvation; importantly, he grants earthly riches as well. That service to the divine will yield possessions is highlighted on the first page of the Gesta: "Si quis animam suam saluam facere uellet, non dubitaret humiliter uiam incipere Domini, ac si denariorum ei deesset copia, diuina ei satis daret misericordia" [GF 1: "If any man wants to save his soul, let him have no hesitation in taking the way of the Lord in humility, and if he lacks money, the divine mercy will give him enough"]. God's reward for services rendered is given in plunder and conquest. After God has helped the Crusaders overcome the enemy, the reward is there for the taking: "Superati sunt itaque, Deo annuente, in illo die inimici nostri. Satis uero recuperati sunt nostri de equis et de aliis multis quae erant illis ualde necessaria" [GF

37: "Thus, by God's will, on that day our enemies were overcome. Our men captured plenty of horses and other things of which they were badly in need"]. This remarkable juxtaposition of holy war and earthly reward, of service to the divine and the expectation of profit, is best expressed in the words uttered by the Crusaders before the Battle of Dorylaeum: "Factus est itaque sermo secretus inter nos laudantes et consulentes atque dicentes: 'Estote omnimodo unanimes in fide Christi et Sanctae Crucis uictoria, quia hodie omnes diuites si Deo placet effecti eritis'" [*GF* 19–20: "For our part we passed a secret message along our line, praising God and saying, 'Stand fast all together, trusting in Christ and in the victory of the Holy Cross. Today, please God, you will all gain much booty'"].[40]

At the heart of the Christian army therefore lie contracts of mutual obligation similar to those upon which the ethical universe of the chansons de geste rests. Such contracts exist between the Christians themselves—for example, between Bohemond and Alexius Comnenus, to whom "si ille fideliter teneret illud sacramentum, iste suum nunquam preteriret" [*GF* 12: "if Bohemond kept his oath faithfully he would never break his own"]. Failure to uphold one's side of the bargain is met with extreme censure, and Alexius's abandonment of the Crusaders at Antioch turns him, in the eyes of the Anonymous, into an "iniquus imperator" [*GF* 6: "that wretch of an emperor"] or "infelix imperator" [*GF* 10: "the wretched emperor"], while his general Tatikios No-Nose becomes "ille inimicus . . . in periurio manet et manebit" [*GF* 35: "that enemy of ours . . . he is a liar, and always will be"]. More important, however, is that this "sacramentum" exists between God and the Christians—they will fight his war for him, and suffer in the process; he will reward that suffering both on earth and in heaven. Crucially, even though the beginning of the work invokes the language of pilgrimage, the *Gesta* conceptualizes Crusade as service owed to the divine: the *crucesignatus* keeps his part of a bargain that casts God as both his spiritual and his secular overlord. The Crusader, on the one hand, is a Christian fighting a spiritual war for the supremacy of his faith over the unbeliever, and he is rewarded with paradise;[41] on the other hand, he confronts his Lord's earthly enemies, reconquers his earthly possessions, and finds a secular reward of plunder strewn across the battlefield. Essentially, the Crusader's duty is to God: the secular lords of the First Crusade may spend almost as much time fighting each other as they do the Saracen, or abandon the army altogether, and the spiritual lords such as Adhemar of Le Puy may go the way of the flesh, but this obligation remains undiminished by the dissent, betrayal, or death of merely human powers.[42]

Like the knights of the chansons, the Crusaders serve one divinity, who rewards them with heaven, and one monarch, who provides them with earthly goods: the Christian God is both of these in the *Gesta*. They serve him on battlefields that echo those of the jongleurs. Even though the Anonymous might often have found himself in the heat of battle, he nevertheless evokes the sights and sounds of warfare with a number of stock phrases, reminiscent of those of the chansons, rather than relying on his own experience: "Iunctis igitur prospere nostris, unus comminus percutiebat alium. Clamor uero resonabat ad celum. Omnes preliabantur insimul. Imbres telorum obnubilabant aerem" [*GF* 36: "Our army joined battle successfully and fought hand-to-hand; the din arose to heaven, for all were fighting at once and the storm of missiles darkened the sky"]; "Rumor quoque et clamor nostrorum et illorum resonabat ad caelum. Pluuiae telorum et sagittarum tegebant polum, et claritatem diei" [*GF* 41: "The din and the shouts of our men and the enemy echoed to heaven, and the shower of missiles and arrows covered the sky and hid the daylight"]. Upon these loud and dark places, where one can hear the Saracens "stridere et garrire ac clamare uehementissimo clamore" [*GF* 40: "gnash their teeth and gabble and howl with very loud cries"], knights roam looking for their prey. As Conor Kostick has pointed out, "The attention of the author of the *Gesta Francorum* was almost entirely fixed on the activities of those he terms *seniores* and *milites*."[43] This is especially so in describing battles: the Anonymous portrays the Crusade almost completely as a sequence of confrontations between mounted warriors, even when horses had become scarce and many knights were reduced to fighting on foot. At Antioch, when hunger and disease had already taken a dreadful toll, and "In tota namque hoste non ualebat aliquis inuenire mille milites, qui equos haberent optimos" [*GF* 34: "In the whole camp you could not find a thousand knights who had managed to keep their horses in really good condition"], the Christians counter the Turkish assaults with cavalry charge upon cavalry charge:

> Fuit itaque ille, undique signo crucis munitus, qualiter leo perpessus famem per tres aut quatuor dies, qui exiens a suis cauernis, rugiens ac sitiens sanguinem pecudum sicut improuide ruit inter agmina gregum, dilanians oues fugientes huc et illuc; ita agebat iste inter agmina Turcorum. Tam uehementer instabat illis, ut linguae uexilli uolitarent super Turcorum capita.

[*GF* 37: So Bohemond, protected on all sides by the sign of the Cross, charged the Turkish forces, like a lion which has been starving for three or four days, which comes roaring out of its cave thirsting for the blood of cattle, and falls upon the flocks careless of its own safety, tearing the sheep as they flee hither and thither. His attack was so fierce that the points of his banner were flying right over the heads of the Turks.]

This relentless focus on chivalric combat continues throughout the work. Knights drive all before them: "Egregius itaque comes Flandrensis . . . occurrit illis una cum Boamundo. Irrueruntque nostri unanimiter super illos. Qui statim arripuerunt fugam, et festinanter uerterunt retro scapulas, ac mortui sunt ex illis plurimi" [*GF* 31: "But the noble count of Flanders . . . made straight for the enemy with Bohemond at his side, and our men charged them in one line. The enemy straightaway took to flight, turning tail in a hurry; many of them were killed"]. Even within the melee they are shown victorious in individual combat: "Paganorum uero gens uidens Christi milites, diuisit se; et fecerunt duo agmina. Nostri autem inuocato Christi nomine, tam acriter inuaserunt illos incredulos, ut quisque miles prosterneret suum" [*GF* 89: "When the pagans saw the Christian knights they split up into two bands, but our men called upon the Name of Christ and charged these misbelievers so fiercely that every knight overthrew his opponent"]. The Crusade is presented as fought above all by knights in the manner familiar to them; the achievements of nonaristocratic infantry is minimalized if not ignored, and we usually hear of them only when they perish.[44] More than indicating the Anonymous's social rank,[45] the primacy of chivalric warfare in the *Gesta* shows him eager to present the Crusade from the very beginning of the movement as a uniquely chivalric affair. The Christians on their way to Jerusalem, at least the ones that matter, are knights, and they wage war against the Saracens in the fashion to which they are accustomed. By reducing the complex military history of the First Crusade to a war of knights against Saracens, the Anonymous makes it contiguous with the chivalric campaigns of the chansons de geste. William of Orange, Roland, Oliver, and the douzepeers are knights above all, their fight against the Saracens waged on horseback, with lance and sword. The Crusaders, the *Gesta* states from the very beginning, tread in the footsteps of Charlemagne: "Isti potentissimi milites et alii plures quos ignoro uenerunt per uiam quam iamdudum Karolus Magnus mirificus rex Franciae aptari fecit usque Constantinopolim" [*GF*

2: "These most valiant knights and many others (whose names I do not know) travelled by the road which Charlemagne, the heroic king of the Franks, had formerly caused to be built to Constantinople"].[46] They do this literally as well as figuratively—they too are Christian knights on their way to fight the pagans. The battlefields of Roncesvalles and Antioch are separate in time and place, but those who walked upon them are very much alike.

The similarity between the heroes of the chansons and the First Crusaders is highlighted by a further act of identification. Not only are the Crusaders Christians who loyally serve God as well as knights who rule the battlefield, they are also Franks.[47] As much as the Anonymous pluralizes the enemy, adding Azymites, Paulicians, Agulani, Kurds, and Persians to the ranks of the Turks and Arabs, so he reduces the Christians to a single ethnic denomination. The Anonymous hardly ever acknowledges the remarkable internationalism of the First Crusade, which brought together Flemings, Provençals, Normans, French, Germans, and Italians under common purpose.[48] He acknowledges this multiethnicity only at the very beginning of the *Gesta*, in the context of the failed Popular Crusade, when "Petrus uero supradictus primus uenit Constantinopolim in kalendis Augusti et cum eo maxima gens Alamannorum. Illic inuenit Lombardos et Longobardos et alios plures congregatos" [*GF* 2: "The aforesaid Peter [the Hermit] was the first to reach Constantinople on 1 August, and many Germans came with him. There they found men from northern and southern Italy and many others gathered together"]. These Germans and Italians choose their own leaders at Nicomedia and march into Asia Minor; there they are decimated at Xerigordon and disappear from the pages of the *Gesta* and of history. These diverse commoners done away with, the chivalric armies that cross the Bosporus shortly afterward are referred to almost exclusively as *Franci* and, less frequently, *Francigenae* [lit. "of Frankish origin"].[49] The use of this terminology to describe the ethnically very diverse second wave of Crusaders is remarkable. The Anonymous certainly knew in great detail the backgrounds of many of those he saw around him and must have known that most were not Franks or even had Frankish origins.[50] He does not, as does Raymond of Aguilers, explain his use of nomenclature.[51] The Anonymous most likely was not a Frank, and as far as we know he never allied himself to any lord who could justifiably be called Frankish, having served the Italian Norman Bohemond and the Provençal Raymond of Toulouse.

To call the Crusaders Franks was not a simple act of reducing the multitudes gathered under the banner of the cross to the dominant ethnic group, for the sake of convenience, to highlight their prominence among the Crusaders, or to hide discord between the many groups who were party to the Crusade enterprise.[52] That the Anonymous abandoned the use of the more geographically definite term "Galli" by the beginning of book 2, where he also abandoned "Alemanni" and "Longobardi," indicates that he was not interested in the primacy of the French as such. Rather, it was an act of identification of the Crusaders with the very Franks of whom the chansons de geste spoke. If Charlemagne's Franks had built the road to Constantinople, the Anonymous's Franks once again trod upon it on their way east. Like the Franks of the chansons, the Crusaders were Christian knights dedicated to and united in service, fighting their lord's disparate pagan enemies to avenge the wrongs done to him and in defense of his earthly possessions. They were therefore the true heirs to these earlier Franks, and their story truly *Gesta Francorum*.[53] Indeed, this identification of the Crusaders with Charlemagne's Franks may be the true purpose of the work's use of the conventions of the chansons de geste.

THE CHANSONS DE GESTE AND THE GESTA FRANCORUM

The Anonymous's use of chanson de geste commonplaces in the *Gesta Francorum* is unremitting. Full of lexical, syntactic, and thematic echoes, the work recasts the Crusaders as the successors to the heroes of the chansons, fighting similar enemies, in a similar way, and for similar reasons. This, of course, immediately raises the question *why* the author of the *Gesta* would go to such lengths to bring to mind the West's mostly imaginary ancestors when describing the deeds of the Crusaders in the East. The Anonymous may have had several reasons for this. To imagine the new Crusade enterprise as an extension of the wars of the chansons associated it with a fashionable genre increasingly popular with Western chivalry. On the most elementary level, this could make the Anonymous's story of the Crusade more appealing; by putting it in line with contemporary narrative trends, the luster of the jongleurs' works would be reflected on it. More important, however, was that it could undoubtedly also help boost the appeal of the still-novel concept of Crusade to a Western audience, and this at a crucial time. The conquest of Jerusalem did not mean the end of the need for Christian manpower in the Levant; rather, it increased it, as Crusaders returning home left the newly conquered areas dangerously exposed. It did, however, rob the Crusade movement of an important teleology. If God had wanted the liberation of the Holy Places, what could serve as a rallying cry now that it had been accomplished? To describe, as the Anonymous did, the First Crusaders as new Franks, and the Crusade as a continuation of the (supposed) earlier wars of the Franks against their Saracen opponents, was to imagine this new movement as part of a long list of confrontations within a far older, ongoing conflict between Christians and the non-Christian others on their borders. If the First Crusade had as its goal Jerusalem, Bethlehem, and Nazareth, this war of "Frank" against "Saracen" was essentially unending.

The continuing wars in the new Crusader states therefore gave the audience of the chansons a chance to take their place in (imagined) history and emulate Charlemagne, the douzepeers, or William of Orange on the shores of Palestine. Morris has suggested that the Anonymous aimed his work especially at an Italian audience, for whom it would have been easy to understand Latin.[54] However, the fact that the Anonymous chose to write the work in Latin may indicate that he imagined a wider audience for the work—wherever Latin was understood, wherever the tale of the First Crusade could be told, and wherever new Crusaders could be recruited. That Bohemond of Taranto chose to distribute copies of the *Gesta* far and wide during his European recruitment campaign of 1104–1106 shows that he considered it useful far outside Italy.

Turning the First Crusade into a chanson de geste of new Franks, however, did more than offer Western chivalry a reason to continue the war against the Saracen beyond the conquest of Jerusalem. Perhaps more important, it allowed the Western Christians to explain and justify their ownership of the newly subjugated lands, especially of those tracts that were not traditionally understood to be part of the inheritance of Christ. The *Gesta* intriguingly discusses the ownership of the land the Christians conquer on their way to Jerusalem. From the moment of their arrival at Constantinople, the First Crusaders were famously compelled to sign an oath of fealty to the Byzantine emperor, in which they swore to surrender any lands conquered to his control. Some echoes of this oath—emphatically decried in the *Gesta*[55]—are found in the beginning of the work, such as when the knight Peter of Aups swears to hold a city "in fidelitate Dei et Sancti

Sepulchri, et seniorum atque imperatoris" [*GF* 26: "in fealty to God and the Holy Sepulchre, and to our leaders and the emperor"].[56] However, the primacy of others here, to whom the emperor is but an afterthought, already heralds a significant shift to come. At Antioch, the Crusaders themselves are firmly established as the rightful owners of the newly occupied regions. This is done in perhaps the most chanson-like passage of the *Gesta*—the remarkable speech Kerbogha's mother addresses to her son. Having arrived at his camp before Antioch, his mother admonishes Kerbogha regarding the folly of attempting battle with the Christians trapped within its walls. Speaking of the Crusaders, she says:

> Hoc autem, karissime, in rei ueritate scias, quoniam isti Christiani filii Christi uocati sunt; et prophetarum ore filii adoptionis et promissionis, et secundum apostolum heredes Christi sunt, quibus Christus hereditates repromissas iam donauit, dicendo per prophetas: "A solis ortu usque ad occasum erunt termini uestri, et nemo stabit contra uos." Et quis potest hic dictis contradicere uel obstare?

> [*GF* 54: Beloved, know also the truth of this, that those Christians are called "sons of Christ" and, by the mouth of the prophets, "sons of adoption and promise" and the apostle says that they are "heirs of Christ," to whom Christ has even now given the promised inheritance, saying by the prophets, "From the rising of the sun to the going down thereof shall be your bounds, and no man shall stand against you." Who can contradict these words or resist them?]

The wording of the passage establishes the Crusaders as the rightful and irresistible owners of the land, which Christ himself has given to them to keep as their own. The emperor, whose troops—as the Anonymous is at pains to remind his audience[57]—abandoned the Crusaders at Antioch, is all but forgotten; the Crusaders will be beholden to nobody in establishing their dominion in the East.[58]

Intriguingly, the use of the conventions of the chansons de geste and the concomitant identification of the Crusaders with the Franks of legend support this emancipation of the Crusader host from the shadow of the emperor and their claim to the ownership of the land. From the very beginning of the work, which shows the Crusaders on the road to Constantinople that Charlemagne built, the audience is reminded of the extent of the Frankish king's lands, which, in memory and imagination, came to include most of the known world, as well as Constantinople and the Near East.[59] Before the emperor's oath of fealty is even brought up, the Anonymous calls attention to the

fact that the empire and all the lands the Crusaders are about to conquer were once subject to the king of the Franks. The continuous
identification of the Crusaders with the Franks that had once sup-
posedly ruled the Levant therefore gives them a right of ownership
certainly as valid or even more so than that of the emperor, whose
claim to the lands the Crusaders conquered was also based on previous tenure. If the Crusaders are the heirs of Christ, and are given the
land by him to rule, they in a more secular legal sense can also claim
it as new Franks, the heirs of Charlemagne, its erstwhile overlord.
The Eastern emperor's rights are therefore nullified, superseded by his
empire's ancient subjection to the Franks, and the Byzantines reduced
to upstart interlopers at best or traitors at worst; indeed, it is as the
latter that they are consistently represented in the *Gesta*.[60] Therefore,
when Kerbogha approaches Antioch, the Crusade leaders send out
emissaries to him not just to discuss the details of the upcoming battle
but also to indignantly ask why he had intruded upon Christian land
and had attacked its population:

> Porro statuerunt omnes maiores nostri concilium, quatinus nuntium
> mitterent ad inimicos Christi Turcos, qui per aliquem interpretem
> interrogaret eos secure eloquio dicens quamobrem superbissime in
> Christianorum introissent terram, et cur castrametati sint, et quare
> Christi seruos occidant et conquassent. Cumque iam finis esset dictis,
> inuenerunt quosdam uiros, Petrum scilicet Heremitam et Herluinum,
> illisque dixerunt haec omnia: "Ite ad execratum Turcorum exercitum,
> et diligenter narrate eis haec omnia, interrogantes eos, cur audacter et
> superbissime introierint terram Christianorum et nostram."

> [*GF* 65–66: All our leaders forthwith held a council and arranged
> to send a messenger to Christ's enemies the Turks, so that he might
> question them through an interpreter, asking confidently why they
> had been so vainglorious as to enter into the Christians' land and
> encamp there, and why they were killing and bullying the servants of
> Christ. When they had ended their council they found certain men,
> Peter the Hermit and Herluin, and said to them, "Go to the accursed
> army of the Turks and give them this whole message in full, asking
> them why they have been so rash and vainglorious as to enter the land
> which belongs to the Christians and to us."]

There is no dispute about to whom the newly conquered territories
truly belong: the Crusaders are not invaders but the rightful owners
of the land, and Kerbogha's army is not a relief force but reduced to a
band of trespassers. The *Gesta* shows the Crusaders to have a double
claim to their conquests: as heirs to Christ, they have a religious and

eschatological claim,[61] while as heirs to Charlemagne and the Franks they have a secular and historical one.[62]

Disregarding possible aesthetic benefits, the use of the conventions of the chanson de geste in the *Gesta* helps to establish the legitimacy of the Crusaders' possession of the new Crusader states as well as to motivate others to join in their defense. At the heart of this intention, and consequently at the heart of the *Gesta*, lie nothing less than the needs of emerging frontier communities that, the hard work of conquest done, now need to turn to the harder work of maintaining political and territorial integrity. No mean feat, and the Anonymous clearly thought it required whatever enthusiasm could be mustered. He therefore complements the religious underpinnings of Crusade with a secular rationale: alongside the simple lay devotion that permeates the work, and that finds its culmination in a religious version of the compact of mutual obligation between lord and vassal that sees the Crusaders as God's warriors, the Anonymous introduces historical concerns and literary representations to motivate the wars in the East. The Crusaders therefore are the heirs of Christ but also heirs of Charlemagne; the Saracens are the enemies of God but also the historical, implacable enemies of the Franks, new or old; and Byzantium is no Christian ally but rather a treacherous Ganelon. Both religious and secular interests are expressed through the chivalric ethos around which the chansons were built: prowess, loyalty, reward, revenge.

Recent study of the *Gesta* has shown Steven Runciman's belief that its author was "a simple soldier, honest according to his lights but credulous and prejudiced" to have underestimated him.[63] The sophisticated Latin of the *Gesta* and the learning the Anonymous included in its pages reveal him to have been a refined author who approached his work with thoughtfulness and purpose; his understanding of chanson commonplaces reveals his sensitivity to the particulars of vernacular culture.[64] The teleology of the *Gesta* furthermore shows its author to have been a man who looked forward as well as back. Completing his work after the Battle of Ascalon,[65] with the help of material he had written previously, he exhibits a subtle understanding of the need to politically and legally establish—as well as to safeguard militarily—the emerging Crusader states, centrally among which, of course, was that of his erstwhile lord, Bohemond of Taranto. The *Gesta* never was, nor was meant to be, a simple war diary. Rather, it was an explanation of and tool for nation building designed to appeal to as broad a swath of Western fervor as possible, most especially among knights, written in a language that facilitated wide distribution. In the way it reflects the concerns of the emerging Crusader states, it is perhaps best understood as "settler writing"—in its own way on a par with other great foundational epics.[66]

It is also within this framework of settler writings, of an appeal from the East to the West for political recognition and military support, that the *Gesta*'s diffusion and popularity must be seen. Bohemond of Taranto is known to have taken the work with him when he set out on his recruiting tour of Europe in late 1104. This was not simply because the *Gesta* narrated the remarkable deeds of the Crusaders, Bohemond's prominent among them—these most likely had already been related by those returning from the East, and were recounted time and again by the man himself.[67] Indeed, the *Gesta*'s great benefit to the cause of Bohemond, as well as to the other states, was that it integrated the details of the campaign and the heroism of the First Crusaders into a narrative framework that drew upon *both* the secular and the religious concerns of the Western fighting classes. If the Crusade had been at heart a religious affair, the Anonymous realized that the survival of Outremer required any and all support it could get—from those wanting heavenly as well as earthly rewards, settlers, penitents, and culture warriors. In depicting this new Christian frontier as the place where all motivations could and had to exist side by side, the *Gesta* introduces a pragmatic note at the very beginning of the Crusade enterprise. It was this practical understanding of political and military realities, rather than its recounting of the events of 1096–1099 or its glorification of his actions, that made the *Gesta* valuable to the prince of Antioch, who by the time of his return to Europe was conscious of the fact that the pursuit of his ambitions in the Eastern Mediterranean required more manpower and resources than could be provided by repentant sinners alone.[68]

CHAPTER 3

Robert of Reims's *Historia Iherosolimitana*

Bohemond of Taranto's first years as prince of Antioch, during which he relentlessly sought to expand his territory, were not very successful. In 1101, Bohemond set out with a small force in support of a local ally threatened by the Danishmend Turks, the Armenian Gabriel of Melitene, and was badly defeated and captured before even reaching Gabriel's town. Although this left his principality in the capable hands of his nephew Tancred, Bohemond remained a prisoner of the Danishmend emir for three years. His plans were once again foiled shortly after his release, when an eastward advance was checked at the Battle of Harran on 7 May 1104. These defeats put a heavy strain on his already limited resources, and increased pressure from the Byzantines, against whom Bohemond stood in defiance of the oath he had sworn in 1097, convinced him to launch an appeal for aid to the West. In this he was remarkably effective; from his arrival at Bari in 1105 to his return to the East two years later, he was feted at courts throughout Europe and everywhere drew recruits to his cause. Such was his appeal that he was granted the hand in marriage of Constance, the daughter of the French king Philip I, in 1106, and was refused entry into England by Henry I lest too many members of the English nobility join him.

By 1107 Bohemond had a substantial army under his command; nevertheless his invasion of Byzantine Illyria foundered, and in 1108 he was forced to sign the Treaty of Devol, in which he subjected himself and his Eastern territories to the authority of the emperor. Thus Bohemond, during the decade after the First Crusade, experienced a

remarkable combination of diplomatic victory and military defeat, of
success in rallying the Western nobility to his cause and failure to turn
this success into lasting political advantage. Although his fame as one
of the First Crusaders undoubtedly contributed to his appeal, it is
also clear that he was very careful to address all concerns in his drive
to whip up Western support. His acceptance in 1105 of the *vexillum
Sancti Petri* from the hands of Pope Paschal II clothed the upcoming
campaign in the guise of holy war if not Crusade. Conversely, Orderic Vitalis also has Bohemond describe to his audience the riches that
could be won in the East.[1] It is within this approach to recruitment
that we must see Bohemond's introduction of the *Gesta Francorum*
into Western Europe.

Bohemond's journey to Europe, and the transmission of the *Gesta*
from East to West, also resulted in the production of new histories
that drew on the Anonymous's work in the years after 1105. Robert, a monk of Reims, composed his *Historia Iherosolimitana* around
1106–1107, a work that was soon followed by the *Historia Ierosolimitana* of Baldric of Bourgueil, the archbishop of Dol (ca. 1107–1108),
and the *Gesta Dei per Francos* of the abbot Guibert of Nogent-sous-
Coucy (ca. 1108–1109).[2] The reliance of these works on the *Gesta* has
led many to see them as created to support Bohemond's recruitment
effort.[3] The dating of the works roughly between Bohemond's arrival
in France and his humiliation at Devol, their generally sympathetic
approach to the prince of Antioch and correspondingly hostile view
of his Byzantine adversaries, and the relationship of the authors to the
court of France to which Bohemond associated himself through Constance in 1106 add further support for this view.[4] A closer look at the
most important and certainly the most popular of these, the work of
Robert of Reims, or Robert the Monk, shows that not only the purpose of the text but also its use of secular literary material to promote
Crusade echo the *Gesta*.[5]

Little more is known about the author of the *Historia Iherosolimitana* than about the anonymous author of its source text. In the
sermo apologeticus attached to the work, he indicates that his name
was Robert, that he was a monk at the monastery of St. Rémi in the
Bishopric of Reims, and that he felt compelled to write his work "per
obedientiam" [*HI* 3; *HFC* 75: "by my vow of obedience"] to an abbot,
Bernard. It has been suggested that he was the Robert who was briefly
abbot of St. Rémi at the end of the eleventh century, who was excom-
municated in 1097 and only reinstated through the help of Baldric of

Bourgueil and Bishop Lambert of Arras in 1100, and who then was prior of Sénuc until his death in 1122. This, however, would render it rather unlikely that he wrote the work because of a vow of obedience to an abbot.[6] Beyond this, evidence of the identity of Robert of Reims is scarce.[7] Even what little we know, however, suggests that Robert wrote from a position that was almost the polar opposite of that of the Anonymous, and the *Historia* shows that this informed how he approached his task of reworking the *Gesta*. If the Anonymous was a southern Italian fighting man who took part in the Crusade with people who intended to settle in the newly conquered territories, Robert was a northern French cleric who most likely never set foot in the East, and whose approach to the holy war was informed by a strong sense of French exceptionalism.

Although Robert uses the *Gesta* extensively in his own work, he makes it clear that he considered his source defective. Above all he thought it incomplete and artistically clumsy; his abbot, he says, had requested that he rework it because "ei admodum displicebat, partim quia initium suum, quod in Clari Montis concilio constitutum fuit, non habebat, partim quia series tam pulcre materiei inculta iacebat, et litteralium compositio dictionum inculta vacillabat" [*HI* 3; *HFC* 75: "he was not happy with it: partly because it did not include the beginning [of the Crusade] which was launched at the Council of Clermont; partly because it did not make the best of the sequence of wonderful events it contained and the composition was uncertain and unsophisticated in its style and expression"].[8] To counter the *Gesta*'s "uncertainness and unsophistication" Robert rewrote the work in an unadorned and heavily paratactic prose that emphasized clarity over erudition, and that he himself admits was likely to irritate the better educated because of its plainness.[9] Beyond the form, the content also needed revision, and it is here that Robert's greatest innovation may be found. He, as well as Baldric of Bourgueil and Guibert of Nogent, the other clerics to rework the *Gesta* in the decade after the conquest of Jerusalem, introduced a theological framework. Recasting the Crusade in a spiritual light, he identifies scriptural parallels and typological precursors to the events of 1096–1099, placing them within universal Christian history and thereby giving spiritual meaning to the recent past. Thus with the *Historia* "the crusading idea . . . passed back into the province of theologians," a reorientation that has been thought to be the most important aspect of Robert's work.[10] However, for all the attention that this introduction of a theological context to the *Gesta* has received, what is often forgotten is that Robert *increased* the use of chanson de geste commonplaces compared with his source text. This has most often been dismissed as a fallacy of the text or its narrator, and where it has been recognized as intentional it has been rejected as meaningless. Robert's most recent translator, Carol Sweetenham, after describing some of the chanson de geste characteristics of the *Historia*, argues that these were meant only to bring color to the work, and that "they prove nothing more than that Robert knew and echoed *chansons de geste* in his work."[11]

This dismissive attitude is unwarranted. If we accept that Robert's introduction of a theological framework was intended to influence his audience's understanding of the Crusade, then we must do so for his extensive use of the chansons as well. Robert's status as a clergyman makes it is easy to assume that his use of scripture was important, and his use of other writings spurious, but we must not forget that he was, after all, trying to sell a war to a wide audience, not merely interpreting the events of the previous decade in a way that would appeal to his fellow monks. Rather, both the new theological framework of the Crusade and the use of secular literary conventions are integral to Robert's message, because both are used to confer upon his audience a special status as divinely and historically chosen, the very basis for his exhortation to Crusade.

One of the reasons Robert says his abbot picked him to rework the *Gesta* was that he was present at the Council of Clermont, and was therefore able to fill an important lacuna in the Anonymous's work. Robert is one of a very few chroniclers to have reported on Urban II's speech, and much of our understanding of the events that set the First Crusade in motion therefore relies on his rendition of the pope's words. It is, however, unlikely that his recollection, put into words more than ten years after the fact, is entirely accurate, and indeed it differs markedly from versions related by other eyewitnesses, in length as well as detail, which might be fairly termed excessive. It is therefore likely that Robert's memory of the event was rather creative—especially because in Urban's great speech Robert already outlines the reasons for and obligation to Crusade that he will expand upon in the rest of his work:

> Gens Francorum, gens transmontana, gens, sicuti in pluribus vestris elucet operibus, a Deo electa et dilecta, tam situ terrarum quam fide catholica, quam honore sancte ecclesie ab universis nationibus segregata: ad vos sermo noster dirigitur. . . . A Iherosolimorum finibus

et urbe Constantinopolitana relatio gravis emersit, et sepissime iam ad aures nostras pervenit, quod vindelicet gens regni Persarum, gens extranea, gens prorsus a Deo aliena, generatio scilicet que non direxit cor suum et non est creditus cum Deo spiritus eius, terras illo-rum Christianorum invaserit, ferro, rapinis, incendio depopulaverit, ipsosque captivos partim in terram suam abduxerit, partimque nece miserabili prostraverit, ecclesiasque Dei aut funditus everterit, aut suorum ritui sacrorum mancipaverit. . . . Quibus igitur ad hoc ulcis-cendum, ad hoc eripiendum labor incumbit, nisi vobis, quibus pre ceteris gentibus contulit Deus insigne decus armorum, magnitudi-nem animorum, agilitatem corporum, virtutem humiliandi verticem capilli vobis resistentium? Moveant vos et incitent animos vestros ad virilitatem gesta predecessorum vestrorum, probitas et magnitudo Karoli Magni regis et Ludovici filii eius aliorumque regum vestro-rum, qui regna paganorum destruxerunt, et in eis fines sancte ecclesie dilataverunt. . . . O fortissimi milites et invictorum propago paren-tum, nolite degenerari, sed virtutis priorum vestrorum reminiscimini.

[*HI* 5–6; *HFC* 79–80: Frenchmen and men from across the moun-tains; men chosen by and beloved of God as is clear from your many achievements; men set apart from all other nations as much by geography as by the Catholic faith and by the honour of the Holy Church—it is to you that we address our sermon, to you that we appeal. . . . Disturbing news has emerged from Jerusalem and the city of Constantinople and is now constantly at the forefront of our mind: namely that the race of Persians, a foreign people and a people rejected by God, indeed a generation that set not their heart aright, and whose spirit was not stedfast with God, has invaded the lands of those Christians, depopulated them by slaughter and plunder and arson, kidnapped some of the Christians and carried them off to their own lands and put others to a wretched death, and has either overthrown the churches of God or turned them over to the rituals of their own religion. . . . So to whom should the task fall of taking vengeance and wresting their conquests from them if not to you— you to whom God has given above other nations outstanding glory in arms, greatness of spirit, fitness of body and the strength to humiliate the hairy scalp of those who resist you? May the deeds of your ances-tors move you and spur your souls to manly courage—the worth and greatness of Charlemagne, his son Louis and your other kings who destroyed the pagan kingdoms and brought them within the bounds of Christendom. . . . Oh most valiant soldiers and descendants of vic-torious ancestors, do not fall short of, but be inspired by, the courage of your forefathers.]

The opening lines of the *Historia* are careful to identify the "gens Francorum" [lit. "Frankish people"] as the target of Urban's Cru-sade appeal. Robert's understanding of who qualifies as Frankish, however, differs markedly from that of the Anonymous.[12] When Bohemond, urging his men to join the Crusade by invoking their ties to the Franks, asks them "Nonne et nos Francigene sumus? Nonne parentes nostri de Francia venerunt, et terram hanc militaribus armis sibi mancipaverunt?" [*HI* 15; *HFC* 92: "After all, are we not [of Frankish origin]? Didn't our parents come from [*Francia*] and take this land for themselves by force of arms?"],[13] he grounds Frankishness in particular geographical origins. The Franks, and the Francia from which they come, are further identified when Robert introduces the French prince Hugh of Vermandois as "frater Philippi regis Francorum, qui ipso tempore Franciam suo subiugabat imperio" [*HI* 13; *HFC* 89: "brother of King Philip I [of the Franks] who at this time [subjected Francia to his authority]"]. Whereas the Anonymous defined Frankishness in the broadest possible terms to incorporate most of Western Christianity, Robert therefore identifies the Franks more specifically as the inhabitants of the France of his day.[14] This more limited definition illustrates the target audience of the work: Robert's message—as was that of Urban II at Clermont—is directed above all to Frenchmen like himself, not to the whole of the Latin West.

While far fewer than those of the Anonymous, Robert's Franks play a role of paramount importance. They, above all others, are called upon to answer the crimes perpetrated by an enemy immediately defined through scripture.[15] The Franks are especially suited for this struggle because of their remarkable military achievements and their excellent pedigree in warfare, seen in the successes of Charlemagne and Louis, which a secular audience must have known primarily through the popular chansons. The importance of both sacred and profane writings in Robert's concept of and exhortation to Crusade is therefore made clear from the very beginning of his work. In Urban's speech, the scriptural is joined to the secular in Crusade as revenge, not defined as in the *Gesta* as vengeance for the wrongs inflicted on God by his enemies but defined as a moral need of *caritas* for other Christians brutalized by the Gentiles.

Throughout the remainder of the *Historia*, Robert expands upon the basic premise of this speech to describe the deeds of the Franks—as in the *Gesta*, almost no reference is made to others partaking in the holy war[16]—on the road to Jerusalem as the continuation and reiteration of two historico-literary traditions. On the one hand, scripture confirms the status of the Crusade as a reflection and continuation of exemplary biblical struggles; it defines the nature of the Crusade as a new Exodus, and the Crusaders as the fulfillment of age-old prophecy. On the other hand, secular martial history gleaned from the chansons de geste demonstrates that the past has proven the Franks chosen for victory; this indicates the suitability of his audience for the struggle at hand and their obligation to continue the wars of their ancestors—"A vobis quidem precipue exigit subsidium, quoniam a Deo vobis collatum est pre cunctis nationibus . . . insigne decus armorum" [*HI* 7; *HFC* 81: "Indeed it is your help [Jerusalem] particularly seeks because God has granted you outstanding glory in war above all other nations"]. Both combine to forge a new chosen people, unparalleled in war and supported by God, an irresistible force that has the power to right the wrongs of the world and take whatever it wants in the process.[17]

THE WONDERS OF GOD AT WORK

Writing in his northern cloister, far from the battlefields of the First Crusade, it was clear to Robert of Reims that the events of 1096–1099 had long been prophesied. Prophecy, or its pagan counterpart soothsaying, had already informed the calculations of Kerbogha's mother in the *Gesta Francorum*;[18] in the *Historia Iherosolimitana*, too, she sees the eventual destruction of her son's mighty army as long established:

> A centum annis et infra invenerunt patres nostri in sacris deorum responsis, et in sortibus et divinationibus suis et animalium extis, quod Christiana gens super nos esset ventura nosque victura. Concordant igitur super hos aruspices, magi et arioli, et numinum nostrorum responsa, et prophetarum dicta, in quibus dicitur: A solis ortu et occasu, ab aquilone et mari, erunt termini vestri, et nullus stabit contra vos.

> [*HI* 63; *HFC* 156: Our forefathers discovered a hundred years and more ago through the sacred oracles of the Gods, in their casting of lots and their divinations and the entrails of animals, that the Christian race would come upon us and defeat us. The soothsayers, mages and diviners, the oracles of our divine powers and the words of the prophets (in which it is said: from the east and from the west, from the north and from the south shall your coast be. There shall no man be able to stand before you) all agree.]

Robert's interpolation of echoes from the books of Psalms and Deuteronomy into the words of Kerbogha's mother indicates, however, that he sees the Crusade prophesied beyond the arcane dealings of augurs and diviners.[19] He emphasizes that scripture, in its *sensus plenior*, anticipated the events of 1096–1099. For instance, when describing the Battle of Dorylaeum, he refers to the Gospel of Luke ("Esurientes etenim suos replevit bonis, divites vero non suos dimisit inanes; deposuit potentes, exaltavit humiles" [*HI* 28; *HFC* 113: "For He hath filled his own with good things and those not his own he hath sent empty away; he hath put down the mighty from their seats, and exalted them of low degree"])[20] and the book of Isaiah ("Hoc est quod per Ysaiam prophetam spopondit sue dilecte Iherusalem: Ponam te in superbiam seculorum, gaudium in generationem et generationem, et suges lac gentium, et mamilla regum lactaberis" [*HI* 28; *HFC* 113: "This is what he promised to his beloved Jerusalem through the Prophet Isaiah: I will make thee an eternal excellency, a joy of many generations. Thou shalt also suck the milk of the Gentiles, and shalt suck the breast of kings"])[21] to put the great victory over the Turks into its proper historical and religious context. Concluding his narrative in book 9 of the *Historia Iherosolimitana*, Robert reiterates that the Frankish triumph he has just recounted was prefigured in divine revelation:

> Cum autem ipsi Domino placuit, adduxit Francigenam gentem ab extremis terre, et per eam ab immundis gentilibus liberare voluit. Hoc a longe per Isaiam prophetam predixerat, cum ait: Adducam filios tuos de longe, argentum eorum et aurum eorum cum eis, in nomine Domini Dei tui, et sancto Israheli, quia glorificavit te. Edificabunt filii peregrinorum muros tuos, et reges eorum ministrabunt tibi. Hec et multa alia invenimus in propheticis libris, que congruunt huic liberationi facte etatibus nostris.

> [*HI* 110; *HFC* 213–14: But when it so pleased God, he led the Frankish race from the ends of the earth with the intention that they should free [Jerusalem] from the filthy Gentiles. He had long ago foretold this through the prophet Isaiah when he said: "I shall bring thy sons from far, their silver and their gold with them, unto the name of the Lord thy God, and to the Holy One of Israel, because he hath glorified thee. And the sons of pilgrims shall build up thy walls, and their kings shall minister unto thee." We have found this and many other things in the books of the prophets which fit exactly the context of the liberation of the city in our era.]

Far from being an isolated event in history, the Crusade fulfilled ancient portents and reiterated biblical history. The first lines of the quotation above, however, also indicate the implications of this: scriptural omens serve to show the hand of God active in the present. There is no accident, coincidence, or fortune of war in the *Historia*; rather, all occurrences show the will of God. At the very beginning of his work, Robert highlights that the Crusade armies set out for the East because God wanted them to. The remarkable enthusiasm that greeted Urban's address at Clermont could only have been the work of God:

> Et ut cunctis clarescat fidelibus quod hec via a Deo non ab homine sit constituta, sicut a multis postea comperimus, ipso die quo hec facta et dicta sunt, fama preconans tante constitutionis totum commovit orbem, ita ut etiam in maritimis Oceani insulis divulgatum esset, quod Iherosolimitanum iter in concilio sic stabilitum fuisset.

> [*HI* 8; *HFC* 82: And, to make it quite clear to all believers that this pilgrimage had been set in train by God rather than men—as we have since established from many sources—on the very day these speeches and deeds took place, the news announcing such an undertaking set the whole world astir so that even in the islands of the sea it was common knowledge that a pilgrimage to Jerusalem had been launched at the Council.]

When the armies gather at Constantinople, Bohemond, who had earlier realized "omnia hec non tantum esse hominum" [*HI* 14; *HFC* 92: "that this could not be the work of men alone"], emphasizes that all are there as a result of divine agency: "O bellatores Dei et indeficientes peregrini sancti Sepulchri, quis ad hec peregrina loca vos adduxit, nisi ille qui filios Israel ex Egypto per mare Rubrum sicco vestigio transduxit?" [*HI* 19; *HFC* 98: "O soldiers of the Lord and tireless pilgrims to the Holy Sepulchre, who was it that led you to these foreign lands if not He who led the sons of Israel from Egypt dry-shod across the Red Sea?"]. Beyond the Bosporus, the Crusaders are wholly guided by and subject to divine will, and they suffer and triumph at God's bidding. The will of God therefore forcefully made manifest that which had been long foretold.[22]

Beyond revealing divine agency on earth, Bohemond's words also indicate that, to Robert the Monk, the Latin journey to and conquest of the Holy Land typologically constituted the Exodus of a new chosen people. References to the books of Exodus, Numbers, and Deuteronomy are frequent throughout the *Historia*, drawing a strong parallel between the efforts of the Crusaders and those of the biblical people of Israel. For instance, after Urban's speech, Adhemar of Le Puy "licet invitus, suscepit quasi alter Moyses ducatum ac regimen dominici populi" [*HI* 8; *HFC* 83: "agreed, albeit unwillingly, to lead and organise the people of God like a second Moses"]; he leads them to "terra . . . que lacte et melle fluit" [*HI* 6; *HFC* 81: "a land flowing with milk and honey"].[23] On their difficult journey God assists the Crusaders in their hour of need, providing them at Antioch with food and drink captured from the Turks: "Sic quoque filiis Israel olim faciebat, cum per terram gentilium regum transire cupiebant, et illi publicum vie regie incessum eis denegabant" [*HI* 38; *HFC* 125: "Just so did He once act for the people of Israel when they wanted to cross the lands of pagan kings who refused to allow them to travel the main road"]. This parallel between the Crusaders and the biblical people of Israel is well understood by Kerbogha's mother, Robert's voice of typological insight, when speaking to her son:

> Fili, Pharaonem regem Egypti quis submersit in mari Rubro cum omni exercitu suo? . . . Ipse idem Deus ostendit quanto amore diligat populum suum, quantaque tutela circumvallet eum, cum dicit: Ecce ego mittam angelum meum, qui precedat te, et custodiat semper. Observa et audi vocem meam, et inimicus ero inimicis tuis, et odientes te affligam, et precedet te angelus meus. Genti nostre iratus est Deus ille, quia nec audimus vocem eius, nec facimus voluntatem, et iccirco de remotis partibus occidentis excitavit in nos gentem suam, deditque ei universam terram hanc in possessionem.

> [*HI* 62; *HFC* 155: Who, my son, sank Pharaoh, King of Egypt, into the Red Sea with his whole army? . . . The same God shows how much he loves his people and how assiduously he surrounds them with his protection when he says: Behold, I send an angel before thee, [who will precede thee and guard thee always. Observe and listen to my voice,] then I will be an enemy unto thine enemies, and an adversary unto thine adversaries. For mine angel shall go before thee. That is the God who is angry with our race because we have not listened to his words or done his will; that is why he has stirred up his people against us from the far-flung lands of the West, and has given all of this land into their possession.][24]

On their march to Jerusalem, the Crusaders are therefore God's chosen people, their progress paved with lines from scripture, their conquest of Jerusalem certain. Against them stand those who, in the words of Kerbogha's mother, have turned away from the word of God, an enemy defined as much through God's disfavor as the Franks are by his favor—truly "filii diaboli" [*HI* 43; *HFC* 130: "the sons of the Devil"]. Their defeat is inevitable, and each Christian victory, every blow against the Saracen, confirms the Franks as the new Israel: "Dux et protector fuisti in misericordia populo tuo quem

redemisti. Nunc, Domine, cognoscimus, quia portas nos in fortitu-
dine tua, ad habitaculum sanctum tuum" [*HI* 28; *HFC* 112: "Thou in
thy mercy hast led forth the people which thou hast redeemed. Now
we realise, God, that Thou art guiding us in Thy strength unto Thy
holy habitation"].[25]

Over the course of this impressive expansion of the theological
context of the Crusade, it is remarkable that Robert the Monk also
subtly alters or reduces the rudimentary theological underpinnings
of the Crusade in the *Gesta*, especially with regard to the role of suffering. The Anonymous considered the suffering of the Crusaders on
the journey to Jerusalem as a double form of repayment. On the one
hand, the Christians of the *Gesta* suffered to fulfill their side of an
agreement of mutual obligation with God, in which they repaid him
for earthly and heavenly rewards with blood, sweat, and tears. On the
other hand, there is also in the *Gesta* a second notion that sees suffering as penitential, as repayment for sins committed. We therefore
have the description of the siege of Nicaea, where "ex pauperrima
gente multi mortui sunt fame pro Christi nomine" [*GF* 17: "many of
the poor starved to death for the Name of Christ"], alongside that
of the siege of Antioch, where "Hanc paupertatem et miseriam pro
nostris delictis concessit nos habere Deus. In tota namque hoste non
ualebat aliquis inuenire mille milites, qui equos haberent optimos"
[*GF* 34: "God granted that we should suffer this poverty and wretchedness because of our sins. In the whole camp you could not find a
thousand knights who had managed to keep their horses in really
good condition"]. The Anonymous therefore combines lay devotion
with traditional penance; throughout, he maintains an approach to
suffering that considers it essentially redemptory, the payment of a
debt owed for the *beneficia* one has received or the *maleficia* one has
committed. Insofar as Christian suffering repays a debt owed, it is
imitatio Christi; this the Anonymous intimates when, at the beginning of his work, he speaks of the time "quem dominus Iesus cotidie
suis demonstrat fidelibus, specialiter in euangelio dicens: 'Si quis uult
post me uenire, abneget semetipsum et tollat crucem suam et sequatur me'" [*GF* 1: "of which the Lord Jesus warns his faithful people
every day, especially in the Gospel where he says, 'If any man will
come after me, let him deny himself, and take up his cross, and follow me'"].

Robert's approach to suffering and to its purpose within the Crusade is strikingly different. At the most basic level, it is remarkable that

Robert limits his descriptions of suffering. Where its source expands upon the anguish of the Crusaders, the *Historia* sometimes remains silent,[26] and more often minimizes the distress of those involved.[27] In the rare occurrences in which his work offers a roughly equivalent description of Christian suffering, Robert is careful not to interpret suffering as penance. In the passage corresponding to the Anonymous's description of the siege of Antioch above, Robert argues that famine and the lack of horses were rather meant to help the Crusaders on their way than to punish them for the sins they had committed:

> Ne illi insolescerent tot victoriis bellorum, opprimebat eos gravi inedia ieiuniorum. In toto namque exercitu mille equi inveniri non poterant ad pugnandum idonei, ut per hoc innotesceret quod in fortitudine equi non haberent fiduciam, sed in se, per quem et quomodo volebat et quando volebat superabant.

> [*HI* 41; *HFC* 128: It was to ensure that they did not get complacent from so many victories that he made them suffer serious pangs of hunger. In the whole army it was impossible to find 1,000 horses in a condition to fight, and by this God wanted to make them realise that they should trust not in their horses but in Him through Whom they were victorious how and when He wanted.][28]

Suffering is to a large extent admonitory in Robert's work, the divine way of showing displeasure with a current course of action as opposed to rectifying past trespasses. This is reiterated in one of the very few passages in which Robert is more expansive in conveying the teleology of suffering than his source had been. At Antioch, God explains, through the mouth of Stephen Valence, the suffering the Crusaders have undergone as follows:

> Nonne tibi videtur quod bene adiuverim eos huc usque, quia illis et Niceam tradidi civitatem, et omnia que eis supervenere bella vincere feci? In obsidione Antiochie eorum miserie condolui; nunc vero ad extremum civitatis ingressum tribui. Omnes tribulationes et impedimenta que passi sunt ideo evenire permisi, quoniam multa nefanda operati sunt cum Christianis mulieribus et paganis, que valde displicent in oculis meis.

> [*HI* 67; *HFC* 161: Is it not obvious to you that I have been helping them all along? I gave them the city of Nicaea and helped them win every battle there was. I looked with pity on their sufferings at the siege of Antioch; eventually I granted them entrance to the city. *I allowed them to suffer all these tribulations and difficulties because they have committed many sins with Christian women—and pagan women—which found grave displeasure in my eyes.*][29]

Suffering therefore does not have the same meaning in the *Historia* as it does in the *Gesta*. In the Anonymous's work, suffering is understood in a fashion that effectively looks backward—it serves to repay a debt to God, resulting either from the Crusader's past behavior or from God's agency on his behalf. It is redemptory at the level of the individual—each after all will carry his own cross. In the *Historia* suffering, much reduced, looks forward resolutely. It does not redeem but admonishes, serves not as penance for the individual but as an indication for the Crusader army to correct its behavior as it continues toward Jerusalem.[30]

Robert therefore moves away from the narrative arc that the Anonymous had included in his work, which led through penitential suffering toward redemption and salvation with the conquest of Jerusalem. Robert's Crusaders thunder on to their unavoidable, divinely ordained destiny, occasionally reminded not to indulge in problematic behavior by the pangs of hunger or the dearth of horses. To a certain degree Robert therefore also moves away from the Anonymous's rudimentary approach to the Crusade as imitatio Christi.[31] It is noteworthy that in a work so earnestly concerned with finding scriptural parallels Robert should choose to minimize the elementary typological parallel his source had identified. This process of negotiation, foregrounding some parallels while letting others fade into the distance, shows Robert's very different conceptualization of the Crusade. As a cleric confronted by successful but violent Christian expansion into the East, he chose to find precedents not in the New Testament but in the Old, not with the meritorious suffering on Calvary but with the travails and territorial appropriations of the biblical people of Israel.[32]

Robert's work therefore emphasizes that the Crusade is the long-foretold work of God and that the Franks are his chosen people and instruments of agency—after all, "quis regum aut principum posset subigere tot civitates et castella, natura, arte, seu humano ingenio premunita, nisi Francorum beata gens, cuius est Dominus Deus eius, populus quem elegit in hereditatem sibi?" [*HI* 4; *HFC* 77: "what king or prince could subjugate so many towns and castles, fortified by nature, design or human ingenuity, if not the blessed nation of the Franks whose God is the LORD; and the people whom he hath chosen for his own inheritance?"].[33] The Crusade of the *Historia* is not as much a story of Christ-like suffering as it is one of the fulfillment of destiny, less a pilgrimage for the redemption of individual sin than a campaign of acquisition of what God had decided should belong to the Franks. It is here that the effect (and the purpose) of Robert's interpretation of the Crusade becomes clear. The justification of Frankish conquest is the fact that they are singled out by God to do his will, and the proof that they are so singled out is conquest. Accordingly, conquest becomes its own justification. On a practical level, this divine mandate confers upon the Franks an *a priori* license to attack and conquer *anyone* with the full knowledge that they are doing the Lord's bidding.

MACCABEES OF THE WEST

Given Robert's attention to the theological backdrop of the Crusade, it is remarkable that he would not only maintain but significantly expand upon the Anonymous's use of the conventions of the chansons de geste. Although it is perhaps counterintuitive for a clergyman to turn to secular literature for inspiration, doing so gave Robert a number of advantages. On the one hand, as a historiographer, the use of chanson de geste commonplaces allowed him to compensate for the distance in time and place separating him from the battlefields of 1096–1099. On the other hand, as a propagandist, it allowed him not only to continue to portray the Crusade as an extension of the imagined Frankish wars against pagans but, more important, to expose within these imagined wars the approving hand of God, demonstrable proof that the Franks are the new Israel.

The Anonymous, for all that Robert deplores his style, had one advantage over the monk of Reims: he was present at the events he described, and his work strongly evokes the myriad sentiments associated with a three-year campaign, the fortunes of which were decidedly mixed. Writing the better part of a decade later, and not having accompanied the Crusaders to the Holy Land, Robert could not call upon memory to express the experience of the road, the camp, and the battlefield. Therefore, to heighten the immediacy of his writing, he greatly expanded the description of the sights and sounds of the campaign. The phrases by which he does so are taken from the chansons. The sun heralds the approach of armies: "Et cum inter tanta agmina enitesceret terribilis fulgor armorum, hunc tamen reverberaret, si posset intueri, splendor animorum. . . . Nam quis carneus oculus loricarum, aut galearum, aut scutorum, aut lancearum, sole radiante, ferre poterat intuitum?" [*HI* 13–14; *HFC* 90–92: "And no matter how much the terrible glint of arms glittered from innumerable columns, the splendour of their courage would still outdo it if it were visible. . . . What human eye could bear the glitter of their breastplates, helmets, shields or lances in brilliant sunshine?"]. The very radiance of the sun on the Crusaders' weapons discomfits the enemy, and in battle it is the harbinger of victory: "Sol vero super hamatas loricas et lanceas radios inferens oculos intuentium reverberabat, et adversariis terrorem immittebat, ut divina testatur Scriptura, quia terribilis est castrorum acies ordinata" [*HI* 73; *HFC* 168: "The sun threw its rays over mailed breastplates and lances which caught its glint, dazzling those who watched, and terrified the enemy: as Holy Scripture says, terrible as an army of siege"].[34] The fighting renders the battlefields dark and wholly cacophonous: "O quantus ibi fragor armorum, quantus strepitus confringentium lancearum, quantus clamor morientium, et quam hilaris vox pugnantium Francorum, militare signum suum altis vocibus conclamantium! Congeminantur ille voces dum eas recipiunt, et recipiendo emittunt concava vallium, cacumina montium, scissure rupium" [*HI* 26; *HFC* 110: "How great was the clash of arms, how loud the splintering sound of lances meeting; what a noise from the dying and how joyful the voice of the Franks as they fought, all shouting their warcry at the tops of their voices! Their voices echoed, bouncing off the sides of the valleys, the summits of the mountains and the clefts in the rock"].[35]

Robert's desire to reproduce the audiovisual experience of Crusade also surfaces in another way: he shares the jongleurs' propensity for direct speech as a way of bringing the audience, at least vicariously, into the events. Although the *Gesta* had included extensive use of direct address, Robert more than doubles its use in the *Historia*. He significantly expands most of the instances of direct speech in the *Gesta* and introduces speeches where there are none in his source. This allows for some stirring motivational orations, especially by Urban II, Bohemond of Taranto, and Adhemar of Le Puy,[36] and even a moving elegy for the death of the heroic Walo II of Chaumont-en-Vexin by his wife.[37] Intriguingly, Robert especially liked to introduce or expand upon dialogue, occasionally between Christians (mostly over primacy),[38] but more often between Christians and Muslims (in which Christians invariably stand defiant)[39] and between Muslims themselves (in which the Christians, it is argued, are much to be feared).[40]

While these descriptions of the sights and sounds of battle bring his audience closer to the experience of the Crusaders, Robert also

uses them to mold the perception of this experience. Every description of shining columns, every glorious image of defiant Christians
making their way inexorably east, further removes the Crusade from
the blood, hunger, and despair that colored the pages of the *Gesta*;
this ties in with Robert's decreased interest in the suffering of the
Crusaders. Direct speech explicitly or implicitly sings the praises of
the Franks and points up the justice of their cause; in this respect it
is notable that Robert puts a number of additional exhortations into
Bohemond's mouth but does not reproduce the part of the *Gesta* in
which he berates William the Carpenter and Peter the Hermit for
desertion.[41]

Robert uses more than narrative technique and style to bring his
history of the Crusade closer—in form and spirit—to the chansons.[42]
His characterization of the warring parties continues the dichotomy
already put in place by his source: diverse, wealthy, morally crooked,
and polytheist Muslims face ethnically cohesive, courageous, deprived
Christians who loyally follow one God.[43] In addition, he adds certain
topoi that the *Gesta* had neglected to include; these allow him to
depict both the Christians as more heroic and the Muslims and their
gods as more unreliable. For one thing, he expands on the descriptions of single combat and introduces a staple of chanson de geste
descriptions of battle, the so-called epic strike.[44] Although the *Historia* very graphically describes the bravery of all the important Christian leaders in individual combat,[45] the honor of the most creative
dismemberment falls to Godfrey of Bouillon:

> Ille exertis brachiis ense nudato eorum cervices amputabat. . . .
> Cumque unus ex eis audacior ceteris, et mole corporis prestantior,
> et viribus, ut alter Golias, robustior, videret ducem sic supra suos
> inmisericorditer sevientem, sanguineis calcaribus urget equum adver-
> sus illum, et mucrone in altum sublato totum super verticem ducis
> transverberat scutum. Et nisi dux ictui umbonem expandisset, et se
> in partem alteram inclinasset, mortis debitum persolvisset. Sed Deus
> militem suum custodivit, eumque scuto sue defensionis munivit. Dux,
> ira vehementi succensus, parat rependere vicem, eiusque tali modo
> appetit cervicem. Ensem elevat, eumque a sinistra parte scapularum
> tanta virtute intorsit, quod pectus medium disiunxit, spinam et vita-
> lia interrupit, et sic lubricus ensis super crus dextrum integer exivit;
> sicque caput integrum cum dextra parte corporis immersit gurgiti,
> partemque que equo presidebat remisit civitati.

> [*HI* 44–45; *HFC* 132–33: He sliced through their necks with his arms
> bare and sword unsheathed. . . . One of them, bolder than the rest,

unusually heavily built and of greater strength rather like another
Goliath, saw the Duke savaging his men mercilessly; he urged his
horse towards him with bloodstained spurs, and lifting his sword
high he sliced through the whole shield of the Duke, which he held
above his head. If the Duke had not parried the blow with the boss
of his shield and twisted over to the other side, he would have paid
the debt of death; as it was God looked after his soldier and defended
him under a protective shield. The Duke, ablaze with furious anger,
prepared to return the blow and thus aimed for his neck. He raised
the sword and plunged it into the left side of his shoulder-blades with
such force that it split the chest down the middle, slashed through the
spine and vital organs and, slippery with blood, came out unbroken
above the right leg. As a result the whole of the head and the right
side slipped down into the water, whilst the part remaining on the
horse was carried back into the city.]

Insofar as Robert intensifies the depiction of the First Crusaders as
heroes of chansons de geste, so, conversely, he renders the Muslims
more in keeping with their literary counterparts. In this regard, Robert includes an interesting addition at the end of the *Historia*. After
the Battle of Ascalon, the Fatimid emir Clement (the historical al-
Musta'li) turns on his divinity for not preventing his defeat at the
hand of the Christians:

> O Mathome, preceptor noster et patrone, ubi est virtus tua? . . . Ut
> quid sic dereliquisti gentem tuam, quam inmisericorditer destruit,
> dissipat, interficit gens pauperrima et pannosa, gens aliarum gen-
> tium peripsema omniumque prorsus hominum fex, rubigo et scoria?
> . . . Que gens ulterius poterit huic nefarie genti resistere, cum gens
> tua contra eam nec ad horam potest subsistere? . . . O Mathome,
> Mathome! Quis unquam venustiori te cultu colitur in delubris auro
> argentoque insignitis, pulchrisque de te imaginibus decoratis, et ceri-
> moniis et sollempnitatibus omnique ritu sacrorum? Sed hoc est quo
> Christiani nobis insultare solent, quia maior est virtus Crucifixi quam
> tua, quoniam ipse potens est in celo et in terra. Apparet autem nunc,
> quoniam qui in eo confidunt vincunt; illi vero vincuntur qui te vener-
> antur. . . . Cuius igitur culpa ita degeneres efficimur, cum omnem tibi
> exhibemus honorem, et nullam nobis rependis vicem?

> [*HI* 106–7; *HFC* 209–10: O Mahommed, our Master and protec-
> tor, where is your strength? . . . Why have you abandoned your
> people like this to be mercilessly destroyed and dispersed and killed
> by a wretchedly poor and ragged people, a people who are the
> scrapings of other races, the lees, rust and slag of the whole human
> race. . . . What nation can resist this appalling race now, since
> your own race cannot withstand them at this hour? . . . O Mahom-
> med, Mahommed, who has ever invested more in the magnificence

of your worship with shrines ornate with gold and silver, deco-
rated with beautiful images of you, and with the ceremonies and
solemnities of every kind of rite? This is what the Christians say to
insult us: that the power of the Crucified One is greater than yours
because he is powerful on earth and in heaven. And it certainly
seems to be the case now that those who place their trust in him
win, whilst those who revere you are defeated. . . . So whose fault is
it that we are reduced to this state? Why should we give you every
honour and receive nothing in return?]

Robert's use of the chanson trope that sees the Saracen turn on his
divinities is especially effective here—at the end of the work it demonstrates not only the final victory of Christian over Muslim but also
of the Christian God over "Mahommed," of destitution over opulence, of weakness over strength, and especially of faith over fickle-
ness. It allows him to further demonize the Muslim as apostate even
to his own religion, while at the same time highlighting the unstoppable nature of the divine will that has led the campaign to successful
completion.

Robert therefore not only continues the *Gesta*'s use of chanson
commonplaces but expands and diversifies it. On an elementary level
this demonstrates the same desire to see in the Crusade a continuation of the older, mostly imagined wars between Frank and Saracen found in his source. That Robert sees the wars of the chansons
as deeply related to the present conflict is shown by the fact that he
refers to the deeds of Charlemagne and Louis the Pious twice at the
very beginning of his work.[46] Connecting the Crusade to the wars
of the Frankish ancestors, which the majority of his audience would
have known from the vernacular chansons whose style and commonplaces he so readily appropriates, of course conveyed to the present
Franks the cachet that the Anonymous had earlier bestowed upon
them. Robert, however, also clearly saw these wars and campaigns as
conveying a call to action. History has shown the Franks unbeaten in
battle, and therefore they especially were called upon to be the shields
of Christianity. This history, even if mostly imagined, carried a moral
imperative: the continuity between the wars of the chansons and the
First Crusade means that the Franks, more than any other people, are
called upon to execute the will of God, because God has chosen them
for this purpose.

It is here that the most innovative aspect of Robert's use of the
chansons emerges most prominently. Whereas the Anonymous, looking forward to the needs of the Crusader states after 1099, saw in

the songs of the jongleurs a secular advantage, Robert uses them to look backward in time to discern a *religious* one. Robert sees in the imagined Frankish past a clear indication of divine favor, finds the hand of God in the victories of Charlemagne and Louis, and turns the chansons into the books of the Maccabees for the West, a sign that the Franks—to whom "ad hoc ulciscendum, ad hoc eripiendum labor incumbit, nisi vobis, quibus pre ceteris gentibus contulit Deus insigne decus armorum, magnitudinem animorum, agilitatem corporum, virtutem humiliandi verticem capilli vobis resistentium" [*HI* 6; *HFC* 80: "God has given above other nations outstanding glory in arms, greatness of spirit, fitness of body and the strength to humiliate the hairy scalp of those who resist you"]—are indeed chosen. Robert's use of the chansons in his work forms an integral part of his strategy within the *Historia*: form, style, and topoi connect his work to a vernacular literature that shows the Franks to be God's elect, the longstanding recipients of divine favor as shown in their victories, both beneficiaries and tools of universal Christian history.

The use of scripture and of the vernacular chansons therefore fulfills two similar and complementary roles within the *Historia*—they are two sides of the same coin. Scripture shows that the Crusade was divinely ordained and prophesied, that those who embarked upon it were a new Israel being led to their Promised Land by the hand of God. The chansons show that God has indeed elevated the Franks, has endowed them with glory crowned in victory and has for centuries relied on them to effect his will in the world; the chansons therefore are to a certain degree continuations of scripture, showing divine agency in the world, separating the elect from all other nations. Insofar as Robert's interpretation and ideology of the Crusade relies upon these two traditions—scripture and the vernacular chansons—his approach is quintessentially literary.

MEN CHOSEN BY AND BELOVED OF GOD

As indicated above, Robert identifies the Franks of which he speaks specifically as his contemporary French; the *Historia Iherosolimitana* consequently presents an uncompromising statement of French exceptionalism. Why, however, would Robert go to such lengths to describe the French as a new Israel, chosen and assisted by God? If it is understandable that a clergyman would seek parallels for the Crusade in scripture, then why does Robert draw so strongly on profane writings as well? Furthermore, why would he emphasize the agency of God while reducing that of the Crusaders, and why would he replace suffering with glory, moving from penitence to unstoppable triumph? Here it is important to bear in mind that Robert, in keeping with the Anonymous, was not only a historiographer but also a propagandist. If the Anonymous called for continued support for the Crusader states in the years following the conquest of Jerusalem, Robert wrote within the context of Bohemond of Taranto's campaign of recruitment of 1104–1106. It would be naïve to consider Robert any less practical than the Anonymous had been.

On the most elementary level, the people Urban called upon at the very beginning of the work are the same upon whom Robert called a decade later. At a time when the Holy Places had been in Christian hands for a number of years, it was important to remind them that Frenchness had always come with its own set of obligations—as the chosen people, as the tools of the divine on earth, the French had a responsibility to fight whomever it was that God set against them. This had been the case at Roncesvalles, when God had kept the sun out so that their ancestors could defeat the Saracens, and had been no less the case at Ascalon. The Crusade was therefore above all a moral obligation, the French assumption of a duty to fight, rather than an opportunity to redeem sins through suffering; at the heart of the holy war lay the will of God, not the piety of the Christian.[47]

Robert's approach to the corollaries of this duty—defeat, suffering, victory, and conquest—flow logically from this premise. Setbacks on the campaign are minimized and become a locus of admonition, not penitence. The victory of the Christians, heroes in the mold of the Franks of yore, is to a certain degree self-evident and serves to continuously reconfirm divine agency and French preeminence. It is perhaps with regard to conquest, however, that Robert is most innovative, and here his ideology of the Crusade has its greatest impact. His approach to conquest, to the ownership of what was won by force of arms, is both far more extensive and subtler than that of his source, which relied on the rights of Westerners as heirs both to Christ and to Charlemagne to stake a claim to lands in the East. In this regard, it is interesting to compare Peter the Hermit and Herluin's mission to Kerbogha as it is represented in the *Gesta* and the *Historia*. Whereas the former refers to the conquered territory as "terram Christianorum et nostram" [*GF* 66: "the land which belongs to the Christians and to us"] and "terra Dei et Christianorum" [*GF* 66: "the land which belongs to God and the Christians"], Robert renders the exchange as follows:

Nulli sapienti mirandum est, si ad Domini nostri Sepulchrum cum armis venimus, gentemque vestram ab istis finibus eliminamus. . . . Terra autem gentis illorum non est, licet diu possiderint, quia nostrorum a priscis temporibus fuit, eisque propter malitiam suam vestra gens adversa abstulit. Que tamen ideo vestra non debet esse, quia diu eam tenuistis; celesti etenim censura nunc est decretum, ut misericorditer reddatur filiis quod iniuste patribus est ablatum. Nec glorietur gens vestra, quia superaverit effeminatam gentem Grecorum, quoniam divina suffragante potentia in cervicibus vestris meritum recompensabitur gladio Francorum.

[*HI* 47–48; *HFC* 137: Nobody with any sense should be surprised at us coming to the Sepulchre of Our Lord as armed men and removing your people from these territories. . . . The land may have belonged to [the Muslims] for a long time but it is not theirs; it belonged to our people originally and your people attacked and maliciously took it away from them, which means that it cannot be yours no matter how long you have had it: for it is set out by divine decree that what was unjustly removed from the fathers shall be restored by divine mercy to the sons. Neither should your people take any pride in having overcome the effeminate Greek race because, by the order of divine power, the payback will be exercised by Frankish swords on your necks.]

This is the only instance in which Robert claims that the Crusaders have a *historical* right to the land as Christians, but even here he introduces two factors that to him are far more important in determining its ownership: the "order of the divine power" and the force of "Frankish swords on your necks." Regardless of ancient claims, the land becomes Christian through the will of God and the violence of the French. That the Crusaders have conquered the land because God wanted them to is obvious both to Christians and to Muslims. Just as the Christian princes argue that Jerusalem "nostra erit non per hominis indulgentiam, sed per celestis censure equitatem. De vultu enim Domini hoc iudicium prodiit, quia Iherusalem nostra erit" [*HI* 48; *HFC* 138: "will be ours not by virtue of human toleration but through the justice of divine decree. It is by God's countenance that Jerusalem will be judged ours"], so Kerbogha's mother admonishes her son:

Quis exhereditavit Seon regem Amorreorum, et Og regem Basan, et omnia regna Canaam, et dedit suis in hereditatem? . . . Genti nostre iratus est Deus ille, quia nec audimus vocem eius, nec facimus voluntatem, et iccirco de remotis partibus occidentis excitavit in nos gentem suam, deditque ei universam terram hanc in possessionem.

[HI 62; HFC 155: Who disinherited Seon, King of the Amorites and Og, the King of Bashan, and all the kingdoms of Canaan and gave it to his own people to inherit? . . . That is the God who is angry with our race because we have not listened to his words or done his will; that is why he has stirred up his people against us from the far-flung lands of the West, and has given all of this land into their possession.]

The divine will allowed for the appropriation of the lands and goods of others, by the first chosen people as well as by the present.[48] One did not need a longstanding claim to take what God had shown he wanted one to take through victory on the battlefield. Here of course we encounter another strong component of what justifies ownership in Robert's writings: the notion that might makes right. The *Historia* glorifies strength, especially the strength of the chosen French, to an uncommon degree. It is after all a gift from God, as Bohemond explains to Pirrus, the Antiochene traitor:

Quanto nos sumus pauciores, tanto et fortiores, vos vero quanto numerosiores, tanto et imbecilliores? . . . Ex hoc igitur conicere potes, quia licet unus Creator creaverit nos et vos, uberiorem tamen sue virtutis prestat habundantiam nobis quam vobis. Certi quippe in illius virtute sumus, quia non solum Antiocham, verum etiam Romaniam totam et Siriam, ipsam etiam Iherusalem obtinebimus.

[HI 52; HFC 143: The fewer we are, the stronger we become; whereas you become weaker as your numbers grow. . . . You can work out from that that, although one Creator brought both us and you into being, he gave a much greater amount of his strength to us than to you. So we are certain that, relying on his strength, we will take not only Antioch but the whole of Anatolia and Syria and Jerusalem itself.]

In the *Historia*, having the strength to take something therefore gives you the right to take it, for it shows divine approval.[49] Rather than any longstanding claim that the Crusaders may have as heirs to Christ or Charlemagne, or as Christians who come to reclaim erstwhile Christian territory,[50] the right to own what they conquer is based on divine will and French power, which in practical terms are wholly interchangeable. This explains the unabashed and unproblematic support for the appropriation of land and goods in Urban's exhortation at Clermont: "Viam sancti Sepulchri incipite, terram illam nefarie genti auferte, *eamque vobis subicite.* Terra illa filiis Israel a Deo in possessionem data fuit, sicut Scriptura dicit que lacte et melle fluit" [*HI* 6; *HFC* 81: "Set out on the road to the Holy Sepulchre, deliver that land from a wicked race and *take it yourselves*—the land which was given by God to the sons of Israel, as Scripture says a land flowing with milk and honey"].[51]

Robert the Monk therefore constructs an elegant logic within his chronicle of the Crusade. The chansons de geste show that the French have been favored by God as a new chosen people; the Crusade is a typological parallel to the travails of the biblical people of Israel on their way to the Promised Land, and demonstrates as well that the French are God's elect and do his bidding. The will of God and the status of the French as chosen both explain and justify the Crusade and the subsequent Latin conquest of much of the Middle East. The reasoning is perfect in its circularity: God willed these campaigns and gave his new chosen people the strength to defeat their enemies, while these victories in turn show that God willed them. For the French who were Robert's audience, the message is clear: aggression and conquest—anywhere, of anything and anybody—carry within them their own validation, as long as they are successful.

Within the context in which the work originated, that of Bohemond's propaganda campaign, the purpose of this logic is twofold, affecting both the interpretation of the past campaign and the ideology of any future one. On the one hand, the Crusader states were established because God wanted them to be. This means that Bohemond's possession of Antioch, and his retention of the city in defiance of his agreement with the emperor Alexius, is divinely mandated: "Eam habeat cui Deus dare voluerit" [*HI* 53; *HFC* 144: "Let the one to whom God decides to give it keep it"].[52] The work therefore functions as an apology for the gathering of earthly riches where the gain should have been spiritual. However, also with an eye toward the future, Robert offers justification for transgressive behavior. Within the logic of his work, where the will of God and French action are effectively interchangeable, any aggression by the chosen people carries a divine imprimatur. This notion must have been especially useful for Bohemond who, in 1104–1106, set out to recruit the French to the banners of the holy war, and attack Byzantium, a *Christian* empire.

The goal of the *Historia* is therefore not merely to ground the Crusade in a theological context but also to expand the applicability of Crusade to all and every battle, against other Christians if need be, as long as it is fought by the chosen French. Robert the Monk constructs a theological framework of Crusade to justify the appropriation of secular goods and territories, and conversely uses secular literature to illustrate the historical validity of that theological framework. This use of the secular and vernacular to prove spiritual truths, and the use then of these truths to justify secular action, suggests that Robert's target audience, at least originally, must have been largely one of laymen. Even though recent criticism has argued for a clerical audience,[53] the remarkable realignment of Crusade from individual penance for sin toward divinely sanctioned appropriation, moving away from pilgrimage toward conquest and thereby opening up the geographical direction of Crusade,[54] as well as the appeal of the chansons de geste as an illustration of the divine election of the French, would be far more effective with an audience of arms bearers steeped in vernacular culture. Even if one takes into account the permeability between the monastic and aristocratic worlds of the twelfth century, which saw a great many of these arms bearers take the cloth, clerics would not gain from an *a priori* justification for the French to take whatever they could, whenever they could.[55]

CHAPTER 4

The Old French Crusade Cycle

Crusade as a War of Families

In the preceding chapters I introduced two approaches to the events of 1096–1099: that of an educated knight living out his last days in the Holy Land and writing in assistance of the nascent Crusader states, and that of a monk with ties to the French crown supporting Bohemond's venture against Byzantium. Both, for reasons very much their own, turn to the chansons de geste to establish the Crusade as a continuation of earlier, imagined wars. The Old French Crusade Cycle, a sequence of poems on the First Crusade, the oldest of which dates from the last quarter of the twelfth century, demonstrates the importance of the chansons de geste in the representation and propagation of the Crusade the better part of a century later.[1] These poems, the *Chanson d'Antioche*, *Les Chétifs*, and the *Chanson de Jérusalem*,[2] draw strongly on Robert of Reims's *Historia Iherosolimitana* and therefore continue the sequence of descent from the writings of the Anonymous; however, they move beyond chanson tropes and themes to take the chanson form as well. The poems in the Cycle illustrate the malleability of the Crusade ideal, as well as the use of the chansons de geste, to suit circumstances—*in casu*, the Western response to the disasters affecting the Crusader states in the second half of the twelfth century.

COUNTERSTRIKE

In the decades following the Battle of Ascalon in 1099, the divisions between the Muslim powers of the Levant continued to benefit the

Latin Christians. Under the rule of capable leaders, the kingdom of Jerusalem consolidated its hold on the Palestinian coast and pushed its borders south and east into Sinai and Transjordan. The princes of Antioch expanded their territories north into Cilicia and east as far as Banyas. Edessa maintained its precarious position on the edge of the Seljuq and Ortuqid lands, while the fall of Tripoli in 1109 led to the creation of a fourth Crusader principality that came to dominate the littoral between Beirut and Latakia. Although Muslim counterattacks could be devastating, such as at Harran in 1104 and at the Field of Blood in 1119, these were insufficient to stop the Latin ascendancy. In 1128, however, Imad ad-Din Zengi, the atabeg of Mosul, added Aleppo to his domain and used the two cities as a base from which to challenge both the rulers of Damascus to the south and the Crusader states to the west. In 1144, making use of the absence of Count Joscelin II and his army, Zengi besieged and conquered Edessa, and by the end of 1145 most of the county up to the city of Turbessel had fallen to his forces.[3]

The destruction of the oldest of the Crusader states caused great consternation in the Christian West, and a forceful response to events swiftly followed. On 1 December 1145, and again on 1 March 1146, Pope Eugenius III directed the encyclical *Quantum praedecessores* to the French king Louis VII and his subjects.[4] The strength of the bull lay in its subtle reiteration and refinement of earlier calls to Crusade. Blaming the loss of Edessa on the sins of Christians both in the West and the Latin East, Eugenius argued that the torch of holy war that had been carried so successfully by the First Crusaders had now fallen to their sons, and he clearly outlined the secular and spiritual benefits associated with taking the cross.[5] The succession of generations, and a sense of responsibility to those who came before, lies at the heart of his appeal. Eugenius himself stands in the footsteps of his papal predecessors who had worked so tirelessly for the liberation of the Holy Places. Just as he aims to live up to their example, so is it up to the secular forces of the West to emulate their forebears: "It will be seen as a great token of nobility and uprightness if those things acquired by the efforts of your fathers are vigorously defended by you, their good sons. But if, God forbid, it should come to pass differently, then the bravery of the fathers will have proved to be diminished in the sons."[6] Eugenius, as a good spiritual father, urges his sons in the Faith to follow the example of Mattathias: "He did not hesitate for a moment to expose himself with his sons and relatives to death and to leave all he had in the world to preserve his ancestral laws; and at length with the help of divine aid and with much labour he and his offspring triumphed powerfully over their enemies."[7]

In *Quantum praedecessores*, Crusade becomes a filial and wider family obligation not just to uphold Christianity in the East but also to preserve the material conquests made in the preceding decades; the continuation of the holy war is owed as much to the ancestors as it is to God. To a certain degree this is a reiteration of the rhetoric of Urban II as we find him in Robert of Reims's *Historia*, where he encouraged those at Clermont: "Moveant vos et incitent animos vestros ad virilitatem gesta predecessorum vestrorum, probitas et magnitudo Karoli Magni regis et Ludovici filii eius aliorumque regum vestrorum" [*HI* 6; *HFC* 80: "May the deeds of your ancestors move you and spur your souls to manly courage—the worth and greatness of Charlemagne, his son Louis and your other kings"]. *Quantum praedecessores* repeats the demand of earlier Crusade appeals that its audience, as Frenchmen and members of the Christian family, should follow the glorious example of countrymen or coreligionists who had come before them. More important, however, Eugenius seems to have added social obligation to historical aspiration. By including filial and familial duty in his Crusade summons, he played upon the developing family traditions of crusading that Jonathan Riley-Smith and Jonathan Phillips have discerned from the turn of the twelfth century onward.[8]

Quantum praedecessores therefore also emphasizes that the enthusiasm or even expectations of families with a history of Crusade could and should serve as motivation to take the cross.[9] This approach of presenting the Crusade both as a literal and as a figurative obligation to family was very successful: there was a widespread response to the papal call to arms, not least from those whose ancestors had been Crusaders, and many kin groups contributed a substantial number of fighters to the armies setting out for the East.[10] The success of papal propaganda did not, however, guarantee the success of the campaign. While the armies of the Second Crusade were well equipped and capably led, the German contingent was defeated by the Seljuq Turks at Dorylaeum on 25 October 1147, and again near Laodicea on 16 November 1147. The French army, led by King Louis VII, was much reduced in its passage through Asia Minor. Upon the arrival of the remaining forces in the Crusader states, heated dissent arose between the Latin lords of the East and the commanders of the Western forces as to where best to apply their strength, and the Christian advance was ultimately halted before Damascus on 28 July 1148.[11]

Despite the ignominious end of the Second Crusade, the ideas within *Quantum praedecessores* were nevertheless deemed important enough to remain part of papal excitatoria for the holy war. The bull was likely distributed once more in 1150, after news of the failure at Damascus had reached the West. Furthermore, Alexander III's Crusade appeals of 1165, 1166, 1169, and 1181 drew strongly on it, and the last of these, *Cor nostrum*, was in turn used by Lucius III in 1184/1185.[12] The notion of Crusade as a family obligation therefore remained current at a time when the fortunes of the Crusader states took a substantial turn for the worse. Zengi was succeeded by his son Nur ed-Din, who, after subjecting Mosul, Aleppo, and Damascus to his rule, turned his attention to the Latins, defeating the army of Jerusalem at the Battle of Huleh in 1157 and the forces of Antioch and Tripoli, together with their Byzantine and Armenian allies, at the Battle of Harim in 1164. Furthermore, in 1163 he sent Shirkuh, the emir of Homs, to Egypt to repel repeated inroads by Amalric of Jerusalem. After defeating the Christian armies near Alexandria in 1167, Shirkuh seized power in the Fatimid caliphate for himself. Upon his death in 1169, he was succeeded as vizier by his nephew Salah ed-Din, or Saladin, who, refusing to submit to Nur ed-Din, in turn took over most of the Zengid territories after Nur ed-Din's death in 1174. This left Egypt and Syria united under powerful leadership, and their strength was quickly turned against the Crusader states. After a number of incursions into the kingdom of Jerusalem, which was increasingly wracked by dissent among the Christian nobility, Saladin's forces confronted its army at the Horns of Hattin on 4 July 1187, and defeated it.[13]

The Battle of Hattin, in which the king of Jerusalem, Guy of Lusignan, was captured and a great number of his nobles were killed, led to the collapse of his kingdom. Deprived of defenders, the coastal cities of the kingdom fell quickly, and Jerusalem itself surrendered to Saladin on 2 October 1187.[14] If the fall of Edessa had occasioned much alarm in the West, Saladin's conquest of the city at the heart of the Christian faith caused even more.[15] In the bull *Audita tremendi*, issued on 29 October 1187, Pope Gregory VIII put the blame for the downfall of Jerusalem squarely on the discord in the Latin East and the sins of its inhabitants, and he called for a new Crusade to reconquer what was lost. Yet the campaigns that set out for the East in the decades

after the fall of Jerusalem did little to alter the new status quo or even
to ameliorate differences between Crusaders and Eastern Christians.
Although the Third Crusade (1189–1192) was well planned and drew
on the royal powers of England and France and the imperial power
of the Holy Roman Empire, it succeeded merely in restoring most
of the kingdom's coastline to Christian control and little else. Much
reduced through infighting during and after the reconquest of Acre in
1191, it famously ended with Richard the Lion-Hearted's frustration
at Beit Nuba.[16] The Fourth Crusade (1202–1204) did not even reach
the Holy Land; rather, the Latin conquest of Constantinople removed
an occasional but still powerful ally from the Christian camp.[17]

The decades after the fall of Edessa were therefore a crucial period
in the history of the Crusades. The declining military and political
fortunes of the Latin states of the Levant required ever-greater numbers of Crusaders to counter; the Christian efforts, however, were
often hamstrung through discord among Crusaders and native Eastern lords alike. At the same time, papal Crusade propaganda emphasized that Crusade could and should be thought of as an obligation to
real and imagined family. The need to recruit Crusaders and to propagate the holy war became more acute, while the notion of Crusade
as filial duty gained traction. In these circumstances the chansons de
geste proved a useful tool once again.

THE OLD FRENCH CRUSADE CYCLE

In the years after the Anonymous and Robert of Reims wrote, the
chanson de geste continued to grow in popularity as well as develop
as a literary genre. As chansons became more widespread, they were
extended, spawned preludes and continuations, and became incorporated into interconnected narratives, inexorably expanding outward
in time, through a lengthy process of cyclification.[18] This process saw
lineage become an increasingly important organizing principle: individual texts were often related to others through the family connections of their characters. During the course of the twelfth century,
many chansons de geste therefore began to coalesce into extensive
narratives of wars between families, and these families' vengeance for
trespasses against them, down the generations. As Bertrand of Bar-
sur-Aube says in *Girart de Vienne* (ca. 1180), these expanded narratives traced the exploits of three noble lineages in particular.[19] The
cycle of chansons known collectively as the *Geste du roi* followed

the house of Charlemagne; it was built on the *Chanson de Roland*, to which were added such works as the *Pèlerinage de Charlemagne* (ca. 1140), *Fierabras* (ca. 1170), and the *Chanson d'Aspremont* (completed before 1190). The cycle referred to as the *Geste de Garin de Monglane* had the dynasty of William of Orange at its heart, and came to include such chansons as the *Couronnement de Louis* (ca. 1130), the *Charroi de Nîmes* (ca. first half of the twelfth century), the *Prise d'Orange* (ca. second half of the twelfth century), and the *Chanson de Guillaume* (ca. 1150–1170).[20] Finally, the *Geste de Doon de Mayence* considered the treacherous line of Ganelon and contained such works as *Girart de Roussillon* (ca. second half of the twelfth century), *Renaud de Montauban* (ca. last quarter of the twelfth century), and *Raoul de Cambrai* (ca. end of the twelfth century). As new branches were added to the chronicles of their deeds, these imagined families swelled; as Howard Bloch has argued, there consequently is a close relationship between textual and familial expansion: "Family relations are coterminous with literary relations; the songs of the deeds of Charlemagne, Doon de Maience, or Garin de Monglane engender poems about the other members of their lineages. . . . Lineage and *geste* are synonymous, as the epic cycle constitutes itself according to a pattern of affiliation between families of heroes and families of poems."[21] The chansons de geste developed into families of epics, and epics about families, at roughly the same time as papal Crusade propaganda, responding to a greater need for manpower in the Latin Middle East, placed increased emphasis on family relations as a motivation for taking the cross. To a certain degree these phenomena are related: both play upon the needs of an aristocracy that was increasingly preoccupied with patrilineal lineage as a social determinant; the concern with family honor, tradition, and prestige that Eugenius III targeted with *Quantum praedecessores* was also expressed in the ever-expanding narratives of family warfare that were popular at the courts of the armigerous aristocracy.[22] It therefore stands to reason that the chanson de geste would once again be used to further the cause of the Crusade.

The oldest of the three Old French chansons de geste that constitute the so-called "historical" First Cycle of the Crusade dates from the last quarter of the twelfth century, and all three were reworked by the first years of the thirteenth, by or for Graindor of Douai. The origins of the oldest and most important, the *Chanson d'Antioche*, have been the subject of intense critical scrutiny ever since Paulin Paris first discussed them in the late nineteenth century.[23] The *Chanson d'Antioche*, a narrative of the history of the First Crusade up to the Battle of Antioch in 1098, was long held to be a reworking of a chanson de geste that was coterminous with the events it describes.[24] It has recently been shown, however, to be far more recent, and a rudimentary Old French or Occitan version of the work appears to have existed only by the last quarter of the twelfth century.[25] This proto-*Chanson d'Antioche* was revised in the late 1100s or early 1200s,[26] when it was amended with additional material from Albert of Aachen's *Historia Ierosolimitana*, Robert of Reims's *Historia Iherosolimitana*, and possibly an unknown third chronicle compiled for the powerful St. Pols of Picardy.[27] Two new compositions were added to complete the Cycle: *Les Chétifs*, a brief chanson without clear literary precedent that details the adventures of a number of Christian prisoners taken at Civetot and their involvement in internecine Muslim conflict,[28] and the *Chanson de Jérusalem*, a continuation up to the Battle of Ascalon, the primary source for which appears to have been the *Chanson d'Antioche* itself.[29]

Little is known about the man who is thought to have reworked the *Chanson d'Antioche* and composed *Les Chétifs* and the *Chanson de Jérusalem*, Graindor of Douai. He is mentioned in the first laisse of the *Chanson d'Antioche*:

> Cil autre jougleor, ki en suelent canter,
> Le vrai coumencement en ont laisié ester.
> Mais Grandor de Douai n'en vot mie oublïer,
> Qui nos a fait les vers tos frés renoveler.

> [CA ll. 12–15: These newfangled *jongleurs* who go around singing it have left out the proper beginning, but Graindor de Douai—who has had all the lines brought up to date for us—has no intention of forgetting it.]

The reference, however, does not clarify Graindor's role in the compilation of the Cycle; the ambiguous "Qui nos a fait les vers tos frés renoveler," which can also translate as "who has made over all the lines for our benefit," suggests both that he may have been an author and a literary patron.[30] Though the man responsible for the Cycle must necessarily remain shrouded in time, the audience to which the Cycle is addressed, and the reason for its composition at the turn of the thirteenth century, are less mysterious. A potential connection of Graindor to the castellans of Douai,[31] together with the possible use of a chronicle linked to the St. Pols and the introduction of a substantial number of Picard family names into the three chansons,[32] suggests that they were originally intended for a northern French audience that most likely included these Picard families. To these the Cycle would have served as vernacular historiography,[33] but perhaps more importantly as propaganda for the Crusade. Laisse 6 of the *Chanson d'Antioche*, painting a bleak picture of the present, urges its audience to take the cross and promises reward in heaven:

> Signor, oiés cançon ki mout fait a loer.
> Cis siecles est mout fel, si nos viut enganer:
> N'i a point de justice, n'i puet on veïr cler,
> Hom n'i est ki foit ait encontre avoir douner.
> Mout i couvient grans gardes pour nos vies sauver;
> Diables nos est prés, qui nos viut enganer;
> Bien nos devriiens mais de ses engiens garder.
> Nostre Sire nos rueve en Jhursalem entrer,
> La desfaee gent ocire et decoper,
> Qui Deu ne voelent croire ne ses sains aorer
> Ne ses coumandemens oïr et ascouter,
> Sa crois et son Sepucre a nule honor garder.
> Mahom et Tiervagan deveriens vergonder
> Et fondre les images et a Dieu aorer
> Et moustiers et eglises et faire et restorer
> Et si del tout en tout le treü aquiter
> Que il n'i ait paien qui mais l'ost demander.
> Li bon baron de France ne volrent arester;
> En tiere de Surie s'alerent desierter.
> La devinrent sauvaje pour lor armes sauver:
> Povertés endurerent, lor cor fisent pener.
> Jesus, li rois de glore, n'en volt nul oublïer,
> Ains les fist en son ciel hautement coroner.

[*CA* ll. 117–40: Sirs, listen to a poem well worth praise. We live in a wicked era, full of treachery; there is no true justice; nobody can see his way clearly; there is no man whose faith is strong enough to keep him on the straight and narrow; we have to take every precaution to save our souls; the Devil is near, seeking to seduce us, and we have to take every care to guard against his wiles. Our Lord asks you to go to Jerusalem to kill and confound the wicked pagans who refuse to believe in God and adore His [saints] or pay heed to His commandments [and who will not maintain his Cross and Sepulchre with any honor. He asks you] to smash and destroy Mohammed and Terva-gant, melt down their images and offer them to Him; to restore the holy churches and ministers; and in the process to make short work of getting rid of the tribute so that no pagan will ever dare demand it again. The noble lords of France did not hesitate. They went to wander through the desert in foreign lands and saved their souls by becoming savages. If anyone willingly allows his body to be broken for God, Jesus King of Glory will not forget him: on the contrary, He will crown him in glory on high.][34]

The Cycle therefore likely sought to promote the Crusades launched to recapture "sa crois et son Sepucre" after the loss of the True Cross at Hattin and the fall of Jerusalem to Saladin. Although the absence of exact dating prevents us from knowing this with absolute certainty, it probably served as part of the propagation of the Fourth Crusade, which was preached widely in Picardy, and in which many Picards and Flemings participated.[35] The subject of the Cycle, the First Crusade, had by the end of the twelfth century served to incite fervor for the holy war for the better part of a hundred years; in using it as an excitatorium, Graindor continued along the path that the Anonymous and Robert of Reims had walked before him. Further in keeping with the earlier works, Graindor turned to the chanson de geste to play upon the tastes of the chivalric aristocracy that formed the heart of Crusade armies. The Old French Crusade Cycle, however, differs from the *Gesta Francorum* and the *Historia Iherosolimitana* in language and form. The use of the vernacular rather than the Latin of the earlier histories facilitated its distribution even among the uneducated and consequently enhanced its impact in northern France and beyond.[36] The form of the *Chanson d'Antioche*, *Les Chétifs*, and the *Chanson de Jérusalem* undoubtedly also contributed to their popularity and circulation: rather than prose narratives that invoke themes and tropes of the chansons de geste, they take the shape of verse chansons de geste themselves. In rendering the history of the First Crusade as a cycle of chansons de geste, Graindor produced the first chansons about the recent past.[37]

The stylistic, formal, and thematic implications of Graindor's casting vernacular history in chanson form are profound and include the turn toward formulaic descriptions of the sights and sounds of battle, the emphasis on individual heroic actions, and the rancorous view of the Muslim and his religion seen in the *Gesta* and *Historia*.[38] The Old French Crusade Cycle, however, propagates an idea of Crusade that differs from its predecessors, especially regarding the role it ascribes to family relations as a motivation to take the cross. The Cycle, written for an audience that likely included a number of powerful Picard families, describes those fighting the First Crusade as tied, and motivated, by bonds of kinship—a "vertical" bond with the divine and a "horizontal" bond with their mortal families. In Graindor's hands, the Crusade becomes a war fought by and for both the macro-family of religion and the micro-family of kin group.

"L'ESTORS ORGILLOUS ET PESANT / DONT LA MERE PLORA PUISEDI SON ENFANT"[39]

In keeping with tradition, the Cycle describes Christians as God's children and him as their Father. God, himself often referred to in familial terms,[40] characteristically addresses Peter the Hermit as "Mes fius de ma car nés" [*CA* l. 300: "Sweet son, flesh of My flesh"]; similarly, the Crusaders are repeatedly referred to as "fils Nostre Segnor" [*CA* Appendix VIII l. 17: "the sons of Our Lord"].[41] The Crusaders therefore are part of an established Christian family of heavenly Father and earthly sons who in turn are spiritual brothers to each other. Beyond this relationship with God, which had driven Crusaders east since the very beginning,[42] Graindor also continually defines the Crusaders by their affiliations with earthly kinsmen. Moving far beyond his sources, he identifies both famous and otherwise unknown First Crusaders as members of secular families. For instance, among the Christians we find:

> Estievenes d'Aubemarle li fius au conte Othon,
> . . .
> Li quens Hues li Maine frere au roi Felippon
> . . .
> Gautiers de Doemart, Bernars li frere Oedon,
> Li quens Rotous del Perce, Andrius li frere Aimon
> . . .
> Et Galerans de Blaves et l'Alemans par non
> Et ses freres Hungiers et dans Raimbaus Creton.
>
> [*CA* ll. 1535–55: Stephen of Albemarle, son of Duke Otto . . . Walter of Domedart; Bernard brother of Eudes; Count Rotrou of Perche and Andrew [brother of Aimon] . . . Lord Hugh the Maisné, brother of King Philip . . . Waleran of Bavaria [the one called the German], his brother Wicher and lord Raimbaut Creton.]

The First Crusaders are therefore as much defined by their place within human kin groups as by their spiritual bond with God. The Old French Crusade Cycle devotes much more attention to these kin groups than had its predecessors; this is further instanced by its description of the anguish of loss the First Crusaders experience at the death of their kinsmen. Witness, for instance, the grief of Conon of Montaigu over his son Gozelo, who dies at Artah:

Encontre son fil vint li peres tout iriés;
Qui adont le veïst, con iert ajenelliés,
Son mort enfant baisoit et devant et detriés.
Entre ses bras le prent, si est sour lui couciés.
"E! Gosse, sire, fius, con dolant me laisiés!
Jou irai au Sepucre; n'i porterés vos piés.
Bien doi estre dolans, maris et coureciés;
Or est de mes enfans li contes abaisciés."

[*CA* ll. 3115–22: [The father, much distraught, came towards his son.
He saw him then, as he fell to his knees, he kissed his dead child on
the front and back. He takes him in his arms, and so bent over him:]
"Ah Gosson my son, you have left me to grieve for you. I am on my
way to the Holy Sepulchre: you will never set foot there. What can I
do but feel grief and anger when the story of my son's life is ended in
this way!"]

Lambert, Conon's other son and Gozelo's brother, who is also a participant in the Crusade, can only urge his father to restrain his grief.[43]

The First Crusaders are therefore sons of God at the same time as
they often are brothers and fathers to those fighting alongside them.
That Graindor does not merely aim to present a more historically
and socially articulated image of the Crusader as a tesseract within a
complex network of relations is highlighted by the fact that all of this
applies to the wholly imaginary Muslim adversaries of the Old French
Crusade Cycle as well. They too are figuratively related to the divine,
if less flatteringly so: just as the Christians are the sons of God, the
Muslims are "la gent a l'avresier" [*CA* l. 4375: "the race of the Devil"],
"la gent Antecris" [*CA* l. 6480: "the people of the Antichrist"]. Theirs
is the lineage of scriptural transgressors, the "linage Judas" [*C* l.103:
"lineage of Judas"] or "linage Chaïn" [*C* l. 674: "lineage of Cain"].
Furthermore, they too are fathers, sons, and brothers to other souls.
To mention only a few among many, the *Chanson d'Antioche* and *Les
Chétifs* speak of Kerbogha and "sa mere, de qui il fu amés; / Calabre
avoit a non, niece fu Josués" [*C* l. 297: "his mother, who loved him,
was called Calabre, and was a niece of Joshua"], whereas in the *Chanson de Jérusalem* we find "li rois Cornumarans / Et Corbadas ses
pere" [*CJ* ll. 122–23: "King Cornumarant and his father Corbadas"]
as well as Lucabel, "ses frere ert de son pere" [*CJ* l. 1450: "who was
the brother of his father"]. As these figures are on the losing side, their
expressions of grief at the death of their family members are more frequent. When told of the death of his son Hisdent, Soliman of Nicaea
cannot hide his misery: "Quant l'entent Solimans, a poi ne pert la

vie; / Il deront ses ceviaus, durement brait et crie: / 'Ahi! biaus sire, fius'" [*CA* ll. 1828–30: "To hear this was a mortal blow to Soliman; he tore his hair, howling and lamenting bitterly: 'Ah! [handsome sir, my son]'"].[44] Muslim sons in turn mourn their fathers: "Li fiers Cornumerans a grant doel de son pere. / Devant Droon d'Amiens li a ocis son frere" [*CJ* ll. 9164–65: "Proud Cornumarant much mourned his father, and killed the brother of Droon of Amiens in front of him"]. Finally, mothers, sisters, and wives do not escape the suffering: when the Christians decapitate the Muslim dead before Antioch and catapult the heads into the city,

> Et li pere et la mere, lor serors, lor amie
> Qui connurent les tiestes, cescuns en brait et crie
> Et maudient la tiere u no jens fu norie!
> Et dist li .I. a l'autre: "N'i porons garir mie!"
>
> [*CA* ll. 3990–93: Fathers and mothers, wives and girlfriends recognized the heads; each shrieked and screamed at the sight, cursing the land that produced such a race and saying to each other: "How can we ever recover?"]

Christians and Muslims are therefore mirrored in the Cycle: all are members of literal and figurative, biological and spiritual, families, forming a matrix of blood and faith that ties them to their like.[45] But for the fact that one side is right and the other is wrong, one serves the true God and one demonic images,[46] this is a struggle of equals.[47] This equality is expressed by the Cycle even on the level of textual structure: we move from the Christian camp in the *Chanson d'Antioche*, to the Muslim in *Les Chétifs*, and back to the Christian in the *Chanson de Jérusalem*.

The First Crusade of the Old French Crusade Cycle is therefore a war of families: of Christian against Muslim but also of the kin groups of which these religions are composed. This representation of the holy war as the struggle between families has a number of important consequences; most notably, conflict between families automatically draws in the concept of vengeance.[48] The notion of Crusade as vengeance for crimes committed against God, the Christian faith, or its adherents had been used since the First Crusade and remained vibrant for centuries; around the time the Old French Crusade Cycle was composed it was used by Innocent III to exhort Crusaders "as sons to take vengeance on injury to their father and as brothers to avenge the destruction of their brothers."[49] Recent critical commentary on the Old French Crusade Cycle, whose three component chansons abound with mentions of revenge, has therefore frequently read the Cycle within this rhetoric of Crusade as Christian vengeance.[50] What this commentary most often ignores, however, is that the drive for vengeance in the Old French Crusade Cycle is *not limited to Christians.* Just as Christian and Muslim are equal in their family ties, so they are in seeking to avenge the injuries done to their kin. As members of spiritual families, human sons and divine fathers both in Christianity and Islam are called upon to redress the insults done to their kind. On the one hand the Christians, powerful and secure in their adherence to the right divinity, journey across the sea to avenge the crimes committed against their spiritual family. The first of these is the Crucifixion. Upon the Cross, Christ himself predicts the arrival of the Latins on eastern shores "por Damedeu vengier" [*CJ* l. 225: "to avenge the Lord God"]: "'Amis,' dist Nostre Sire, 'saces veraiement / Que de dela la mer venront novele gent / Qui de la mort lor Pere prendront le venjement'" [*CA* ll. 201–4: "'My friend,' said Our Lord, 'be assured that a new race will come from over the sea to avenge the death of their Father'"]; "Si fil le venjeront as brans d'acier forbis. / Içou dist Nostre Sire qui en la crois fu mis" [*CA* ll. 1675–76: "Our God and Father who was hanged on the Cross said that He would be avenged by His sons with swords of shining steel"].[51] Beyond the vengeance of God, retribution of the injuries inflicted upon the Christian family also involves avenging brothers in the faith; upon finding the Muslim slaughter of Christians at St. Simeon, the Latins are quick to seek redress:

Al pont des nés paserent por prendre vengison!
...
Li dus garde a senestre pardevers une aree
Et voit Claret de Nike a la barbe mellee
Qui a .I. Crestiën ot la tieste copee.
Quant li bons dus le voit, forment li desagree;
Il a estrains les dens, s'a la teste crolee:
"Cuvers, mar le toucastes! Vostre vie est alee!"

[*CA* ll. 4310–57: They crossed the bridge to seek vengeance. . . . [Duke Godfrey] glanced to the left and saw Calet of [Nicaea], him of the grizzled beard, on the other side of the battlefield; he had just beheaded a Christian. The duke was enraged at the sight: he gnashed his teeth in rage and swore, "You made a mistake when you killed him, you coward! You will pay with your life!"][52]

On the other hand, if the Christians' Saracen opponents have no similar insults upon their religion to avenge, they have all the more Muslim
blood for which to seek redress. Lacking the prowess of the Christian
and misguided in their faith, however, the Muslims of the Old French
Crusade Cycle do not have the ability to avenge their losses. While
they often state their desire to avenge the devastation wrought upon
their coreligionists, they are never able do so;[53] rather, they are left
calling vainly upon their gods to avenge *them*. Corbadas, the unfortunate king of Jerusalem, rages against the inevitable:

> "Ahi!" dist il, "caitif! Mal Crestiën gloton!
> Con vos alés querant vo grant perditïon,
> Car tot serés ocis, mis a destrutïon.
> Ja n'en arés garant de vostre Deu Jhesum.
> Mahons a grant vertu en qui nos affïon.
> De vos nos vengera, qui qu'en poist ne qui non."

> [*CJ* ll. 3155–60: "Alas!" he says, "wretches! Evil gluttonous Chris-
> tians! How you set about seeking your own great downfall, because
> you will all be killed and turned to destruction. You will never be
> protected by your God Jesus. Mohammed, of great virtue, in whom
> we put our faith, will avenge us upon you, come what may."][54]

The two religious families in the Old French Crusade Cycle are therefore contrasted in their ability to take care of their members. While
the ascendant Christian family is formidable enough to avenge the
injuries inflicted upon both its human and its divine members, the
Muslim one is so devoid of power that its only recourse is to trust in
feeble patresfamilias.

If spiritual families are called upon to avenge the injuries done to
them, earthly families are as well. The Christians devote almost as
much attention to avenging their human kin group as they do the
affronts to God. In *Les Chétifs*, for instance, Baldwin of Bauvais seeks
revenge for the death of his brother Ernoul, who was slain by the serpent Sathanas: "Car li dels de sen frere li done hardement; / Or aproce
li termes qu'en prendra vengement" [C ll. 2300–2301: "Because the
suffering of his brother hurt him gravely, now nears the time when he
will avenge it"].[55] Similarly, Hugh of St. Pol attacks the Saracens to
avenge the death of his son before Jerusalem; his opponent is sent to
the grave with the words "de le mort Engerran t'ai gerredon rendu!"
[*CJ* l. 8776: "I have paid you back for the death of Enguerrand!"].
Garsion, the Muslim king of Antioch, voices how the desire to avenge
family affects the Christian conquests in the East; in conflating literal

and figurative fathers and sons, he highlights how intimately connected Graindor considered the human kin groups besieging the Syrian city and the greater Christian family to be:

Quant jou fui de jouvent, si conquis ces regnés.
Mout ai de Crestiëns ocis et afolés.
Or me heent li fil que il on engenrés
Pour lor peres ke j'ai et ocis et tués.
Mais or me repent jou que tant les ai grevés,
Par les enfans cuic estre encor desbaretés
Et mes fius Sansadones aussi desiretés.

[CA ll. 5554–60: When I was a young man I conquered these lands.
In the process I inflicted death and suffering on large numbers of
Christians. Now their sons hate me [because I have killed and slain
their fathers]. But now I am sorry for what I made them go through.
I expect I shall be killed and dispossessed by their children, and my
son Sansadoine declared a prisoner.]

Les Crestiëns ai mis a grant destrutïon.
Or me heent li fil pour iceste ocison,
Ma cité ont asise entor et environ.

[CA ll. 5598–600: I slaughtered Christians right, left and centre as I
hastened onwards. Now their sons hate me for the death I dealt out,
and have put a siege right around my city.]

Inasmuch as personal vendetta spurs on the Christians, the Muslims
too are driven by the thirst for vengeance; as they suffer more than
the Westerners on the field of battle, they have even more to avenge.
As the *Chanson d'Antioche*, *Les Chétifs*, and the *Chanson de Jérusalem* discuss the capture of Saracen cities and the destruction of their
ruling families, so do they tell of the Muslims' vain efforts to attain
redress for their grievances. From the earliest pages of the *Chanson
d'Antioche*, injured Saracens seek vengeance: Soliman of Nicaea, who
loses his sons Hisdent and Tornicant and his nephew Corsolt, futilely
seeks to avenge all three. He calls upon his soldiers to capture Bohemond and Tancred and return them to him alive: "Ne l'ociés vous
mie mais soiés le prendant, / Et tous sains et tous saus les amenés
avant. / Si en ferons justice por Hisdeus mon enfant!" [CA ll. 2446–
48: "Do not kill them on any account—bring them back here to me
in one piece so I can take revenge on them for the death of my son
Hisdent"]. He associates the ability to avenge his nephew Corsolt,
who dies shortly after, with his right to hold land: "'Biaus niés,' ce
dist li rois, 'con mar vous voi morir! / Se ne vous puis vengier, ne doi

tiere tenir'" [*CA* ll. 2600–2601: "'My handsome nephew,' said Soliman, 'what a way to see you die! [If I cannot avenge you, I should not hold any lands]'"]. His consequent failure to exact vengeance for his slain kinsman heralds the loss of his city.[56] Finally, when his other son Tornicant is killed, he can only rage in despair and charge the enemy, imploring Mohammed to avenge his death.[57] *Les Chétifs*, which starts out with the sultan of Baghdad seeking vengeance on his coreligionist Kerbogha for the death of his son Brohadas, who has died at Antioch, through a trial by combat between Richard of Caumont and two of the sultan's best warriors, continues with the family of those warriors seeking their own redress when Richard defeats them:

> Lÿons de la Montaigne ot molt son cuer irié
> Por Sorgalé son oncle, qui le cief ot trencié;
> Il joste son linage, qui molt sont courecié,
> Plus furent de .X. mil quant sont aparellié.

> [*C* ll. 1209–12: The Lion of the Mountain was much angered in his
> heart over his uncle Sorgalé, whose head was cut off; he urged on
> his family, who came up in great numbers; there were more than ten
> thousand when they were equipped.]

Les Chétifs therefore discusses vengeance *outside* the context of Crusade: of Muslims upon other Muslims or their Christian proxies. The final text of the Cycle, the *Chanson de Jérusalem*, also is full of Muslims seeking to avenge their losses as the Christians besiege and capture Jerusalem, defeating the combined armies of Islam.[58] The fundamental inability of the Saracens to halt, overturn, or avenge their conquest of the Holy Land leads them to rely on the succeeding generations to do so. If the words of Garsion of Antioch show that the Crusaders redress the injuries done to their ancestors, for the Muslims too this is a war that continues through successive generations:

> Cil qui a or .X. femes, si penst de l'engenrer,
> Si croistera nos pules por crestïens mater;
> Li enfant qui venront feront molt a douter,
> Des Frans nous vengeront, nel vos quier a celer,
> De le gent maleoite qui no loi velt fauser.

> [*C* ll. 150–54: He who now has ten wives, should think of mak-
> ing them pregnant, so that our children can grow up to defeat the
> Christians; the children that will come will do many fearsome things,
> and—I do not think to hide it from you—will avenge us upon the
> Franks, upon the accursed people that wants to overthrow our law.][59]

The Crusade is therefore not just a war of legitimate vengeance in which the Latins avenge the insults done to God and Christianity. Rather it is a war between families, earthly and heavenly, in which an attack upon one's religious community and injury to kinsmen drive *both* Christians and Muslims to seek redress, and in which sons continue the struggle of their fathers. It is a war of eternal tit for tat, with the opening shot fired by the "lineage of Judas" at the Crucifixion, the fortunes of which are inconstant: if the Old French Crusade Cycle showed the ascendant Christians avenging their God and their kin alike while their Muslim enemies can do nothing but invoke their gods in vain and rely on the vigor of future descendants, the events preceding the Cycle's composition saw Islam once again with the upper hand.

The notion of Crusade as an ongoing war between families, wherein each act invites its own retribution, also affects what both sides stand to gain or lose. In the Old French Crusade Cycle, the heavenly reward due to the Crusader is tied to his ability to exact revenge: "Qui hui ens en cest jor Damedeu vengera / En son saint paradis son cief coronera. / Les mals que avés fais tos les vos pardonra!" [*CJ* ll. 2175–77: "He will crown the head of whoever avenges God here today in his holy paradise, and he will forgive you for all the bad things you have done!"].[60] A more important issue at stake, however, is patrimony, the land that both families claim and only one can possess. Both sides in the Old French Crusade Cycle want to expand into each other's lands, to take the other's ancestral domains. As the Christians conquer the Holy Land, so the Saracens state their desire to cross the sea and subject Europe. "Par force woel aler outre mer a Pavie, / France vaurai conquerre et Puille et Romenie" [*CJ* ll. 4342–43: "I want to go across the sea to Pavia in force, I would like to conquer France and Apulia and Romania"], says the sultan before the climactic battle of Jerusalem; or again, to Peter the Hermit, "Puis venras avoec moi por France conquester. / . . . / A cest premier passage en irons oltre mer: / Por Crestïens destruire vaurai oltre passer" [*CJ* ll. 7097–100: "Afterwards you will come with me to conquer France. . . . With that first passage we will cross the sea: I would like to cross over to destroy the Christians"].[61] Yet while both sides in this unending conflict aim to take over the lands in the other's possession, of course only the Christian can be successful. It is, however, remarkable how little, compared with the *Gesta* and the *Historia*, the Crusaders of the Old French Crusade Cycle express the desire to settle or occupy the land.[62] Rather, the Christian right to the land is portrayed as a matter of principle: their claim is the oldest, has been violated, and must now be restored. Before the Battle of Antioch, the bishop of Le Puy stakes out the Christian case as follows:

> Mandés a Corbaran, cui li cors Dieu cravent,
> Que cis regnes est nostres d'ancïen tenement.
> Nostre ancisour le tinrent jadis tot quitement
> Mais lor gent lor tolirent par lor esforcement.
> Or i sont venu cil a cui l'onors apent.
> Prés somes del mostrer que il n'i ont nïent.
> U a .XX. chevaliers u a .X. ensement
> U a .I. cors a cors qui mout ait hardement.

> [*CA* ll. 9011–18: Let us send an embassy to Corbaran (God crush him!). Our message will be that this kingdom is ours by ancient right but their people took it by force; now we, the rightful holders of the fief, have come. We are ready to prove that they have no claim with 20 knights, or just with ten, or one very brave knight in single combat.]

When Peter the Hermit conveys the message to Kerbogha he adds, "Or i sont cil venu qui claiment l'ireté. / . . . / Cil ki vencus sera s'en voist en son regné / Sains et saus et delivres trestout en quiteé" [*CA* ll. 9074–79: "Now [they] have come to claim their inheritance. . . . The one who loses will go back to his kingdom safe, sound and free, all claims cancelled"].[63] The war between the Christians and the Saracens is therefore also an ancient territorial dispute: the Christian family has had its rights violated, and now its sons come to reclaim those rights, to restore the inheritance to its rightful proprietors. If for the Crusaders ownership of the land is a matter of principle and of legal dispute to be settled by judicial combat if possible, it is very different for the Saracens; as little as the Christians talk about their winning the land, as much do the Muslims discuss their losing it.[64] Furthermore, throughout the Old French Crusade Cycle, the Saracens associate land with family and the loss of the one with that of the other. Soliman of Nicaea, the first to be stripped of his possessions by the Crusaders, complains as follows:

> Mes dex me contralie.
> Ma tere ont par esfort et ma cité garnie,
> Et mes enfans ocis—au cuer en ai hascie—
> Et ont pris mon avoir et ma cité saisie.

> [*CA* ll. 2701–4: My god has turned against me. The Christian forces have taken my lands, my wife, my children and my prosperous city.]

Il ont ma cité prise, dont je sui mout dolans
Ma femme m'ont tolue et ans .II. mes enfans.

[CA ll. 6369–70: They took my city. I am in the depths of despair.
They deprived me of my wife and both my children.][65]

Because of this close relationship between Muslim territory and Muslim family in the Old French Crusade Cycle, the Christian takeover of the Holy Land becomes the chronicle of the annihilation of a number of noble Saracen houses. Just as Soliman loses both his city and his sons, so Garsion loses Antioch, his sons, and eventually his life; all of the sultan of Baghdad's sixteen sons are killed, while Corbadas loses his son Cornumarant and Jerusalem alike. In the battle for the Holy Land, one family must eclipse another; the Christians' resumption of their rightful claim over the land means that the competing claimant must be destroyed. In this context it is not a little symbolic that in the climactic battle for Jerusalem Godfrey of Bouillon and his brothers, who will rule the city after the Crusade, extinguish the lineage of the sultan who was its erstwhile overlord.[66]

THE PURPOSE OF THE OLD FRENCH CRUSADE CYCLE

The cycle of Old French chansons de geste about the First Crusade, compiled in the later years of the twelfth century or the first of the thirteenth, is therefore above all else concerned with family. Written most likely for an audience that included a number of powerful Picard families, it tells of how the Crusaders, members of the greater Christian family as well as fathers, brothers, and sons within earthly kin groups, fight a Muslim enemy that is defined within families of his own. This conflict between families originated when one, the Saracen, insulted and killed the Father and leader of the other, and illegally occupied his land. The Chanson d'Antioche, Les Chétifs, and the Chanson de Jérusalem see that family return to claim its patrimony; this in turn invites yet more revenge from the Saracens who are wronged in the process. Crusade therefore becomes a virtually unending sequence of strike and counterstrike in which both sides are called upon to continue the war of their Father/fathers. This notion of Crusade as a family obligation moves the works beyond the rhetoric of Christian vengeance for pagan insult that had existed from the beginning of the Crusade period, and by which it has often been judged. Rather, in propagating the Crusade as a duty to literal and figurative kin groups, Graindor follows the encyclical *Quantum praedecesso-res*, which called upon the Christian West to continue the struggle of its fathers, and which had strongly influenced papal rhetoric on the Crusades ever since its first issue in 1145. Furthermore, Graindor's choice of a form with which to promulgate this notion of holy war as an obligation to family was a wise one, as the chansons de geste had throughout the twelfth century become the preferred medium for dis-cussing conflicts between dynasties, even if those conflicts involved the imagined houses of the Carolingian Empire. Graindor's use of the genre to discuss very real and near-contemporary conflict, while innovative, was therefore also quite appropriate. This, together with the ease with which the vernacular chansons could be disseminated and the popularity of the genre among an aristocratic audience preoc-cupied with dynastic prestige, served to amplify the effect and value of the Old French Crusade Cycle as Crusade propaganda. In all, the Cycle shows both how papal notions of Crusade were spread down to the grassroots level and the endurance of such notions among a lay audience.

A number of additional benefits accrued to the propagation of Cru-sade as a war of families in the years following the disastrous Battle of Hattin in 1187. It is clear from the Old French Crusade Cycle that there are not one but two kin groups that each consider the Holy Land its patrimony; although the Christians are its rightful owners through a claim dating back to the incarnation of Christ, to the Saracens too the land is intimately associated with the well-being of their kin. Any action against this joint inheritance therefore necessarily invites a reaction, and as both sides call upon their descendants to continue their struggle, the war becomes cyclical, continuous, and in need of constant reinforcement. Importantly, the cyclical nature of the Cru-sade makes it susceptible to the fortunes of war: just as the Saracens struck the first blow when they crucified Christ and took his inheri-tance, which the Christians then took back during the First Crusade, this conquest itself invites Saracen counterstrikes, which the Chris-tians in turn need to avenge once more. The Muslim reoccupation of the Holy Land under Saladin,[67] the outrages done to the Cross and the Sepulchre referred to at the beginning of the *Chanson d'Antioche*, are therefore both parallel to and the logical consequence of the Sar-acen actions that led to the First Crusade. It therefore once again becomes a historic and social necessity for the Christian to avenge this, to take his place in the age-old struggle between the Christian and Muslim families; those taking the cross after Hattin therefore are not only following in the footsteps of the First Crusaders, they are in a very real sense their equals.

Finally, the propagation of Crusade as a family war also serves as a call for unity among the Christians who are to fight it. The period leading up to the fall of Jerusalem was one of increasing fractiousness, both between and among the Eastern and Western Latins; these divisions strongly affected the ability of the Third Crusade to restore the status quo ante. The Old French Crusade Cycle not only represents the Crusader army as a family of families, it also exerts no small effort to show it as united in purpose, one force harmoniously composed of many nationalities and social classes. The historic hostilities between the Crusader army and the Byzantine Empire are much reduced; even though the emperor remains as duplicitous as he had been in the *Gesta* and the *Historia*, Tatikios No-Nose becomes a staunch friend of the Crusaders and "Cil de Constantinoble—tot furent compaignon" [*CJ* l. 3131: "those of Constantinople—all were companions"] remain with the army until the conquest of Jerusalem.[68] The Old French Crusade Cycle, far more than the *Gesta* and the *Historia*, emphasizes the diversity of the Crusader host, brought together from a great many countries under common purpose.[69] The historical divisions that plagued the First Crusade, such as that the between Tancred of Hauteville and Baldwin of Boulogne and that between Raymond of Toulouse and Bohemond of Taranto, are largely omitted.[70] Intriguingly, the Cycle also depicts the three estates together at war: in addition to the chivalric aristocracy and the clergy that had been the subject of its sources, the Old French Crusade Cycle devotes much attention to the commoners on Crusade. The lower-class Tafurs, while referred to in terms hardly more flattering than those reserved for the Muslim enemy,[71] make their way to the holy city under their own king; the final battle of Jerusalem sees the three estates fighting alongside each other and defeating the combined armies of Islam together: "Chevalier et ribaut—gent i avoit assés" [*CJ* l. 6697: "Knights and rogues—there were many men"].[72] In the years after 1187, the Old French Crusade Cycle's promotion of Crusade as a duty to kin group is therefore not only a call for the reinvigoration of an age-old struggle by a new generation but also an appeal for unity within the Christian family. It is perhaps here that we see how clearly Graindor understood what was required to keep the Saracen lineage at bay: as military setbacks took the True Cross from

Christian hands and drove the Latins from the holy city of Jerusalem, only a unified Christian family, tied together by kinship and united across ethnic and social boundaries, could undo the disasters and safeguard its hold on the land. The decades following the completion of the Cycle saw continuing dissent between and among Western and Eastern Christians accompany the collapse of Latin dominion in the Levant, and proved him right.

PART II

Chivalric Romance
in Crusade Propaganda

CHAPTER 5

The Challenge of Romance and the Thirteenth Century

CHIVALRIC ROMANCE

More than a century ago, Gaston Paris noted that "la croisade n'aurait pas eu lieu sans la Chanson de Roland."[1] By this he meant that both flowed from similar sociopolitical and religious circumstances, that "les mêmes faits psychologiques provoquèrent les chansons de geste et les croisades."[2] Crusade and the chansons de geste were not, however, merely two parallel children of the same spirit of piety and confrontationalism. Their progress intertwined: as demonstrated in the preceding chapters, the chanson de geste was used in excitatoria in the years following the First Crusade to make the novel concept of Crusade both understandable and appealing to an audience of the chivalric aristocracy, whose participation was crucial to maintaining and expanding the Latin conquests in the Fertile Crescent. Whereas in the first decade after the fall of Jerusalem to the Crusader armies the genre was used to unite disparate forces under a common purpose and to give these forces the right of ownership both of the Holy Places and beyond, by the end of the twelfth century the chansons served to present Crusade as a war between families to revive aristocratic interest after the disastrous losses of 1187.

The following years saw continued use of the chansons de geste in Crusade excitatoria. As the twelfth century drew to a close, a Norman cleric who accompanied Richard I of England on the Third Crusade of 1189–1192 described the deeds of the monarch and his army in a work known as the *Estoire de la Guerre Sainte.*[3] Seeking to praise

Richard's successes and exculpate him for his failures, Ambroise, who began his work after 1192 and completed it before 1199, made extensive use of the formal and thematic commonplaces of the chanson de geste to shape his narrative.[4] Beyond commendation of Richard the Lion-Hearted and condemnation of his enemies, however, Ambroise sought to encourage further expeditions to the Levant, and here too the chansons, and the deeds they described, played an important part. For instance, if future Crusaders would like to avoid the internal divisions that had, as Ambroise argued, prevented the Christian armies from reconquering Jerusalem, they would do well to take heed of the past:

> Quant li vaillant reis Charlemaines,
> Qui tant conquist terres et regnes,
> Ala josteier en Espaine
> Ou il amena la preuz compaine
> Qui fu vendu al roi Marsille
> Par Guenelon, dont France avile;
> E quant il refu en Sesoigne
> Ou il fist meinte grant besoigne,
> E il desconfist Guiteclin,
> E mist les Senes a declin,
> Par la force de maint prodome;
> E quant il mena l'ost par Rome,
> Quant Agolant, par grant emprise,
> Fu par mer arivé a Rise,
> En Calabre, la riche terre;
> E quant Sulie a l'autre guerre
> Refu perdue e reconquisse
> E Antioche si fud assise,
> E es granz ostz e es batailles
> Sor les Turcs e sor les chenailles
> Dont tant i ot mortes e mates;
> La n'avoit estrifs ne barates,
> Lores a cel tens në anceis,
> Qui erent Norman ou Franceis,
> Qui Peitevin, ne ki Breton,
> Qui Mansel, ne ki Burgoinon,
> Ne ki Flamenc, ne qui Engleis;
> Illoc n'i aveit point de jangleis,
> Ne point de s'entreramponouent
> Mais tote honors en reportouent;
> Cil erent tuit apelé Franc
> E brun e bai e sor e blanc,
> E par pechié quant descordouent,
> E li prince les racordouent,

E erent tuit a une acorde,
Si que poi i doroit descorde;
E ausi deussent icist faire
E si guverner lor affaire
Que hom i peust essample prendre
Non pas li uns l'autre entreprendre.

[When the valiant king Charlemagne, who conquered so many lands
and countries, went to campaign in Spain, taking with him the noble
band who were sold to Marsile by Ganelon to the dishonour of
France, and when he, Charlemagne, had returned to Saxony, where
he did many great deeds and defeated Guiteclin, bringing about the
fall of the Saxons by the strength of many valiant men and when
he led his army to Rome, when Agoland, through a great undertaking had arrived at Reggio in the rich land of Calabria, when, in
another war, Syria was lost and reconquered and Antioch besieged,
in the great armies and the battles against the Turks and the pagan
hordes, when many were killed and conquered, there was no bicker-
ing and quarrelling, at that time and before; then there was neither
Norman nor French, Poitevin nor Breton, Mansel nor Burgundian,
Flemish nor English; there was no malicious gossip nor insulting of
one another; everyone came back with all honour and all were called
Franks, whether brown or red, swarthy or white, and when through
sin they disagreed the princes brought them back into agreement with
each other, and all were of one mind so that disagreement lasted little
time. This is how things should be done and the affairs of today dealt
with, that men may follow this example and not attack each other.][5]

It is noteworthy that Ambroise juxtaposes the events of the *Chanson
de Roland*, the *Chanson des Saisnes*, and the *Chanson d'Aspremont*
with those of the First Crusade as examples to emulate; as did the
anonymous author of the *Gesta* and Robert of Reims, he presents
the campaigns of Charlemagne and those of the First Crusaders as
deeply related. It is intriguing to see, however, not only that Ambroise
associates the deeds of Charlemagne with those of the First Crusaders but also that he likely found these deeds in similar sources, as it
appears Ambroise knew of the events of 1096–1099 from the *Chanson d'Antioche*. Ambroise, after all, speaks of the siege of Antioch but
not of the many events that occurred *after* that siege, or even of the
conquest of Jerusalem, the goal and the culmination of the First Crusade. Of the many sources of the siege of Antioch, only the *Chanson
d'Antioche* omits the terrible internal divisions among the Crusader
armies, allowing it to function as an image of unity to the following
generations.[6] Furthermore, speaking of the French who had stoked
the fires of dissent during the Third Crusade, he mentions:

E de gent si desmesuree
N'iert ja bone chançon chantee,
N'ovraine feite que Deu veie,
Si com il fist a l'autre veie,
Quant Antioche fud assise
E nostre gent par force enz mise—
Dont l'en raconte encore l'estorie,
De cels qui Deus dona victorie,
De Buiamont e de Tancré—
C'erent pelerin esmeré—
E de Godefrei de Buillon,
E de hauz princes de grant non,
E des autres qui lors i furent
Qui Deus servirent e mururent
Tant qu'il lor rendi lor servise
A lur gré e a lur devise,
E lor ovraines suzhauça
Par tantes feiz e eshauça,
E il e totes lor lignees;
Si en sunt encore eshaucees.

[Never will a good song be sung about such uncontrolled men, nor will God look upon their deeds as on those who went on a different pilgrimage, when Antioch was besieged and taken by force by our men. The story is still told of those for whom God gave the victory, of Bohemond and Tancred, who were distinguished pilgrims, and of Godfrey of Bouillon and high princes of high renown and of the others who died in the service of God, so that He gave back to them according to their desires and plans. He raised their deeds to great heights and they and all their family are exalted and still honoured.][7]

As opposed to the First Crusaders who besieged Antioch, God will not smile upon the French, and no *song* will be made that will enshrine their deeds in memory. The story of Bohemond, Godfrey, and their companions of which Ambroise speaks is therefore probably the *Chanson d'Antioche*.[8] Ambroise's notable reference to Godfrey of Bouillon makes it furthermore likely that he knew the *Chanson d'Antioche* in Graindor's redaction rather than in a possible earlier form, as the *Chanson d'Antioche* drew heavily on Albert of Aachen's *Historia Ierosolimitana* and shared its sympathy for the Lotharingian duke.[9] This illustrates the swift distribution of the *Chanson d'Antioche* outside Picardy; even before the turn of the thirteenth century, its popularity in both the clerical and aristocratic circles around Richard I must have been great enough not only for Ambroise to be aware of the work but also for him to be confident that his audience would be too. It also demonstrates how the *Chanson d'Antioche* influenced late twelfth-century understanding of the Crusade, both in Ambroise's foregrounding of the siege of Antioch within the history of the First Crusade and in his mention of the families of its participants, which echoes the *Chanson d'Antioche*'s depiction of the Crusade as family warfare.

Crusade excitatoria continued to utilize the stylistic and thematic tropes of the chansons de geste to encourage their audience to take the cross after the turn of the thirteenth century. Insofar as their works served to propagate the Crusade, Robert of Clari, who wrote an account of the Fourth Crusade, and Jean of Joinville, who accompanied Louis IX on the Seventh Crusade and related his experiences in the *Vie de Saint Louis*, drew upon the chansons;[10] so did the author of the *Estoire d'Eracles* (ca. 1205–1234), an Old French translation of William of Tyre's chronicle of the Latin kingdom of Jerusalem, *Historia Rerum in Partibus Transmarinis Gestarum*;[11] while circa 1212–1213, William of Tudela, following the example of the *Chanson d'Antioche*, wrote a history of the early years of the Albigensian Crusade, the *Canso de la Crozada*, in the shape of a chanson de geste.[12] The First Old French Crusade Cycle was greatly expanded, and by 1266–1268 Humbert of Romans, in *De Praedicatione Sanctae Crucis contra Saracenos*, listed the *Gesta Caroli Magni in Hispania*, more commonly known as the *Pseudo-Turpin Chronicle*, among the exempla to use to whip up fervor for the holy war.[13] As the popularity of the chansons endured, so did their usefulness to Crusade propaganda.

We see in the Old French Crusade Cycle, however, that by the last decades of the twelfth century certain literary developments were afoot. Perhaps a rationale for multiple authorship of the Cycle is the changing role of women in its component texts. Whereas the oldest, the *Chanson d'Antioche*, reserves only a limited role to women, as objects of affection left behind or at best as helping to alleviate the stress of battle,[14] by the end of the *Chanson de Jérusalem* they themselves have become motivations for Crusade:

> Les dames lor escrïent, "Ne soiés pas lanier!
> Li vallés por s'amie, li hom por sa moillier!"
> . . .
> Les dames s'escrïerent, qui de l'ost Deu sont la,
> De le vile conquerre u Dex resuscita—
> Tos jors avra s'amor qui bien le vengera.

[*CJ* ll. 3512–88: The ladies cried to them: "Don't be cowardly! The youth for his beloved, the man for his wife!" . . . The ladies cried out that they who were there in the army of God to conquer the city where God came back to life, and would avenge him well, would always have their love.]

While the chansons de geste had included amorous relationships from early on, love itself did not usually constitute a motivation to fight in the poems;[15] though occupying no more than five lines among the more than thirty thousand in the First Cycle, the passage above illustrates the growing popularity of a genre of which it was a driving factor: chivalric romance. Chivalric romance, which rose to prominence alongside the chansons,[16] is traditionally assumed to have originated with the writings of Chrétien de Troyes, whose first known poem, *Erec et Enide*, was completed circa 1170. As a genre it emphasized the achievements and amorous interests of the individual; unlike that of the chanson de geste, the protagonist of romance does not fight for the expansion or survival of his political, religious, or social group:

> The hero is not desperately defending his homeland but chooses to go out from a secure bastion of wealth and privilege (such as the Arthurian court) to seek adventures by which the values of chivalry and service to ladies (not only being in love but "being a lover," a social grace as much as a private emotion) will be submitted to test and proved. . . . The action is no longer "real" or historical; there are elements of the marvellous; geography is vague; time is unreal. The knight is not impelled by dynastic or territorial ambitions, but chooses to go out on adventures because that is how he proves the values by which he lives—proves his reality, his identity, in fact. Feats of arms, arbitrary in themselves, are the means of self-realization. . . . Above all, the hero now thinks and feels as well as acts; there is an inner consciousness to be explored. He is in love.[17]

Chivalric romance, like the chansons de geste written both about and primarily for the chivalric aristocracy, addressed the way the knighthood of the later twelfth century regarded itself, and especially how it wished to be regarded by others. For an audience increasingly preoccupied with courtliness, it depicts chivalry as the individual demonstration of ideal valor. Typically, a member of the knightly class will set out on a journey or "quest" to solve a problem confronting him. On this journey—a "practically uninterrupted series of adventures"[18]—he will demonstrate his superior qualities and adherence to social, military, and religious principles through feats of arms, often against marvelous or magical opposition in otherworldly places.

These principles include prowess, loyalty, generosity, and courtesy; however, the most definitive principle is courtly love, the service in word and deed to ladies by lovers deemed inferior, a love closely related to the *fin' amors* pioneered by the troubadours.[19]

The popularity of chivalric romance quickly spread beyond the court of Champagne, where Chrétien had composed *Erec*, and within decades romances in Anglo-Norman (e.g., *Gui de Warewic*, early thirteenth century), Middle Dutch (e.g., *De Roman van Walewein*, ca. 1260), Middle High German (e.g., Hartmann of Aue's *Iwein*, ca. 1202; Wolfram of Eschenbach's *Parzifal*, ca. 1210), and even Old Norse (the mid-thirteenth-century *riddarasögur*, e.g., *Erex saga* and *Parcevals saga*) had appeared. As more romances were written, some abandoned the verse form of the earliest works, and by 1230 the extensive Vulgate or *Lancelot-Grail* Cycle chronicled the rise and fall of Arthur and the Round Table in five books of prose.[20] Although chivalric romance was primarily concerned with the "Matter of Britain"—the legends of Arthur and the Knights of the Round Table—works on the adventures of unrelated protagonists quickly appeared (e.g., *King Horn*, ca. 1225; *Ipomadon*, before 1191).[21] In the centuries following Chrétien's work, romance evolved into a literature of extraordinary wealth, diversity, and flexibility, broaching issues as wide-ranging as the passionate, adulterous love of Lancelot for Guenevere or Tristan for Isolde, Parzifal's quest both for the Grail and its meaning, Havelok the Dane's search for origins, and Gawain's stinging failure in *Sir Gawain and the Green Knight*.[22]

Given the use of the chansons de geste in Crusade excitatoria, it would not be surprising to find chivalric romance to be employed in the service of holy war as well. If the chansons were popular among the very aristocracy that was relied upon to fight the campaigns in the East, chivalric romances were equally so. The structure of romance furthermore invited comparison with Crusade: after all, they spoke of journeys from the safety of home to far away countries, secular pilgrimages to prove individual perfection in the crucible of battle, normally followed by a return to the home left behind.[23] Nevertheless, chivalric romance was not immediately used to propagate the Crusade, even after Saladin's conquest of Jerusalem, in the years when romance experienced a meteoric rise in popularity. This was because of the problematic nature of the aspect that, more than any other, differentiated romance from chanson de geste: courtly love and service to ladies.

PECCATIS EXIGENTIBUS

From its beginning at the court of Marie of Champagne in the second half of the twelfth century, the love of the romances, while passionate and full of abandon, was also deeply troubling from a religious point of view. The countess of Champagne's chaplain, Andreas Capellanus, who wrote *De Amore* (ca.1170–1174) at roughly the same time as Chrétien wrote his early romances, argued that courtly love was unlike any other, in part because it could not take place within the bonds of marriage:

> But I am greatly surprised that you wish to misapply the term "love" to that marital affection which husband and wife are expected to feel for each other after marriage, since everybody knows that love can have no place between husband and wife. They may be bound to each other by a great and immoderate affection, but their feeling cannot take the place of love, because it cannot fit under the true definition of love. For what is love but an inordinate desire to receive passionately a furtive and hidden embrace? But what embrace between husband and wife can be furtive, I ask you, since they may be said to belong to each other and may satisfy all of each other's desires without fear that anybody will object?[24]

It is this hidden, transgressive love that animates the pages of Chrétien's *Le Chevalier de la Charrette*, which speaks of Lancelot's love for Guenevere, the wife of his lord, Arthur, and which contends that *not* to give in to your paramour is a sin, while suicide for love is a virtue. Although not all courtly love is adulterous (for instance, Chrétien's work *Le Chevalier au Lion*, written roughly simultaneously with *Le Chevalier de la Charrette*, discusses the marriage of Yvain with Laudine, the widow of a man he has defeated in battle), very much of it is extramarital.[25] The upending of traditional morals within courtly love would of course be problematic for those with Pauline sensitivities; Andreas himself acknowledges that the love of which he speaks disregards religious guidelines:

> Now for many reasons any wise man is bound to avoid all the deeds of love and to oppose all its mandates. The first of these reasons is one which it is not right for anyone to oppose, for no man, so long as he devotes himself to the service of love, can please God by any other works, even if they are good ones. For God hates, and in both testaments commands the punishment of, those whom he sees engaged in the works of Venus outside the bonds of wedlock or caught in the toils of any sort of passion. What good therefore can be found in a thing in which nothing is done except what is contrary to the will of

God? Alas what an affliction it is and what bitterness to our hearts when we grieve constantly to see men reject the things of heaven for the sake of the foul and shameful act of Venus![26]

In other words, by its strongly extramarital nature, courtly love defies the will of God and in effect strays into sin. It is an irony of history that the years that saw chivalric romance, exultant in the overthrow of traditional morals through sinful courtly love, become widely popular throughout Western Europe also saw the Latin West sensitive once again to the effects of sin on society.

It did not take long for the disastrous defeat at Hattin, the fall of Jerusalem, and the loss of most of the Christian littoral of the Eastern Mediterranean to be blamed on the sins of the Christians. Sin, and especially the sin of the Eastern Latins, had caused God to withdraw his favor from them, giving way to Saladin's successes. The anonymous author of the *Itinerarium Peregrinorum et Gesta Regis Ricardi*, likely an English Crusader writing during or shortly after the Third Crusade,[27] described the events leading up to the disasters of 1187 as follows:

Then the Lord's hand was aroused against His people—if we can properly call them "His," as their immoral behaviour, disgraceful lifestyle, and foul vices had made them strangers to Him. For shameful practices had broken out in the East, so that everywhere everyone threw off the veil of decency and openly turned aside to filthy things. It would take a long time to describe their murders, robberies and adulteries. . . . Suffice it to say that when the Ancient Enemy spread the spirit of corruption far and wide, he particularly seized on Syria. So the region from which other areas had received religion now became an example of all immorality.[28]

From its very beginning in the last years of the eleventh century, sin had been thought perhaps the greatest threat to the success of the Crusade—after all, it was an armed pilgrimage engaged in for the *remission* of sin—and failures were habitually ascribed to the transgressions of its participants.[29] Among the offenses that invited the wrath of God, sexual misbehavior, notably extramarital or illicit sex, featured prominently.[30] Just as the author of the *Itinerarium Peregrinorum* blamed the fall of most of the kingdom of Jerusalem on the "adulteries" of the Easterners, Henry of Huntingdon had blamed the defeats of the Second Crusade on the fornication perpetrated by the French and German armies, and the sexual activities of the Franks had been thought the cause of their misfortunes at Antioch.[31] It is

therefore not surprising that magnates and princes planning to set
out on Crusade sought to regulate the sexual behavior of those who
were to accompany them: for instance, the Geddington ordinances of
1188, in which Henry II of England instituted the "Saladin tithe" in
preparation for his own campaign, also prevented any women other
than laundresses of high moral standing to join it.[32] Furthermore,
the sensuality that the courtly love of the chivalric romances cham-
pioned had for many years been attributed to the Muslim adversary.
Drawing upon a longstanding clerical tradition that represented the
prophet Muhammad as a heresiarch who appealed to his followers by
indulging their hedonistic desires,[33] Crusade propaganda had from its
earliest days depicted the Saracen as steeped in the sin of *luxuria*.[34]
The passionate, often illicit love of the romances was therefore wholly
troublesome in the context of Crusade: not only did it contribute to
the disasters that befell both the Crusader states and the armies that
came to their aid, it also invoked the specter of the enemy itself, reducing the Christian to the level of his debauched Saracen opponent.

REMEDIA AMORIS

Where the concerns of the chansons de geste, such as the loyalty
between lord and vassal, patrilineal inheritance, and duty to family
were easily and successfully incorporated into the call to Crusade,
this was far less straightforward for the deleterious courtly love at
the heart of chivalric romance.[35] This of course made romance of
only limited use to Crusade propaganda. The reluctance with which
Crusade excitatoria of the twelfth and thirteenth centuries touched
on the notion of secular love is revealed in the songs of the Occitan troubadours and northern French trouvères. A number of these,
known as *chansons de croisade* and ranging in form from the topical
sirventes to *pastorelas* and the discussion poems known as *tensos*,
consider the effect of the Crusade on their surroundings or aim to
encourage their audience to take the cross.[36] However, even though
troubadours and trouvères shared an interest in fin' amors with the
poets of the romances, they from very early on struggle to combine
secular love for women with the holy war. In "Ahi! Amours, com dure
departie," Conon of Béthune (ca. 1150–1220), a knight from Artois
in northern France who participated in both the Third and the Fourth
Crusade, describes how the Crusader is himself divided between his

obligations, forcing him to leave the heart behind with his lady, while the body sets out to the East:

> Ahi! Amors, com dure departie
> Me convenra faire de le meillour
> Ki onkes fust amee ne servie!
> Deus me ramaint a li, par se douchour,
> Si voirement ke m'en part a dolour!
> Las! c'ai jou dit? Ja n'e m'en part jou mie!
> Se li cors vait server nostre Seignour,
> Li cuers remaint dou tout en se baillie.

> [ll. 1–8: Oh, Love! How hard will it be for me to have to leave the best woman who was ever loved or served! May God, in his kindness, lead me back to her as I leave her in sorrow. Alas! What have I said? I am not really leaving her at all! If my body is going off to serve Our Lord, my heart remains entirely within her sway.][37]

Expressing what a great many undoubtedly experienced, Conon's Crusader will fight on the Syrian battlefield while holding on to the memory of what he has left behind; the separation between lover and beloved is therefore spatial and temporal. Some poets, however, see Crusade not as an impediment but as an end to love, inevitably turning the lover away from his beloved. For instance, in "A la fontana del vergier," the troubadour Marcabru (fl. 1130–1150)[38] describes coming upon a lady whose knight has joined the French contingent of the Second Crusade:

> A la fontana del vergier,
> on l'erb' es vertz josta.l gravier,
> a l'ombra d'un fust domesgier,
> en aiziment de blancas flors
> e de novelh chant costumier,
> trobey sola, ses companhier,
> selha que no vol mon solatz.

> [ll. 1–7: By the spring in the orchard, where the grass is green beside the bank, in the shade of a fruit tree, with its pretty white flowers and the usual spring birdsong, I came across that young woman who, alone and without companion, does not want my company.][39]

The traditional setting of love poetry contrasts sharply with the loneliness of the lady and her desire to stay alone. We find that her isolation, even among these magnificent surroundings, is only half self-inflicted—her beloved has left her to fight alongside Louis VII.

The blame for his leaving—for turning away from her and toward the
Holy Land—lies with both God and the French king:

> Dels huelhs ploret josta la fon
> e del cor sospiret preon.
> "Jhesus," dis elha, "reys del mon,
> per vos mi creys ma gran dolors,
> quar vostra anta mi cofon,
> quar li mellor de tot est mon
> vos van servir, mas a vos platz.
> Ab vos s'en vai lo mieus amicx,
> lo belhs e.l gens e.l pros e.l ricx;
> sai m'en reman lo grans destrix,
> lo deziriers soven e.ls plors.
> Ay! mala fos reys Lozoïcx,
> que fai los mans e los prezicx
> per que.l dols m'es el cor intratz!"

> [ll. 15–28: Beside the spring she wept and sighed from the bottom of
> her heart; "Jesus," she said, "king of the world, because of you my
> great sorrow is increasing, for your shame is my undoing: the best of
> all this world are going to serve you, since it is your will. My love, the
> handsome, courtly, brave and noble, departs with you; great distress,
> frequent longing and tears stay here with me. Oh! Cursed be King
> Louis, who orders the call to arms and the preaching which are the
> cause of this grief entering my heart!"][40]

The separation between the lovers is psychological as well as physical.
The poem presents the knight with a stark choice: on the one hand the
love of ladies and the orchards and riverbanks of home, on the other
the love of God, loyalty to the king of France, and the hard life of
the campaign. Marcabru, who appears supportive of the holy war,[41]
suggests that those taking the cross must abandon the former to turn
toward the latter, even if it means leaving behind a broken heart.[42]

A third group of poets solves the problem of courtly love by
making the divine itself the object of love, using the language of
fin' amors to speak of service to God and the Virgin Mary, maintaining the allure of the language while removing any problematic
licentiousness. Illuminating in this respect is the poetry of Thibaut
IV, count palatine of Champagne (1201–1253). Thibaut was both a
prolific creator of love poetry and an energetic Crusader who participated in the Albigensian Crusade in 1226 and led his own campaign to the Holy Land in 1239–1240. A number of his works are
classified as chansons de croisade; as William Chester Jordan has
pointed out, these show an intriguing psychological and spiritual

development.[43] As could perhaps be expected in the writings of a man renowned as a lover, the separation between lover and beloved as a result of Crusade is an important theme. In "Dame, ensi est qu'il m'en couvient aler," for instance, the poet goes so far as to question why the Holy Land exists, since it does so much damage to those united in love:

Dame, ensi est qu'il m'en couvient aler
et departir de ma douce contree
ou tant ai maus apris a endurer,
quant je vous lais, droiz est que je me hee.
Dex, por quoi fu la terre d'Outremer
qui tant amanz avra fet desevrer,
dont puis ne fu l'amors reconfortee,
ne ne porent leur joie remenbrer!

[ll. 1–8: Lady, since I must go away / And leave the sweet country / Where I learned to endure such suffering, / And leave you, it is only right that I hate myself. / God! Why does the Holy Land exist / Which will separate so many lovers / Who, afterward, will have no comfort from love, / Nor will they be able to remember their joy!][44]

The poet then adds, however, that he, while removed from his earthly beloved, simply cannot live without love: "Ja sanz amor ne porroie durer, / tant par i truis fermement ma pensee, / ne mes fins cuers ne m'en let retorner" [ll. 9–11: "I could never last without love, / So completely is my thought devoted to it, / Nor could my true heart let me renounce it"].[45] The incompatibility of Crusade and secular love, combined with the poet's inability *not* to love, leads him to devote his love to God and the Virgin Mary:

a vous me rent, biax Peres Jhesu Criz!
Si bon seigneur avoir je ne porroie;
cil qui vous sert ne puet estre esbahiz.
Bien doit mes cuers estre liez et dolanz:
dolanz de ce que je part de ma dame,
et liez de ce que je sui desirranz
de servir Dieu, qui est mes cuers et m'ame.
Iceste amor est trop fine et puissanz,
par la couvient venir les plus sachanz;
c'est li rubiz, l'esmeraude et la jame
qui touz guerist les vix pechiez puanz.
Dame des ciex, granz roine puissanz,
au grant besoing me soiez secoranz!
De vos amer puisse avoir droite flamme,
quant dame pert, par dame me soit aidanz!

[ll. 30–44: I render myself to you, good Father of Jesus Christ! /
Such a good lord I could never find on earth; / He who serves you is
immune to fear. / It is fitting that my heart be joyous and doleful: /
Doleful for leaving my lady, / And joyous, desirous / Of serving God,
who is my heart and my soul. / This love is surpassingly true and
powerful, / And by its path come the most learned; / It is the ruby,
the emerald, the gem / Which cures us all of ugly, foul-smelling sin. /
Lady of the heavens, great, powerful queen, / Greatly am I in need of
succour! / May I be inflamed with love for you! / When I lose a lady,
by a lady may I be helped!][46]

A new love replaces that of his lady and removes the poet from "foul-
smelling sin"; it combines ardent, armed service to God with love service to the Virgin Mary, who supersedes his erstwhile beloved as the
object of his courtly affections.[47] The twelfth- and thirteenth-century
poetry of the troubadours and trouvères therefore strongly emphasizes the physical, psychological, and spiritual *incompatibility* of secular fin' amors and holy war: not only does Crusade divide lovers in
time and space, taking the cross also requires that the knight devote
himself to God rather than to a lady, and courtly love usually survives
only if rendered less problematic by transferring it to those who, like
the Virgin Mary, are spiritually acceptable.[48] Given the reluctance of
the poets to include secular love in their call to Crusade, it is not surprising to find chivalric romance—a genre that combined courtly love
with adventure and the definition of self through clash of arms—used
only sparingly in excitatoria of the twelfth and thirteenth centuries.
Where chivalric romance was used in propaganda, it too occurred
almost uniquely in ways that emphasized the separation in time and
space between the knight's commitment to secular love and commitment to holy war, or that rendered courtly love wholly unproblematic. A discussion of a number of episodes in the early continuations
of the Old French Crusade Cycle, and of the mid-thirteenth-century
chivalric biography *L'histore de Gille de Chyn*, will serve to illustrate
this trend.

THE EARLY CONTINUATIONS TO THE FIRST
OLD FRENCH CRUSADE CYCLE

In the years following the completion of the historical cycle of the
First Crusade Cycle, a number of branches were added that expanded
the Cycle backward in time.[49] Dating from as early as the last years
of the twelfth century to the middle of the thirteenth, they traced the

lineage of Godfrey of Bouillon, the first Advocate of the Holy Sepulchre, back to his mythical ancestor the Swan Knight.[50] Even though
they are far more fantastic, these additional branches maintained the
dual function of the historical cycle as vernacular historiography and
Crusade propaganda;[51] furthermore, as they were composed when
chivalric romance experienced a great rise in popularity, they show
the subtle effect of the new genre on the chansons de geste of the
Crusade.

Two of these early branches explore the very origin of the Boulogne line, the mysterious birth of Elias, the Swan Knight.[52] Gaston
Paris has dated the oldest of these, *Elioxe*, which draws on Alta Silva's
Dolopathos, sive de Rege et Septem Sapientibus of circa 1190, to the
last years of the twelfth century or the first of the thirteenth.[53] In it,
Elioxe, wife to King Lothair of Hungary, gives birth to seven children, only to die in childbirth. Lothair's mother Matrosilie, who had
despised the match, has the children, six boys and a girl, all of whom
were born wearing gold necklaces, taken to the forest to die. A hermit finds them and raises them until the moment at which another of
Matrosilie's servants chances upon the hermitage. Instructed by her
to obtain the necklaces, he succeeds only in taking those of the boys,
who turn into swans. While feeding her brothers, the girl is found
by Lothair's seneschal; at his urging the king speaks to her, and she
tells him what has happened. The mother's treachery is discovered,
and five of the six boys are returned to human form; the sixth, whose
chain had been melted down to make a dish, must remain a swan.
One of the five, now known as the Swan Knight, then sets out with
his bird brother toward Nijmeghen, where the dynasty of Godfrey of
Bouillon will be established.

The second version, *Beatrix*, which has not been conclusively dated
but draws on both *Dolopathos* and *Elioxe*, offers an interesting comparison.[54] The anonymous author reimagined the tale to focus especially on the Swan Knight, and in doing so invoked certain echoes of
contemporary chivalric romance. In the *Beatrix*—which purports to
counter the lies of those "ki vous cantent de la reonde table" [l. 14:
"who sing to you about the Round Table"][55] by telling the salutary
story of Godfrey's ancestry—a boy, Elias, is left behind when his five
brothers and sister are turned into swans. Raised by the hermit, Elias
bears a striking resemblance to Perceval in Chrétien's *Le Conte du
Graal*. When finally forced to leave the woods, he too "houme fol et
sauvaje mervelles resambloit" [l. 889: "resembled a crazy man and a

wonderful savage"]; he too thinks his name is "Biaus Fius" [l. 910: "Beautiful Son"], as he is only ever called that; and he too is comically stunned by the outside world, reacting, for instance, to the appearance of a horse as follows: "'Dex! Aidiés!' fait li enfes qui nul mal n'i pensoit. / 'Quel beste voi jou la? Je ne sai que ce soit. / Espoir c'est li cevaus dont mes peres parloit'" [ll. 883–85: "'God! Help!' says the child, who did not think badly of it. 'What animal do I see there? I do not know what it is. I hope it is the horse of which my father spoke'"].[56] More important, if Elias leaves the woods a Perceval, he does so to become a Lancelot: he too must fight an enemy in one-on-one combat in defense of a lady. However, whereas in Chrétien's *Le Chevalier de la Charrette* Lancelot fights to defend his beloved Guenevere against Meleagant's charge of adultery, Elias fights to clear his mother, whom the *Beatrix* resurrects, against spurious charges leveled by her evil mother-in-law, Matabrune.[57] Elias's channeling of Chrétien's heroes therefore does not serve his development as a knight or courtly love but rather serves the interests of his family: although he might look the country bumpkin, Elias quickly kills his grandmother's champion, rallies his father's forces to defeat her, reconciles his parents, turns nearly all of his siblings back to human form, and is finally crowned king. While the *Beatrix* echoes *Le Chevalier de la Charrette*, the work removes the most problematic aspect of Chrétien's poem by focusing on the relation between (natural) son and mother, not (illicit) lover and beloved. Whatever echoes of romance exist in the work serve to emphasize the passing of generations and the construction of a dynasty, not to prove the chivalric or amorous qualities of its protagonist.

This pattern continues in the branches that follow the *Beatrix*. In *Le Chevalier au Cygne* (composed before 1218),[58] the Swan Knight's travails as a *chevalier errant* result in his acquiring a fief, a wife, and a daughter. Continuing his aid of mothers under duress, the Swan Knight, having arrived at the emperor Otto's court, vows to defend the rights of the elderly duchess of Bouillon against Duke Regnier of Saxony. After the Swan Knight defeats Regnier, the duchess of Bouillon decides to enter a monastery and therefore arranges the marriage of her daughter to her champion at the court of the emperor:

> "Gentius rois de bon aire, por Deu a moi entent.
> Grant honor m'as hui faite, Jhesus de Belliënt,
> Et cis frans cevaliers par son fier hardement.
> Sire, recoif ma terre et cest baron le rent,

Et si prenge ma fille par le tien loement.
Et jo devenrai none al mostier saint Lorent."
"Certes," dist l'emperere, "jo l'otroi bonement.
La terre li rendrai sans nul arestement."
Li Cevaliers le Cisne se drece isnelement;
La pucele recoit et quanqu'a li apent.

[ll. 1268–77: "Kind, noble king, by God, listen to me. You have
done me great honor today, upon Jesus of Bethlehem, as well as
this brave knight [the Swan Knight] for his impressive boldness. My
lord, receive my land, and give it back to this brave man, and let him
take my daughter with your consent. And I will become a nun in the
monastery of St. Laurent." "Certainly," said the emperor, "I willingly grant it. I will give him the land back without delay." The Swan
Knight approaches without delay; he receives the girl and whatever
belongs to her.][59]

The marriage between the Swan Knight and the girl, which establishes
the link between the mythical hero and the territory of Bouillon, pro-
duces a daughter, Ida. Continuing the progress of the generations, *Les
Enfances Godefroi* sees her married to the count of Boulogne and giving birth to Eustace, Godfrey and Baldwin, all of whom grow up to be
exemplary knights. Perhaps the most interesting episode in this branch,
which ends with Godfrey preparing to depart for the East, sees the
future Advocate of the Holy Sepulchre defending the rights of a lady,
this time against the challenge of her cousin Guion. Godfrey, in keeping with his father's precedent, defeats Guion easily, but when the lady
"Son castel et s'onor li met en sa baillie" [l. 2140: "puts her castle and
her honor at his command"], he shows his fundamental difference from
the heroes of romance, and kindly refuses—after all, he is meant for
greater things. Therefore, while the rise of chivalric romance added
some magic and adventure in the service of ladies to the early continuations of the Old French Crusade Cycle, it notably does not add
courtly love. The Swan Knight champions not lovers but mothers: his
own in the *Beatrix*, that of his future wife in *Le Chevalier au Cygne*.
His grandson Godfrey, in *Les Enfances Godefroi*, defends the rights of
the lady for the sake of justice, not love. The early continuations of the
Old French Crusade Cycle are singularly uninterested in matters of the
heart; the ancestry of the Advocate of the Holy Sepulchre must be as
untouched by sinful desire as the man himself.

Perhaps more important, however, than the early continuators'
inability to include fin' amors in the pages of their works is the fact
that they chose to go backward rather than forward in time. They

were certainly not unique in creating an enfances or a lineage for the hero of a cycle, but by doing so here they divide the universe of the Old French Crusade Cycle in time and space. First, there is a European past, the world of the Swan Knight, Ida, Nijmeghen, and Bouillon, a world infused with adventure and service to ladies, no matter how devoid of courtly love that service is. This is followed in time by a Middle Eastern present, the world of Godfrey, Tancred, Antioch, and Jerusalem, a world of duty and service to God. The continuators of the Old French Crusade Cycle thereby echo the troubadours and trouvères: both speak of a life, of women abandoned on the way to Outremer by those who will now devote themselves to God and the expiation of sin. Over three generations, the family of Godfrey of Bouillon leaves the delights of home for suffering abroad—the pattern so heart-wrenchingly repeated, on an individual and temporally condensed level, in the chansons de croisade.

L'HISTORE DE GILLE DE CHYN

Another who exchanges the love of a lady, in a world celebrating the virtues of chivalric romance, for duty and suffering in a Latin East redolent of the chansons de geste is the hero of the mid-thirteenth-century *L'histore de Gille de Chyn*,[60] an early Old French verse biography of Gilles of Chin, the lord of Berlaymont, a knight and sometime Crusader from Hainault who was killed in a tournament on 12 August 1137.[61] *Gille de Chyn* was completed between 1230 and 1240 by a man who refers to himself in the last lines of his work as Gautier of Tournai;[62] though little is known of him, he demonstrates extensive knowledge of the chivalric literature of his time throughout the 5,550 lines of his poem, and it has been suggested that he was a professional minstrel.[63] He likely wrote *Gille de Chyn*, which he claims to have based on an earlier work by Gautier le Cordier,[64] at the behest of the Abbey of St. Ghislain in Hainault, where Gilles of Chin was buried and which had benefited substantially from his generosity,[65] and the poem therefore probably served to highlight the continuing ties of the monastery to the descendants of the man whose remains rested within its confines.[66] However, Gautier's imaginative portrayal of Gilles—by the time of composition dead for a century—as a paragon of chivalry undoubtedly did not only mean to praise but also to inspire, to serve as an example to the knighthood of Hainault, which could only aim to emulate the achievements of the lord of Berlaymont.[67]

Born so scrawny as to make even his father dislike him,[68] Gilles of Chin as a young man displays martial abilities that belie his earlier physical frailty. Demonstrating his skill in the tournaments staged in and around Hainault, he earns the love and admiration not only of his parents but also of the local nobility.[69] As he adds victory to victory, others flock to join him, and soon we find him surrounded by both friends and minstrels, talking about love, wandering from tournament to tournament.[70] Gilles is here described almost as a knight errant:

> Iii. ans toz plains ainsi ala
> Gilles de Chyn, que ne fina
> De marce en marce de l'errer,
> Por son pris guerre et aloser.

> [ll. 387–90: For three full years did Gilles of Chin travel this way, and he did not cease to roam from march to march to pursue his reputation and to make it illustrious.][71]

In keeping with romance convention, a lady soon falls in love with him: when the wife of the count of Duras informs him of her feelings, Gilles swears to be her knight forever, and he happily wears the love tokens she gives him.[72] As their love grows, the countess implores him to keep it hidden, as disclosure would inexorably lead to disaster:

> En vostre cuer l'amor tenés,
> Nient en la langhe; ce savés
> Que puis que l'amours est seüe
> A .iiii., ou a .iii. conneüe,
> Ne puet pas estre longement
> Sans grant anui et sans tourment.

> [ll. 1180–85: Keep the love in your heart and not on your tongue; understand that when the love is known to four, or known to three, it cannot long continue without great trouble and without torment.]

The adulterous love between Gilles and the countess of Duras remains secret and is notably never consummated; regardless, it drives the knight to distraction[73] and inspires him to ever-greater exploits in the lists,[74] culminating in victory and the amassing of great wealth at a tournament at Trazegnies.[75] However, soon after Gilles has become the consummate courtly knight, driven by fin' amors to best all, he experiences a remarkable transformation. Lying in bed at night, he is visited by Christ, who shows him his wounds and leaves him a letter.[76] Unable to decipher the missive, Gilles brings it to a monastery, where a priest interprets it:

Par sez lettrez vous prie et mande,
Et aprez chou si vous commande
La crois a prendre sans targier;
Si alez sa honte vengier
Des Turs felons, qui pas ne voient,
Et des Guïs qui pas ne croient
A nul fuer s'incarnatïon,
Sa mort ne sa surrectïon.

. . .

Qui por s'amor sont en la terre
En painne, en travail et en guerre.
Ce sont sez fillez et si fil
Qui por lui tienent cest escil.
Qui por s'amor iluec morra
En Paradis posés sera
O sez fix et o sez amis;
Avuec sez angles sera mis.

[ll. 1780–99: With his letter he implores and commands you, and
afterward he also orders you to take the cross without delay; by doing
so you will go to avenge his shame upon the wicked Turks who do
not see, and upon the Jews who do not in any way believe in, his
incarnation, his death, or his resurrection. . . . Those who for love of
him suffer pain, hard work, and war in that land, those are his sons
and daughters. Those who undergo this torment for him, who die
there for love of him, will be put in paradise with his sons and his
friends; he will be placed among his angels.]

To the great dismay of all, Gilles immediately takes the cross.[77] When
he bids his adieus to the countess of Duras, she at first tries to dissuade
him, for he surely could not *truly* love his lady if he contemplates going
on Crusade; however, emphasizing that "por mez peciez / Et por les
siens, bien le saciez, / Ai entreprise ceste voie" [ll. 1958–60: "for my sins
and for hers, as you well know, have I undertaken this voyage"], Gilles
finally persuades her to give him leave to go. Although Gilles, as a tournament knight, may have a great many things to atone for,[78] his mention that the sins he seeks to redress are both his and hers suggests that
their adulterous relationship ranks highly among them. The moment
Gilles departs for the Holy Land, having promised the countess that he
will love no other while on Crusade, therefore marks the end of courtly
love in *Gille de Chyn*. Though he will return to the tournament after
coming back from Crusade, he will never again set eyes on the countess, and though we find a number of women in the remaining pages of
the work, their relationships to Gilles will be vastly different. His turn
toward spiritual salvation is above all one away from sinful fin' amors.

Trotter has observed that, as the action of *Gille de Chyn* moves from northwestern Europe to the Eastern Mediterranean, the work abandons a romance style to take on one more reminiscent of the chansons.[79] As Gilles travels to the Holy Land via Brindisi, he trades the martial play of the tournament in service of a lady for the war against the Saracen in service of established dynastical hierarchies. After arriving in Acre, he rides to Caesarea, frees a number of Christian prisoners from their Muslim captors before "Assur" (Tyre?), and then spends the night at Toron;[80] having traveled throughout the kingdom of Jerusalem, he enters the service of the king. Gilles takes the field against the Turks when they cross into the territory of his new lord.[81] Exhorting his men to "deservir le tresor / Que Dix noz garde en Paradis" [ll. 2397–98: "earn the treasure which God keeps for us in paradise"], he defeats the Muslim army in an encounter strongly reminiscent of those of the chansons:

A une haute vois escrie:
"Ha Saint Sepulcres! Dix, aïe!"
Puis met la main au branc d'acier.
Qui li veïst Turs detrenchier,
Verser, caïr, morir et braire,
Il peüst bien por voir retraire
C'onquez nus hom tant Turc n'ocist
Comme Gilles de Cyn la fist.
. . .
Un Turc i ot quis conduisoit,
Qui merveillez d'armez faisoit.
Gilles de Cyn le vait ferir,
Si roidement par tel aïr
Le cief li fait del bu voler
Toise et demie, sans fausser.
A terre en est li cors caüs,
Dez crestiens lieve li hus.

[ll. 2404–35: He cries out with a loud voice: "Oh Holy Sepulchre! God, come to our aid!" Then he takes his iron sword in his hand. Whoever sees him cut up the Turks, sees them be knocked down, fall, die and cry out, he can well relate as truth that no man ever killed as many Turks as Gilles of Chin did there. . . . A Turk rode there who performed wondrous deeds of arms. Gilles of Chin moved to strike him so forcibly with such violence that he made his head fly from his trunk for more than a *toise*, without lie. The body fell to the ground, and cheers erupted from the Christians.]

In battle after battle, Gilles drives the Saracens back; when not safeguarding the kingdom of Jerusalem from invasion, he is protecting pilgrims from both human and animal adversaries. Consequently, "par lui est rengeneree / Toute la terre d'outremer" [ll. 2853–54: "all of the land across the sea was regenerated by him"]. Thoroughly impressed, the king decides that Gilles should by rights rule the country, and he offers the knight the crown of Jerusalem, an offer politely but resolutely refused.[82] As he was in Hainault, Gilles is recognized the best of all in the kingdom of Jerusalem, and this again leads to a married woman declaring her love for him, this time the queen of Jerusalem herself. Whereas Gilles had reciprocated the feelings of the countess of Duras, however, now he is wholly unwilling to do so. The queen's many entreaties are to no avail, and she eventually turns hostile. When he tells her he cannot return her love, as his thoughts are elsewhere, this is her reply:

"Voire," fait ele, "en .i. garchon;
Voz traiés de mauvais archon,
N'a point de fer en vostre flece,
En vous a mout vilaine tece;
N'aiez cure de teil mestier
Car trop em porriez avillier."

[ll. 3549–54: "Truly," she says, "with a boy; you draw a bad bow, and your arrow does not have an iron tip, which is a heinous default in you; you should not care for such business, because you can be made too vile by it."]

In response to the queen's accusation, Gilles emphasizes his heterosexuality and declares that he has left his heart behind in Hainault.[83] Unplacated, the queen develops a furious hatred for him and seeks his death.[84] Although her plan fails, Gilles is enraged; even the king's suggestion to burn his wife alive cannot keep the knight in his service,[85] and he joins the forces of the prince of Antioch. Having also dispatched the Saracen enemies of this second lord in suitably epic fashion,[86] he ends his Crusade and returns home.

Gautier of Tournai's description of Gilles of Chin's Crusade constructs the Latin territories in the Levant as the opposite of the Hainault of his birth. In the West Gilles relentlessly pursues reputation and worldly gain in the lists and finds purpose in courtly love. In the East he fights the Saracen to protect pilgrims, safeguard the territory of his secular lords in both Jerusalem and Antioch, and cleanse his soul from sin; he turns down the opportunity to acquire territories in the area and notably spends all he has on charity.[87] Furthermore, rather than motivating him to do great deeds, a woman wants him dead. This opposition, between a Western Europe preoccupied with the concerns of chivalric romance and a Middle East where such concerns cannot last among those of the chansons de geste, is further instanced in the way Gautier of Tournai integrates literary borrowings into his work. It is perhaps not surprising that Gautier finds inspiration in earlier works on the Crusade to narrate Gilles's deeds across the sea, and it is likely that his description of Gilles's fight with a lion that threatens the inhabitants of the kingdom of Jerusalem draws on *Les Chétifs*.[88] He does, however, also include a number of episodes drawn from romance writings, adapting them to fit the environment of the Crusade frontier. The queen's accusation echoes Marie de France's lai of *Lanval*;[89] but whereas Lanval is saved from death by his otherworldly beloved, no lady will save Gilles when the queen's thoughts turn to bloodshed. Furthermore, the king's answer to the queen's transgression is to indicate that Gilles's service is more important to him than her life: here the lady, far from driving men to better themselves, is perceived as an impediment to the relationship between the king and Gilles, a contract of mutual obligation by which the kingdom of Jerusalem had been safeguarded. For this relationship to continue, and for the kingdom to remain inviolate, the lady must be physically removed, and the king is willing to subordinate matters of the heart to matters of state. In another episode Gilles, having left Jerusalem for Antioch, comes upon a lion fighting a serpent, and when Gilles slays the serpent, the thankful lion joins him on the road. Gautier here likely draws upon Chrétien de Troyes's *Yvain*, which sees a lion similarly join forces with his savior.[90] Whereas Chrétien's lion accompanies Yvain on a number of adventures, however, and contributes to his definition as *Le Chevalier au Lion*, this lion—the second in the work—almost immediately succumbs to the risks inherent to life in the Middle East: when Gilles confronts yet another Muslim host, "I. Turs le fiert parmi le cors / D'une lance bien aceree / Devant Gille en la meslee" [ll. 4200–4202: "a Turk struck him through the body with a lance well-covered in steel, right before Gilles in the melee"]. Gautier therefore includes a number of borrowings from romance works into *Gille de Chyn*, only to demonstrate their incompatibility with the Crusade frontier: there, no mystical beloved will rescue Gilles from a queen whose love, turned to wrath, endangers the safety of her kingdom, and his lion will fall to the arms of the Saracens.

The extent to which Crusade serves as an antidote to especially the fin' amors of chivalric romance in *Gille de Chyn* is demonstrated

not only by the description of Gilles's experiences in the kingdom
of Jerusalem and the principality of Antioch but to a certain extent
also by their aftermath. After his Crusade, Gilles again takes up most
of the activities he had earlier left behind, the tournament in particular. He does not, however, engage in matters of the heart ever
again. Upon reaching Europe he, as had Godfrey of Bouillon in *Les
Enfances Godefroi*, champions the cause of an heiress threatened by
powerful outside forces,[91] but Gilles's return to the service of ladies
is as devoid of courtly love as was Godfrey's—after his defeat of the
lady's enemies, he quickly continues his journey home. There he finds
the countess of Duras dead,[92] and shortly before his death in a tournament he marries a lady described as a suitable match, but otherwise
mostly disregarded.[93]

The mid-thirteenth-century *Gille de Chyn* therefore employs the
formal and thematic commonplaces of both the chanson de geste and
chivalric romance to build an opposition between Western Europe
and the Crusade battlefields of the Middle East. The work, a description of a life that should be both admired and imitated, associates
the former with chivalric romance: here Gilles wanders from place to
place to prove his mettle and finds solace in the service of ladies and
courtly love. He must abandon these pastimes as he takes the cross:
the frontiers of Christianity are a place of the interreligious warfare of
the chansons, where the preoccupations of romance both literally and
figuratively cannot survive. The fact that Gilles resumes his participation in the tournament and his service of ladies upon his return home
but no longer engages in—or even talks about—fin' amors, suggests
that the opposition between chivalric romance and chanson de geste
in *Gille de Chyn* is not only one of space but also one of time. The life
of the wandering courtly lover preoccupies the young Gilles, but with
the passing of time he must turn to weightier issues: to armed service
of both heavenly Lord and secular lords, and to a marriage that will
allow the dynasty of Berlaymont to continue. Chivalric romance is
therefore used to shape not only the Western Europe in which Gilles
is born but also to a certain extent his youth.

Although chivalric romance quickly became popular among the aristocracy upon whose continued commitment the future of the holy
war depended, the sinful fin' amors that lay at its heart made it difficult to use in Crusade propaganda. Crusade excitatoria written in
the decades after the appearance of the romances, such as the early

continuations of the First Old French Crusade Cycle and the mid-thirteenth-century *Gille de Chyn*, include elements of romance sparingly, and above all to paint an elaborate "before" picture. In keeping with the songs of the troubadours and trouvères, they include adventure and service to ladies in all that must be left behind on the road to the Holy Land. Accordingly, these fit into an essentially salvific structure: when taking the cross the knight must change the familial for the strange, the West for the East, service to ladies for service to God, adventure for duty, the phenomenal for the sublime. Crusade *excitatoria* from this time by and large include it to show that it *cannot* be part of Crusade—that the world of romance and the world of Crusade must be temporally, geographically, and teleologically separate. This changed, however, as the fate of the Crusader states as well as secular attitudes took a turn in the later years of the thirteenth century and the beginning of the fourteenth. The need to recruit men began to outweigh the dislike of "sinful" romance that Crusade propaganda harbored at first. Thus would the boundary between Crusade and romance collapse, reframing the Crusade frontier as a land of adventure and courtly love.

CHAPTER 6

Nicolaus of Jeroschin and the Fourteenth-Century Crusade

AFTER ACRE

The fall of Acre, Latin Christianity's last great outpost on the Palestinian shore, to the forces of the Mamluk sultan al-Ashraf Khalil in 1291 signaled the final demise of the states that had existed in one form or another since the successes of the First Crusade of 1096–1099.[1] Along with the refugees, the last chance to counter Egyptian dominance over the Holy Places vanished over the horizon. The psychological effect on the Latins of the loss of this last foothold, and the final denial of what had started as the *Gesta Dei per Francos*, was devastating.[2] Equally damaging was its effect on the Crusade in the Eastern Mediterranean: beyond the activities of the Orders of the Hospital and the Temple, which faced a constant struggle to hold on to their bases in the Levant and the Aegean, few Western Crusaders turned toward the Middle East for the better part of half a century, despite frantic planning and the taking of the cross by king after king.

Traumatic as the effect of the fall of Acre was, it did not mean the end of the Crusade as such, and the movement first voiced by Urban at Clermont continued to influence the fourteenth-century imagination. Increasingly organized campaigns set out to the East from 1343 onward, and by the end of the fourteenth century the Crusade to the Holy Land had once again become an important part of Western European foreign policy. Furthermore, two other theaters of Crusade, the Baltic and Spain, did not suffer the setbacks of the Levantine Crusade, and may even have benefited from them. The German Order, having moved its activities north, commenced a methodical program of conquest and annexation of Prussian, Lithuanian, and Livonian lands that would not end until 1410. In Spain, campaigns against the Moors made further inroads into Muslim territory and led to the capture of the important town of Algeciras in March 1344. Even if there were no expeditions of note to the Holy Land in the early decades of the fourteenth century, the Baltic and Spain allowed aspiring Crusaders to continue to campaign almost at will.[3]

Although the holy war continued vigorously after the fall of Acre, the fourteenth-century Crusade differed in several important respects from its late twelfth- and thirteenth-century predecessors. The shifting political sands of Europe prevented some of the traditional driving forces of the Crusade—the English and French monarchies, and the papacy itself—from maintaining their earlier leadership roles, as they found themselves increasingly entangled in wider European conflicts and domestic distractions. In England, Edward I had engaged in a policy of territorial expansion that pitched him against the Welsh,[4] the French,[5] and the Scots;[6] this left little time or energy to recapture the Holy Land. Although his son Edward II took the cross in 1313,[7] his reign was turbulent, and most of his attention was drawn to the war with the Scots and the conflict with the English nobility that would lead to his imprisonment and death. Edward III had his eyes on a larger, more immediate prize: the prosecution of his "Just Quarrel" would lead to Crécy and Poitiers, not to Jerusalem.

France under Louis IX had taken an especially prominent role in the Crusade to the Holy Land, and at the turn of the new century the memory of the Saint King's expeditions to Damietta and Tunis was still vivid.[8] Although Philip IV (1285–1314) made a conscious effort to strengthen the image of the French monarchy as the lynchpin of the Crusade, he did not follow in the footsteps of his grandfather, nor did he ever make substantial preparations for a campaign.[9] His priorities lay instead with the comprehensive reform of his kingdom,[10] where his considerable achievements made equally considerable demands on his time and finances. His sons' Crusade planning was similarly limited: Philip V (1317–1322) and Charles IV (1322–1328) confined themselves to organizing, if not executing, a limited *passagium particulare* to relieve the Turkish pressure on Armenia.[11] While Charles IV's successor, Philip VI (1328–1350), contemplated a larger Crusade, he abandoned his plans in 1336, shortly before the outbreak of the Hundred Years' War.[12]

Finally, the papacy too found itself distracted from the cause d'Outremer in the first decades of the fourteenth century. Philip IV of France's heavy taxation of the church[13] led to a series of virulent quarrels with the firebrand Boniface VIII (1294–1303), the assault on Boniface by supporters of the French king at Anagni in September 1303, and the pope's death on 11 October. A successor, Clement V (1305–1314), proved rather more amenable to the suggestions of the French king and moved the papal court to Avignon, but here French influence limited the independence of papal planning and decision making. Consequently, papal interest in crusading during the first decades of the fourteenth century consisted of little more than rubber-stamping what little effort the French mustered. While a more determined line was taken under Benedict XII (1334–1342) and Clement VI (1342–1352), valuable time had been lost, and when in 1337 England and France commenced what was to become the Hundred Years' War, papal initiative lost the support of the two most powerful Western European nations. When in 1378 the Western Schism created a rival obedience in Rome, whatever Crusade enthusiasm the papacy could still rally was finally turned against other Christians.

The great powers to which Latin Christians had for the past few centuries looked to organize and execute Crusade campaigns therefore spent the decades after the turn of the century repositioning themselves within Europe. They would not be the driving forces behind the fourteenth-century Crusade: kings would not lead their hosts east as had Richard the Lion-Hearted, Frederick Barbarossa, and Louis IX. Those expeditions that did set out to fight the Saracen were smaller, often locally organized, and heavily reliant on the recruitment of the single knight or nobleman. These knights and noblemen, still the core of Crusade armies, did not journey to the East to fulfill their obligations within seigniorial armies. They set out on Crusade mostly for individual reasons, drawn to the frontiers of Christianity by their own piety, greed, or thirst for adventure. Even though individual interests had motivated Crusaders since the very beginning, the fourteenth-century Crusade differed from its predecessors even in this respect, as the knights of the fourteenth century were very different from those that came before them.

Although it may be an exaggeration to suggest that chivalry had entered an irreversible decline by the turn of the century,[14] it is nevertheless true that certain factors threatened the status of knighthood at this time, leading to what Peter Dembowski has referred to as "the crisis of real chivalry."[15] The late thirteenth and fourteenth centuries saw great changes in the practice of warfare. The direct confrontation of open battle, ideally suited to the chivalric way, was increasingly avoided, more emphasis falling on siege warfare and the economic warfare of the *chevauchée*.[16] Furthermore, in the relatively rare cases in which full-scale battle was joined, the dominance of the chivalric heavy cavalry was increasingly challenged by skilled infantry and missile troops drawn mostly from the middle and lower classes. The defeat of chivalric armies by infantry formations—such as at Stirling Bridge (1297), Courtrai (1302), Crécy (1346), and Sempach (1386)—further undermined the military justification of chivalry's social supremacy: its function as a bulwark against enemies and as protector of the land and people.[17] In addition to these military developments, the ubiquitous wars of the period saw ever-greater evidence of the dark side of knighthood, as knights, sometimes fighting as mercenaries, inflicted a reign of violence on most of Western Europe, often to subsidize an ever more costly chivalric way of life. These were signs, it was thought, of a degeneration of knightly morals and prowess. Contemporary critics, both clerical and chivalric, excoriated knighthood "not merely . . . for involvement in wholesale pillaging in war, but for a much more wholesale abandonment of what they thought had been the hardy, ascetic discipline and tradition of the chivalry of old times, for the softness of noble ways, for the extravagance of noble living, for its arrogance and vainglory, its love of luxury and its perennial quest for funds to support continuing and conspicuous waste."[18] The criticism leveled at knighthood did not, however, aim to do away with the institution, and even its harshest critics most often remained convinced of the importance of chivalry in society. What fourteenth-century commentators desired above all was reform that would return chivalry to its erstwhile greatness. This desire for reform did not embrace the changing times; rather it was reactionary or nostalgic in nature. It "appealed to the example of the chivalrous past in offering the pattern for reformation."[19] Chivalric reform was to be based on the models found in the literary sources of chivalric excellence; this reform movement has consequently been called a first "chivalric renaissance."[20] Models for reform were found in a wide range of works. The fourteenth-century cult of the Nine Worthies, the paragons of pagan, Jewish, and Christian chivalry, first identified by Jacques of Longuyon in the *Voeux du Paon* of circa 1312 (Hector, Alexander, Caesar, Joshua, David, Judas Maccabeus,

Arthur, Charlemagne, and Godfrey of Bouillon), perhaps best illustrates the sources deemed worthy for chivalric instruction: from the
Old Testament, to the epics of the matters of France and Rome, to
chivalric romances.[21]

Romance, especially Arthurian romance, was a genre that from
the very beginning had illustrated good chivalric behavior. Among
the adventures were found the perfect courtesy of Gawain, the perfect
prowess of Lancelot, and the spiritual perfection of Galahad. Knights,
themselves often readers of romance,[22] could find in these abundant
examples to emulate. Romance had played an important role in chivalric pageantry and play-acting from roughly the second quarter
of the thirteenth century onward, when jousts and tournaments frequently became cloaked in romance, mostly Arthurian, garb. In 1223,
on the occasion of the knighting of the sons of the lord of Beirut,
a tournament in Arthurian dress was held in Cyprus.[23] Seven years
later, in 1240, the famed Bavarian knight Ulrich of Liechtenstein and
six of his companions, dressed as King Arthur and his knights, traveled around Germany daring all to joust; those who proved themselves a match were allowed into the Order of the Round Table.[24]
Festive Round Tables were celebrated throughout France, England,
and the Holy Roman Empire; often these were organized by powerful
magnates or even monarchs, such as Roger Mortimer's Round Table
at Kenilworth in 1279, Edward I's at Nevyn in 1284, and Edward
III's at Windsor in 1344.[25] Perhaps typical of this use of Arthurian romance for purposes of entertainment and performance is the
description of the festivities held at Acre in 1286: "It was the loveliest
festival anyone had seen for a hundred years, with amusements and
jousts with blunted lances. They re-enacted the stories of the Round
Table and also of the Queen of Feminie, with knights dressed up like
women jousting together. Then they had nuns who were dressed as
monks and who jousted together, and they role-played Lancelot and
Tristan and Pilamedes and many other fair and delightful and pleas-
ant scenes."[26]

It was, however, acknowledged early on that Arthurian romance
could serve as a model for reform. Edward I likely found in the
Round Table an expression of a model relationship between knights
and their monarch,[27] while the 1278 tourney at Ham, which featured such Arthurian characters as Guenevere and Kay, "was undertaken . . . in order to foster honor, prowess, and courtesy, which were
then decaying."[28] The potential of romance as an example for reform

came to the foreground as the late medieval "crisis of real chivalry" unfolded. Romance became increasingly important in chivalric theory and practice: formal codes of chivalry, composed with primarily reformist intent, began including romance elements in the description of good knighthood.[29] A telling example is the French knight Geoffroi of Charny's popular *Livre de Chevalerie*, written around 1352 as a manual for the members of the chivalric Order of the Star. Geoffroi insisted that the good knight should love loyally and set out to accomplish deeds of arms in honor of his lady, thereby mirroring the behavior of Arthur's companions. Indeed, almost at the very beginning of his work he highlights romance *Frauendienst* as an important part of a chivalric education:

> There is another category of men-at-arms who when they begin are
> so naïve that they are unaware of the great honor that they could win
> through deeds of arms; nevertheless they succeed so well because
> they put their hearts into winning the love of a lady. And they are
> so fortunate that their ladies themselves, from the great honor and
> superb qualities that reside in them, do not want to let them tarry nor
> delay in any way the winning of that honor to be achieved by deeds
> of arms, and advise them on this and then command them to set out
> and put all their efforts into winning renown and great honor where
> it is to be sought by valiant men; these ladies urge them on to reach
> beyond any of their earlier aspirations. Such naïve men-at-arms may
> nevertheless be so fortunate as to encounter such good adventures
> that their deeds of prowess and achievements in a number of places
> and fields of battle are held to be of great account. And they should
> be praised and honored, and so also should the noble ladies who have
> inspired them and through whom they have made their name. And
> one should indeed honor, serve, and truly love these noble ladies and
> others whom I hold to be ladies who inspire men to great achieve-
> ment, and it is thanks to such ladies that men become good knights
> and men-at-arms.[30]

Indeed, adventure in the service of ladies is instrumental in transforming a "naïve" knight into a good knight who is renowned for his prowess. Its advantage is not restricted to young knights newly entering the profession of arms; well-established knights, too, can reap the benefits of fighting in a lady's service.[31] By urging both aspirant knights and their senior colleagues to seek adventure as Frauendienst, Geoffroi has them engage in the staples of romance.

Not all knights looked kindly upon romance love service as a means for achieving good knighthood. Philippe of Mézières, for instance, strongly disapproved of "ceulx qui veilent devenir preux comment qu'il aille, et font leur moyens d'amer par amours pour parvenir a vaillance" ["those who want to become worthy any which way, and go through courtly love to reach valiance"].[32] Nevertheless, there is ample evidence to suggest that knights took the turn to romance to heart. It did not guarantee favorable results: Sir Thomas Gray, in the *Scalacronica*, relates how at the siege of Norham Castle Sir William Marmion, who had been given a gilded helmet by his beloved and had been told to make it renowned, attacked the Scottish army by himself. Lancelot may have been victorious in such a situation, but Sir William barely escaped with his life.[33] There are many instances, however, of more successful application.[34] The biography of Boucicaut, arguably the most famous knight of the late fourteenth and early fifteenth centuries, shows him taking to love at the very beginning of his chivalric career and fighting his way across Europe in the service of his lady. The anonymous author of the work explicitly connects Boucicaut's love service with the Arthurian romances and suggests that he was hardly alone:

> Amours oste paour et donne hardement, fait oublier toute peine et prendre en gré tout le traveil que on porte pour la chose amee. Et qu'il soit vray, qui veult lire les histories des vaillans trespassez, assez trouvera de ce preuve, si comme on lit de Lancelot, de Tristan et de plusieurs autres que Amours fist bons et a renommee attaindre; et mesmement en noz vivans assez de nobles hommes en France et d'autre part en veons et avons veu, si comme on dit de messire Othe de Gransson, du bon connestable de Sensarre et d'autres assez, qui lonc seroit a dire, lesquieulx le service d'Amours ot fait devenir vaillans et bien moriginez.

> [Love removes fear and gives courage, makes one forget all trouble and accept all the work done for the beloved. And that this is true, everyone who wants to read the histories of the valiant dead can find enough of this matter, as one can read of Lancelot, of Tristan, and of many others that love made good and made achieve renown; and even in our lifetimes we see and have seen enough noblemen of France and of other regions, whom the service of love has made brave and well known, such as is said of Sir Otho of Grandson, of the good constable of Sancerre, and of many others, which would be lengthy to relate.][35]

In other words, Boucicaut, in seeking out adventure in the service of ladies, walks a path previously tread upon by such illustrious knights as the Savoyard knight Otho of Grandson (ca. 1340–1397), the constable of France Louis of Sancerre (1342–1402), and many others, a path ultimately traceable to that of Tristan and Lancelot as found in chivalric romance. From the pages of Boucicaut's biography we find that this romance-inspired service of ladies applies not only to the object of one's own affections but to *all* ladies: the foundational document of Boucicaut's chivalric order, the Order of the White Lady on the Green Shield, explicitly stated that its members must "tenu de droit de vouloir garder et deffendre l'onneur, l'estat, les biens, la renommee et la louange de toutes dames et damoiselles de noble lignee" ["willingly guard and defend the honor, the estate, the goods, the renown and the praise of all ladies and young ladies of noble lineage"].[36]

Boucicaut's Order of the White Lady brings us to yet another way in which romance influenced chivalric practice in the later Middle Ages. By the middle of the fourteenth century, a great number of secular orders of chivalry had been created. While typically founded with the rather serious purpose of tying its members to their lords with a renewed bond of loyalty backed by the fear of dishonor in the eyes of their peers, these often explicitly drew their inspiration from the pages of romance. The Order of the Garter, established by Edward III in 1348, aimed to revive Arthur's Round Table, while John II of France's Order of the Star, which was created in 1352, imitated the Order of the Free Palace from *Perceforest*.[37] The statutes of some of these lay chivalric confraternities stipulated that their members should periodically gather to have their adventures recorded in a book, a practice that Maurice Keen has associated with romance: "The making of books such as these . . . was clearly inspired by the account in the romance of *Merlin* of how, when he left Arthur's court, a knight of the Round Table had to swear that 'he would tell on his return all that had happened to him . . . be it to his honour or his shame. And by this means was made judgement of the prowess of each.'"[38] Keen has with much perspicacity discussed a great many of these secular orders of knighthood.[39] Perhaps most important for our purposes, however, is one he does not include: the chivalric order called the Societas Templois, which was founded in or before 1337 by Otto IV of Austria.[40] Though bearing a similar name, this "Society of the Temple," whose purpose was to assist the Teutonic brothers in their wars in the Baltic,[41] and which counted important nobles from the Holy Roman Empire in its ranks,[42] did not aim to revive the Order of the Temple, which had been dissolved exactly twenty-five years earlier. Rather the order, whose members were called "Tempelaise" or "Tempeloiser," drew inspiration for its name from romance, in this case from Wolfram of Eschenbach's *Parzifal*, where we find "Tempeleise" burdened with the protection of the Grail.[43]

In short, as knighthood entered a period of military and social crisis in the late thirteenth century and throughout the fourteenth century, romance began to find its way into chivalric theory and practice. Literary representations of almost flawless knights became an ideal through which knighthood sought to reform itself in an attempt to regain its former glory. Codes of knighthood such as Geoffroi of Charny's influential *Livre* outlined how the search for adventure and the service of ladies could benefit a knight; these lessons were carried into the field by knights such as Sir William Marmion and Boucicaut, the Spanish hero Don Pero Niño, and the knights on the pages of Froissart's *Chroniques*.[44] Knights founded secular orders that formally required Frauendienst and the search for adventure from their members; often these orders explicitly imitated romance orders such as those of the Round Table and the Free Palace. Romance in the later Middle Ages became, therefore, a tool for nostalgic reform and chivalric revival.

The crisis both of the Crusade and of chivalry in the first years of the fourteenth century undermined barriers that had been upheld for more than a century. As chivalry increasingly defined itself by reference to romance, a door was opened through which romance could be used to present and propagate Crusade. Fourteenth-century propaganda writings began strongly associating Crusade with chivalric romance, and would redefine the Crusader, the battlefield, and the concept of holy war itself in romance terms to convince an often unwilling Latin aristocracy to take the cross.

THE CRUSADE IN THE BALTIC AND THE ORIGINS
OF THE ORDENSTAAT

Among the first to play upon the changing interests of European chivalry to benefit its Crusade ventures was the Order of the Teutonic Knights of St. Mary's Hospital in Jerusalem, better known as the Teutonic or German Order, which in the first decades of the fourteenth century aggressively expanded its territories south of the Baltic Sea.[45] Originally founded in 1190 as a field hospital catering to the needs of German participants in the siege of Acre, the German Order quickly followed the older and more established Hospital of St.

John in complementing the care of the sick with the protection of the healthy, becoming a military order in 1198. In the first century of its history, the order actively participated in the defense of the Crusader kingdoms, safeguarding the roads to the Holy Places and protecting pilgrims. The loss of Acre, however, strongly affected the religious orders that were sworn to its defense. The most powerful of them, the Templars, became embroiled in the web of inertia and recrimination that would lead to their dissolution little more than twenty years later, in 1312. The Hospitallers increasingly withdrew into insignificance, first on Rhodes and later on Malta. The German Order, forced to rethink its long-term goals, moved its activities from the Mediterranean to the far northeast frontier of Latin Christianity; in doing so, it chose a path toward empire.

The Teutonic Knights had first become involved in the defense— and the politics—of the Eastern Christian frontier soon after the foundation of their order. In 1211, the Hungarian king Andrew II invited them to participate in the defense of Transylvania against the pagan Cumans.[46] In 1225, Duke Conrad of Mazovia asked the order to help defend his lands against the aggressive pagan Prussians, offering Kulmerland in southern Prussia for its efforts. By 1226, the order had persuaded the emperor to recognize it as sovereign ruler of Kulmerland, and its rights over the territory were confirmed by the papacy eight years later.[47] Under the guise of protecting local Christians while fighting and converting the Prussians, the brothers had laid the groundwork for the *Ordenstaat.*

The surrender of Kulmerland to the Teutonic Order introduced a highly efficient and aggressive new element to the fighting that had been going on for generations between Christians and pagans in northeastern Europe.[48] Soon after its arrival, the order launched a wide-ranging program of conquest and settlement. Its gains were impressive: by the middle of the 1280s—little more than fifty years after the arrival of the brothers in the area—Prussia was firmly in the order's hands. At about this time, Livonia to the northeast also came under its sway. This left the lands of the powerful Lithuanians clamped in a vise between the order's holdings. By the middle of the 1270s the brothers had already turned their attention to the Lithuanians. These, however, proved a far more tenacious enemy than either the Prussians or the Livonians had been. The autocratic rule of Mindaugas, which extended from the early decades of the thirteenth century to his murder in 1263, had left Lithuania with significant

political organization and stability, and the Lithuanians had themselves set out to expand their territories, pushing to the south and
southeast into the "Black Rus." The order's confrontation with the
Lithuanians therefore pitched the two ascendant powers in the region
against each other and cast them into warfare that would last more
than a hundred years. Although the order eventually succeeded in
connecting its holdings in Prussia to the west with those in Livonia to
the northeast through the conquest of Lithuanian Samogitia, it would
ultimately be unable to overcome its enemy.[49]

The German Order's wars with the Lithuanians were character-
ized by two complicating factors. First, the terrain on which they
were fought was particularly unforgiving. Lithuanian Samogitia was
a land of dense forests, rivers, and marshes, and the nature of the
terrain allowed for military activity only in the short periods when
the winter cold or an extended period of summer heat made it accessible.[50] This prevented extended, large-scale campaigns and limited
the warfare to two relatively brief and exceedingly difficult forays
per year, referred to as the winter and summer *Reisen*. The Reisen
did not usually seek direct confrontation with the enemy forces but
rather focused on economic warfare and methodical annexation of
territory. Most often, the aim of the *Winterreisen* was the destruction of enemy settlements and the abduction of their inhabitants. The
Sommerreisen sought to increase the order's hold on the Lithuanian
lands by constructing fortresses and outposts in strategic locations or
by destroying those of its opponents.

The second problem confronting the order was its chronic shortage
of fighters. The manpower available to the order at the onset of the
wars in Lithuanian Samogitia was quite limited. William Urban estimates the number of Teutonic Knights at "probably eight hundred to a
thousand in Prussia and perhaps only five hundred in Livonia, including those past the age of military usefulness"; in addition to these, the
order could field "sergeants and mercenaries in a ratio of ten for each
knight [and] the secular knights and militia of German and Polish
origin and the native knights and militia."[51] Even these numbers were
decidedly insufficient to conduct offensive operations without leaving the hinterland unguarded. Any conquests would stretch resources
increasingly thin. To find the men needed to accompany the German
Order on the strenuous Reisen or to defend its outposts against enemy
reprisal, an appeal was made to Western crusading enthusiasm. Since
the middle of the thirteenth century, Western fighters had occasionally

come to the aid of the order—indeed, its great castle of Königsberg was built in honor of King Ottokar of Bohemia, who had led a group of Crusaders to Prussia in 1254.[52] The order, however, began consistently seeking to draw large numbers of Crusaders to the summer and winter Reisen only in the early fourteenth century, when the difficulty and intractability of the Lithuanian wars had become obvious.

To attract Western support, the order presented the Crusade in the Baltic in a way that would appeal to those who would be of greatest help—knights and those aspiring to the chivalric life. Though monks themselves, the German brothers understood that, in the troubled decades after the ignominious end of the Crusader states, those able to make the journey to the inhospitable Baltic frontier often needed motivation beyond religious devotion to actually do so.[53] They therefore began accompanying their Crusade expeditions with festivities and spectacles that aimed to satisfy the secular interests of the chivalric aristocracy. The Reisen "were preceded and followed by carefully organized programmes of feasting, jousting, sightseeing, and hunting. Most importantly, there was the *Ehrentisch*, the table of honour at which, in the second half of the fourteenth century, those who had distinguished themselves in fighting against the Lithuanians were feasted and awarded prizes."[54] Those crusading in the Baltic could therefore expect not just to redeem their vows but also to enjoy the order's generous hospitality and the opportunity to win honor in the presence of other notables. Adding this dimension of spectacle and festivity to the Baltic Crusade played on the longstanding chivalric desire to win both worldly renown and heavenly recompense, and appears to have been quite effective: "The first crusaders to arrive in Prussia at the beginning of the fourteenth century, after a thirty-year interval, were Rhinelanders, under the count of Homberg. . . . Bohemians reached Prussia in 1323, Alsatians in 1324, Englishmen and Walloons in 1329, Austrians and Frenchmen in 1336, Bavarians and Hollanders in 1337, Hungarians and Burgundians in 1344, and in the second half of the century Occitanians, Scots and Italians."[55]

The innovations the order made to draw volunteers to the Baltic went beyond the addition of formal spectacle and festivities to Crusade expeditions; perhaps more important, it attempted to alter the way the Crusade itself was understood. In some of their spectacles, but especially in their literature, they began associating Crusade with chivalric romance, with adventure and the service of ladies. The Teutonic Order was quite aware of the growing importance of romance to Western chivalry and showed itself ready to exploit it. In the second part of the fourteenth century, for instance, an essential part of the spectacle with which it dazzled those who decided to fulfill their Crusade vows in the Baltic was the abovementioned Ehrentisch. This Table of Honor was usually held at the very beginning or end of a Reise; the participants deemed worthy of the highest honor were seated at a high table, publicly celebrated, and awarded badges with the inscription "Honeur vainc tout."[56] Strongly reminiscent of Arthur's Round Table,[57] the Ehrentisch appealed—and was meant to appeal—to the reformist sentiments that also underpinned many of the secular orders of chivalry. The secular orders had often demanded that their members seek adventure and return to have their deeds recorded and judged, a practice taken from romance. Here, then, was an almost Arthurian undertaking in foreign lands, for which there would be a reward of honor and public recognition. Much like the secular orders, the Ehrentisch was pageantry with a mission. The Teutonic Order's appropriation of romance themes furthermore went beyond spectacle and ritual. The order also used elements of romance in representing its presence in the Baltic, its goals, and its wars to the outside world, and, more important, to possible Crusaders. We find a good example of this use of romance in the order's propaganda in Nicolaus of Jeroschin's *Krônike von Prûzinlant*, a sweeping history of the order's Baltic endeavor written circa 1331–1344. To fully understand Nicolaus's work, however, we must first turn to its source, Peter of Duisburg's *Chronica Terre Prussie*, as well as the milieu in which both works originated.

NICOLAUS OF JEROSCHIN'S KRÔNIKE VON PRÛZINLANT

The German brothers' precarious position on the edge of Christianity—geographically and, after the controversy surrounding the military religious orders at the beginning of the fourteenth century, psychologically—required careful management of public opinion. The outside world from which the order drew support, and to a certain extent the brothers themselves, needed to be told why an order created for the defense of the Holy Land would find itself on the shores of the Baltic. During the period of transition in the late thirteenth and early fourteenth centuries, the order intensified its literary production in an attempt to explain its actions and justify its wars.[58] Most of these propaganda writings took the form of vernacular verse translations of episodes from the Old Testament, saint's lives, and histories. The production of verse treatments of the Bible and *vitae* served to emphasize Prussia's role as a center of orthodox devotion. At the same time, biblical books such as Ezra and Nehemiah and the lives of martyred saints such as St. Martina and St. Barbara recalled the persecution of God's people at the hands of its enemies,[59] the rectification of which had been a driving force of the Crusade movement ever since Urban II first spoke at Clermont.[60] By writing histories, the order was able to interpret, shape, and present events in the best possible light. This undoubtedly is what Werner of Orseln, the order's grandmaster between 1324 and 1330, had in mind when he instructed the priest Peter of Duisburg to write its official history.

The result was the *Chronica Terre Prussie*, or *Chronicle of the Land of Prussia*, which Peter completed in 1326.[61] In three books of Latin prose, it traces the history of the order from its origins to the time of writing, while a fourth book describes the most important events of the wider Western world at the time. In the course of telling the history of the order's conquest of Prussia, Peter illustrated the theoretical basis for and justice of its wars, by reference to examples from the Old Testament, most notably the Maccabees, whom he mentions twenty-five times in his work. For instance, he invites his audience to observe similarities between the Teutonic Knights and the biblical holy warriors: "Attende, qualiter fratres ut Judas Machabeus loca sancta terre Prussie, que gentes prius per ydolatriam polluerunt, mundaverunt, et sacrificatur in eis quotidie deo sacrificium laudis et honoris" [CTP 23: "Hear how the brothers, like Judas Maccabeus, purified the holy places of the Prussian land, that people beforehand polluted with idolatry, and how in them every day a sacrifice of praise and honor is made to God"]. Confronted with such a magnificent history as that of the order, he invokes his own inability to do it justice:

Longum et supra ingenii mei parvitatem esset singulariter enarrare, quam potenter et magnifice, quam eleganter et strenue magister et fratres predicti, tanquam alteri Machabei, in ampliando fines Cristianorum et dilatando, in impugnando hostes, in expugnando municiones ingesserint manus suas, quorum prelia et triumphos usque ad finem seculi narrabit omnis ecclesia sanctorum.

[CTP 66: It would be long, and would go beyond the smallness of my powers, to tell in detail how powerfully and magnificently, how elegantly and vigorously, the master and the aforesaid brothers, whose battles and victories will be talked about by the whole church of the

saints until the end of time, put their hands to work like new Maccabees, when enlarging and broadening the borders of the Christians,
when fighting their enemies, and when destroying fortifications.]

Moreover, a (fictional) letter to the order that Peter ascribed to Pope
Gregory IX uses 1 Maccabees 3:58 to exhort the brothers: "Accingi-
mini et estote filii potentes, estote parati, ut pugnetis adversus nacio-
nes, que convenient disperdere nos et sancta nostra, quoniam melius
est nobis mori in bello, quam videre mala gentis nostre et sanctorum"
[CTP 38: "Prepare yourselves and be powerful sons, be ready, so that
you may fight against the nations that come together to destroy us
and our holy things, because it is better for us to die in battle than
to see the misfortune of our people and our holy things"]. Further
on, the missive also cites 1 Maccabees 4:8 to steel their resolve: "Ne
timueritis multitudinem eorum et impetum eorum ne formidetis.
Mementote, qualiter salvi facti sunt patres nostri in mari rubro, cum
persequeretur eos Farao cum exercitu multo" [CTP 38: "Do not be
afraid of their numbers and do not fear their attack. Remember how
our forefathers were saved in the Red Sea, when Pharaoh pursued
them with a great army"].[62]

The Maccabee material had already had a certain history of use
in Crusade propaganda, mostly to illustrate the concept of the *militia Dei*[63] and, more specifically, the notion of the warrior-monk, but
Mary Fischer has noted the *Chronica*'s uniqueness in applying it as
a justification for war.[64] However, Peter's close association of the
order's actions with the struggle of Judas Maccabeus, whose deeds
earned him a place among the Nine Worthies of chivalry, was perhaps
characteristic of—and gained added meaning in—an age that sought
inspiration for chivalric excellence in written sources. Indeed, the use
of this material was most likely calculated to achieve three things.
Obviously, a first goal was to explain the order's actions by situating
them within a larger framework of almost everlasting struggle against
the unbeliever—indeed, in some way the very struggle that the pages
of the Old Testament describes. A second was to highlight the very
chivalric nature of the struggle in the Baltic. This was no common-
er's war—it was a battlefield of men very much like the famed knight
Judas Maccabeus. This then led to a third: to describe the chivalry of
the order, so very much like that of one of the Nine Worthies, as an
emulation of the perfect knighthood that was so desired by Western
chivalry.[65]

It is very likely that this intricate and astute message was aimed at knights both religious and secular, both to the Teutonic brothers themselves as a form of *Selbstdeutung*, or self-definition,[66] and to possible recruits and allies as a clarion call to join the Crusade. What effect the work had on the order itself remains unknown, but Peter's chronicle probably was only moderately successful in achieving its goal of attracting Crusaders, and enjoyed only limited distribution.[67] Perhaps in the fourteenth century a chronicle in Latin could be of only so much use in convincing Crusaders to travel to the far reaches of the Christian world to fight; more likely, in its timing Peter's message of resolutely religious chivalry simply did not resonate with a lay audience—after all, this was only a few years following the harsh censure of the military orders, which had culminated in the dissolution of the Templars.

To overcome these barriers, Werner of Orseln's successor, Lothar of Brunswick, the grandmaster between 1331 and 1335, commissioned one of the order's chaplains, Nicolaus of Jeroschin, to translate the work into Middle High German. If little is known about Peter of Duisburg beyond his priesthood and the suggestion of western German heritage implied in the geographical cognomen, somewhat more can be gleaned about Nicolaus. Likely of eastern German, Prussian, or Polish extraction,[68] and perhaps not a native speaker of German,[69] he was probably born before the turn of the fourteenth century and served the order for about three decades until his death around 1344.[70] He is assumed to have been the author of two works, both of which clearly fit within the order's early fourteenth-century propaganda effort. The first, written around 1327–1329, was a Middle High German life of St. Adalbert, a translation of Johannes Canaparius's Latin life of the saint, who had come from Prague to convert the Prussians to the Christian faith and had been martyred in 997.[71] This work apparently was sufficiently pleasing to the order for Lothar of Brunswick to entrust him with the translation of Peter's work a few years later. The fruit of Nicolaus's efforts, the *Krônike von Prûzinlant*, or *Chronicle of Prussia*, was completed in 1344. It is a translation in verse, consisting of 27,738 lines. The use of verse probably had the same goal as the use of Middle High German: to appeal to a far wider audience than Peter's often dense Latin prose had. Indeed, from the very beginning, Nicolaus points out that the project of translation was undertaken

ûf daz er sus bedûten
mug *allen dûtschin lûten*
dî wundir unde zeichin gots,
dî nâch gûte sîns gebots
in Prûzinlande sin geschên.

[*KVP* ll. 161–65: so that it might explain to *all German people* the
signs and miracles which God in His goodness performed in Prussia.
(my italics)]

Nicolaus cast his net wider: he aimed to reach the whole of the
order's German-speaking hinterland. His choice of form supported
the goal of widespread dissemination as much as his choice of language; verse made the work not only more esthetically pleasing, but
also easier to memorize by preachers. The many surviving copies
of the *Krônike* are a measure of Nicolaus's success, and they suggest a far more widespread distribution than that of Peter's Latin
chronicle.[72]

In his attempt to reach all those willing and able to assist the German brothers, however, Nicolaus went beyond the use of German
and the introduction of a more agreeable and effective form. Peter of
Duisburg had set out to illustrate in his *Chronica* the justified, orthodox, and chivalric character of the order's wars in the Baltic; to do
this he had relied uniquely on Old Testament typology, most notably
on the books of the Maccabees, and had studiously avoided reference
to secular literature to make his case. He had even uttered a certain
disapproval of such writings as unbefitting the members of the order.
The Virgin Mary herself had complained about their recitation during mealtime. Speaking to brother Herman Sarrazin, she laments:

> Hoc movet me ad turbacionem, quod dilecti filii mei, fratres tui, de
> domo Theutonica non referebant quondam in collacionibus suis, nisi
> de filio meo et me et de gestis sanctorum; modo non referunt, nisi de
> factis regum et principum et seculi vanitate, ita quod filius meus et
> ego et sanctorum vita raro vel nunquam recitatur.

> [*CTP* 95: This disturbs me, that my beloved sons, your brothers, of
> the German house used not to relate anything during their meals that
> did not deal with my son or with the acts of the saints; now they do
> not relate anything that does not deal with the deeds of kings and
> princes and with worldly vanity, so that my son and I, and the lives of
> the saints, are rarely or never read.]

Peter did not cross the boundary between sacred and profane in either
apology or exhortation. The Baltic Crusades, in his view, were the

continuation of the age-old conflict between believer and unbeliever; his representation played upon the chivalric interests of knights both secular and religious, but ultimately did so within a strictly biblical framework. Although Nicolaus retained the imprint of the Maccabees in the *Krônike*, he was far more flexible with regard to other sources. Indeed, a second reason for his choice of verse over prose may be a desire to echo secular chivalric verse epic, which would increase its appeal to a knightly audience. More important, it appears that Nicolaus was aware of the transition chivalry was undergoing at the time he made his translation, and of the consequent need to move beyond religious appeal and simple implication of glorious martial endeavor. He therefore introduced words, themes, and even structure strongly reminiscent of chivalric romance to make the wars on the Prussian frontier both understandable and appealing to his audience.

A first instance can be found in Nicolaus's discussion of the journey to Prussia of the abovementioned Herman Sarrazin, a new recruit to the order who was singularly devoted to the Virgin Mary.[73] Peter had treated the matter somewhat cursorily and had followed his description of Herman's journey with the invective against the brothers' reading literature on secular subjects mentioned above.[74] Nicolaus expands greatly on Peter's version; he introduces innovative wording and what may perhaps be called a certain thematic crescendo. Herman's love for the Virgin Mary, he says, preceded his departure for the order's lands:

> Der selbe, dô der dâ bevorn
> in werltlîchir wîse was,
> dô pflag er stête, als ich las,
> daz er Marîen gotis trût,
> sîn tochtir, mûtir und sîn brût,
> sô rechte lîb hatte î,
> daz er des mit nichte lî,
> swer in durch iren namen bat
> iz wêre dit odir dat,
> den bitter er gewerte,
> swes er an im gerte,
> ob im der macht ôt nicht gebrach.

[*KVP* ll. 10330–41: When he still belonged to the world he was so devoted to the Virgin Mary, God's beloved, His daughter, His mother and His bride that he never refused anything that was asked of him in her name, whatever it was; he granted any request that he was capable of fulfilling.]

Herman's love of the Virgin is then further qualified and put to the test in the description of his journey to Prussia. Traveling toward the East, he chances upon some knights, one of whom challenges him to individual combat in honor of his lady:

> Dô diz hôrte Sarrazin,
> der rede bleib er unvorzait.
> Er hofte an dî zarte mait,
> dî er in lîbe hatte irkorn
> und îr zu dînste zich gesworn,
> Marîen ich dô meine.
> Durch dî sûze reine
> stapft er ûf dî bane,
> und allis zwîfils âne
> sprencte er den rittir an
> und stach in sundir wân
> in dem êrsten rîtin,
> daz man in sach glîtin
> mit valle ûf dî erde.
> Dî wâpin mit dem pferde
> er den armin dâ vorgab
> und reit alsô her ab.

[*KVP* ll. 10398–414: When Sarrazin heard this he made his mind up. He put his trust in the tender maiden he had chosen and in whose service he had dedicated himself, I mean Mary of course. In the name of the pure Virgin he marched into the arena, confidently attacked the knight, unseated him with his lance at the first attempt and knocked him to the ground. He gave the arms and the horse to the poor and rode away.]

The knight's love of the Virgin Mary guarantees his success. But he does not love the Virgin Mary merely in the traditional way: he has "chosen her in love," has sworn himself to her service, and fights in her honor—a religious version, as it were, of the Frauendienst, the love service to ladies of chivalric romance.

This love service to the Virgin Mary is rewarded; this reward too is drawn from romance. After Herman Sarrazin's arrival in Prussia, the Virgin whom Herman has so loyally served "in touginlîchim trôste / ofte mit im kôste" [*KVP* ll. 10423–24: "secretly consoled him and often spoke to him"]. Shortly before Herman's death in battle, the Virgin forewarns him of his death with the words:

> Lîber vrûnt, ich lade dich
> zu der wirtschaft mînes suns,
> dâ dû dich vroien salt mit uns

in êwigir sêlikeit.

[*KVP* ll. 10742–45: Dear friend, I invite you to my son's table, where you will rejoice with us in eternal blessedness.]

As in chivalric romance, the reward for Herman's service is a secret one, and the Virgin Mary refers to him as her "lîber vrunt" ["sweet friend"], the "doux ami" of the French tradition. In other words, Nicolaus infuses the story of Herman Sarrazin with language and themes drawn from romance. It is also important to note that the romance content of Herman's story increases the closer he gets to Prussia. At home, Herman loves the Virgin Mary; on the road, he has chosen her in love, devoted himself to her service, and fights in her honor; while in Prussia itself, his devotion is reciprocated, the Virgin gives him a secret reward and refers to him as her "sweet friend." The geographical location itself appears to contribute to the romance nature of the action.[75]

Horst Wenzel and Mary Fischer have focused on the fact that Sarrazin traveled to Prussia to become a Teutonic Knight and have found in this passage merely an attempt at Selbstdeutung, or self-definition, by the order, a way for it to define itself in terms a lay audience could understand.[76] Fischer argues that Nicolaus's wording in the Sarrazin episode is intended only to show the incompatibility of worldly chivalry with the life of the German brothers, that "familiar terminology is used to make the idea of service to God as an alternative to secular chivalry acceptable to a lay audience."[77] A passage found a little earlier in the work, however, complicates Wenzel's and Fischer's approach. In it, Nicolaus discusses a battle between Christians and Prussians before Kulm. The townspeople, venturing out to retrieve their dead, chance upon a Christian survivor, barely alive. When they want to take him inside the town for treatment, he resists and demands to be left there, as the Virgin Mary has appeared to him:

Zujungist sî ouch zu mir quam
und dô sî des intsebete,
daz ich dennoch lebete,
mit alsulchim trôste
sî lîblîch zu mir kôste:
"Ô vil lîber kempfe mîn,
nû lîd vrôlîch dise pîn.
An dem drittin tage
volendit sich dîn clage,
want dû den irsterbin solt

und den himilischen solt
mit wunnen alzû grôz intpfân,
als alle dî intpfangin hân,
dî durch mich hî ir lebin
hân in den tôt gegebin."

[*KVP* ll. 7258–72: Finally she came to me and when she realised I
was still alive she spoke sweetly and comfortingly to me: "My dear
warrior, bear this suffering cheerfully. On the third day your complaints will be at an end because you will die and receive your heavenly wages with indescribable joy, as all these who gave up their lives
for me have done already."]

There are many parallels between this scene and the Sarrazin episode. Quite apart from the fact that the passages are very similar
in content—the Virgin directly speaking to a man, telling him of
his impending death, and informing him of the glory that awaits
him in the afterlife—the wording is similar and carries the same
romance connotations. Whereas with Herman Sarrazin Mary "in
touginlîchim trôste / ofte mit im kôste" ["often comforted him in
secret"], here she "mit alsulchim trôste / sî lîblîch zu mir kôste"
["spoke sweetly and comfortingly to me"]. Furthermore, Mary calls
the Teutonic brother "lîber vrunt" ["sweet friend"] and the Kulmer townsman "vil lîber kempfe mîn" ["my dear warrior"]. The
romance notion of a lady giving sweet comfort to someone she calls
her friend is here mirrored in a lady's giving sweet comfort to one
she refers to as *her warrior*. The use of the word "kempfe," which
besides "warrior" means "champion" (in the sense of "duelist"),
strengthens the idea of the man's fight against the unbeliever as an
act of love service for the Virgin.[78]

In other words, romance wording is used in both the Sarrazin
passage and that of the Kulmer townsman. This calls into question
Fischer's and Wenzel's explanation of its use solely as a tool of Selbstdeutung; indeed, if Herman Sarrazin eventually becomes a knight-
brother, there is no indication that the Kulmer townsman is anything
more than just a Kulmer townsman, a Christian in no apparent way
connected to the order. The use of romance phraseology is therefore
not connected to membership in the order; rather, it appears related
to the *location* of the action. As we have seen, the romance nature
of Sarrazin's story increases as he gets closer to the Prussian frontier, the very frontier on which the episode of the man from Kulm
takes place. The Prussian setting, rather than any social quality of the

protagonists, is what brings about the affections of the Virgin Mary and the romance language of her address.

That romance wording and romance themes are not limited to the religious, such as Sarrazin and his fellow brothers, is further borne out by the fact that the Baltic frontier offers not only the reward of the attention of the Virgin Mary but also far more secular adventures and incentives. For example, Nicolaus further associates the Baltic Crusade with chivalric romance by introducing what Geraldine Heng has accurately termed "a prime instrument in the narrational machinery of medieval romance—the chivalric rescue of aristocratic maidens."[79] Time and time again, Nicolaus introduces damsels in distress where there are none in Peter's original. In one instance, the Teutonic Knights and their fellow Crusaders kill a number of Lithuanians; in Peter's words, "multos Cristianos captos redemerunt" [CTP 166: "they freed many captured Christians"]. Nicolaus sees them "lôsende juncvrouwin, / vrouwin unde kindir vil / ûz iren banden" [KVP ll. 21261–63: "freeing many damsels, ladies, and children, from their shackles"].[80] Another instance shows the aftermath of a successful raid by the Lithuanian grand duke Vytenis ("Witêne") on the order's lands. In Peter's words, "ultra mille et ducentos captos cristianos homines secum duxit" [CTP 176: "he led more than twelve hundred captured Christian men with him"]; later on, he looks upon "Cristianos captos, qui ligati astiterunt ibi" [CTP 176: "the captured Christians, who stood there tied up"]. Nicolaus's parallels are, respectively:

> sô hatte er gevangen
> juncvrouwin, kinder, wîbe
> wol drîzênhundirt lîbe,
> dî man in den stundin
> treib dâ hin gebundin.

[KVP ll. 23575–79: And so he had captured almost thirteen hundred damsels, children, and women, and driven them, bound up, away from there.][81]

> zuletzt wart er ouch schouwin
> juncvrouwin unde vrouwin,
> der vil vor im dô stûndin
> jâmirlîch gebundin.

[KVP ll. 23602–5: Finally he was also shown the damsels and ladies, of which many stood before him, bound piteously.][82]

Where women are explicitly mentioned in the source text, Nicolaus takes the occasion to ply the heartstrings. An invasion by Swantopolk of Pomerania ended, according to Peter, with the enemy "mulieres et parvulos in captivitatem perpetuam deducentes" [*CTP* 69: "leading away the women and the little ones into everlasting captivity"]. Nicolaus, sparing no pathos, turns it into the following:

> Ouch wurdin harte jêmirlîch
> ir wîb gevangin und dî kint,
> dî vil arbeitlîchin sint
> mûstin blîbin ouch behaft
> in êwiclîchir eiginschaft.
> Dâ mochte man jâmir schouwin
> an den edlin vrouwin,
> dî dâ irzogin wârin zart,
> daz dî mûstin nû sô hart
> lîdin manchis smachtis pîn
> und dâbî betwungin sîn
> zu pflegelîchir arbeit
> in vil strengir hertekeit.

[*KVP* ll. 6208–20: Their wives and children were taken prisoner in scenes of great wretchedness and kept as slaves in perpetual captivity. It was pitiful to see these noble women who had been brought up as gentlewomen and now had to suffer such painful humiliation and were brutally forced to work.]

In short, where Peter describes faceless Christian captives of mostly undefined gender, Nicolaus's work translates these quite literally into damsels in distress.[83] In doing so, Nicolaus not only turns those who fight in the Baltic almost into romance heroes but also suggests that Prussia is a place where romance adventure belongs to the realm of possibility. The Baltic Crusade, then, is a war in which both spiritual and romance rewards are on offer, in which one can both fight for the salvation of one's soul and find romance adventure. In a passage without clear parallel in Peter's *Chronica Terre Prussie*,[84] Nicolaus urges his audience to take action by juxtaposing religious and secular motivations. The two, it appears, go hand in hand:

> Rechchit um des himels lôn
> des jâmirs stric:
> des lastirs blic
> an den reinen vrouwen,
> juncvrouwen,
> sî ûch ein schric

zu der râche widdirbic!

[*KVP* ll. 23737–43: Avenge, for the reward of heaven, the pitiful trappings: let the look of dishonor upon the pure ladies, damsels, also be a spur for vengeance!][85]

Romance, of course, not only trades in Frauendienst, it also speaks of adventure, and a third way in which Nicolaus associates the events in Prussia with chivalric romance is by referring to them simply as "adventures." Describing, for instance, the siege of Bartinstein, a stronghold of the order, he says: "Dêswâr in menlîchir tucht / geschach dâ ebintûre vil" [*KVP* ll. 12384–85: "They had many heroic adventures"]. Peter refers to "mirifica facta" [*CTP* 111: "wonderful deeds"]. In another instance, a raider named Mucke, who has pursued a pagan troop deep into enemy territory, rouses his companions by asking: "Wer weiz, waz ebbintuire / an der dît ungehuire / uns noch geschên von gote sol!" [*KVP* ll. 26134–36: "Who knows what adventures with the heathens may still be waiting for us if God wills it!"]. Once again Peter's original is far less explicit, and Mucke urges his men on with the words: "Videamus, si possumus aliquid proficere circa ipsos" [*CTP* 190: "Let us see if we can accomplish something in the vicinity of these men"]. By unequivocally referring to the deeds done on the Baltic frontier as adventure, Nicolaus continues his interpretation of the Prussian Crusade along romance lines. Interestingly, here too he depicts the secular and the religious as running hand in hand—Mucke after all speaks of finding adventure "if God wills it."

A fourth and final way in which Nicolaus puts aspects of chivalric romance to use to redraw the Crusade in the Baltic is structural. The Middle High German text differs from the Latin in the way in which the narrative is organized. As we have seen above, Peter's *Chronica* is subdivided into four books: book I ("De Origine Ordinis Domus Theutonice") tells the history of the origins of the order; book II ("De Adventu fratrum Domus Theutonice in Terram Prussie") follows the order's transition from the Holy Land to Prussia; book III ("De Bellis Fratrum Domus Theutonice contra Pruthenos") discusses the wars of the order, first against the Prussians, then later against the Livonians and Lithuanians; and book IV ("De Incidentibus") is a collection of sketches of the most important persons and events in the wider European sphere from the order's inception to the time of writing. Nicolaus's translation, on the other hand, does not follow Peter's division into books but mingles them together, using only chronology as an organizing tool.[86] He moves back and forth between the events in the Baltic and the situation outside the order's lands; the immediate effect is one of increased contextualization, simultaneity and parallelism. He explains his reasoning for using this structural method, which he calls "braiding," as follows:

> Nû sol ich ouch betichtin,
> betichtinde intrichtin,
> intrichtine beschrîbin,
> beschrîbinde întrîbin
> und înbrengen dirre schrift,
> alse mir der schrifte gift
> mit wârheit urkunde gît,
> waz pêbste unde keisre sît
> sîn gewesin von der zît,
> daz der ordin mit begrift
> des dûtschin hûsis wart gestift;
> ouch darzû wol ebin trift,
> daz ich herînvlichte
> ein teil der geschichte
> *durch hovelîchiz sagin*
> di bî irin tagin
> in der werlde sîn irgân,
> und ouch was sî selbe hân
> prûvelichir tât getân.

[*KVP* ll. 1192–210: Now I will also compose, explain by compos-ing, describe by explaining, take apart by describing, and insert in this writing, as the gift of the writing truthfully testifies, under the rule of which popes and emperors the order of the German house was founded in the beginning; for that purpose, too, it is fitting that, *for the sake of courtly expression*, I braid in a piece of the history that happened in the world during their days, and also [tell] what they have demonstrably done themselves.][87]

What he means by this "courtly expression" may be clarified by the fact that Nicolaus's method of "braiding" is strongly reminiscent of the literary technique termed, by Ferdinand Lot and subsequent schol-arship,[88] "entrelacement" (quite by accident the exact French word for Nicolaus's "învlichtin"). Entrelacement, a practice whereby various temporally parallel storylines are interwoven with the narrative voice moving back and forth between them, is most often associated with Arthurian romance, and Chrétien de Troyes himself most likely pio-neered the technique in his last work, the *Conte du Graal*.[89] The result of Nicolaus's modification of the work to fit "courtly expression," in other words, is that he makes it more structurally similar to romance.

This structural reorganization may perhaps also be seen as moving the work closer to romance in a second way. A chronicle's primary purpose is the creation of a timeline, but what Nicolaus's work also does by constantly paralleling Prussia with the rest of Europe is to create space: it creates a here and a there, two places that distinctly exist simultaneously. Crusaders, or knights such as Herman Sarrazin, come from the European heartland to the Baltic frontier, and in most cases return to it. Doing so, they descend into a world of ever-increasing danger and adventure and return to one of safety and stability; accordingly, they travel between the two poles that Northrop Frye has identified as central features of the "mental landscape of romance."[90] Here the ability of romance to influence the geographical and political understanding of the Crusade in the later Middle Ages, which I discuss in greater detail below, already breaks the surface.

Nicolaus's approach is therefore decidedly different from Peter's: by portraying the Crusade in the Baltic as love service to a heavenly lady, by peppering the Prussian frontier with damsels in distress and secular adventure, and by altering the structure of his work to resemble that of the tales of Arthur, he associates the wars in the Baltic with chivalric romance. Importantly, in his presentation of the Baltic Crusade, romance adventure and service to God are not opposites or alternatives, as Fischer would have it. Rather, they run seamlessly together. Nicolaus speaks of a world in which knights rescue damsels "um des himels lôn" and find adventure "von gote"; here traditionally secular deeds reap a heavenly reward. He who comes to the order's aid in the Baltic can find adventure and serve ladies as well as earn salvation. It is here that we find the great innovation of Nicolaus's chronicle. Although he was not the first churchman to use vernacular, secular literature as a source of inspiration when propagating Crusade, Nicolaus turned to a genre whose often profane nature had rendered it problematic ever since its origins in the twelfth century. He furthermore used romance not merely as a source of historical parallel and example, but rather sought to associate the very ethic of romance knighthood with that of Crusade, to combine the desires of the armed pilgrim with those of the secular adventurer, and to turn the Baltic frontier into a place where one could find fulfillment for both.

CRUSADE AND ROMANCE IN SUCHENWIRT'S VON HERZOG ALBRECHTS RITTERSCHAFT

The *Krônike von Prûzinlant* was sanctioned and circulated by the Teutonic Order; however, the international nature of the Baltic Crusade in the fourteenth century also likely helped spread the work's ideas. Crusaders from all over Western Christianity joined the German brothers. On their return home after an often brief winter or summer campaign, many would have taken the order's message with them, and in turn convinced others to take the cross in Prussia. As such, both Crusade preaching by the order and the simple fact of interaction between Crusaders and their environs may have contributed to the dissemination of the *Krônike*'s concept of Crusade. Nicolaus's description of the Baltic wars did not merely give Western knights yet more motivation for taking the cross, it may also have influenced how they understood those wars, as hinted at in a poem composed by Peter Suchenwirt. Suchenwirt, who lived from circa 1320 to 1395, was one of the finest practitioners of heraldic poetry of his time. While he may have been in the service of Louis of Hungary and Burgrave Albert of Nuremberg early on in his career, from 1372 until his death he was attached to the Austrian court as court poet and herald. Fifty-two works have been ascribed to him; these are mostly death laments and *Ehrenreden*—poems combining panegyrics of the great deeds and virtues of knights with elaborate descriptions of their arms and helmets—on some of the principal nobles of the empire. Importantly, most of these nobles appear to have belonged to the Societas Templois, the chivalric order founded by the duke of Austria in 1337;[91] this has led Cain van d'Elden to suggest that Suchenwirt may have functioned as official herald to the Societas Templois as well as to the house that had created it.[92]

When, in 1377, Suchenwirt accompanied the young Duke Albert III of Austria on a Reise to Lithuania, he may have done so not only to witness the heroic acts of his patron but also to see the Societas Templois itself in action—after all, its purpose included the assistance of the order in its Baltic wars. Shortly after, he completed a verse description of this journey, entitled *Von Herzog Albrechts Ritterschaft*.[93] The somewhat misleading title of the poem—*About Duke Albert's Knighthood*—is explained by the fact that Albert of Austria was not motivated to travel to Prussia solely to fight the pagan. Rather, he wanted to be dubbed a knight while on Crusade, which would confer additional honor onto the proceedings. In keeping with the nature of warfare in the Baltic, which favored short, destructive incursions into enemy territory over long, drawn-out campaigns, Albert's journey into pagan lands was brief. Only eight days were spent plodding through the horrific terrain, and with the exception of the massacre of a Lithuanian wedding party, very little appears to have been accomplished. Suchenwirt's description of the events, however, clearly illustrates how the duke and his companions understood the Crusade, or wanted it to be understood. Especially interesting is the way it treats Crusade, romance, and space.

In keeping with Nicolaus's *Krônike*, the service of ladies and the search for adventure clearly play an important role in the duke's Crusade. Suchenwirt describes some of the Crusaders setting out into the lands of the Lithuanians as motivated by love:

schapel und strauzzenfedern
fûrt dâ manig stolzer helt,
der sich zu liebe hêt geselt
durch vreuden trôst, durch minne prunst:
dem was geschancht in lieber gunst
golt, silber, edelstain;
perlein grôz unde chlain
sach man auf hauben liechtgevar,
chrenz und chlainât offenwar,
daz er gab gegen der sune glast.

[ll. 246–55: Many of the proud heroes / who were in the service of love, / driven by their ardor and hopes of joy, / wore garlands and wreaths of ostrich feathers. / As signs of favor they had been given / gold, silver, jewels, / pearls large and small, / wreaths and ornaments, / all of which they bore on their helmets, / glittering in the sun.]

These knights appear to have regarded the Crusade quite literally as an adventure. When, immediately after having crossed into pagan lands, they decide to seek out the enemy, Suchenwirt says:

Als daz mâl ein ende nam,
vil manig ritter lobsam
rait auz durch abenteure.
Daz lant daz was mit feure
entzundet und verprunen auch;
von dampf und auch von grôzem rauch
macht niemant wol gesehen[.]

[ll. 412–17: After the meal / many worthy knights / rode out to seek adventure. / They set the land afire / and burned it / until the smoke was so thick / one could hardly see.]

Perhaps even more interesting than these romance descriptions of Crusade—or descriptions of romance Crusade—is how Suchenwirt creates space in *Von Herzog Albrechts Ritterschaft*. He distinguishes three distinct worlds in the poem: a world of ladies, a world of men, and a world of beasts. The Crusaders travel among these—from the world of ladies to that of men to that of beasts and back again. The poet describes a number of stops Duke Albert and his companions make. At the first of these, Breslau, they are made welcome by ladies:

> di zîrten iren stolzen leib
> zu vrauden manigerlaie,
> recht als der chûle Maie
> blûmet anger und den walt.
> Man sach dâ freude manikvalt
> mit schimphen, tanzen, lachen;
> waz trauren chunde swachen,
> des vlizzen sich die vrauen zart[.]

[ll. 56–63: They blessed the proud knights / with all manner of happiness / just as cool May / brings meadow and forest into bloom. / There was great joy / in joking, dancing, and laughing / and the sweet ladies took pains to dispel / whatever cares might have burdened those knights.]

No local men take part in these festivities; the town might as well be inhabited by ladies alone. The same is true of the second town the Crusaders visit on their way to the Prussian frontier, Thorn. There,

> Dem edel fursten reiche
> pat man gar tugentleiche
> di vrauen dâ zu gaste;
> dâ sach man widerglaste
> von mundelein und von wangen;
> mit perlein, porten, spangen
> di vrauen sich dâ zîrten
> und gên der lust vlôrîrten;
> chrôn, schapel, unde chrenze
> sach man, und vil der tenze
> mit zuchten und mit êren.

[ll. 69–79: The fine and noble prince [the duke] / was courteously offered / the ladies' hospitality. / Their dainty mouths and cheeks / were a shining splendor and / they adorned themselves / for the joyous occasion / with pearls, waistbands and brooches, / with tiaras, chaplets and wreaths. / And the dances! / How many there were, all fine and decorous."]

Once again there is not a single man in sight; only wonderfully adorned ladies are there to receive the Crusaders. The first stops on the road to the Baltic frontier, then, are populated uniquely by ladies; they constitute a sort of world of women. This changes as soon as they enter the lands of the Teutonic Order:

> Von dan begund man chêren
> gên Mergenburch hin fur sich paz.
> Der maister dâ mit hause saz;
> Weinreich von Chniprôd ist sein nam.
> Der edel herre tugentsam
> dem fursten und den seinen
> liez grôze zucht erscheinen
> mit hôchen êren, daz ist wâr;
> man trûg sô mildikleichen dar
> gût getranch und reiche chost;
> wî man sich solt vor schanden rôst
> bewaren mit der milde,
> des phlag man dâ zwispilde.
> Darnâch zog man zu Chunigesperch;
> dâ sach man hôcher herren werk
> mit grôzer milde offenwar[.]

> [ll. 80–95: From here [Thorn] they went on / to Marienburg. / The grandmaster had his seat there. / Winrich von Kniprode was his name. / This noble and virtuous lord / most graciously received / the prince and his men, / showing them great honor. / They were most generously feted / with good drink and fine food. / Through generosity one guards himself / against the blemish of dishonor / and here there was a double show! / Then they went to Koenigsberg / and here too the great lords / gave great display of generosity.]

Once again, two cities are visited, Marienburg and Königsberg; all present, however, are men, and not a single woman is mentioned. The virtues on display—boundless generosity extended by all sides—are less courtly, and more chivalric. Of course, since the Teutonic Order was a monastic order, this is perhaps to be expected; nevertheless, the contrast with the description of Breslau and Thorn is marked. The cities of Marienburg and Königsberg, the heart of the Ordenstaat, constitute a parallel world of men.

From this second world, then, the Crusaders cross into the territory of the pagan Lithuanians. Here the poem notably changes in tone. Suchenwirt's descriptions become far more realistic, even gritty. In the words of David Tinsley, the crossing into enemy territory "is accompanied by harrowing descriptions of the hardships Albrecht's party had to endure, including swamps with impassable deadfalls, thickets impossible to penetrate, as well as drowning, illness, injury, and starving horses."[94] It is a dangerous region populated by people closely likened to animals. When the Crusaders attack, their enemy resembles the prey of a hunting party:

Dâ sach man wûchsten, prennen,
slahen, schiezzen und rennen
haid ein, pusch ein, unverzagt,
recht als der füchs und hasen jagt.
Sô fluhen si der widervart!

[ll. 363–67: There we laid waste and burned, / slew and speared, charging / boldly through thicket and meadow. / It was like chasing foxes and rabbits; / just so did they flee!]

Conversely, when the pagans take the initiative, they resemble predatory animals, striking and retreating back to their lairs:

des nachts si chômen selten wider!
Mit lauter stim si schrieren
geleich den wilden tieren;
si stâchen leut, si schuzzen ros,
und fluchen wider auf daz mos[.]

[ll. 308–12: Still there was little rest that night / for screaming loudly / like wild beasts the pagans / stabbed men, speared horses / and then fled back into the marsh.]

The return journey simply reverses the sequence. From this dark and threatening world of beast-like men, the Crusaders cross back into the world of men, Königsberg, and from there go back into the world of ladies, arriving in the town of Sweidnitz, where they are welcomed by the duchess:

ir herz sich freut des fursten junch;
ez was ain stam und ain ursprunch:
von Ôsterreich ist si geporn.
Di furstin edel und auzerchorn
hêt megde vil und vrauen zart
von purt und auch von edler art,
di chunden sich erpieten wol
mit zuchten, als man pilleich sol.
Mit hâhem mût man vreuden phlag;
daz wert unz an den vîrden tag[.]

[ll. 533–42: Her heart rejoiced in the young prince, / for she had been born in Austria / of the same family and lineage. / The noble and

splendid princess / had many maids and lovely ladies, / noble by birth
and also by nature, / who served as gracious hostesses. / For four days
/ there was courteous and high-spirited joy.]

Suchenwirt's description of these three worlds is interesting on many
levels. The most obvious one is, of course, that this man's world of
Teutonic Knights and their knightly allies is quite literally the thing
standing between the world of ladies and the pagan beasts. The Baltic
Crusade is therefore aimed not just at fighting the unbelievers but also
implicitly at protecting the feminine, in towns such as Breslau, Thorn,
and Schweidnitz. Second, the journey from the safety and happiness
of Germany and the world of ladies into the dark, dangerous world of
violence and adventure and back again mirrors the journey between
the world of light and the world of darkness that Frye suggests lies at
the very heart of romance; we have found Nicolaus introducing a similar spatial structure in the *Krônike von Prûzinlant*. Accordingly, the
creation of space in Suchenwirt's poem illustrates how the notions of
romance and Crusade brought together in Nicolaus's chronicle could
influence a geographical understanding of the world in the later Middle Ages. Both the *Krônike* and Suchenwirt's *Von Herzog Albrechts
Ritterschaft* describe on the one hand a European heartland, a place
of courtliness, happiness, and peace, and on the other an undefined,
dark, and dangerous pagan frontier, the home of both Crusade and
adventure in service of ladies.

The comparison between Nicolaus of Jeroschin's *Krônike von
Prûzinlant* and Peter of Duisburg's *Chronica Terre Prussie* therefore
shows how, in a time of continuing conflict and undiminished need
for manpower on the frontiers, the German Order shaped its message
to appeal to the changing concerns of the knightly class. A new concept of Crusade in the Baltic that closely tied it to chivalric romance
appears to have spread across fourteenth-century Europe, propelled
by preachers and returning Crusaders. As Suchenwirt's work shows,
this association influenced the fourteenth-century understanding of
the Crusade frontier as a place of adventure and Frauendienst. Nevertheless, this new understanding also affected Crusade battlefields
other than Prussia: little more than a decade after Nicolaus translated Peter of Duisburg's chronicle into Middle High German, we
find a number of Old French poems belonging to what is commonly
referred to as the Second Old French Crusade Cycle exhibiting a similar phenomenon.

CHAPTER 7

Adventure and the East in the Second Old French Crusade Cycle

The title "Second Old French Crusade Cycle" has traditionally been used to refer to four late-medieval chansons de geste on the Crusades. Three of these are poems: *La Chanson du Chevalier au Cygne et de Godefroid de Bouillon* (shortened here to *Godefroi de Bouillon* to avoid confusion with the early thirteenth-century *Le Chevalier au Cygne*), a new redaction in 35,180 lines of much of the material from the First Old French Crusade Cycle;[1] *Baudouin de Sébourc*, a somewhat fantastic history of the life and times of the third ruler of Jerusalem, Baldwin of Bourg in 26,360 verses;[2] and *Le Bâtard de Bouillon*, whose 6,554 recovered verses describe the adventures of Baldwin I of Jerusalem's bastard son.[3] Added to these is a fourth fragmentary text in prose, *Saladin*, which recounts the rise of the eponymous hero from his early youth to his adventures in both the Holy Land and France.[4] This Cycle, a mixed bag of *remaniements* and inventive new additions, has garnered on the whole little critical attention since Gaston Paris first associated the texts with each other in the late nineteenth century.[5] Within this limited critical framework, scholars have intensely debated the authorship, the dates, and sequence of composition of the texts, and even the validity of the very notion of a "Second Cycle."

Of the four texts, only the three poems can be dated with some degree of certainty. *Saladin* is more problematic; while it is usually associated with the three others, it appears only in prose form in fifteenth-century manuscripts.[6] The date of its origin is unclear, as is whether there existed an earlier version in verse, and it has been suggested that the text may have been part of the First rather than the

Second Cycle, and thus the oldest of the four by far.[7] Regardless of the
problems associated with *Saladin*, much recent work has proposed
probable dates and places of composition as well as authors of the
components of this Second Cycle. E. R. Labande, who presented an
initial scholarly treatment of *Baudouin de Sébourc*, assumed that his
subject text had been written earliest, probably somewhere between
1314 and roughly the middle of the fourteenth century, as the poem's
most complete version is found in a manuscript datable to about 1350.[8]
He considered the *Bâtard de Bouillon* to be a continuation of this first
text; it must therefore have been written after *Baudouin de Sébourc*
but, since it is found in the same manuscript, also before circa 1350.
Godefroi de Bouillon was third in line, written circa 1344–1356.[9]
Labande does not treat *Saladin* in much detail, merely summarizing
its contents, but his reference to the fifteenth-century manuscripts of
Jehan d'Avesnes, in which *Saladin* is found, as the "résumé des continuations"[10] of *Baudouin de Sébourc* suggests that he considers there
to be a linear connection between at least *Baudouin de Sébourc*, the
Bâtard de Bouillon, and *Saladin*. Labande proposed that *Baudouin
de Sébourc* was composed by two poets in the area of Valenciennes
in Hainault, the first a "bon vivant" who started the poem between
1314 and 1350, and a more serious second writer, who took over
after about 17,000 verses and did away with much of the humor.[11]
He assumes the *Bâtard de Bouillon* to have been written in the same
region by a poet sharing certain affinities with, but probably not iden-
tifiable with, the second author of *Baudouin de Sébourc*.[12] Labande
does not elaborate on the authors of the other works; nevertheless, he
acknowledges a certain similarity in language between *Godefroi de
Bouillon*, the *Bâtard de Bouillon*, and *Baudouin de Sébourc* which,
combined with their roughly similar dates of composition, leads him
to speculate that they might well have been the product of the same
literary "atelier."[13]

Fifteen years after Labande, Suzanne Duparc-Quioc published
a strongly differing opinion. Basing her research on the frequent
annonces and *rappels* in the poems—references to and mentions of
one text in another—she deduced that the oldest of the works was not
Baudouin de Sébourc but rather *Godefroi de Bouillon*.[14] She placed
its composition after 1350, with some verses definitely written only
after 7 December 1355,[15] and that of the other works between 1360
and 1370.[16] Duparc-Quioc considers the four texts of the Second
Cycle to be the work of only two authors: one who wrote *Godefroi*

de Bouillon and a second writer who aimed to complete the work of the first, and who composed the *Bâtard de Bouillon, Baudouin de Sébourc,* and *Saladin.*[17] She too does not doubt Hainault as the place of origin of the texts.

A third and slightly more complex approach has been proposed by Robert L. Cook and Larry S. Crist. Cook, writing on the *Bâtard de Bouillon, Baudouin de Sébourc,* and *Godefroi de Bouillon,* argues that the composition of the works cannot be understood as linearly connected in the way Labande and Duparc-Quioc thought them to be, with one poem giving rise to another in a temporal sequence that stretched throughout the fourteenth century. Rather, he sees the three poems as separate developments of materials dating back to the thirteenth century, slowly assimilated to one another during the course of successive rewritings and adaptations. An original date or sequence of composition is therefore almost impossible to devise.[18] Nevertheless, the manuscript tradition provides some ways of determining the date of the texts, and the works as we have them now can be dated roughly to 1350 for *Baudouin de Sébourc* and the *Bâtard de Bouillon* and to 1355 for *Godefroi de Bouillon.*[19] If we can tentatively date the poems, it is, however, far harder to establish their authorship. The cooperative nature of the development of the Second Crusade Cycle makes a convincing attribution of the works to any one, or two, or even three authors very difficult. Cook and Crist develop Labande's theme of an atelier of writers from francophone Hainault at the source of the three poems.[20] If Cook and Crist are confident in connecting *Baudouin de Sébourc,* the *Bâtard de Bouillon,* and *Godefroi de Bouillon,* they are less certain about the place of *Saladin,* arguing that there is too little extant evidence to draw convincing conclusions as to the date of origin of a proto-*Saladin,* its place within this Second Cycle, or whether there existed a proto-*Saladin* to begin with.[21]

The Second Crusade Cycle is therefore a collection of four texts: three, *Godefroi de Bouillon, Baudouin de Sébourc,* and the *Bâtard de Bouillon,* were written in the form they have come down to us circa 1350 to 1370, in "laisses monorimées" of alexandrines, by more than one unknown author, probably in Hainault,[22] while the fourth, *Saladin,* is of indeterminate date and authorship but has certain strong connections to the three poems.[23] Although they are decidedly more imaginative, and include romance tropes such as love and adventure within their depiction of Crusade, the works of the Second Old French Crusade Cycle are connected to those of the First not only by their subject matter and (if we discount the prose *Saladin*) form but also by their purpose as both historiography of and propaganda for the Crusades. The fourteenth-century works too were "poems with historical pretensions";[24] their often fantastic nature notwithstanding, they were likely considered as true a record of events as the *Chanson d'Antioche*.[25] The status of *Godefroi de Bouillon* as a remaniement of the First Old French Crusade Cycle, and the place of the *Bâtard de Bouillon*, *Baudouin de Sébourc*, and even *Saladin* within the historical framework already outlined by that Cycle, suggest that these texts too functioned as vernacular historiography. Undoubtedly they benefited from the aura of historicity that had surrounded the Crusade chansons for centuries, and the veneer of legitimacy covered even those passages that are now considered outré.[26] Furthermore, the later works continued the propaganda function of the earlier. They remain filled with praiseworthy examples to emulate,[27] such as Godfrey of Bouillon in *Godefroi de Bouillon*, Baldwin of Sébourc in *Baudouin de Sébourc*, and Baldwin I in the *Bâtard de Bouillon*, and replete with commonplaces of Crusade propaganda as old as the movement itself, from representations of fighting in the Holy Land as the fulfillment of the obligation of Christian knighthood to avenge their Lord's death,[28] to reiterations of the everlasting heavenly benefit those who take the cross might win for themselves, and even for friends and family.[29] Cook has furthermore pointed out that the works' inclusion of romance elements too could benefit their capacity to serve as propaganda. He notes the frequency of liaisons between Christian men and Muslim women in the works—between Godfrey of Bouillon and Florie, and Baldwin I and Margalie in *Godefroi de Bouillon*; between Baldwin I again and Sinamonde, and the Bastard of Bouillon and Ludie in the *Bâtard de Bouillon*; and between Baldwin of Sébourc and Ivorine in *Baudouin de Sébourc*. Each of the women finds matters of the heart more important than the tenets of her faith, and most abandon their religion to be with their beloved.[30] Cook discerns a certain purpose to this:

> Peut-être s'agit-il d'une tentative réelle pour suggérer qu'à la Guerre Sainte il y avait non seulement la gloire ou des terres à gagner, mais aussi des femmes, moralement semblables à celles qu'on devait quitter. . . . On peut se demander si les histoires de Florie et d'Ivorine, de Margalie et de Sinamonde, dans le Deuxième Cycle de la Croisade, n'ont pas pu servir à faire naître, chez certains auditeurs au moins, le désir d'entreprendre une Croisade qui promettait des rencontres

amoureuses, analogues à celles qu'on connaissait grâce à des romans qui n'ont rien à voir avec la délivrance de Jérusalem.[31]

Not only the fin' amors between the Crusaders and Eastern ladies in the later Crusade chansons could serve to attract volunteers, however. The drive for adventure too was used to propagate fighting in the East in *Baudouin de Sébourc* and the *Bâtard de Bouillon*, through the identification of crusading with knight-errantry and of the theater of war with a romance otherworld, an "Arthurian East."

BAUDOUIN DE SÉBOURC

Baudouin de Sébourc, an imaginative history of the third ruler of Jerusalem, Baldwin of Bourg,[32] is both the tale of the fictional wars of the House of Nijmeghen-Boulogne against Godfrey of Frisia, and a bildungsroman tracing the life of its prodigal son Baldwin, from his origins as a nameless foundling to his days as a knight errant and his final reabsorption into the fold of the Boulogne family. The narrative snakes alongside these two currents, dynamically constructing itself between Baldwin's life as a wandering adventurer in the Christian and Muslim spheres[33] and the story of the family from which he is initially removed and into which he is later reintroduced. These poles effectively represent the worlds of romance and epic in the poem: Baldwin's adventures, while rendered in the chanson form of single-rhyme alexandrine laisses, are romance in content, a story of illicit love, wanderings and individual glory, whereas the dynastic struggles of the House of Nijmeghen-Boulogne constitute an epic family history. Beyond narrative variety, these two worlds embody opposites that define the propaganda message of the text. The opposition between family epic and individual romance is also one between normative and transgressive behavior: although his family's wars against Godfrey are just and righteous, Baldwin's deeds are described as roguish if not criminal. Furthermore, the opposition between individual and family, transgressive and normative, is also associated with the difference between adventurous fighting in the East and true Crusade.

Baldwin's family is engaged in a struggle that few would have considered unjust: the recovery of its heritage from Godfrey, the duke of Frisia, who has usurped power in Nijmeghen after Baldwin's father, Ernoul, dies on Crusade. Throughout the various stages of the conflict between the House of Nijmeghen-Boulogne and Godfrey there is little doubt as to the justice of the former and the evil of the latter.[34]

The family's patina of righteousness does not, however, attach to Baldwin, who was sent to Boulogne for safekeeping as an infant and left stranded at Sébourc, where he is raised. By the time he reaches adulthood, he has fathered thirty bastard sons, including one with the lord of Sébourc's daughter, and he is forced to leave pursued by the man who reared him. He follows his desire to the Flemish court, where he elopes with Blanche, the sister of the count of Flanders, and is in turn pursued by her brother. A pariah in his home region, he turns to what is effectively the life of a mercenary. It is at this time, when Baldwin unknowingly enters the service of his brothers against Godfrey, that he starts to be called ".j. homs aventureus" [BS 1:263, l. 860: "an adventurer," lit. "an adventurous man"].[35]

If Baldwin's leaving Sébourc and eloping with Blanche, not to mention the possibly mercenary quality of his adventure, do not provoke the poet's overt censure, what does is the fact that Baldwin's adventures are most often inspired by adulterous desire. He departs for the East when Blanche is captured by Godfrey of Frisia, exclaiming: "S'une femme ai perdue, Diex le me rendera! / Si ceste-ci ne vient, une autre revenra!" [BS 1:294, ll. 965–66: "If I have lost a woman, God will give her back to me! And if this one won't come back, another one will!"]. Upon his arrival near the Eastern city of Baudas (Baghdad), Baldwin almost immediately replaces Blanche with Ivorine, the daughter of the Old Man of the Mountain. In this case, however, there is a decided authorial, and indeed Authorial, intervention: a lion, who serves him as a faithful friend, fellow fighter, and even mount, tears Ivorine apart, proving to be an angel sent to point out God's displeasure with Baldwin's actions.[36] Only then does Baldwin recognize the error of his ways;[37] it is this realization and rejection of previous behavior that sets in motion the process of reabsorption, as he returns to his wife and finds his place among his kin. Baldwin's life of adventure is therefore morally erring as well as spatially errant;[38] yet the struggle of the Nijmeghen-Boulogne family is just, and no sooner does Baldwin give up the error of his ways than he is reintegrated into the righteous cause of his family.

The two poles of romance/transgression and epic/normativity are furthermore also associated with adventuring in the East as opposed to genuine Crusade. The poem begins with the Crusade and eventual death in the East of Baldwin's father, Ernoul of Nijmeghen, who, concerned about the salvation of the souls of his beloved wife and parents, decides to go "outre mer pour Sarrasins grever" [BS 1:9, l. 279:

"across the sea, to hurt the Saracens"]. Baldwin of Sébourc himself
goes to the East no fewer than three times, but on only one of these
occasions does he actually go there on Crusade. He leaves for a first
time immediately after Blanche's capture, but not to fight with the
Christian host against the Muslims. Rather, he goes there to serve as
a "chevalier d'aventure," to seek his fortune, apparently in the service
of his brother, Glorians of Cyprus.[39] He arrives in Muslim lands only
when the ship that is supposed to bring him to Cyprus is destroyed
at sea. His second journey to the East also seems to have secular
motives: he has to return to the Lady of Ponthieu, whom he had found
in the East, and who had asked him to tell her family of her well-
being and conversion to Islam, to deliver her his findings; he is concerned for Ivorine; and he is eager to fight the lion-angel that roams
around Abilant (Babylon). He then departs for the East a third and
final time after he has been reintegrated into the Nijmeghen-Boulogne
family, and it is only then that he formally decides to go on Crusade
to "Vengier le mort Jhésu qui morut à tourment" [BS 2:408, l. 291:
"Avenge the death of Jesus who died in agony"].[40] In short, there is an
explicitly stated difference between the eastward expeditions undertaken from within the family context and those attempted from without: the former are described as Crusades, the latter are not—they are
merely adventures on Eastern soil.

Baudouin de Sébourc therefore moves between an epic world of
just struggle and genuine, declared Crusade and a romance world of
scarcely commendable individual advancement, love, and adventure.
To a certain extent we have already seen this in earlier works that
shift from the folly of romance to the more serious business of Crusade.[41] Here, however, the walls separating the worlds are very thin,
almost nonexistent beyond the formality of the nomenclature. Baudouin de Sébourc does its utmost to minimize the practical difference
between the "licit" deeds done in the East and those less ethically
elevated. The feats done from within the epic framework of family
struggle are effectively the same as those done from within that of
romance: they occur in the same place, against the same enemies,
and with the same spiritual consequences. They are indistinguishable
from one another beyond the motivation expressed for them; there is
no practical difference between fighting in the East on a formal Crusade and going there on an amorous adventure.

To be sure, the epic and the romance parts of Baudouin de Sébourc
share a theater of operations, a Middle East that, as we shall see

below, is closely associated with the Arthurian otherworld. When they are in the East, both formal Crusader and amorous adventurer face the same opposition, both fight the magical or supernatural enemies that are characteristic of Arthurian romance, and the Saracen opponent of the chanson de geste. It is not surprising to find Baldwin, the man of adventure, fighting a giant lion that turns out to be an angel. However, Baldwin's father, Ernoul of Nijmeghen, who at the beginning of the work sets out on Crusade, finds his end in the maw of a giant snake. Having won the trust of the man who has defeated and captured him, the Red Lion of Abilant, Ernoul is sent on a diplomatic mission:

> Par terre païenie va Ernous chevauchant;
> Mais par desous .j. mont, delez .j. desrubant,
> Leur sali au matin .j. serpent par devant,
> Qui du mont de Tigris va à val descendant:
> A Ernoul est venus, qu'il a trouvé devant.
> Quant Ernous vi le beste, si va Dieu réclamant;
> Il a traite l'espée, qui avoit bon taillant;
> Au serpent a geté .j. cop merveille grant:
> Sus le dos le féri, mais ne valut noiant,
> Nient plus comme une englume ne va le cuir passant.
> Li serpens de sa keue le va estoriant;
> A terre l'abati; adont le va hapant,
> Tout ensi c'uns leus va le mouton engoulant.
> S'en va a tout le Roy, sus le mont remontant:
> Là endroit va le beste le bon Roi dévourant,
> Et laissa le chief coy, mengua le remanant.

[*BS* 1:40–41, ll. 264–79: Ernoul rode through the pagan land, but at the base of a mountain, next to a ravine, one morning a serpent jumped in front of them, which descending from the Tigris Mountain into the valley, had come to Ernoul, whom it had found in front of him. When Ernoul saw the beast, he called upon God; he drew his sword, which was razor-sharp; he struck a marvelous blow on the serpent: he struck it on the back, but to no avail, the skin took no more damage than an anvil would. The serpent attacked him with its tail, and struck him to the ground; then it grabbed him, just as a lion swallows a sheep. And so it befell the king, when they had gone up the mountain again: there the beast devoured the good king, and he left his head, and ate the rest.][42]

In *Baudouin de Sébourc* the adversaries of romance make their way into the epic of the Crusade. The opposite is also true, however, and when he ventures East Baldwin fights the same Saracen opponents

as his father. His great enemy is the same Red Lion who had ended
Ernoul of Nijmeghen's Crusade: the two great wars fought by Baldwin during his first two journeys to the East are against the Red Lion's
vassal, the lord of Italie, and the Red Lion himself, whom he eventually kills. Baldwin succeeds where his father had not, and Baldwin's
adventures are presented as the logical continuation of his father's
failed Crusade.

If the opposition father and son face are the same, and their battlefields are the same, the results of their efforts are also closely related.
Ernoul of Nijmeghen departs on Crusade because of the spiritual benefits it accrues: the souls of his wife and parents will be saved if he
fights in the East. But *Baudouin de Sébourc* does not stop with this
original perspective on the crusader indulgence. The poem suggests
that even adventure in the East has spiritual benefits. Although Baldwin's adulterous behavior in the East is frowned upon by God, during
his stay there he at some point becomes a virtual saint. Soon after his
arrival in the city of Baudas, he is transformed into a figure somewhat
reminiscent of St. Alexis, struck down by a mystery illness:

> S'ot une maladie, au vouloir Jhésu-Cris,
> Dont telle punasie rendoit ichius marchis
> Que devant l'uis ne passe crestiens, né Juïs,
> Qu'il n'estoupe son nés; de ce soiiés tout fis.

> [*BS* 1:332, ll. 115–18: Therefore, through the will of Jesus Christ, he
> was struck down with a sickness, the foulness of which changed this
> marquess so that no Christian or Jew would pass before him without
> turning his nose, be sure of that.]

Finding mercy neither with the Muslim ruler of the city nor with the
local Christians, Baldwin is left to waste away on the streets, until
he is eventually taken in by a poor cobbler. Soon afterward the city's
Christians come under threat from the Muslim ruler, who says that he
will destroy them all unless they perform two seemingly impossible
tasks: first, removing the keystone from their monastery wall without toppling the structure; and second, making Mount Tyrus higher.
They accomplish the first task with God's help; the second one, however, needs the intercession of Baldwin of Sébourc:

> Bonne gent, entendés; vous arrés garison!
> Mais che ne sera mie pour vous, né pour vo non;
> Ains ert pour un saint homme, de bonne norrechon,
> Qui est en cheste ville, droit à une maison
> Chest le bon chavetier. Or vous mande Jhésum:

Alés à son hostel, pour cheure le preud'om;
Si li faites honnour et révération.

[*BS* 1:343, ll. 494–500: Listen, good people: you will be saved! But it
will not at all be because of you or your name; it will be because of a
holy man, of good breeding, who is in this town, in front of the house
of the good cobbler. Jesus commands you to do this: go to his dwell-
ing place, for the sake of the valiant man; thus you will do him honor
and reverence.]

They find Baldwin in the house of the cobbler, and immediately afterward "Et nous fait la cronnike dire et autoriser / Que Diex a le prière
Bauduin, le gerrier, / Fist li montaigne aleir, et partir, et cangier" [*BS*
1:345, ll. 573–75: "And the chronicle tells and swears us, that God,
in response to the prayer of Baldwin, the warrior, made the mountain
go up, and separate, and change"]. This truly makes Baldwin into a
saint: he is referred to not only as "homme de sainte vie" [*BS* 1:343, l.
511: "a man of holy life"] but also as "sains hons" [*BS* 1:345, l. 551:
"a holy man"], and it is said that "A éureus se tient qui sa cote souil-
lie / Poet frotter, et baisier, et touchier une fie; / Bien croient que lor
puist garir de maladie" [*BS* 1:344, ll. 529–31: "He who could scratch
and kiss his dirty mantle, or touch a part, thought himself lucky; they
really thought that it could cure their illness"]. It is possible that the
poet or poets of *Baudouin de Sébourc* found it desirable to expand
upon the purported saintliness of its eponymous hero to attach divine
favor to the family of Nijmeghen-Boulogne or to the kings of Jerusalem. It is important, however, that Baldwin's saintly status is associated with his presence in the Levant, given the fact that his time as a
holy man coincides with his time there. He becomes a "sains hons"
almost immediately upon his arrival in the East, and he reverts back
to the saintly life after Ivorine has been killed by the lion. Before
returning to his ancestral home, he becomes a hermit, living outside
Abilant (Babylon) for seven years. The fact that mention of Baldwin's
sanctity is limited to his stay in the Middle East is not coinciden-
tal; his presence there itself plays an essential role. The Holy Land
presents Baldwin with a great many opportunities for adventure and
romance while simultaneously offering him a chance for redemption
and even sanctity.

These elements make Crusade and adventure in the East appear
very much the same in *Baudouin de Sébourc*. Both Crusader and
adventurer fight in the East against the same enemies, and both
reap spiritual benefits from their actions there. These similarities in

content and purpose nullify the gap between the two worlds of epic and romance, between normative and transgressive, between genuine Crusade and the adventure for personal gain. Here, the war in the East becomes an action in which the *utile* and the *dulce* are the same thing: the Crusader is made to look like the adventurer, and the adventurer like the Crusader. Even those whose primary interest is not in the saving of souls or the recapture of Christ's patrimony—the lovers, the rogues—have a place in the holy enterprise, and conversely those who go on Crusade will not be starved of the adventures of romance.

LE BÂTARD DE BOUILLON

If the action of *Baudouin de Sébourc* straddles the Mediterranean, and Baldwin of Sébourc is engaged in love and war in both Europe and the Levant, the *Bâtard de Bouillon* is focused entirely on events in the Holy Land. The work recounts what happened after Baldwin of Sébourc joined the Crusader army of Baldwin I of Jerusalem, as we find "Bauduin de Sebourc qui coer ot de lion, / Et si .xxx. bastars qui furent de grant non" [*BB* ll. 15–16: "Baldwin of Sébourc, who had the heart of a lion, and his thirty bastard sons who had a great reputation"] fighting for the king of Jerusalem. If we discount its last lines, which mention Tancred's journey to the West (ll. 6343–546), the *Bâtard de Bouillon* can be roughly divided into two major parts. The first part (ll. 1–3743) depicts Baldwin I's fictional war against Mecca, in which he defeats the Saracen lords Saudoine, Esclamart, Marbrun, Taillefer, and Ector, and courts their sister Sinamonde. The fruit of the "bons delis" of the king of Jerusalem and the princess of Mecca is the eponymous Bastard of Bouillon. His campaign completed, Baldwin goes to find the kingdom of Arthur, Faërie, which lies beyond the Red Sea. He finds it and is magnificently welcomed by the once and future king; although it appears he has spent only a short time at Arthur's court, upon his return he finds he has been away for five years. The second part concerns the deeds of his illegitimate son, the Bastard, whom Baldwin leaves in Mecca (ll. 3744–6342). The young man grows up to be quite temperamental,[43] and he kills first his cousin in Mecca and then his half-brother Orry in Jerusalem. Only the intervention of Hugh of Tiberias saves the Bastard's life. Banned from Jerusalem forever, he joins Hugh in his struggles with the Muslim lords of Orbrie and Babylon and falls in love with Ludie, the daughter of the lord of Orbrie, whom he marries but who eventually betrays him. Both parts of the *Bâtard de Bouillon* therefore seamlessly integrate holy war and romantic adventure—the father fights the lords of Mecca and conquers Sinamonde, the son helps expand the lands of Hugh of Tiberias while (less successfully) pursuing his own Saracen princess. Both conquer the East with the sword and in the bedroom.

Beyond his dalliance with Sinamonde, Baldwin's path moves from conquest to adventure as soon as he moves beyond Mecca. The king and twelve companions leave the army and journey into Faërie, the land of Arthur. Even though they claim to continue the holy war across the Red Sea,[44] the purpose of their voyage soon changes:

> Si con li .xiij. prinche ensamble cheminoient,
> Outre le Rouge Mer, en tel lieu s'embatoient
> C'une nuee vint, en coi il se boutoient;
> Che fu forte aventure, car si s'ebleuissoient
> Que l'un d'encoste l'autre ravoir moult hautement crioient,
> Par non et par sournon vistement se huchoient,
> Et de fies en autre moult hautement huoient.

> [*BB* ll. 3366–72: When the thirteen princes traveled together, across the Red Sea, they came to a place where a cloud came down that enveloped them; that was a great adventure, because they were so dazzled that one truly doubted to see the other again, they quickly called one another by name and surname, and out of concern they shouted very loudly at one another.]

The remainder of the passage continues in the vein of romance adventure as events serve to test the worth, not of Baldwin himself, but of one of his knights, the convert Hugh of Tiberias, who is found to be the best knight in Christendom. Soon after Hugh is separated from his companions, he finds and blows a horn inscribed with the following:

> Nuls hons du firmament
> Ne me porroit sonner pour or ne pour argent,
> Se che n'est flour du monde, passant de hardement
> Tout le monde a .j. jour, tant con li chielx comprent;
> Mais quant chius venra chi, moy prenge vistement,
> .I. son en getera melodieusement.

> [*BB* ll. 3437–42: No man in the whole universe can make me sing, not for gold or silver, if he is not the flower of the world, surpassing in boldness the whole world, such as the heavens hold it, in one day; but when he will come here, he will quickly take me and throw a melodious sound out of me.][45]

Upon arriving at Arthur's court, they find that the once and future king's garden contains a special rose, which can be picked only by "li plus prex" [*BB* l. 3625: "the most valiant"]. The rose is protected by two fearsome golden automata. Baldwin and his knights try to defeat the golden men; all fail except Hugh, who is finally recognized as the best of all. The rose and horn, the tests to find the best of all possible knights, underscore the turn from epic to romance; the wars of the crusading king have seamlessly turned into adventure in the land of Faërie. That this union of holy war and romance adventure will continue even with Baldwin's descendants is made clear when Arthur presents the Bastard of Bouillon with his horse and suit of armor. When Baldwin is ready to return to Mecca, Arthur accosts him:

> "Sire," che dist li roys, "entendés a moi cha:
> Veschi .j. haubregon que li miens corps porta
> Jadis en maint estour, quant li miens corp regna.
> Roys, pour amour de vous, qui estes venus cha,
> Le donrai vostre fil: vos corps li portera,
> Le bastart Bauduin, que vos corps engenra
> Ens ou corps Synamonde, qui tant de biauté a:
> Sachiés par armeüre ja faussés ne sera.
> Et mon riche destrier Blanchart il avera,
> Ca sachiés de chertain, tel chevalier n'i a
> Ou regne de Surie, ne jamais n'averra."

> [*BB* ll. 3656–66: "My lord," says the king, "listen to me: here is a suit of armor that my body wore in many battles, when I [lit. "my body"] still ruled. My king, out of love for you who have come here, I will give it to your son: your body will carry him, Baldwin's bastard, whom your body created in the body of Sinamonde, who is so beautiful: know that he will never be let down by his armor. And he will have Blanchart, my good warhorse, and be sure of this, that no knight in the kingdom of Syria has the like, or ever will."]

This transfer of Arthur's horse and armor to the Bastard is of some symbolic significance: now that the time of Arthur has passed, the Bastard will continue where he left off. The Bastard of Bouillon, the subject of most of the remainder of the *Bâtard de Bouillon*, is presented as the spiritual heir to Arthur even before we have met him.

The Bastard's actions as a Crusader and as an adventurer parallel those of Baldwin of Sébourc. The dynamic of *Baudouin de Sébourc* runs between two poles or worlds: one that is epic in nature, associated with family, Crusade, and normativity; and another of a romance character, associated with individual advancement, love, adventure, and transgression. Baldwin of Sébourc leaves the former of these worlds under a cloud of resentment concerning his dealings with the daughter of the lord of Sébourc and Blanche of Flanders, finds adventure throughout the latter world, and is eventually reabsorbed into the former. A similar framework can be found in the lines relating the deeds of the Bastard. The Bastard, too, commits two crimes that result in his exile from the epic world of his father's crusading court: he kills his cousin and his half-brother Orry. Baldwin of Sébourc ends up in the service of his brothers and later finds his battles in the East; the Bastard, already in the East, falls in with Hugh of Tiberias and engages in his war with the lord of Orbrie. Both Baldwin and the Bastard have amorous motives: the former, as we have seen, pursues his passions from Blanche to Ivorine; the latter fights the lord of Orbrie and Corsabrins of Montoscur because of his love for Ludie. After their adventures, both return to the epic world. Baldwin is recognized as belonging to the Nijmeghen-Boulogne family, returns to claim his heritage, and departs on Crusade; the Bastard is recalled to Jerusalem when his father, Baldwin I, is dying, reconciles with him, and retakes his place in the history of the Crusader kingdom. Importantly, adventure is once again closely related to Crusade: whereas Baldwin fought his father's enemies and received roughly the same benefits, the Bastard fights only Saracens and refuses to convert to Islam even to win the hand of his beloved.

There are marked differences between the two, of course. Baldwin of Sébourc's fascination with the opposite sex is mere rakishness compared with the Bastard's penchant for bloodshed, and Baldwin's success with women stands in marked contrast to the pastiche of fin' amors we find in the *Bâtard de Bouillon*, which tells of the Bastard's wooing of a woman who does not return his sentiments, complete with his making his way to Ludie's rooms only to be betrayed and captured. Nevertheless, there are strong similarities between the *Bâtard de Bouillon* and *Baudouin de Sébourc*, not only in that both seek to juxtapose and integrate romance adventure and Crusader warfare, but also in the way they achieve this. It is made clear that Crusaders—in this case Baldwin I of Jerusalem—will encounter adventure on Crusade and that conversely adventurers—such as the Bastard—have a place in the Crusade too. A penchant for describing protagonists as delinquents before they become full-fledged Crusaders appears to suggest that those who have run afoul of the boundaries of acceptable behavior can nevertheless become Crusaders. It

is likely that this message struck home in a time filled with random
violence, when incessant warfare throughout Europe was a breeding
ground for chequered pasts.[46]

THE GEOGRAPHY OF ROMANCE

As the act of crusading becomes synonymous with adventure and
the pursuit of fin' amors in *Baudouin de Sébourc* and the *Bâtard de
Bouillon*, so does the physical terrain of the holy wars, the Middle
East on which the Crusader states were built, become increasingly
identified with the world of Arthur. When Baldwin of Sébourc leaves
the West after the capture of Blanche of Flanders to join his brother
Glorians of Cyprus, his ship is wrecked in a storm, and he finds himself not far from the city of Baudas (Baghdad). Immediately upon his
entering the Crusade frontier, reference is made to the adventures of
Arthur and his knights, whom Baldwin will now surpass:

> Mais il i trouvera aventure pesant:
> Ains tèle ne trouva Perchevaus, né Gorhant,
> Anselos, né Gawans, né tout li conquérant
> Qui au tamps d'Arturs furent aventure quérant[.]
>
> [*BS* 1:300, ll. 1174–77: But he found great adventure, the like of
> which not Perceval, nor Gorhant, nor Lancelot, nor Gawain nor all
> the conquerors who looked for adventure in Arthur's time found.]

The implication that, arriving in the East, Baldwin has entered the
world of Arthurian romance is strengthened by the fact that his most
prominent adventures there—his wooing of Ivorine and his confrontation with the lion near Abilant—draw upon Arthurian antecedents.
Before Baldwin has seen Ivorine, he is told by the Caliph of Baudas
that the girl has a particular quality:

> Né jamais ne doit rire, né joie démener
> Tant qu'elle verra en ichel lieu entrer
> Fleur de chevalerie à ruistes cos donner,
> Et chellui qui n'ara en che monde son per.
>
> [*BS* 1:349, ll. 710–13: She cannot laugh or be joyful until she sees the
> flower of chivalry, who can strike heavy blows, come into this place,
> and the one who does not have his equal in the world.]

Here, the romance trope of supernatural events drawing forth the
best of all possible knights works to the advantage of Baldwin of
Sébourc, and upon seeing him the girl laughs, proving him to be the

flower of chivalry. Beyond the recurrence of the commonplace, what is noteworthy is that the appearance of a girl who laughs only when she sees the best of all knights has a precedent in Chrétien de Troyes's *Perceval*. Perceval, upon entering Arthur's court for the first time, finds a similar girl:

> Ceste pucele ne rira
> Jusque tant que ele verra
> Celui qui de chevalerie
> Avra tote la seignorie.

> [This girl will not laugh until she will see the one that will have full mastery over all knighthood.][47]

If Baldwin is identified with Perceval while in the East, he is also identified with another of Chrétien's knights: after the lion of Abilant submits and then fights alongside Baldwin, "Baudouin paraît maintenant destiné à une carrière semblable à celle d'Yvain."[48] The lion—a parallel to the lion that is defeated by and then serves Yvain in *Yvain*—is a romance creature roaming an Arthurian otherworld. It and Ivorine, the echoes of Chrétien, mark Baldwin as part of the East, the world of romance. Consequently, the moment the lion destroys Ivorine and turns into an angel Baldwin's time in this Arthurian otherworld has come to an end.

The *Bâtard de Bouillon* goes even further in identifying the East with the lands of Arthur. After about a thousand lines of the poem, the poet lists the most important cities in the Levant conquered by the Crusaders "Quant il ont conquesté le Temple Psalemon, / Et Nikes, Anthioche, et Acre, et Escalon, / Acre, Surtre, et Orbrie, *et la chit(e) d'Avalon*" [BB ll. 1121–23: "When they conquered the Temple of Salomon, and Nicaea, Antioch, and Acre, and Ascalon, Acre, Surtre, and Orbrie, *and the city of Avalon*" (my italics)]. Virtually all of these were wrested from the Muslims by the First Crusade; they are mentioned in historically logical succession. If one follows the road taken by the Crusader armies from Asia Minor into the Holy Land, one finds Nicaea, Antioch, Acre, and Ascalon; between Antioch and Acre lies "Surtre" (Sur/Tyrus); "Orbrie" is harder to identify but may refer to La Forbie, south of Ascalon, the site of an important Christian defeat in 1244. The poet therefore had some knowledge of the geography of the Crusade; this makes the fact that he introduces the city of Avalon in his list of Crusader victories all the more surprising, and indicates a conscious effort to conflate the lands of the Crusade with those of Arthur.

Continuing farther south in the description of the Levant, one reaches the Red Sea and Egypt, and it is here that this conflation reaches its apogee: beyond the Red Sea lies the land of Arthur himself. The princes of Mecca, when asked what lies to the west of their city, reply:

> Le nostre anchisserie
> Avoit oï retraire que che est Faërie,
> Et que le terre Artus et Morgue la jolie
> Marchist au les dela; ains n'i ala galie
> Qui puis au les decha en retournast en vie.

> [BB ll. 3308–12: Our ancestors have heard say that it is the land of Faërie, and that the country of Arthur and of beautiful Morgana lies there; no galley has ever gone there and returned safely.]

Baldwin and his knights cross into this strange land, and it is there that they meet

> Artus, le noble conquerant,
> Richement couronnés de couronne luisant;
> .II. fees gratieuses l'aloient adestrant:
> L'une fu sa soer Morgue, qui a prisier fist tant,
> Et li autre Oriande, qui le corps ot plaisant.

> [BB ll. 3549–53: Arthur, the noble conqueror, richly crowned with a resplendant crown; two graceful fairies went by his side: one was his sister Morgana, who is so praiseworthy, and the other Oriande, who has such a pleasing body.]

In the *Bâtard de Bouillon* as well the Holy Land is portrayed as closely associated with the lands of Arthur. Jerusalem itself and the Christian strongholds are but a stone's throw from Avalon, and Arthur's land of Faërie lies just across the Red Sea. This identification strengthens the association of Crusade and adventure. If the East truly is the land of Arthur, then traveling or fighting there is the stuff of romance.[49]

This identification of the Crusade frontier as the locus of courtly love and adventure in *Baudouin de Sébourc* and the *Bâtard de Bouillon* may have implications for late medieval chansons de geste beyond the Second Old French Crusade Cycle. William Kibler has observed that the works of the Second Crusade Cycle are not the only later chansons to incorporate aspects of chivalric romance; others such as *Huon de Bordeaux* and *Tristan de Nanteuil* do as well.[50] He suggests that these works are the products of an unfortunate conflation of the two genres and proposes referring to them as *chansons d'aventure*.[51]

The fact, however, that similar processes are at work both in the Second Crusade Cycle and in non-chanson works such as Nicolaus of Jeroschin's *Krônike von Prûzinlant* and Suchenwirt's *Von Herzog Albrechts Ritterschaft* suggests that the increasing import of chivalric romance in the late medieval chansons de geste may result not so much from a breakdown of established genre boundaries as from a changing perspective on holy war. The conflict with the religious other had been a preoccupation of the chansons de geste since the *Chanson de Roland,* and remained a preoccupation of the later chansons. As the holy war and the frontiers of Christianity upon which it was fought were increasingly propagated and thought of in romance terms,[52] the later chansons de geste may therefore have come to include more elements of romance as a corollary—the result of thematic, rather than generic development.[53]

When discussing the appearance of Arthur himself in the *Bâtard de Bouillon,* Cook remarks: "What is distinctive about the Arthurian episode in the *Bâtard,* beyond its potential cyclical implications, is the ease with which the redactor(s) slipped into the romance world for the sake of a required shift in emphasis."[54] He is right of course, but we might expand on his comment to acknowledge the ease with which the poets or redactors of *Baudouin de Sébourc* and the *Bâtard de Bouillon* slipped into the romance world while describing supposed episodes of Crusade history. It is important to remember that the works of the Second Crusade Cycle served as both vernacular histories and Crusade propaganda. By erasing the barriers between romance adventure and Crusade, the Cycle served to propagate the holy war by associating it with a popular, accessible literature. In the *Bâtard de Bouillon* and *Baudouin de Sébourc,* crusading is equated with adventure, and the geographical theater of the Crusades with the world of Arthur; Cook has furthermore suggested that the description of women in the Second Crusade Cycle was designed to draw Crusaders to the East with the promise of romantic love. In a time of transition for the Crusade, when the fall of Acre had made the will of God rather more obscure, these were powerful incentives to a chivalry that looked increasingly toward romance for self-validation.

CHAPTER 8

The Ideal Crusader
in *La Prise d'Alixandre*

THE CRUSADES OF PETER I OF CYPRUS

After the fall of Acre, the remaining Christian powers of the East—the military orders, the Cypriots, and the European potentates of the Aegean, which included the Venetian, Pisan, and Genoan merchant empires—did not have the luxury to neglect the war against their aggressive Muslim neighbors. Nevertheless, their actions in the early years of the fourteenth century, such as the Hospitaller *passagium* of 1309–1310 and the Byzantine-Venetian-Hospitaller operation of 1334, had enjoyed little success.[1] In 1343, however, the new and energetic Pope Clement VI responded to Hospitaller and Cypriot demands for assistance by creating a naval league, made up of his own, Venetian, and Cypriot forces. Although the fleet's numbers were modest, its commanders were able, and on 28 October 1344 the coalition forces succeeded in occupying the strategically important town of Smyrna on the Turkish shore of the Aegean.[2] Militarily far from overwhelming, the victory was nevertheless significant: after half a century of defeat at the hands of their Muslim opponents, the Christians had regained some degree of initiative, and the conquest of Smyrna breathed new life into the Crusade to the Holy Land.[3]

In the following years, the charismatic Peter of Lusignan, the second son of the king of Cyprus Hugh IV, harnessed resurgent enthusiasm for the Crusade and led the Christians to the most notable successes of the century. Impulsive and with a certain love of adventure,[4] he immediately began implementing a highly aggressive foreign policy when he ascended to the throne as Peter I in 1359. His receipt of the fortified coastal town of Gorigos on the south coast of Asia Minor from the Armenian king Leo V in 1360 offered him a base of operations from which to attack the neighboring Muslim powers. These— the most powerful Turkish ruler in Asia Minor, the Grand Qaraman Ibrahim Bey, as well as the smaller emirates of Alaya, Tekke, and Monovgat—assembled a sizable force with which to face this new threat on their shores.[5] The king of Cyprus struck first, however, and in 1361 he led a fleet of 126 ships against Adalia, or Satalia, a port city of vital importance to the emir of Tekke,[6] and took it with relative ease. The Muslim alliance collapsed, and the emirs of Monovgat and Alaya even went so far as to offer to accept Cypriot sovereignty and pay a yearly tribute.[7] More important, Peter's reputation as the true *athleta Christi* was made. This reputation would become increasingly significant the more Peter had to rely on Western money and manpower to continue his conquests.

There had always been foreigners among Peter's contingents;[8] however, Western participation in his campaigns was to rise dramatically after the Treaty of Brétigny in 1360. The treaty arranged an armistice in the Hundred Years' War between England and France and freed a whole generation experienced in and in many ways dependent on war from their commitments on the Continent.[9] It is unclear whether Peter targeted these specifically for recruitment, but he left Cyprus on 24 October 1362 to seek aid from the princes of Europe.[10] He was received magnificently wherever he went,[11] even winning the king of France John II to his cause,[12] and while the enthusiastic John died in May of the following year, to be succeeded by Charles V, who was not similarly inclined, there was no dearth of converts to the king of Cyprus's plans. When he finally returned to Cyprus he brought with him an army drawn from all over Europe, large enough to allow him to direct his attention to one of the Eastern Mediterranean's most radiant lights.[13] Alexandria on Egypt's Mediterranean coast was not expecting an attack. When the Crusader fleet first appeared in its Old Harbor on 9–10 October 1365,[14] the surprise was complete, and Alexandria fell easily; the whirlwind of plunder and death that followed was reminiscent of the fall of Jerusalem in 1099.[15]

Preoccupation with booty, however, prevented the Christian army from properly securing its conquest, which left the Crusaders in a precarious situation. With Mamluk reinforcements on the way and the army's thirst for plunder quenched, very few were willing to continue the fight, and under heavy protest from the king of Cyprus the decision to retreat was made.[16] Even though the Christian occupation of Alexandria was brief, it was an important psychological victory: one of the greatest cities of the Mediterranean world, the very heart of the Mamluk sultanate, had been taken and ravaged, with minimal losses, the vast wealth of its *funduqs* looted. Decisive action by a united Christianity against its Muslim adversary was shown still to be possible, and Peter's fame spread far and wide.[17]

The retreat from Alexandria did not stop Peter in his tracks. In November 1366, his fleet attacked and sacked Tripoli on the Syrian coast, and in June 1367 a similar assault was launched against Tortosa and Latakia.[18] The crusading zeal of the king of Cyprus ended only with his murder by some disaffected vassals in the early hours of 16 January 1369.[19] The failure to exploit the victory at Alexandria, the lackluster success of the campaign of Amadeo of Savoy of 1366–1367, and the murder of Peter I of Cyprus cost the Crusade the momentum it had built up over the preceding two and a half decades. Peter's actions had, however, left a lasting impression on the imagination of the Christian West. Even though the Crusade, lacking the energetic and purposeful leadership it needed, again ground to a halt in the years following Peter's death, his successes convinced much of the West that Crusade still was a cause worth pursuing. Foremost among these was Guillaume de Machaut, whose *Prise d'Alixandre* served to extol the king, his victories, and the Christian war against the Muslim.

MACHAUT'S MAGNUM OPUS

When, in the years after the death of Peter I of Cyprus, Guillaume de Machaut (ca. 1300–1377) composed *La Prise d'Alixandre*, he had already built an illustrious and very productive career, one that had turned him into "the most important French artist of his generation," a "pioneering musician and poet,"[20] who had won the patronage of some of the most prominent nobles of the time. Born at the beginning of the fourteenth century in Champagne into a family of little social standing,[21] he attended the cathedral school at Reims, and most likely studied theology at university.[22] Machaut quickly came to the attention of John of Luxembourg, the king of Bohemia, probably in the late teens or early twenties of the fourteenth century.[23] As his private secretary and confidant, Machaut accompanied the king on his campaigns and travels throughout Europe, at least until the early 1340s, when blindness forced the king to hand over most of his temporal power to his son. During these years Machaut composed his first great works, *Le Dit dou Vergier, Le Jugement dou Roy de Behaingne,* and *Le Remède de Fortune*.[24] After John of Luxembourg's death at the battle of Crécy in 1346, Machaut became attached first to the court of the king's daughter Bonne (to whom he dedicated the *Remède de Fortune,* and upon whom he may have modeled one of the characters in *Le Jugement dou Roy de Navarre*),[25] and then of Charles, nicknamed "the Bad," king of Navarre and count of Evreux. Machaut joined Charles the Bad's entourage probably in 1349 or 1350, almost immediately after the death of Bonne, and would stay by his side at least until the king's imprisonment in 1356 after a failed plot to murder his sovereign and father-in-law, the king of France.

Machaut's two great works of this period, *Le Jugement dou Roy de Navarre* and *Le Confort d'Ami,* frame their relationship as much as they reflect the varying fortunes of the king, the former a *dit* of amorous debates dated 9 November 1349,[26] the latter a prison poem probably written in October 1357, when Machaut's patron had been imprisoned for more than a year. While *Le Confort d'Ami* suggests that Machaut remained emotionally attached to Charles of Navarre throughout his imprisonment, in this period Machaut seems to have shifted his loyalties to the century's most prominent benefactor of the arts, John of Berry, brother to the French king.[27] Machaut's first work for his new patron resembled, at least in intent, the last one he had composed for Charles of Navarre: the *Fonteinne Amoureuse* was written as a consolation to John of Berry when he was a hostage in England after the Treaty of Brétigny in 1360. It is likely that Machaut became acquainted with Peter I of Cyprus around this time. Machaut was at Reims during the coronation of Charles V of France on 19 May 1364, an event also attended by Peter, who at that time was on his first European trip aimed at garnering support for his Crusade enterprises. Machaut appears to have developed an excellent rapport with him,[28] and the poet retained a lasting impression of the king as one of the great figures of his time, an impression that would translate into his last great poem.

La Prise d'Alixandre, which can be dated with fair certainty to the early 1370s,[29] has usually been understood as a chivalric biography of Peter of Lusignan. Probably written either for the French

king Charles V or the Holy Roman emperor Charles IV,[30] its 8,888
lines describe the full story of Peter's life and achievements, from his
birth to his European journeys in search of support, his campaigns
in the East, and his eventual murder.[31] Machaut seems to have based
his writing on the most accurate sources available to him, including letters, three of which he faithfully includes in his text, and the
testimony of informants.[32] Machaut's conscientious use of source
material and the triviality of his errors have earned great credibil-
ity for the *Prise*;[33] this has meant, on the one hand, that virtually
every scholar of the later Middle Ages has assigned pride of place to
Machaut's work among contemporary sources,[34] and, on the other,
that "because of its subject, critics have usually regarded the work
as more history than poem."[35] Few have approached the *Prise* as a
literary work;[36] consigning the work to the realm of historiography, scholars have very nearly ignored its merits as a poem, with an
internal dynamic or purpose that differentiates it from traditional
historical writing.

   D. G. Lanoue has argued that the *Prise*, rather than the merely
descriptive chivalric biography or historical work it is usually thought
to be, must be understood as an epic with a distinctly propagandistic
purpose.[37] In his view, the poem's opening sequence, a drawn-out,
almost mythological description of Peter I of Cyprus's birth, sets it
outside traditional historiographical writing;[38] no mere chronicle, the
Prise instead proffers a heroic epic that the Christian world would do
well to imitate:

> The fact that Alexandria, "civitas prepotens et opulentissima," fell to a
> small and outnumbered contingent of Christian knights, had enormous
> symbolic value for Machaut's contemporaries and certainly fanned the
> flame of crusading fervour in subsequent years. For a poet setting out
> to write a panoramic historical epic in 1370 or thereabouts, the recent
> conquest of Alexandria would have provided a subject charged with
> emotional and political connotations. . . . If Machaut's epic is read as
> an instructive mirror for courtly audiences of the 1370s, his portrayal
> of Peter's crusade appears obviously significant. In the first place, the
> poet's decision to elevate Peter of Lusignan to the status of epic hero
> has clear political ramifications. A knight who avoided involving
> himself in the internecine fighting within Christendom, Peter instead
> fought vigorously against what was perceived at the time to be the
> common enemy. Viewed as a chivalric model, Machaut's hero answers
> the contemporary need for Christian unity in the face of the Turk's
> escalating encroachments throughout the century.[39]

Lanoue therefore suggests that Machaut intended the tale (and the extraordinarily flattering portrait) of Peter of Lusignan to draw people away from the struggles within Europe and back to the holy war against the infidel. The work was thus meant to propagate the Crusade as much as to illustrate a worthy life; as the text was written for either Charles V of France or the emperor Charles IV, this message must have been aimed at the halls of power. The image of the ideal Crusader Machaut propagates in the *Prise* is, however, far from traditional, and earlier centuries would not likely have approved of it.

La Prise d'Alixandre begins with an almost mythological description of the birth of Peter I of Cyprus, who was put on this world with a very specific purpose. In the earliest lines, Mars is found to bemoan the passing of his champions, the Nine Worthies:

mi bon et chier amy sont mort
et fine par piteuse mort
ce sont li bons rois alixandres
qui conquist angleterre et flandres
et tant quist terre et mer parfonde
quil fu signeur de tout le monde
hector et cesar julius
et puis judas machabeus
david . josue . charlemainne
et artus qui ot moult de peinne
et dux godefroy de buillon
qui par son or et son billon
son sens . sa force . et sa vaillance
et de son grant bien lexcellence
mist toute en sa subjection
la terre de promission
ou au mains la plus grant partie
en la fin y laissa la vie

[ll. 45–62: My virtuous and good friends now all lie cold / And finished by a pitiful death. / These are the good king Alexander, / Who conquered England and Flanders, / And campaigned through so much of earth and ocean / He became lord of all the world; / Hector and Julius Caesar, / And afterward Judah Maccabee; / David, Joshua, Charlemagne, / And Arthur, who suffered mightily, / And Duke Godfrey of Bouillon, / Who, through his gold and wealth, / His cunning, his power, his valor, / And the excellence of his great virtue, / Made subject to him / All of the promised land, / Or at least its greater part; / There in the end he laid down his life.]

The present time sees the world without the blessing of a great man, but Mars does not stop at that. Godfrey's conquest of the Holy Land carries with it an ethical imperative:

> si deveriens tuit labourer
> au bon godefroy restorer
> et querir homme qui sceust
> maintenir sa terre et deust

> [ll. 63–66: Thus we must, all of us, struggle / To restore his land to noble Godfrey / And seek out some man who has the power / And the duty to maintain that domain.]

This challenge may not have been lost on Machaut's audience, but of course Mars is addressing the pantheon. His fellow gods agree and implore Nature to create the being perfectly suited to achieving the reconquest of the Holy Land. Nature obeys, and she decides that this perfect Crusader should be made from the conjunction of two gods: "lors de mars et venus ensamble / fist conjunction ce me samble" [ll. 73–74: "To do so she effected a conjunction / Of Mars and Venus, it seems"]. This preamble already sets out the main lines of what Machaut suggests the ideal Crusader to be: the man whom the gods have predestined to free the Holy Land is a combination of Mars and Venus, a fighter as well as a lover. Given such auguries, Peter of Lusignan cannot but develop into the consummate fighter and lover of his age, and Machaut repeatedly highlights the Cypriot king's amorousness and martial ability. Peter developed an interest in the opposite sex fairly early on:

> quant il ot laage de .ix. ans
> que de norrice fu exens
> et laissa lestat de innocence
> et prist a avoir congnoissance
> toutes ses inclinations
> et ses ymaginations
> tuit si penser tuit si desir
> furent en faire le plaisir
> de dames et de damoiselles
> moult li furent plaisans et belles

> [ll. 263–78: After he reached the age of nine / And quit his nurse, / And left behind the state of innocence / And he began to have understanding, / All of his inclinations, / All of what he imagined, / All his thoughts, all his desires / Were directed toward what would afford pleasure / To ladies and young women. / These he found very appealing and attractive.]

When Peter goes on his first great journey to Europe to garner support for his Crusade enterprise, his amorousness follows him. He is graciously received by the household of the Holy Roman emperor:

> la fu liement receus
> honnourez . servis . et veus
> fu delles en fais et en dis
> que ce li sambloit paradis

[ll. 1133–36: There he was joyfully received, / Honored, served, and looked after / By the women, in both word and deed, / And so he thought this paradise itself.]

The king's presence in fact inflames the court of the emperor, as we are told: "mais il ni avoit nesun deus / ne delles . qui chiere joieuse / neust . et pensee amoureuse" [ll. 1184–86: "Yet there was not a single man / Or lady who was not pleased / And had thoughts of romance"]. The thought of love will follow this son of Venus wherever he goes, be it in Christendom or beyond.

Also on this journey, Peter's martial prowess comes prominently into play, especially his jousting ability. Throughout the description of his journey through Europe, we are told that none was his match:

> et quant il estoit bien armez
> bien montez et bien acesmes
> la lance eu pong lescut au col
> il ni avoit sage ne fol
> qui ne deist a grant murmure
> cil roys fu nez en larmeure
> tant estoit gens . joins . lons et drois
> hardis puissans en tous endrois
> jamais ne refusast nelui
> a peinnes veoit on que lui
> car il estoit toudis errans
> puis ci puis la dessus les rans
> il sen venoit lance sous fautre
> sabatoit lun ci et la lautre
> encontre lui riens ne duroit
> de son bien chascuns murmuroit
> et se seingnoit de la merveille
> chascuns de son bien se merveille
> et je meismes men merveil
> quant a li pense et je mesviel

[ll. 855–74: And whenever he was fully armed, / Well mounted, with his equipment in order, / The lance in his fist, the shield around his neck, / There was no one, wise man or fool, / Who didn't say and loudly: / "The king was born in his armor." / He was so noble, elegant, tall, and straight, / Brave, powerful in every respect. / He refused combat to no man. / In fact, it was difficult to glimpse him / Because the man was always on the move, / First here, then there, in the lists. / He rode with his lance mounted, / Threw down one man here, then another there. / No one could stand up to him. / Everyone spoke of his virtue, / And crossed themselves for the miracle's sake. / Every man found his virtue remarkable, / And I marvel myself about all this / When I think about him, and I am moved.]

Excellence on the battlefield and amorous prowess are of course only to be expected of the son of Mars and Venus, and it is also what we can probably expect to find in a chivalric biography of this type. It is remarkable, however, that so much of the description of Peter's qualities closely echoes romance. On the one hand, "his string of first prizes in tournaments recalls similar achievements in romance by Lancelot, Gawain, Partenopus de Blois, Amadas, Gliglois, Guilhem de Nevers, the Châtelain de Couci, and others."[40] Even his grand tour of the banquet halls and bedrooms of Europe seems to follow a certain romance pattern. While traveling, "Peter and his friends consciously seek to maintain an atmosphere of pomp and elegance, to live up to the highest ideals of romance found in books";[41] they travel from place to place, and everywhere there is love to be found in the arms of the castellan's daughter, or even in the arms of the daughter of the Holy Roman emperor.

This brings us to a second aspect of Machaut's description of Peter I of Cyprus. For if his ideal Crusader is described first and foremost as a son of the classical tradition, he also appears to be in some sense a romance character. Beyond these two allusions to romance and the Arthurian paradigm, a third may be found in the fact that it takes the poet almost fourteen hundred lines to reveal that he is indeed speaking of the man who "de chipre et de jherusalem / fu roys . pierre lappella lem" [ll. 1394–95: "Of Cyprus and of Jerusalem / He was the king; Pierre was he named"]. This echoes the Arthurian "unknown knight" motif found in, among other works, the *Chevalier de la Charrette*, where Lancelot's name is withheld until line 3661; in Renaut of Beaujeu's *Li Biaus Descouneüs*, where the eponymous hero is only identified as Guinglain halfway through the work; and in *Sir Gawain and the Green Knight*, where we find the name of Gawain's magical opponent, Bertilak of Hautdesert, only in the final verses of the poem. Machaut may therefore set Peter up as a romance *bel inconnu*. We find a fourth specific allusion to Arthurian romance in that the king of Cyprus is surrounded by councilors whom Machaut himself associates with Arthurian heroes. Also fighting on the beach at Alexandria are Peter's two trusted advisers:

> Aussi perceval de coulongne
> qui a basti ceste besongne
> moult hardiement se combat
> quan quil ataint tue et abat
> riens nest qui contre ses cops dure
> sespee qui est bonne et dure
> et taillant . scet bien mettre en ouevre
> bien se deffent et bien se cuevre
> nil ne doubte mort ne prison
> fors deshonneur et mesprison
> . . .
> Messires bremons de la vote
> estoit la com chastiaus sus mote
> fors . et fermes . et deffensables
> plus que gauvains li combatables

[ll. 2381–96: And in addition Perceval of Coulonges, / Who had conceived their plan, / Fought with much courage as well; / He slew and cut down whatever man he reached. / None could endure under his strokes. / His sword, which is good and strong / And sharp, knew quite readily what to do. / He defended and protected himself well. / The man feared neither death nor capture, / Only dishonor and ignominy. / . . . / My lord Brémont de la Voulte / Like a castle above a moat there stood firm; / Strong, secure, and able in the defense, / Surpassing even the warrior Gawain.]

The scene presents us with two of Peter's subjects and associates who, we are told, truly resemble Arthur's knights, fighting side by side with their king. One through monumental coincidence is named Perceval, while Machaut associates the other with Gawain, thereby drawing both the knights and their lord into the Arthurian realm.[42] Insofar as the king of Cyprus is depicted as Arthurian, his excursions and campaigns away from his native island are presented as adventures or even quests.[43] Peter of Cyprus is therefore not only the son of Mars and Venus; Machaut also intended his ideal Crusader to be seen as an Arthur-like character, a romance hero seeking adventure, devoted as much to ladies as to the idea of Crusade.

The desire for love and the commitment to Crusade, the two aspects that drive Peter forward, are brought together in the dynamic of honor that permeates the work. Throughout the *Prise*, Machaut presents Peter I of Cyprus, the ideal Crusader, as preoccupied almost ad absurdum with honor;[44] honor within the context of the Crusade is, however, not a goal by itself in Machaut's writings. In a passage in the *Dit dou Lion* where Machaut describes the virtues of taking the cross, he talks about those knights who never catch the eyes of ladies:

> Lors s'en aloient outre mer
> En Chypre, en terre de Labour,
> A grans frais et à grand labour,
> Pour demourer deux ans ou trois.
> Ci cerchoient tous les destrois
> Du païs et des aventures,
> Dont ils avoient de moult dures.
> Si qu'il estoient si vassaux
> Ès batailles et ès assaus,
> Et si fiers en trestout fais d'armes,
> Que les nouvelles a leurs dames
> De leur entreprise venoient;
> Dont assez plus chier les tenoient.
> Et quant estoient revenu,
> Les dames souvent et menu
> Les appelloient doucement
> Et prioient courtoisement
> Que leur deissent des nouvelles.
> . . .
> Et quant venoit au congié prendre,
> Il n'estoient pas à aprendre.
> Ains disoient: savez comment,
> Ma dame, à vous me recommant.
> Vous povez seur moy commander
> Et moy penre, sans demander:
> Car vostre sui entièrement
> Pour faire vo commandement,
> A tant s'en partoient de la.
> Après chascuns disoit: vela
> Celui qui vainqui la bataille
> Entre Illande et Cornuaille.
> L'autre disoit: par Saint Thomas!
> Mais plus il revient de Damas
> D'Anthioche ou de Damiette.
> Et d'Escauvaire ou Dieu Mori
> Tout droit, et de Jherusalem.
> Dieu pri qu'il le gart de mal an!
> Car s'il vit, s'iert ans Alexandres.
> —Aussi fust il en Alexandres,
> Dit l'autre, et ou mont de Synay.
> —Et l'autre disoit; si n'ay
> Homme, qui à li se compert,

Ne dont tant de bien nous appert;
Car il fu jusqu'à l'Arbre sec
Oû li oisel pendent au bec.

[Then they went across the sea, to Cyprus, to the land of suffering,
at great cost and effort, to stay there for two or three years. There
they sought out all the corners of the land and adventures, of which
they had many difficult ones. And they were so bold in battles and
assaults, and so proud in all manner of deeds of arms, that the news
of their exploits came to their ladies; which made these think more
highly of them. And when they came back, the ladies often discreetly
called them, and courteously asked them to tell them some news. . . .
And when it came to saying goodbye, there was nothing they still
had to learn. And so they said: "Know how much I consign myself
to you, my lady. You can command me, and hang me without asking: because I am entirely yours, to do what you want." And when
they left there, afterwards everyone said: "See there the one who won
the battle between Ireland and Cornwall." The other said: "By St.-
Thomas! What's more, he has just returned from Damascus, from
Antioch or Damietta, and straight from Calvary where God died,
and from Jerusalem. May God guard him from misfortune. Because
if he lives, he will be an Alexander."—"He also was in Alexandria,"
says the other, "and on Mount Sinai"—And the other said: "There is
no man that compares to him, nor to whom we owe so much good;
because he has been to the Dry Tree, where the birds hang from their
beaks."][45]

The knights' exploits have won them honor and renown; men sing
their praises when they see them walking by, and women learn of
their great deeds. The honor won in the *Dit dou Lion* is the same as
the one that motivates virtually all the action in the *Prise*. This honor
is not just its own reward; a knight's honor, even when won on Crusade, rather more importantly works as an emollient with the opposite sex. Honor, love, and war are therefore elegantly interwoven, and
form the triangular framework upon which Crusade rests in the *Prise*.
    We therefore find, in a text that quite probably was meant to prop-
agate the Crusade as much as to relate recent history, a portrait of the
ideal man for reconquering the Holy Land: Peter I of Cyprus is the
son of Mars and Venus, an outstanding fighter and a man devoted
from early age to the art of love, and also a quasi-Arthurian figure of
romance, looking for adventure in order to gain the honor that will
bring him the respect of man and lady alike. The battlefields of the
Crusade are then the places par excellence on which to bring all of
this to bear. The passage from the *Dit dou Lion* above offers insight

into Machaut's attitude toward the Crusade venture: the Crusade is a crucible, a proving ground where one can find the adventure necessary to gain honor and love. To a certain extent therefore, in the *Dit*, Machaut turns the holy war into just another adventure, shorn of the spiritual value it was granted in previous centuries. Machaut presents the Crusade in similar terms in the *Prise*: the Crusade frontier will be where adventure is found, honor won, and ladies and love served. Indeed, Machaut intimates that these things more than anything else were on Peter's mind during the conquest of Alexandria; when the king is unable to prevent the Crusaders from withdrawing after the fall of the city,

> lors dist . *honneur . amours . et dames*
> *que direz vous quant vous verrez*
> *ces gens qui sont si esserrez*
> *certes jamais naront honnour*
> *par droit . fors toute deshonnour .*
> . . .
> Li roys monta en sa galee
> a cuer triste a face esplouree
> trop fu courcies trop fu dolens
> il navoit dalixandre a lens
> personne qui fust si dolente
> il se complaint il se demente
> des yex pleure dou cuer souspire
> homs vivans ne vous saroit dire
> son meschief . trop se desconforte
> et dist *honneur or yes tu morte*
> *certes dou tout perdu tavons*
> *sans recouvrer . biens le savons*

[ll. 3558–84: Then he said: "*Honor, love and ladies! / What will you say when you see / These men drawn up here in their ranks? / Surely they will never have any claim / On honor but complete dishonor instead.*" / . . . / The king embarked on his galley, / His heart heavy, his face covered with tears. / He was quite angry and full of sorrow. / There was no man this miserable / From Alexandria to Lens. / He bemoaned his lot, he went mad, / Crying from his eyes, sighing from the heart. / No man alive could describe / His misfortune; he was quite disconsolate / And said: "*Honor, now you lie dead! / Surely we've forfeited you for good; / We'll never regain you—well we know it*" (my italics).]

Seeing a great Crusade victory snatched away from him, Machaut's Peter does not resort to theological arguments; what he really laments is the honor that is lost, and the ladies and love that remain unserved.

Moreover, it is not only in Peter that Crusade, honor, and love are associated: Machaut shows that those who fight alongside the king of Cyprus do so for similar reasons. Fighting among Peter's troops is a certain Jean of Biauvillier, "qui moult amoit / armes . honneur . honneste vie / et croy quil avoit belle amie" [ll. 5880–82: "who loved arms, / Honor, and honest living very much, / And I believe he had a pretty lady"]. Those who storm the gates of Alexandria are similarly described:

> la li assaus recommensa
> la li plus couars savansa
> la se moustra chevalerie
> la vit on qui avoit amie
> la chascuns si bien le faisoit
> qua dieu et au monde plaisoit

> [ll. 2883–88: There the assault began again; / There even the biggest coward moved forward; / There chivalry displayed itself; / *There were seen those with lovers*; / There every man did so well / It pleased God and the whole world" (my italics).]

Here the battlefields of the Crusade are once again where honor can be found and ladies can be served. They are a proving ground where knights can test their mettle, a place where one can find romance adventure. Machaut presents his notion of the Crusade-as-adventure as complementary to the traditional notion of the Crusade as service to God. In the above passage, the amorous knights before Alexandria fight so well that "it pleased God and the whole world." Their love service is not seen as replacing or in any way compromising the service they owe God; rather, the one continues where the other leaves off or, even better, they are one and the same. Peter places service to God and the quest for personal honor on the same level when he seeks advice: "or me donnez votre conseil / si bon . que dieux y ait honnour / et nous ni aiens deshonnour" [ll. 2632–34: "Give me counsel now good enough / To bring God honor / And permit us to avoid shame"]. And just so does Brémont of la Voulte associate the cause of God with that of one's own honor when he tells his men that

> je vous menray procheinnement
> en tele place et en tel lieu
> contre les anemis de dieu
> que je ne say nen mer nen terre
> si bon lieu pour honneur conquerre

[ll. 3698–702: Soon I will lead you / Into a place and country /
Against the enemies of God / Like no other I know on sea or land /
No destination better for the winning of honor.][46]

Machaut therefore makes common cause of the religious and romance
functions of the Crusade in the *Prise*: fighting in the East not only
serves God and satisfies his honor, it also demonstrates personal honor
and elevates one's standing with the female sex. As a consequence, he
adds an altruistic veneer to an essentially selfish value system.

Guillaume de Machaut, writing in the third quarter of the fourteenth century, describes the Crusade and Crusaders in recognizable
terms: here, too, Crusade and romance are identified. From the beginning we know that the ideal Crusader, the man devised by nature to
liberate the Holy Land, must not merely be a pious warrior concerned
with the salvation of his soul and the restitution of Christ's inheritance: he must also be an almost Arthurian character concerned not
merely with love and adventure but with the honor that will earn him
acclaim and status. Not only Peter but also the rank and file of his
army fight not merely for their faith but equally for their ladies and
honor. In Machaut's form of Crusade propaganda, there is no political or religious urgency or necessity to the Crusade, and there is little
that is truly holy about holy war.

Conclusion

A Christian soldier, a devoted lover, could fear nothing, think of
nothing, but his duty to Heaven, and his devoir to his lady.
—Sir Walter Scott, *The Talisman* (1825)

Both the initial successes of the Crusade and the failures and defeats
that beset it in the following centuries required continued recruitment of new fighters for the holy war. The Levantine principalities
that arose after the First Crusade of 1096–1099 needed a continuous
flow of men and money to maintain their precarious independence on
the edge of the Islamic world. As they crumbled under the military
might of their Muslim neighbors, yet more volunteers were needed,
first to halt the advance of the enemy and recover what was lost, and
eventually also to weaken him elsewhere and so expedite the eventual
triumph. As I have demonstrated, the long duration of the need for
recruitment forced those advocating continued Christian engagement
in Crusade to be creative. Although Crusade was always a primarily
religious undertaking, propagandists invoked a range of other interests in seeking to convince Latin Christians to take the cross. Insofar
as the chivalric aristocracy was, from the very beginning, the most
important audience of their appeals, these other interests were above
all those that mattered to knights.

The chansons de geste and chivalric romance addressed the central
concerns of knighthood and were popular among aristocratic audiences, providing an effective tool for propagandists seeking to cast the
net of persuasion beyond the appeal to individual piety. In the decade
after the fall of Jerusalem in 1099, historiographical works that propagated the holy war turned to the chansons, vernacular songs that
frequently depicted confrontations between Christian Franks and
non-Christian Saracens, to urge their audience to continue what the

First Crusaders had set in motion. The *Gesta Francorum*, an eyewitness account of the events of 1096–1099 completed by early 1101, utilized the formal and thematic characteristics of the chansons to depict the Crusaders as new Franks and the Crusade as a continuation of the wars of Charlemagne; as such, its anonymous author not only proposed additional justification for the Christian conquest of much of the Middle East but also provided a motivation to fight that extended beyond the goals of the First Crusade. Within a decade, Robert of Reims reworked the *Gesta Francorum*, including a new theological approach to the Crusade and also extending the imprint of the chansons. The *Historia Iherosolimitana* (ca. 1106–1107) depicted the French as a new Israel whose actions carried the divine imprimatur; this national exceptionalism turned *all* the wars of the French into holy wars—a message especially useful for ambitious men such as Bohemond of Taranto, who sought to expand his dominion into the Christian Byzantine Empire. In the later twelfth century, when papal Crusade appeals called upon the Latin West to follow in the footsteps of its ancestors, the chansons' preoccupation with warfare between extended families and duty to kin groups again made them useful. Redacted in the wake of the conquest of much of the Crusader states by the forces of Saladin—a sequence of events with terrible theological implications—the works of the First Old French Crusade Cycle (late twelfth or early thirteenth century), which adopted the form of chansons, again related the events of the First Crusade. Urging their audience to undo the Muslim advance, they depicted the Crusade as a conflict between spiritual and secular kin groups, participation in which is a duty owed as much to earthly family as it is to God.

The later Middle Ages saw Crusade propaganda turn also to chivalric romance, a genre that developed alongside the chansons de geste in the last quarter of the twelfth century and devoted more attention to amorous desire, the service of ladies, and individual adventure in faraway lands. Though its interest in sinful—for extramarital—courtly love at first limited its use in Crusade propaganda, writers who sought to exhort their audience to take the cross increasingly utilized the commonplaces of romance to present the holy war as a journey of chivalric self-realization, an opportunity to prove one's qualities on the farthest edges of the Christian world. Nicolaus of Jeroschin, who composed the *Krônike von Prûzinlant* (ca. 1331–1344) as part of the propaganda effort of the Teutonic Order, portrayed his order's long wars in the Baltic as divinely sanctioned adventures in which Christians could free aristocratic damsels from the grasp of the unbeliever, entwining piety and courtliness in his appeal to Western chivalry. The works of the Second Old French Crusade Cycle further developed Nicolaus's identification of the Crusade frontier with a romance otherworld; *Baudouin de Sébourc* and *Le Bâtard de Bouillon* (ca. 1350–1370) do not differentiate between Crusade and adventure, and the latter locates Avalon and Arthur's court in the southern Levant and Egypt. By the end of the fourteenth century, Guillaume de Machaut's *La Prise d'Alixandre* (completed in the early 1370s) depicted the ideal Crusader as son to both Mars and Venus, a heroic figure who is both lover and fighter, and who sets out for the East as much to satiate his thirst for adventure as to fight his Lord's battles.

As this book has demonstrated, for the better part of three centuries historiographical works that propagated the Crusade appropriated the genre characteristics of chivalric literature to spur their audience to action. Writing in both Latin and the vernacular, from the Middle East to the Baltic and northern France, their authors turned to both chansons de geste and chivalric romance to complement the appeal to individual piety and present Western chivalry with secular motivations to take the cross. Although I have focused on the excitatoria themselves and not on audience reception of their message, the often great popularity of the works suggest that their presentation of the Crusade was an appealing one. It affected the way some Western audiences thought of the holy war: for instance, the new ideal of the Crusader as both adventurer and courtly lover propagated in the fourteenth century was widespread enough for some of the most important contemporary thinkers to comment on it. I pointed out at the beginning of this book John Gower's bitter complaints, in both *Mirour de l'Omme* (ca. 1376–1379) and *Confessio Amantis* (ca. 1386–1390). Geoffrey Chaucer, a friend of Gower, weighed in as well. Already in his first major poetic work, *The Book of the Duchess* (ca. 1369–1372), Chaucer's Black Knight praises the White Lady for having the good grace not to make excessive demands of her suitors:

Hyr lust to holde no wyght in honde,
Ne, be thou siker, she wolde not fonde
To holde no wyght in balaunce
By half word ne by countenaunce—
But if men wolde upon hir lye—
Ne sende men into Walakye,
To Pruyse, and into Tartarye,
To Alysaundre, ne into Turkye,

And byd hym faste anoon that he
Goo hoodles into the Drye Se
And come hom by the Carrenar,
And seye, "Sir, be now ryght war
That I may of yow here seyn
Worshyp or that ye come ageyn!"
She ne used no suche knakkes smale.[1]

Wallachia, Prussia, Alexandria, and Turkey saw intense Crusade activity in the second half of the fourteenth century; Tartary, or the Mongol Empire, was considered a possible ally against the joint Muslim enemy, and the hope of Christian–Mongol cooperation was "the persistent theme of fourteenth-century crusading propaganda circulating in the West."[2] The Black Knight of *The Book of the Duchess* is therefore praising his Lady for not requiring that men go to the battlefields of the holy war to win her approval. This compliment could have meant something only if Chaucer's audience knew ladies who *did* make such demands as well as men who set out to win their love on the Crusade frontier.

For his part, Chaucer represented those crusading lovers in the character of the Squire in his great work of late-medieval social commentary, the *Canterbury Tales* (ca. 1388–1400). The Squire, who follows his father, the Knight, a rather more old-fashioned Crusader,[3] on the Canterbury pilgrimage, is said to have participated in the "chyvacie / In Flaundres, in Artoys, and Pycardie," better known as Bishop Despenser's Crusade of 1383, "in hope to stonden in his lady grace."[4] His Tale, set at the court of Genghiz Khan "in the land of Tartarye,"[5] elegantly intertwines Crusade and romance. It speaks of a magical ring that allows the wearer to understand the birds, a sword that both heals and kills, a mirror that provides insight into the minds of men, and a flying horse made of brass; discusses the heartbreak of a lovesick falcon; and if completed (which it mercifully was not) would have depicted to its audience Cambalo's fight to win the affections of his sister Canacee. This world of magic and love is, however, also identified as the Crusade frontier, and the Squire's narrative is riddled with references to the holy war. The magical gifts are sent to the court of Cambyuskan by "the kyng of Arabe and of Inde,"[6] who has been identified as either the sultan of the Mamluk Empire, which crushed the last remnants of the Crusader states,[7] or Prester John, the shadowy, powerful Christian ruler beyond the lands of the Saracens, who, it was rumored, sought to join the Latins to liberate the Holy Places.[8] Furthermore, the falcon, mourning the loss of her paramour the tercel,

does so on a tree "for drye as whit as chalk."[9] This Dry Tree is important in Crusader iconology; its return to health would signify the final
victory of the Crusaders over their opponents in the Holy Land. Sir
John Mandeville finds it two miles from Hebron: "And som prophecie
seith that a prince, lord of the west syde of the worlde, shal come and
wynne the Londe of Promission with the help of Cristen men. And he
shal do synge a messe under the drie tre, and hit shal wexe grene and
bere fruyt and leves. And by that miracle many Sarysynes and Jewes
and other shal be turned to Cristen feythe."[10] The Dry Tree, so legend
had it, would quite literally bear the fruit of the Crusaders' efforts,
and it is not without irony that Chaucer transforms it into the perch
of a lovesick bird. Finally, the Squire would have Cambalo fight for
Canacee "in lystes with the bretheren two."[11] Haldeen Braddy has
pointed out that Chaucer most likely knew of the episode, described
in the *Anonimalle Chronicle* for the year 1377, in which one English
knight successfully took the field against two Indian brothers, who
had come to Spain to disprove the Christian faith through combat.[12]
In other words, whereas Gower complained about knights becoming
Crusaders for all the wrong reasons, Chaucer shows us one such in
the *Canterbury Tales*: a Squire who takes the cross to win the favor of
his beloved, and whose Tale takes place in a land that is both th*e terre
d'aventures* of chivalric romance and the frontier between Christendom and Islam.

Chaucer's and Gower's comments on the Crusade evince the effec-
tiveness of late medieval Crusade propaganda, which associated the
holy war with chivalric romance. By the end of the fourteenth century, a new generation of knights had come to think of Crusade as an
act of love service to ladies, performed in a faraway land of magic and
adventure. However, even successful propaganda could not guarantee
the triumph of Latin Christianity over its adversaries; rather, it may
have contributed to the utter ruin of the Levantine Crusade. After a
half century marked by early successes and increasing involvement on
the part of the Western European aristocracy, the fourteenth-century
Crusade to the Holy Land came to a brutal end in 1396, only a few
years after Gower and Chaucer wrote.

From the middle of the fourteenth century on, ever-growing numbers
of Ottoman Turks had begun crossing the Bosporus, putting increasing pressure on the Catholic kingdoms of the Balkan; the defeat of the
Serbs at Cernomen (1371) and Kosovo Polje (1389) left the Turks at the
gates of Hungary. The Hungarian king Sigismund sent out embassies

requesting help from the Catholic princes of the West and found a receptive audience,[13] above all in Pope Boniface IX (1389–1404)[14] and Philip the Bold, the ambitious duke of Burgundy.[15] A magnificent army, consisting of the best Western chivalry had to offer, was raised: some ten thousand French and Burgundians, a thousand English and six thousand Germans, under the command of the duke's son John of Nevers. Together with thirteen thousand Styrians, Bohemians, Poles, and Italians, sixty thousand Hungarians, and ten thousand Wallachians, the Crusader forces combined to form an enormous army perhaps one hundred thousand strong.[16] Even if that number is exaggerated, the army was probably the greatest Crusader force seen for centuries.[17]

The assembled armies moved toward the Turkish frontier and enjoyed some initial successes at Widdin and Rahova, two outposts that they overcame easily. The first significant obstacle they faced was the fortified town of Nicopolis; the Crusaders laid siege, but having neglected to bring the equipment necessary to take the town by force, the army resorted to starve the garrison into submission. This was necessarily a slow process, during which discipline quickly deteriorated, especially among the younger members of the Franco-Burgundian contingent;[18] like the Squire, they spent their time dancing, feasting, and reveling in outward splendor. Thus did these young knights lead the Christians to disaster. When the Ottoman sultan Bayezid finally appeared to reinforce Nicopolis, their desire for worldly honor got the better of them, and they insisted on being the first to attack the Turks.[19] To reach Bayezid's main force, however, they had to fight through two sheltering cordons of lightly armed troops; when they finally reached their goal, the Ottoman cavalry quickly defeated them in their depleted condition.[20] The flower of Western crusading chivalry was destroyed, a defeat that sent almost as great a shudder through Latin Christianity as had the fall of Acre a century earlier.[21] Now, however, the effect was different: rather than provoking a deep grudge against the Saracens and igniting a burning desire to recapture the Holy Places, this defeat sapped the Western will to continue the struggle.[22] The earth that swallowed the Christian army at Nicopolis took with it almost three hundred years of Crusade to the Middle East.

The *idea* of Crusade, however, survived this devastation. Fighting in Spain persisted with undiminished zeal, and the German Order continued to be a powerful force in the Baltic even after the expansion of the Ordenstaat was checked at Tannenberg.[23] Furthermore,

Crusade was invoked whenever, over the following centuries, Christian powers confronted their non-Christian neighbors. As the rhetoric of Crusade endured (even if it was applied to wars that had little to do with the conquest of the Holy Land) so did the romance notion of holy war that saw Crusaders fighting both for the faith and for love on battlefields brimming with adventure. We find it, for instance, in Torquato Tasso's *Gerusalemme Liberata*, written almost two hundred years later, during the incessant wars between the Christian nations of Europe and the Ottoman Empire.[24]

In the years after the Battle of Nicopolis, the Ottomans continued their expansion unabated. Their armies swept across the Balkans, conquered Belgrade in 1521, and besieged Vienna in 1529 and 1532;[25] their navies controlled the Eastern Mediterranean and vied for supremacy with Christian maritime powers such as Venice, Portugal, and Spain. Successful military resistance against the Ottoman ascendancy was rare, but the empire's growing power was finally halted at the siege of Malta (1565) and, a few years later, at the Battle of Lepanto (1571). Both Christian victories reignited Christian hope in the face of the Ottoman juggernaut: on Malta, the island stronghold of the Order of the Hospital, a numerically superior Turkish enemy had been decisively defeated, while the great naval engagement near Lepanto saw a united Holy League of Christian forces comprehensively destroy the Ottoman fleet.[26]

Tasso completed *Gerusalemme Liberata* only a few years after the Battle of Lepanto, in 1575.[27] The avowed purpose of Tasso's poem, which sought to rival Ludovico Ariosto's epic *Orlando Furioso*,[28] is one familiar by now: to incite Western Europe to continue the war against its Muslim adversaries, which had taken so bright a turn in the preceding years. Tasso addressed his patron, Alfonso of Este, the duke of Ferrara, as follows:

È ben ragion, s'egli avverrà ch'in pace
il buon popol di Cristo unqua si veda
e con navi e cavalli al fero Trace
cerchi ritôr la grande ingiusta preda,
ch'a te lo scretto in terra, o se ti piace,
l'alto imperio de' mari a te conceda.
Emulo di Goffredo, i nostri carmi
in tanto ascolta e t'apparecchia a l'armi.

[It well accords with reason that, if at peace / Christ's holy folk should find itself some day, / ready to make the fierce Thracian

release, / by force of ships and steeds, his unjust prey, / Earth's sceptre
should be yours or, if you please, / yours on the seas the undisputed
sway. / Meanwhile, be you as Godfrey was of yore. / Attend my song
and gird yourself for war.][29]

If the goal of *Gerusalemme Liberata* is to move his audience to emulate Godfrey of Bouillon and continue the holy war against the "fierce
Thracian" or Turk, Tasso uses a tried and tested touchstone to do
so—the successful First Crusade, of which the *Gesta Francorum*,
Historia Iherosolimitana, and First Old French Crusade Cycle had
spoken before, and for which he drew material from the *Historia* of
William of Tyre.[30]

In Tasso's hands the history of the First Crusade is transformed
into an impassioned "heroic poem"[31] in which the Crusaders, both
pious knights and courtly lovers, must fight not to be swept away by
the magic and adventure with which the Holy Land overflows. Tasso's army of the First Crusade adds to the historical ranks of Godfrey, Bohemond, and Tancred the rather more fantastical figures of
Rinaldo, Dudon, and the band known as "gli avventurieri" ["the
Adventurers.]"[32] As the army advances from Antioch to Jerusalem,
the Crusaders' amorousness quickly threatens to distract them from
their goals. Tancred falls in love with the Saracen warrior Clorinda,
whom he first sights near a well:

> Quivi a lui d'improviso una donzella
> tutta, fuor che la fronte, armata apparse:
> era pagana, e là venuta anch'ella
> per l'istessa cagion di ristorarse.
> Egli mirolla ed ammirò la bella
> sembianza, e d'essa si compiacque e n'arse.
> Oh maraviglia! Amor ch'a pena è nato,
> già grande vola e già trionfa armato.

> [There, all at once, appeared to him a maid, / clad in full armour, all
> except her face. / Pagan she was. She too had sought the shade / to
> find, like him, refreshment in that place. / He saw her. He admired.
> He surveyed / her fair semblance. He burned for it apace. / O marvel-
> lous! Love, scarcely born, takes wing, / at once full grown, in arms,
> and triumphing!][33]

He relentlessly pursues his heroic beloved, on and off the battlefield;
his ardent love turns into mourning when he mistakenly kills her after
she has burned the Christian siege tower before the walls of Jerusalem. Furthermore, the Saracen sorceress Armida,[34] sent to sow discord

among the Christians, seduces Rinaldo. Originally intending to kill him, she instead falls in love with him and, Circe-like, takes him to the Fortunate Isles, whence he must be saved by Charles and Hubald. Only after his escape from the control of Armida, and the end of Tancred's preoccupation with Clorinda, are the Christian forces, reunited under common purpose, able to conquer Jerusalem.

Like fourteenth-century Crusade propaganda, *Gerusalemme Liberata* therefore imagines the Holy Land as a realm of love, magic, and adventure. In Tasso's work—Crusade propaganda for a different era—the Crusade frontier has added menace: although the Crusaders are lovers and adventurers in their own right, the land itself threatens to drown them in their amorousness and divert them from their conquest. That threat can be averted only by turning love into conquest. Like the Saracen princesses of the Second Old French Crusade Cycle, the women of *Gerusalemme Liberata* are won for Christianity. Clorinda accepts baptism before dying, and Armida converts out of love for Rinaldo:

> Si parla e prega: e i preghi bagna e scalda
> or di lagrime rare, or di sospiri;
> onde sì come suol nevosa falda
> dov'arda il sole o tepid'aura spiri,
> così l'ira che 'n lei parea sì salda
> solvesi e restan sol gli altri desiri.
> —Ecco l'ancilla tua: d'essa a tuo senno
> dispon,—gli disse—e le fia legge il cenno.—

> [So speaks he and so prays, and with his sighs / and precious tears warms and anoints his prayers; / and as a shower of snowflakes melts and dies / in burning sunlight or the warm spring airs, / so now her violent rage dissolves and dies, / to leave only her other passions' cares: / "Behold your handmaid," says she, "let your will / dispose of her and be her master still."][35]

As the land is taken by the Christians, the women are Christianized, and love itself becomes a tool of acquisition just like the sword. The Crusaders' struggle with the licentiousness of the land is therefore both domesticating and salvific: as Christian host conquers Saracen land, Christian man conquers Saracen woman, and both can now enter the celestial as well as the earthly Jerusalem.

Long after the Crusade campaigns, and campaigns reminiscent of the Crusades, had come to an end, much of the ever-shifting and inconstant ideology of holy war survived in popular memory and imagination. The conflation of Crusade and chivalric romance, which brought together holy war in service to God and adventure in service to ladies, originated in late-medieval propaganda that responded to the incessant need for recruits to fill the ranks of the Crusader armies. It endured in the early modern period in such works as Tasso's *Gerusalemme Liberata* as the spirit of Crusade outlasted the pious desires in which it had originated. It lived on when even that spirit had passed, when the Romantics, seeking kindling in the passions of the Middle Ages, would again reconstruct the Crusader as both holy warrior and courtly lover, his sojourn in the Holy Land one of both conquest and adventure.[36] Through them, it has survived to this day.

INTRODUCTION

1. Elizabeth Siberry notes Gower's support of the Crusade in the *Vox Clamantis* (ca. 1380) and in "In Praise of Peace" (ca. 1386–1390); see Siberry, "Criticism of Crusading."

2. See, e.g., book III, ll. 2516–46, and book IV, ll. 1666–82, of the *Confessio Amantis*; Gower, *Complete Works*, 2:294–95 and 2:346, respectively.

3. Gower, *Mirour de l'Omme*, 312–14.

4. This is perhaps best illustrated by the fourteenth-century knight Geoffroi of Charny, for whom "the man to whom God by His grace grants high honor in this world and in the end the soul's acceptance in paradise . . . could not ask for more from God." Geoffroi de Charny, *Book of Chivalry*, 165. On the connection between the drive for honor and the service to God, see Keen, *Chivalry*, 53–56.

5. The issue continued to occupy Gower even later in life. Book IV, ll. 1620–33, of the *Confessio Amantis* touches upon the same subject: "Forthi who secheth loves grace, / Wher that these worthi wommen are, / He mai noght thanne himselve spare / Upon this travail forto serve, / Wherof that he mai thonk deserve, / There as these men of Armes be, / Somtime over the grete Se: / So that be londe and ek be Schipe / He mot travaile for worschipe / And make manye hastyf rodes / Somtime in Prus, somtime in Rodes, / And somtime into Tartarie; / So that these heraldz on him crie, / 'Vailant, vailant, lo, wher he goth!'" See Gower, *Complete Works*, 2:345.

6. Housley provides an informative survey of the scholarship on Crusader motivations; see Housley, *Contesting the Crusades*, 24–38 and 75–98.

7. Housley, *Contesting the Crusades*, 29 and 77–79.

8. See, e.g., Riley-Smith, *First Crusaders*; Bull, *Knightly Piety*.

9. Bull, *Knightly Piety*, 9–10; see also 286.

10. Bréhier, *Église et Orient*, 48.

11. Lloyd, *English Society and the Crusades*, 96.

12. Lloyd, *English Society and the Crusades*, 96. See also Guard, *Chivalry, Kingship and Crusade*, 160–64; and Trotter, "Mythologie arthurienne." For a contrasting view of the propaganda value of chanson de geste

and romance, see Hardman and Ailes, "Crusading, Chivalry and the Saracen World," 64–65; and Daniel, *Heroes and Saracens*, 267.

13. David Trotter, for instance, remarks that chansons could urge audiences to imitate ancestors elevated to "saints qui occuperont des 'sieges el grignor pareïs'"; Lloyd speaks of the "sacred cause" to which romances could draw their audiences; while Timothy Guard suggests that they highlight the impossibility of penance by other than physical means, thereby "impressing upon knightly audiences the devotional context of their decision to embark." See Trotter, "Mythologie arthurienne," 157; Lloyd, *English Society and the Crusades*, 96; and Guard, *Chivalry, Kingship and Crusade*, 161–62. Guard also notes that the "precise recruitment value [of the romances] is difficult to ascertain, but taken up with enthusiasm such models possessed strong resonance, teaching the integral tenets of Christian knighthood and mirroring the energy of contemporary chivalry"; see Guard, *Chivalry, Kingship and Crusade*, 163.

14. See, e.g., Maier, *Crusade Propaganda and Ideology*; and Smith, *Crusading in the Age of Joinville*, 75–108.

15. Spiegel, *Romancing the Past*, 5.

16. On the definition of Crusade, see Housley, *Contesting the Crusades*, 1–23.

17. Cf. Geert Claassens: "Unlike the story of the *expeditio crucis* that was not accessible to the *illiterati* the Cycle de la Croisade was accessible to an unschooled public and as such it functioned as a parallel historiography. Such parallelism also emanates from the mutual textual relationships between the Latin chronicles and the Cycle de la Croisade. . . . I am certain that medieval audiences must have viewed the stories in the cycle as an account of 'wie es eigentlich gewesen' (Leopold von Ranke): exact reports of how things really were." See Claassens, "Cycle de la Croisade," 186. On the correlation between the Cycle and the Latin chronicles, see Richard, "Arrière-plan historique." Even participants in the Crusade themselves invoked them as sources of historical knowledge; for instance, in the *Estoire de la Guerre Sainte*, an eyewitness account of the Third Crusade written ca. 1192–1199, Ambroise turned to the *Chanson d'Antioche* to describe the events of the First Crusade; see my chapter 5.

18. Bull and Kempf, "Introduction," 5–6; Housley, *Contesting the Crusades*, 2–3 and 17.

19. See, e.g., Nicholson, *Love, War, and the Grail*; Trotter, *Medieval French Literature*; Heng, *Empire of Magic*; Kinoshita, *Medieval Boundaries*, 15–73; Housley, *Contesting the Crusades*, 81 and 88–89; Ashe, "'A Prayer and a Warcry'"; and Ashe, "Ideal of Knighthood."

20. Along these lines, Sharon Kinoshita has argued with regard to the *Chanson de Roland* that "the crusading ethos presumed to permeate the poem from the outset is, instead, produced during the course of it"; see Kinoshita, *Medieval Boundaries*, 15–45, here 15.

CHAPTER 1

1. On the term "Latin," see Bartlett, *Making of Europe*, 18–23.
2. Some clearly even did so before the fall of Jerusalem. Raymond of Aguilers argues that before its capture, "the crusaders gave up hope of God's mercy and so marched down to the plain of Jordan. There they gathered palms, and were baptized in the Jordan River; and since they had viewed Jerusalem, they planned to give up the siege, go to Jaffa, and, in whatsoever manner they could, return home." Raymond d'Aguilers, *Historia Francorum*, 120–21.
3. This would lead to the creation of a fourth Crusader state, the county of Tripoli, in 1109. See Mayer, *Crusades*, 67–68; and Barber, *Crusader States*, 92–96.
4. See Runciman, *Kingdom of Jerusalem*, 3–70.
5. For an outstanding overview of the processes involved, see Prawer, *Crusader Institutions*.
6. See Barber, *Crusader States*, 50–64; and Runciman, *Kingdom of Jerusalem*, 71 and 81–86.
7. This appears to have happened quite quickly; at the end of his chronicle, which he completed ca. 1127, Fulcher of Chartres could say the following: "For we who were Occidentals have now become Orientals. He who was a Roman or a Frank has in this land been made into a Galilean or a Palestinian. He who was of Rheims or Chartres has now become a citizen of Tyre or Antioch. We have already forgotten the places of our birth; already these are unknown to many of us or not mentioned any more. Some already possess homes or households by inheritance. Some have taken wives not only of their own people but Syrians or Armenians or even Saracens who have obtained the grace of baptism. One has his father-in-law as well as his daughter-in-law living with him, or his own child if not his step-son or step-father. Out here there are grandchildren and great-grandchildren. Some tend vineyards, others till fields. People use the eloquence and idioms of diverse languages in conversing back and forth. Words of different languages have become common property known to each nationality, and mutual faith unites those who are ignorant of their descent." Fulcher of Chartres, *Expedition to Jerusalem*, 271–72.
8. Raymond d'Aguilers, *Historia Francorum*, 84.
9. Runciman, *Kingdom of Jerusalem*, 6–7.
10. This need for men is instanced by the desperate letter of Patriarch Daimbert of Jerusalem to the Germans dated April 1100. See Barber and Bate, *Letters from the East*, 37–38.
11. These included men who had taken the cross after Clermont but had not joined the armies on their way east, and others who had set out on the First Crusade but had returned home before its completion. See Riley-Smith, *Short History*, 34–36; Riley-Smith, *First Crusade*, 120–34; and Mayer, *Crusades*, 63–65.
12. See Erdmann, *Origin of the Idea of Crusade*; for an interesting counterpoint, see Bull, *Knightly Piety*, 21–69.

13. Robert of Reims, *History of the First Crusade*, 80–81. In excerpts of Robert's work below, translations are taken from this edition, abbreviated as *HFC*. The Latin original is from Robert of Reims, *Historia Iherosolimitana*; all further references to Robert's work, unless otherwise stated, will be to this edition, abbreviated to *HI*. Both the original and the translation will be cited in the text parenthetically.

14. Tyerman, *Invention of the Crusades*, 8–29.

15. See Ní Chléirigh, "*Nova Peregrinatio.*"

16. See Hill, *Gesta Francorum*. All further references to the work, unless otherwise stated, will be to this edition, and will be cited in the text parenthetically, abbreviated as *GF*.

17. Petrus Tudebodus, *Historia de Hierosolymitano Itinere*.

18. Albert of Aachen, *Historia Ierosolimitana*; Ralph of Caen, *Gesta Tancredi*.

19. Guibert of Nogent, *Gesta Dei per Francos*; Baldric of Bourgueil, *Historia Ierosolimitana*. On Guibert, see Rubenstein, "Guibert of Nogent, Albert of Aachen and Fulcher of Chartres"; on Baldric, see Biddlecombe, "Baldric of Bourgueil and the *Familia Christi.*"

20. Riley-Smith, *First Crusade*, 22–23; Riley-Smith, *Short History*, 37.

21. See, e.g., Raymond d'Aguilers, *Historia Francorum*, 93–97.

22. E.g., *HI* 6, 19, 27–28, and 62; see also my chapter 3.

23. Guibert of Nogent, *Gesta Dei per Francos*, 142.

24. Bartlett, *Making of Europe*, 5–59 and 111–16.

25. In Albert's work vengeance is blind to religious creed, and he describes vengeance exacted upon Christians as well as Muslims. As to the former see, e.g., Albert of Aachen, *Historia Ierosolimitana*, 15–16, 19, and 23; as to the latter see, e.g., 37–39, 213, 243, 247, 289, 385–87, 393, 409, 441, 449, 489, 547, and 581. The Muslims, too, seek vengeance when possible: e.g., on pp. 37 and 215. For more on vengeance as a driving force in Crusade, see Riley-Smith, *First Crusade*, 54–57; and Throop, *Crusading as an Act of Vengeance*. On the terminology of vengeance in Crusade sources, see Throop, "Zeal, Anger and Vengeance."

26. These words obviously contradict Urban II's privilege to the pilgrims: "Whoever goes on the journey to free the church of God in Jerusalem out of devotion alone, and not for the gaining of glory or money, can substitute the journey for all penance for sin." See Peters, *First Crusade*, 37.

27. Riley-Smith, *First Crusade*, 40.

28. The oldest chansons are thought to be the *Chanson de Roland* and *Gormond et Isembart*. The oldest extant manuscript of the *Roland*, Oxford Digby 23, can be dated to 1150; based on internal characteristics, the work in its present form was probably completed ca. 1060–1100. See Suard, *Chanson de Geste*, 15–18; Burgess, *Song of Roland*, 8; Calin, *Muse for Heroes*, 14–15; and Gaunt, *Retelling the Tale*, 25. Only 661 lines of a twelfth-century manuscript of *Gormond et Isembart* have survived; the song has been dated to as early as 1068. See Jones, *Introduction to the Chansons de Geste*, 40–41; and Holmes, *History of Old French Literature*, 91–92.

29. Gaston Paris, *Histoire poétique*; see also Jones, *Introduction to the Chansons de Geste*, 3–6; Daniel, *Heroes and Saracens*, 3; and Innes, *Epic*, 90.

30. Bédier, *Légendes épiques*; see also Jones, *Introduction to the Chansons de Geste*, 3–6; and Gaunt, *Retelling the Tale*, 33.

31. Gaunt, *Retelling the Tale*, 25–37.

32. Leverage, *Reception and Memory*, 293.

33. Suard, *Chanson de Geste*, 12. They range from an average of a dozen in the *Chanson de Roland* to 1140 in laisse 74 of *Huon de Bordeaux*.

34. Bédier, *Chanson de Roland*, 22 and 4, respectively. Here and later in the text I have quoted from the *Chanson de Roland* and given later examples in notes. I chose the *Chanson de Roland* over other chansons not only because of its quality but more important because it predates the works discussed later, showing that the ideas it embodies existed before the anonymous author of the *GF* completed his work. The original is taken from Bédier, *Chanson de Roland*, and the translation from Burgess, *Song of Roland*. All future references to the *Chanson de Roland* are to these editions, and will be cited in the text parenthetically, abbreviated as *CR*.

35. Suard, *Chanson de Geste*, 10–11.

36. Holmes, *History of Old French Literature*, 66.

37. Suard, *Chanson de Geste*, 53; Holmes, *History of Old French Literature*, 97–98.

38. In the words of Debra Higgs Strickland, the chansons de geste were "the major imaginative arena for the creation of the medieval Saracen"; Strickland, *Saracens, Demons, and Jews*, 166.

39. The chansons' discussion of the faith ranges from uncomplicated statements of Christian supremacy such as Roland's famous "Paien unt tort e chrestiens unt dreit" [*CR* l. 1015: "The pagans are wrong and the Christians are right"] to subtle reflections of contemporary scriptural knowledge and religious practice; see Schulze-Busacker, "Expression de la foi." The late twelfth-century *Fierabras*, for instance, expands upon the cult of the relics (especially those held at St. Denis) and religious conversion; the work also sees Charlemagne assume a more confrontational position toward God. See Le Person, *Fierabras*; and Ailes, "Faith in *Fierabras*."

40. God's assistance is famously made clear in *CR* when he holds back the darkness so that Charlemagne can exact his revenge upon the Saracens at ll. 2458–59. The Franks' final reward is shown in Roland's ascent into heaven at ll. 2389–96: "Sun destre guant a Deu en puroffrit. / Seint Gabriel de sa main l'ad pris. / Desur sun braz teneit le chef enclin; / Juntes ses mains est alet a sa fin. / Deus tramist sun angle Cherubin / E seint Michel del Peril; / Ensembl'od els sent Gabriel i vint. / L'anme del cunte portent en pareïs." ["He proffered his right glove to God; / Saint Gabriel took it from his hand. / Roland laid his head down over his arm; / With his hands joined he went to his end. / God sent down his angel Cherubin / And with him Saint Michael of the Peril. / With them both came Saint Gabriel. / They bear the count's soul to paradise"]. Here, the relationship to the early indulgences of Leo IV (847–855) and John VIII (872–882), who promised paradise to those killed

fighting the Muslims in Spain, should be noted. See Allen and Amt, *Crusades: A Reader*, 19–20.

41. Roland, for instance, is said to have won Charlemagne his empire: see *CR* ll. 2322–34.

42. See, e.g., Charlemagne's destruction of the Saracens in laisses 178–81, ll. 2418–87, of *CR*. Roland also sees this as Charlemagne's duty: "Venget li reis, si nus purrat venger" [l. 1744: "Let the king come, then he can avenge our deaths"].

43. On the increasing number of traitor narratives in the chansons de geste of the twelfth century, see Kay, *Chansons de Geste in the Age of Romance*, 175–99.

44. Jones, *Introduction to the Chansons de Geste*, 19. Andrew Cowell has examined the gift giving upon which this system of exchange was built from an anthropological angle, and he observes that it could serve to *enforce* indebtedness: "Aggressive giving as a recruitment tool served essentially to 'de-pluralize' relationships between a lord, his various followers, and their other potential relationships, and to create the unity necessary for action." Publicly performed giving as substitute for physical repression was especially prevalent in the early Middle Ages, when the relationship between between lord and vassal was legally ill-defined. See Cowell, *Medieval Warrior Aristocracy*, 36.

45. Suard, *Chanson de Geste*, 36.

46. On the military practices of medieval chivalry, see Verbruggen, *Art of Warfare in Western Europe*, 19–110; and Keen, *Chivalry*, 23–27.

47. E.g., *CR* ll. 1261–82: "E Gerins fiert Malprimis de Brigal. / . . . / E sis cumpainz Gerers fiert l'amurafle. / . . . / Sansun li dux, il vait ferir l'almaçur. / . . . / E Anseïs laiset le cheval curre, / Si vait ferir Turgis de Turteluse" ["And Gerin strikes Malprimis of Brigal; / . . . / And his companion Gerer strikes the Emir; / . . . / Duke Samson goes to strike the almaçor. / . . . / Then Anseis gives his horse full rein / And goes to strike Turgis of Turteluse"]. See also Daniel, *Heroes and Saracens*, 104–10.

48. Some of these "noble Saracens," such as Fierabras in *Fierabras* (ca. 1170) and Otinel in *Otinel* (late twelfth century), will eventually be baptized and integrated within the Frankish fold. See Schulze-Busacker, "Expression de la foi," 111–14; Ailes, "Faith in *Fierabras*," 131–33; and Hardman and Ailes, "Crusading, Chivalry and the Saracen World."

49. Daniel, *Heroes and Saracens*, 72–87 and 156–59; and Cohen, *Medieval Identity Machines*, 208–9.

50. See also Tolan, *Saracens*, 125–26. On the Saracen as "monstrous," see Strickland, *Saracens, Demons, and Jews*, 159–60.

51. Daniel, *Heroes and Saracens*, 121–78; Tolan, *Saracens*, 105–34, esp. 125; Kay, *Chansons de Geste in the Age of Romance*, 50; Jones, *Introduction to the Chansons de Geste*, 21–22; Kangas, "Inimicus Dei et Sanctae Christianitatis," 138–42; and Strickland, *Saracens, Demons, and Jews*, 165–68, esp. 166.

52. Daniel, *Heroes and Saracens*, 173–77; Ailes, "Faith in *Fierabras*," 125–26.

53. Daniel, *Heroes and Saracens*, 179–210; see also Tolan, *Sons of Ishmael*, 66–78.

54. For the audience of the chansons de geste, see Leverage, *Reception and Memory*, 23–105.

55. E.g., the Provençal *Girart de Roussillon* (ca. 1150) and the Middle High German *Rolandslied* of Konrad der Pfaffe (twelfth century). See Combarieu du Grès and Gourian, *Chanson de Girart de Roussillon*; and Konrad der Pfaffe, *Priest Konrad's Song of Roland*.

56. Keen suggests that the participation of knights in the Crusades almost *ab origine* made these an important factor in the development of the chivalric ideal. See Keen, *Chivalry*, 44–63.

57. Peters, *First Crusade*, 44–45; see also Asbridge, *First Crusade*, 49–50.

58. Robert the Monk, writing with the benefit of hindsight, has Urban say the following: "Et non precipimus aut suademus, ut senes aut inbecilles et usui armorum minime idonei hoc iter arripiant, nec mulieres sine coniugibus suis aut fratribus aut legitimis testimoniis ullatenus incedant. Tales enim magis sunt impedimento quam adiumento, plus oneri quam utilitati" [*HI* 7; *HFC* 81–82: "We are not forcing or persuading the old, the simple-minded or those unsuited to battle to undertake this pilgrimage; neither should a woman set out under any circumstances without her husband, brother or other legitimate guarantor. That is because such pilgrims are more of a hindrance than a help, a burden rather than of any practical use"].

59. On lay piety and chivalric literature, see Kaeuper, *Chivalry and Violence*, 45–62; on the wider interaction between chivalric ideology and lay theology, see Kaeuper, *Holy Warriors*.

60. This, of course, was especially so for the French, who had constituted a large proportion of the First Crusaders and had been the original target of the speech at Clermont; Jonathan Riley-Smith says that the First Crusade was "largely a French enterprise." Riley-Smith, *First Crusade*, 86.

61. Riley-Smith, *First Crusaders*, 81–105.

62. On the often complex nature of the relationship between vassal and overlord, and the representation of social hierarchy and political power in the chansons de geste, see Kay, *Chansons de Geste in the Age of Romance*, 116–44.

63. See also Laura Ashe, "'A Prayer and a Warcry.'"

CHAPTER 2

1. See Flori, *Chroniqueurs et propagandistes*, 9 and 49–59; and Morris, "*Gesta Francorum* as Narrative History," 55. *Dixit* Kostick: "It was the version of events that had the greatest impact in its day and it provided the basic materials for the even more widespread circulation of later twelfth century histories of the First Crusade. These, in turn, greatly influenced nineteenth century historians and popular twentieth century accounts: so that it is no exaggeration to say that the *Gesta Francorum* is the font from which springs the great rivers of writing on the First Crusade." Kostick, "Further Discussion," 1.

2. *GF* ix. Colin Morris has the composition completed before the end of 1099; see Morris, "*Gesta Francorum* as Narrative History," 66.

3. In all, we find Bohemond referred to as "dominus" eleven times in the *GF*; see Flori, *Chroniqueurs et propagandistes*, 70, n. 15.

4. Flori, *Chroniqueurs et propagandistes*, 67–82. The author's partisanship toward Bohemond has led Flori to refer to the *GF* as "l'épopée de Bohémond"; see Flori, *Chroniqueurs et propagandistes*, 78.

5. Hagenmeyer, *Anonymi Gesta Francorum*.

6. E.g., "They located, followed, and drove the enemy to death in the Orontes," or "But why make a longer story of it? There was a fight, our troops fled, and we lost almost three hundred men and no one knows how much in spoils and arms." Raymond d'Aguilers, *Historia Francorum*, 32 and 42, respectively. Moreover, Raymond does not describe the important Battle of Ascalon in any detail, glossing over the episode with: "We could neither estimate the amount of costly goods nor compute the sum total of arms and tents seized." Raymond d'Aguilers, *Historia Francorum*, 135.

7. *GF* xi; for a recent view, see Kostick, "Further Discussion."

8. *GF* 7–8.

9. *GF* xi–xii; Kostick, "Further Discussion," 4–8.

10. Morris, "*Gesta Francorum* as Narrative History," 64–67.

11. Hagenmeyer, *Anonymi Gesta Francorum*, 17.

12. Flori, *Chroniqueurs et propagandistes*, 83–106; Kostick, "Further Discussion," 8–11.

13. Runciman, *Kingdom of Jerusalem*, 47; and Flori, "Guerre sainte et rétributions spirituelles," 621. Nicholas Paul has argued against Bohemond's use of written propaganda such as the *GF*; see Paul, "Warlord's Wisdom."

14. Raymond d'Aguilers, *Historia Francorum*, 7–8.

15. Flori, *Chroniqueurs et propagandistes*, 105–6.

16. Wolf, "Crusade and Narrative," 210; see also Morris, "*Gesta Francorum* as Narrative History," 66–67.

17. Kostick, "Further Discussion," 2.

18. Consider, e.g., that he completely bypasses the fraught history of Peter Bartholomew and the Holy Lance on *GF* 59–60. Hagenmeyer (*dixit* Morris, "*Gesta Francorum* as Narrative History," 58) sees in this a lack of foresight and therefore an indication of hasty composition; the Anonymous was, however, a strong partisan of Bohemond, and Bohemond lent little credence to the veracity of the Lance. Why then did the Anonymous miss the chance to revel in Peter Bartholomew's sad fate? It is likely that he here digresses from Bohemond's party line to avoid issues that served only to sow division and muddle the waters of the Crusade.

19. *GF* xv.

20. Bennett, "First Crusaders' Images of Muslims."

21. Morris, "*Gesta Francorum* as Narrative History," 60–64.

22. Morris has come closest to expanding the interpretation of the use of chanson conventions in the *Gesta* beyond the aesthetic, arguing that the Anonymous may have wanted to please the southern Italian aristocracy: "He was bringing to his hearers a real-life epic. While this method of writing may well

have been natural to him, and have reflected the cultural background from which he came, it is also possible that it was in part deliberately adopted as an approach to his audience. His links with Bohemund suggest that he may initially have had an Italian audience in mind, and the similarity between Latin and the various Italian vernaculars was probably close enough to enable them to understand the narrative, just as Italian congregations, before Vatican II, could often understand the Latin Mass." Indicative of the status of the discussion on the *Gesta*, Kostick recently turned Morris's suggestion back to the eternal question of identity: "This explanation suffers from being unnecessarily complicated. Given that there were literate knights in the era and on the crusade, if a text looks like it was shaped by the culture of the secular nobility rather than that of the clergy, then by Occam's Razor if no better criteria, it would be more logical to simply attribute it to a knight than a cleric adopting a style that would appeal to knights." Morris, *"Gesta Francorum* as Narrative History," 63–64; and Kostick, "Further Discussion," 4.

23. *GF* 6–10. The Anonymous's knowledge of Byzantine structures of government is also seen, e.g., in his inclusion of "corpalatium" for "kyriopalatios" on *GF* 10.

24. As, e.g., when he speaks of the Turks, "qui putabant terrere gentem Francorum minis suarum sagittarum, sicut terruerunt Arabes, Saracenos, et Hermenios, Suranios et Grecos" [*GF* 21: "who thought that they would strike terror into the Franks, as they had done into the Arabs and Saracens, Armenians, Syrians and Greeks, by the menace of their arrows"], he likely refers to the recent conquests of Alp Aslan and Malik Shah I.

25. *GF* 49; see also Bennett, "First Crusaders' Images of Muslims," 108–9.

26. The Anonymous also uses very large numbers to make the Christian victories more impressive; e.g., the enemy is said to number more than 360,000 at Dorylaeum and 200,000 at Ascalon. See *GF* 20 and 96, respectively.

27. *GF* 49, n. 6.

28. See, for instance, the letters of Anselm of Ribemont to Manasses of Reims dated November 1097 and July 1098, and the letter of the Christian magnates to the West of September 1099; see Barber and Bate, *Letters from the East*, 18–21, 26–30, and 33–37, respectively.

29. See chapter 1.

30. See also Bennett, "First Crusaders' Images of Muslims," 115; and Morris, *"Gesta Francorum* as Narrative History," 63. Interestingly, this is the *Gesta*'s longest discourse on religion. See my chapter 1 on the chanson trope.

31. E.g., Raymond of Aguilers, who refers to the Muslim deity only as Allah, and to whom Muslims are "those who have followed the Koran in order to worship Allah of the Turks." Raymond's knowledge of Islam is surprisingly nuanced. He acknowledges the role of the caliph, whom he refers to as "of Mohammed's stock" and shows an understanding of the difference between Sunni and Shia in his description of the Turkish offer to the Fatimid ruler to "worship Ali, kinsman of Mohammed whom he worshipped." Raymond d'Aguilers, *Historia Francorum*, 68, 90, and 89, respectively.

32. See also Bennett, "First Crusaders' Images of Muslims," 116.

33. Hodgson, *Women, Crusading and the Holy Land*, 190–96.

34. "Feminae quoque nostrae in illa die fuerunt nobis in maximo refugio, quae afferebant ad bibendum aquam nostris preliatoribus, et fortiter semper confortabant illos, pugnantes et defendentes" [*GF* 19: "The women in our camp were a great help to us that day, for they brought up water for the fighting men to drink, and gallantly encouraged those who were fighting and defending them"].

35. Wolf, "Crusade and Narrative," 208–9.

36. "He probably remembered it by ear and did not collate it with the Vulgate"; see *GF* 2, n. 1.

37. See also *GF* 62 and 96; this is expanded to "inimici Dei et sanctae christianitatis" ["enemies of God and holy Christendom"] on *GF* 32.

38. Compare to *CR* ll. 1314–16, when Margariz attacks Oliver: "L'escut li freint suz la bucle d'or mer, / Lez le costet li conduist sun espiet. / Deus le guarit, qu'el cors ne l'ad tuchet" ["He breaks his shield beneath the pure gold boss / And his thrusting spear shaved his side. / God prevented a wound to his body"].

39. On those who did die in battle, see *GF* 40.

40. This echoes Roland's words before the battle of Roncesvalles: "Seignurs barons, suef, le pas tenant! / Cist paien vont grant martirie querant. / Encoi avrum un eschec bel e gent" [*CR* ll. 1165–67: "My lord barons, gently, not too fast! / These pagans are heading for great slaughter; / Today our spoils will be fine and noble"].

41. The words of Bohemond sum this up well: "Vade quam citius potes ut uir fortis, et esto acer in adiutorium Dei Sanctique Sepulchri. Et reuera scias quia hoc bellum carnale non est sed spirituale. Esto igitur fortissimus athleta Christi" [*GF* 36–37: "Charge at top speed, like a brave man, and fight valiantly for God and the Holy Sepulchre, for you know in truth that this is no war of the flesh, but of the spirit. So be very brave, as becomes a champion of Christ"].

42. Here the dispute between Tancred of Hauteville and Baldwin of Boulogne or between Raymond of Toulouse and Bohemond of Taranto, and the desertions of Stephen of Blois and Hugh of Vermandois on the road to Jerusalem, should be noted. The Anonymous is very reluctant to talk about confrontations between the Christian magnates. See Kostick, "Further Discussion," 5–6.

43. Kostick, "Further Discussion," 5.

44. E.g., the unfortunates of the Popular Crusade; see *GF* 3–5, 17.

45. Kostick, "Further Discussion," 6–8.

46. For Charlemagne's journey to Jerusalem and Constantinople the Anonymous may have drawn on the *Descriptio Qualiter Karolus Magnus* (ca. 1080), although the tale may have circulated orally; see Gabriele, *Empire of Memory*, 51–70.

47. On the term "Frank," see Bartlett, *Making of Europe*, 101–5; Kinoshita, *Medieval Boundaries*, 29–31; and Kinoshita, "Crusades and Identity," 94–95. On its use in the histories of the First Crusade, see Gabriele, *Empire of Memory*, 154–57; and Bull, "Overlapping and Competing Identities."

48. In this respect he is unlike his fellow chronicler of the First Crusade, Fulcher of Chartres, for whom the ethnic difference between Crusaders is almost a point of pride. He, for instance, describes the Crusader camp after the Battle of Dorylaeum as follows: "And whoever heard of such a mixture of languages in one army? There were present Franks, Flemings, Frisians, Gauls, Allobroges, Lotharingians, Alemanni, Bavarians, Normans, English, Scots, Aquitanians, Italians, Dacians, Apulians, Iberians, Bretons, Greeks, and Armenians. If any Briton or Teuton wished to question me I could neither reply nor understand." Fulcher of Chartres, *Expedition to Jerusalem*, 88.

49. The Anonymous refers to *Francigenae* on GF 34, 52, 68, 91, and 96; see also Bull, "Overlapping and Competing Identities," 197, n. 6. He furthermore mentions the presence of southern Italians at Antioch on GF 71, while Bohemond refers to William the Carpenter and Peter the Hermit as "O infelix et infamia totius Franciae, dedecus et scelus Galliarum" [GF 33: "You wretched disgrace to the whole Frankish army—you dishonourable blot on all the people of Gaul!"].

50. E.g., on Bohemond's army: "Tandem transfretauit mare cum suo execitu, et cum eo Tancredus Marchisi filius, et Richardus princeps, ac Rainulfus frater eius, et Rotbertus de Ansa, et Hermannus de Canni, et Rotbertus de Surda Valle, et Rotbertus filius Tostani, et Hunfredus filius Radulfi, et Ricardus filius comitis Rainulfi, et comes de Russignolo cum fratribus suis, et Boello Carnotensis, et Alberedus de Cagnano, et Hunfredus de Monte Scabioso" [GF 7: "Thereafter he crossed the sea with his army, and with him went Tancred son of the Marquis, Richard of the Principality and Ranulf his brother, Robert of Anse, Herman of Cannes, Robert of Sourdeval, Robert Fitz-Toustan, Humphrey Fitz-Ralph, Richard son of Count Ranulf, the count of Russignolo and his brothers, Boel of Chartres, Aubré of Cagnano and Humphrey of Monte Scaglioso"].

51. Unlike the Anonymous, Raymond does differentiate between Flemings, Provençals, and Franks as a cover term: "Among the auxiliary group were the Count of Flanders and some Provençals, a name applied to all those from Burgundy, Auvergne, Gascony, and Gothia. I call to your attention that all others in our army are called Franks, but the enemy makes no distinction and uses Franks for all." Raymond d'Aguilers, *Historia Francorum*, 34. This does not stop him from referring to Normans and Germans where needed, as for instance on pp. 25 and 79, respectively. That the use of the term "Frank" was far from common in the first years after the capture of Jerusalem is suggested by the fact that another Norman, Ralph of Caen, rarely uses the term, preferring Gaul, and refers to the component parts of the army almost twenty years after the completion of the GF. For instance, he describes the discord at Antioch, which the GF bypasses, as follows: "The men of Narbonne, Auvergne, Gascony, and all of the people of Provence were on one side. The remainder of Gaul, and especially the Normans, were with the men of Apulia. The Bretons, Swabians, Huns, Ruthenians and others protected those whom they heard speaking their language outside the walls." Ralph of Caen, *Gesta Tancredi*, 117–18.

52. Or, as Kostick suggests, to hide the dissent in the ranks; see Kostick, "Further Discussion," 5–6.

53. *Gesta Francorum* is the title the Anonymous set out to give to his work; see Morris "*Gesta Francorum* as Narrative History," 55.

54. Morris, "*Gesta Francorum* as Narrative History," 63–64.

55. E.g., "Tam fortes et tam duri milites, cur hoc fecerunt? Propterea igitur, quia multi coacti erant necessitate" [*GF* 12: "But why did such brave and determined knights do a thing like this? It must have been because they were driven by desperate need"].

56. Hill understands the unnamed city to have been Placentia; see *GF* 25, n. 5.

57. *GF* 34–35.

58. On the Crusaders' "fantasies of entitlement" to the land, see also Burgwinkle, "Utopia and Its Uses," 552–55.

59. Roland, speaking of his sword Durendal before Roncesvalles, famously reminisces how it has helped him serve his king: "Jo l'en cunquis e Anjou e Bretaigne,/ Si l'en cunquis e Peitou e le Maine;/ Jo l'en cunquis Normendie la franche, / Si l'en cunquis Provence e Equitaigne / E Lumbardie e trestute Romaine; / Jo l'en cunquis Baiver e tute Flandres / E Burguigne e trestute Puillanie, / Costentinnoble, dunt il out la fiance, / E en Saisonie fait il ço qu'il demandet; / Jo l'en cunquis e Escoce e Vales islonde / E Engletere, que il teneit sa cambre" [*CR* ll. 2322–32: "With it I conquered Anjou and Brittany / And with it I conquered Poitou and Maine; / With it I conquered Normandy the free / And with it I conquered Provence and Aquitaine / And Lombardy and all Romagna. / With it I conquered Bavaria and all Flanders / And Burgundy and all Apulia. / And *Constantinople, which renders homage to him.* / In Saxony his commands are obeyed. / With it I conquered Scotland and Ireland / And England, which became his domain"]. My italics. Gabriele points out that, before the First Crusade, most of Europe and the Middle East was thought to have belonged to Charlemagne; see Gabriele, *Empire of Memory*, 31–37.

60. Byzantine treachery toward the Crusaders begins the moment they enter their territory: "Dux illius loci . . . mox mala cogitatio cor eius tetigit, illosque apprehendit, ac iussit Constantinopolim imperatori caute duci, quo ei fidelitatem facerent" [*GF* 6: "the governor of that place . . . immediately devised a treacherous plan, and he arrested them and sent them under guard to the emperor at Constantinople, so that they might swear fealty to him"]. The emperor himself continues this abominable behavior after their arrival in Constantinople: "Tunc imperator anxians et bulliens ira, cogitabat quemadmodum callide fraudulenterque comprehenderet hos Christi milites" [*GF* 11: "Then the emperor, who was troubled in mind and fairly seething with rage, was planning how to entrap these Christian knights by fraud and cunning"]. Even before they cross the Bosporus, he aims to destroy the Crusaders, keeping some of the Nicaean prisoners of war "ut illos ad Francorum nocumenta et obstacula paratos haberet" [*GF* 17: "so that he could have them ready to injure the Franks and obstruct their crusade"] and sending as his representative to the Crusader army "inimicus Tetigus" [*GF* 34: "our

enemy Tatikios"], "ille inimicus . . . in periurio manet et manebit" [*GF* 35: "that enemy of ours . . . he is a liar, and always will be"].

61. On eschatology and the First Crusade, see Rubenstein, *Armies of Heaven*; and Buc, *Holy War, Martyrdom, and Terror*, 53–54 and 101–2.

62. Ralph of Caen plays upon the same dual justification when describing Baldwin I of Jerusalem: "Indeed, his bearing showed with ease his descent from Charlemagne and that fact that he was born divinely as one who was to take his seat on David's throne." Ralph of Caen, *Gesta Tancredi*, 61.

63. Runciman, *First Crusade*, 329.

64. Morris, "*Gesta Francorum* as Narrative History," 67.

65. The Anonymous likely worked with and rewrote material he had accumulated over a number of years; Emily Albu has demonstrated that the *GF* was composed in stages. See Albu, "Probing the Passions of a Norman on Crusade."

66. Note Bartlett's description of the "literature of conquest" accompanying settlement on the frontiers of Latin Europe; see Bartlett, *Making of Europe*, 96–101.

67. See Paul, "Warlord's Wisdom," 556–60.

68. It is furthermore possible that Bohemond had learned the value of the chansons de geste to propagate his affairs from his father Robert Guiscard; see Grégoire and de Keyser, "*Chanson de Roland* et Byzance."

CHAPTER 3

1. Orderic Vitalis, *Ecclesiastical History*, 3:6.70–71; see also Paul, "Warlord's Wisdom," 558–59.

2. Kempf and Bull propose a later date of completion of the *Historia Iherosolimitana*, around 1110; see *HI* xxxv–xxxviii. See also Naus, "*Historia Iherosolimitana* of Robert the Monk," esp. 113–14.

3. See *HFC* 4–7.

4. *HFC* 5–7.

5. There are eighty-four extant manuscripts of the *HI*, and the work has known a wide geographical distribution. For an extensive description of these, see *HI* xlii–xlvii; see also Kempf, "Textual Archaeology," 117.

6. *HFC* 3–4.

7. For a more extensive biography of Robert, see *HI* xvii–xli; and Riley-Smith, *First Crusade*, 135–36.

8. Others shared this jaundiced view. Guibert of Nogent, in his introductory letter to Lysiardus, writes of his work that "si aliquotiens me a vulgari grammatica peregrinari contigerit, idcirco fecerim, quod vitia, immo illud humi serpens eloquium praecedentis corrigebam historiae." Guibert of Nogent, *Gesta Dei per Francos*, 117–18.

9. *HI* 3. On the style of Robert's work, see *HFC* 64–65.

10. Riley-Smith, *First Crusade*, 139; see also Kempf, "Textual Archaeology," 118–19.

11. *HFC* 41. Sweetenham also argues: "Although [Robert] has some links with the vernacular tradition, these are probably stylistic and via the *GF* rather than direct." See *HFC* 28.

12. On the flexibility of the term "Franci" in early Crusade historiography, see Bull, "Overlapping and Competing Identities."

13. Toward the end of the work, Robert highlights the flaw in Bohemond's claim to Frankishness: "Habuitque a patre suo, qui Francigena fuit, optima principia, sed a matre, que Apuliensis extitit, retinuit vestigia" [*HI* 92; *HFC* 191: "He had inherited the highest principles from his French father; but they were tainted by elements from his Apulian mother"].

14. As Kempf and Bull point out, Robert presents the Crusade as "a specifically French achievement"; see *HI* xv.

15. Here Ps. 78:8, which tells of a just new generation superseding a corrupt older one: "And might not be as their fathers, a stubborn and rebellious generation; a generation that set not their heart aright, and whose spirit was not steadfast with God."

16. Following his source text, Robert includes Italians and Germans among the Popular Crusade on *HI* 9 (cf. *GF* 2–4) and mentions the presence of Italians at Antioch on *HI* 78 (cf. *GF* 71).

17. The notion of Frankish chosenness is an old one and has received close attention from Ernst Kantorowicz and Mary Garrison. See Kantorowicz, *Laudes Regiae*, 56–58; and Garrison, "Franks as the New Israel."

18. See *GF* 55.

19. *In casu* Ps. 106:3 and Deut. 11:24–5; see *HI* 63, n. 105–6.

20. Robert here includes Luke 1:52–53; see *HI* 28, n. 41–42.

21. The reference is to Isa. 60:15–16; see *HI* 29, n. 44.

22. This is not limited to Robert; as Sweetenham has pointed out, similar sentiments explain Guibert of Nogent's naming of his work *Gesta Dei per Francos*; see *HFC* 51.

23. Robert here cites Exod. 3:8 and Num. 13:28; see *HI* 6, n. 12.

24. Robert here cites Exod. 23:20–23; see *HI* 62, n. 100–101.

25. Robert here cites Exod. 15:13; see *HI* 28, n. 40. Especially the description of the aftermath of the Battle of Dorylaeum repeatedly refers to Exodus.

26. E.g., the Anonymous describes the return of Alexius's army to Constantinople as follows: "Voluissent noluissent nostri reuersi sunt retrorsum, dolentes amarissime usque ad mortem; fueruntque mortui multi ex peregrinis languentes nec ualentes fortiter militiam sequi; remanebantque morientes in uia" [*GF* 65: "So, willy-nilly, our friends retreated, grieving very bitterly even to death, and many of the sick pilgrims died because they had not the strength to follow the army, so they lay down to die by the wayside"]. Robert elides this in the corresponding passage on *HI* 66.

27. Compare, e.g., the Anonymous's description of the journey to Iconium, "Nos itaque persequebamur eos per deserta et inaquosam et inhabitabilem terram, ex qua uix uiui euasimus uel exiuimus. Fames uero et sitis undique coartabant nos, nihilque penitus nobis erat ad edendum, nisi fortes uellentes et fricantes spicas manibus nostris, tali cibo quam miserrime uiuebamus" [*GF* 23: "We therefore pursued them through a land which was deserted,

waterless and uninhabitable, from which we barely emerged or escaped alive, for we suffered greatly from hunger and thirst, and found nothing at all to eat except prickly plants which we gathered and rubbed between our hands. On such food we survived wretchedly enough"], to that of Robert, "Nostri enim invenerunt terram illam desertam, inaquosam, omnibus bonis peregrinam. Vellebant spicas segetum iam ad maturitatem proximantium, et inter manus confricando expilabant, talique cibo famem utcumque mitigabant" [*HI* 30; *HFC* 115: "For our men found this land to be empty of water and provisions alike. They tore off nearly ripe ears of corn and hulled them by rubbing them in their hands, appeasing their hunger as far as they could with such food"]. Compare also the Anonymous's observation "Ibi quidem sunt mortui multi ex nostris, non habentes pretium unde tam carum emere potuissent. Willelmus igitur Carpentarius et Petrus Heremita, pro immensa infelicitate ac miseria ipsa, latenter recesserunt" [*GF* 33: "Many of our people died there, not having the means to buy at so dear a rate. Because of this great wretchedness and misery William the Carpenter and Peter the Hermit fled away secretly"] vs. "Propter quod multi ibi fame perierunt, qui unde aliquid emerent non habuerunt. . . . Petrus enim Heremita et Guilelmus Carpentarius nocturno elapsu in fugam versi sunt, et a sacra fidelium Dei societate disiuncti sunt" [*HI* 40; *HFC* 127: "The result was that many died of hunger because they had nothing they could eat. . . . In fact Peter the Hermit and William the Carpenter fled, escaping by night, and left the sacred company of God's faithful"].

28. Compare also *GF* 62–63 vs. *HI* 64–65; here, while the description of the suffering is maintained, Robert no longer argues, as did the Anonymous, that it occurred "pro Christi nomine" [*GF* 62: "for the Name of Christ"].

29. My italics. Compare *GF* 58: "Bene adiuui vos, et amodo adiuuabo. Ego permisi uos habere Niceam ciuitatem, et omnia deuincere bella, et conduxi uos huc usque, et condolui vestrae miseriae quam passi fuistis in obsidione Antiochiae. Ecce in auxilio oportuno, misi uos sanos et incolumes in ciuitatem, et ecce multam prauamque dilectionem operantes cum Christianis et prauis paganis mulieribus, unde immensus foetor ascendit in caelum" ["I have given you great help, and I will help you hereafter. I granted you the city of Nicea, and victory in all your battles, and I have led you hither and suffered with you in all the troubles which you have endured in the siege of Antioch. Behold, I gave you timely help and put you safe and sound into the city of Antioch, but you are satisfying your filthy lusts both with Christians and with loose pagan women, so that a great stench goes up to Heaven"].

30. I disagree with Sweetenham when she says that in the *HI* "through their sufferings on Crusade they do penance for their sins" (*HFC* 55). The lines to which she refers to demonstrate this, those uttered by Bohemond at Constantinople before the army's crossing into Asia Minor on *HI* 19; *HFC* 98, do not suffice in this regard. Nevertheless, redemption from sin is still possible in the work, but it is tied up with the journey and not the suffering en route—as Urban II himself says to his audience at Clermont, "Arripite igitur viam hanc in remissione peccatorum vestrorum" [*HI* 7; *HFC* 81: "Seize on this road to obtain the remission of your sins"]. This is achieved, in

accordance with traditional approaches to pilgrimage, upon reaching one's destination, and the Christians "gratias referentes capitalitia sua obtulerunt" [*HI* 100; *HFC* 201: "laid down their mortal sins"] at Jerusalem. Remission is also achieved through martyrdom, as in the case of Walo, although his wife's imploration on *HI* 50–51 perhaps shows this not to be a guarantee. That martyrdom is not defined as resulting from the suffering on the journey is further shown on *HI* 11; *HFC* 86: "Deus vero, ut credimus, recepit eos intra septa semper virentis Paradisi, quoniam noluerunt a fide sua peregrinari" ["And God did indeed, as we believe, receive their souls into eternal Paradise because they refused to be turned away from belief in Him"]. A further separation between sins and suffering is perhaps uttered by St. Andrew through Peter Bartholomew at Antioch: "Mandat vobis sanctus Andreas ne timeatis sed confitemini et penitentiam agite a malis operibus vestris, quoniam infra V dies super inimicis vestris iterum triumphabitis" [*HI* 68; *HFC* 163: "Saint Andrew orders you not to be afraid, but to confess and do penance for your sins, because five days from now you will triumph again over your enemies"].

31. This shift is, perhaps most symbolically, also demonstrated in Robert's parallel to the Anonymous's invocation of the obligation to shoulder one's cross and follow Christ. Robert, oddly, turns it into a literal marker of identity: "Quicumque ergo huius sancte peregrinationis animum habuerit, et Deo sponsionem inde fecerit, eique se libaturum hostiam vivam, sanctam et bene placentem devoverit, signum dominice crucis in fronte sua sive in pectore preferat. . . . Tales quippe bifaria operatione complebunt illud Domini preceptum, quod ipse iubet per Evangelium: Qui non baiulat crucem suam et venit post me, non est me dignus" [*HI* 7–8; *HFC* 82: "Anyone who has a mind to undertake this holy pilgrimage, and enters into that bargain with God, and devotes himself as a living sacrifice, holy and acceptable, shall wear the sign of the Cross on his forehead or his chest. . . . Such men will bring to pass through this double symbolism what God himself orders in the Gospel: he that taketh not his cross, and followeth after me, is not worthy of me"].

32. To illustrate, one can compare the number of references to the Old Testament (including Genesis, Exodus, Leviticus, Numbers, Deuteronomy, Maccabees, the books of the Prophets, the books of Wisdom, and Psalms) to the number of references to the New Testament (the Gospels, the Acts of the Apostles, Epistles, and the book of Revelation) in Robert's work. In *HI*, the most recent edition, Kempf and Bull note sixty-nine references to the Old Testament and only eighteen to the New Testament.

33. Robert here cites Ps. 32:12; see *HI* 4, n. 3. He notably interpolates "of the Franks" into his citation.

34. See also *HI* 29–30. Robert here cites Song of Sol. 6:3 and 9; see *HI* 73, n. 124.

35. Also, e.g., "Evolat sanguis de corporibus vulneratorum; evolat pulvis agitatus equorum pedibus discurrentium. Ether obnubilatur, et, quasi crepusculum fieret, obtenebratur" [*HI* 76–77; *HFC* 172: "Blood spun away from the bodies of the wounded; dust spun away from the feet of the galloping horses. The air was clouded and darkened as if at dusk"].

36. *HI* 5–8 (cf. *GF* 1–2). See also *HI* 14–15, 19, 39, 74, and 77.

37. *HI* 50–51.

38. See, e.g., *HI* 52–54 (cf. *GF* 44–45), 17–18 (cf. *GF* 9), and 19–20.

39. See, e.g., *HI* 47–48, 51–52, and 70–72 (cf. *GF* 66–67).

40. See, e.g., *HI* 29–30 (cf. *GF* 22–23), 59–60 (cf. *GF* 50–51), and 61–64 (cf. *GF* 53–56).

41. *GF* 33–34; *HI* 40–41.

42. Here it should also be noted that Robert occasionally introduces verse into his prose chronicle; see *HFC* 65–66.

43. On the depiction of Muslim diversity, which exceeds even that of the *GF*, see, e.g., *HI* 27 and 58. Their supposed polytheism is referred to on *HI* 61–64 and 70; they are, of course, once again unsuccessful in their attempts to convert the Franks (*HI* 71). Muslim wealth is referred to, e.g., on *HI* 28 and 74. For Muslim luxury and lechery, see *HI* 60–61 and 76. Nevertheless, once again Muslims still would make good soldiers if only they were Christian (*HI* 35). In *HI* the Crusaders have the social and ethnic cohesion they have in the *GF*, if for somewhat different reasons—Robert, as seen above, closely identifies the Franks of which the *HI* speaks with his French countrymen. They are young and energetic (e.g., *HI* 75–76, 77, and 88) and tied together through kinship (*HI* 15) as well as friendship (*HI* 15–16 and 75). As seen above, they suffer similar privations to those of the *GF*, although Robert is somewhat less interested in drawing attention to these.

44. See chapter 1.

45. See, e.g., Hugh of Vermandois on *HI* 76, Robert of Normandy, Tancred, Godfrey, and Eustace of Boulogne on *HI* 105.

46. The first instance is found in Urban II's speech on *HI* 6, and was referred to at the beginning of this chapter. Furthermore, shortly afterward, the Christian armies are said to travel "per viam scilicet quam Karolus Magnus incomparabilis rex Francorum olim suo exercitui fieri usque Constantinopolim precepit" [*HI* 9; *HFC* 84: "doubtless following the same route as Charlemagne the incomparable king of the Franks once followed on his pilgrimage to Constantinople"].

47. Here it is important to remember that Urban mentions the sins of the Crusaders only once in his speech, whereas he invokes the will of God and the special obligation of the French to fight five times. Also, Robert follows up Urban's speech with his forgiving of the sins of those present, further reducing the redemption of sin as a driving factor in Crusade. See *HI* 5–8.

48. As Robert points out, when describing a successful foraging raid during the siege of Antioch: "Esurientes bonis implebat, quibus adversarios suos spoliabat. Sic quoque filiis Israel olim faciebat, cum per terram gentilium regum transire cupiebant, et illi publicam vie regie incessum eis denigabant. Omnes pari modo qui contra illos accipiebant gladium, gladio peribant; et eorum terra et facultates dabantur eis in possessionem" [*HI* 38; *HFC* 125: "He filled the hungry with good things plundered from their enemies. Just so did He once act for the people of Israel when they wanted to cross the lands of pagan kings who refused to allow them to travel the main road. In exactly the same way all who drew swords on them perished by the sword; and their lands and property were given over to them"].

49. Conquest therefore becomes closely associated with judicial combat, which Robert unsurprisingly makes explicit when Peter the Hermit and Herluin address Kerbogha: "Quod si aput te equi ponderis sunt ius et ratio ut voluptuosa voluntas, fiat inter tuos et nostros determinata pugna, et victoribus absque alio sanguinis dispendio tota hec concedatur patria" [*HI* 70; *HFC* 165: "If law and reason carry the same weight with you as the luxury of getting your own way, let a combat take place between your men and ours and this whole country be conceded to the victors without further bloodshed"].

50. This is how Sweetenham interprets Robert's notion of Crusade; see *HFC* 49.

51. My italics.

52. Robert is arguably even more critical of the Byzantines than the Anonymous had been. He also makes it clear that the Byzantine emperor has no rights to Antioch; see, e.g., *HI* 79.

53. See *HI* xiv; and Riley-Smith, *First Crusade*, 148.

54. It should, after all, not be forgotten that "it was the goal of Jerusalem that made the Crusade a pilgrimage"; Riley-Smith, *First Crusade*, 22.

55. To assume so would necessitate a high degree of anxiety at the prospect of Christian violence, which Robert does not display; he, for instance, does not condemn atrocities such as the cannibalism of Ma'arra or the massacres at Jerusalem. See *HI* 88 and 99–100.

CHAPTER 4

1. I will use "First Cycle of the Crusade," and "Old French Crusade Cycle" to refer to the "historical cycle" around which the remaining poems of the Old French Crusade Cycle were built. On these later additions to the three original chansons, see Edgington and Sweetenham, *Chanson d'Antioche*, 24–26; Suard, *Chanson de Geste*, 93; and Trotter, *Medieval French Literature*, 108–10.

2. Nelson, *Chanson d'Antioche*; Myers, *Chétifs*; and Thorp, *Chanson de Jérusalem*. All further references to these three works will be to these editions and will be cited in the text parenthetically, abbreviated as *CA*, *C*, and *CJ*, respectively. The translation of *CA* is taken from Edgington and Sweetenham, *Chanson d'Antioche*; the translations of *C* and *CJ* are my own.

3. See Barber, *Crusader States*, 174–99. The remainder of the county was sold to the Byzantine emperor in 1150 and fell to the Muslims within the year.

4. See Housley, *Fighting for the Cross*, 8. The bull was used beyond France as well; see Phillips, *Second Crusade*, 59.

5. Eugenius extends the protection of the church upon the Crusaders' property, prevents suits being brought against it in their absence, and absolves them from the need to pay interest on loans. The spiritual reward is no less impressive: "By the authority of omnipotent God and that of Blessed Peter the Prince of the Apostles conceded to us by God, we grant remission of and absolution from sins, as instituted by our aforementioned predecessor, in

such a way that whosoever devoutly begins and completes so holy a journey or dies on it will obtain absolution from all his sins of which he has made confession with a contrite and humble heart; and he will receive the fruit of everlasting recompense from the rewarder of all good people." See Phillips, *Second Crusade*, 281–82.

6. Phillips, *Second Crusade*, 281.

7. Phillips, *Second Crusade*, 281.

8. Riley-Smith, *First Crusaders*, 93–105; Phillips, *Second Crusade*, 99–103.

9. Riley-Smith, "Family Traditions," 101–8; Phillips, *Second Crusade*, 52. On the role of family history in the decision to take the cross, see also Paul, *To Follow in Their Footsteps*.

10. See, e.g., Riley-Smith, "Family Traditions," 103–4; and Riley-Smith, *First Crusaders*, 169–88.

11. Phillips, *Second Crusade*, 168–227.

12. Phillips, *Second Crusade*, 37.

13. See Barber, *Crusader States*, 289–323.

14. Jaffa, Arsuf, Caesarea, Haifa, Sidon, Gibelet, and Beirut all fell between 10 July and 6 August 1187; see Barber, *Crusader States*, 307–8.

15. Schein, *Gateway to the Heavenly Jerusalem*, 159–87.

16. Gillingham, *Richard I*, 208.

17. See Queller and Madden, *Fourth Crusade*.

18. Sunderland has noted three stages in the development of Old French literary cycles. A first saw "the continuation of existing literary texts in the twelfth century to produce longer narrative sequences," with the important caveat that "many of these 'additions' are in fact transmitted only by later cyclical manuscripts, but they have been dated to an earlier period by their editors, allowing us to discern the gradual agglomeration of material." During a second stage, "existing groups of material were adapted and extended through the addition of further texts to 'complete' sequences," often through the addition of works detailing the *enfances* and *morts* of important characters. Finally, the third stage "is the recopying of the material to produce a cyclical manuscript." This process of cyclification was by and large quite slow: "at least fifty and often hundreds of years separate the writing of individual source texts and the production of cyclical manuscripts." See Sunderland, *Old French Narrative Cycles*, 4–7. Bloch has noted that the progression of this cyclification most often expanded the body of chansons backward in time: "The earlier a character or event can be situated chronologically within the global cycle, the later, generally speaking, the date of its addition to the cycle." Bloch, *Etymologies and Genealogies*, 94.

19. Suard, *Chanson de Geste*, 80–82; Bloch, *Etymologies and Genealogies*, 93–96; and Sunderland, *Old French Narrative Cycles*, 4–5.

20. Sunderland has pointed out that even though parts of the *Chanson de Guillaume* can be dated to the early twelfth century, the text that has come down to us is a later compound poem, making the *Couronnement de Louis* the oldest of the *Geste de Garin de Monglane*. See Sunderland, *Old French Narrative Cycles*, 4.

21. Bloch, *Etymologies and Genealogies*, 94.

22. This concern, especially in Flanders and Picardy, where the Old French Crusade Cycle was compiled, is also reflected in the remarkable number of vernacular lay genealogies that were written there, especially in the early decades of the thirteenth century. See Sweetenham, "Antioch and Flanders," 141. On the growing importance of patrilineal kinship as of the eleventh century, see Bloch, *Etymologies and Genealogies*, 64–91; and Keen, *Chivalry*, 143–61, esp. 160–61.

23. Alexis-Paulin Paris, *Nouvelles études*.

24. See Duparc-Quioc, *Chanson d'Antioche*, 2:217; and Kleber, "Graindor de Douai," 66–75. The historical evidence for the existence of its supposed early composer, Richard the Pilgrim, is scanty at best, and there is no proof that the version of the *CA* that preceded this was a chanson de geste. See Edgington and Sweetenham, *Chanson d'Antioche*, 4–5 and 9–12; and Cook, "*Chanson d'Antioche*," 23–27.

25. As Susan Edgington and Carol Sweetenham note, this late twelfth-century version may have drawn on older vernacular, non-chanson material, such as the writings of Gregory Bechada and possibly the *Canso d'Antioca*. See Edgington and Sweetenham, *Chanson d'Antioche*, 12–13; see also Sweetenham and Patterson, *Canso d'Antioca*, 51–78.

26. See Duparc-Quioc, *Chanson d'Antioche*, 2:132–39; Sweetenham, "Antioch and Flanders," 136–51; Throop, *Crusading as an Act of Vengeance*, 200–201; and Edgington and Sweetenham, *Chanson d'Antioche*, 34. The texts offer some possible circumstantial indications as to the date of the Cycle's composition. Laisse 6 of *CA* implies that the Saracens at the time of writing occupy the Holy Places and possess the Cross, imposing a tribute on Christian visitors (*CA* ll. 117–40). The mention of "tribute" implies that these lines postdate the Treaty of Ramla, which opened up Jerusalem to Christian pilgrims, in 1192. The sense of astonishment and urgency reflected in the *CJ* furthermore suggests a date rather not too long after the events of 1187: "Se nos Jerusalem ralons or reperdant / Tos nos pelerinages ne vaura .I. bezant / Ne quan que avons fait ne pris jo mie .I. gant" [*CJ* ll. 5381–83: "If, having lost it, we now do not go back to Jerusalem, all of our pilgrimages will not be worth one bezant, and all that we have done and conquered not even one glove"]. See also *CJ* ll. 5545–47, 6626–30, and 6733–34. Finally, the remarkably benevolent way in which the Old French Crusade Cycle approaches the Byzantines may indicate a date before the Latin conquest of Constantinople. It is therefore likely that the Cycle was completed in the period 1192–1204.

27. Edgington and Sweetenham, *Chanson d'Antioche*, 15–24. The St. Pols play a far more extensive role in the Old French Crusade Cycle than they had in the First Crusade; see Sweetenham, "Antioch and Flanders," 139–42.

28. *C* xi–xxxv; Edgington and Sweetenham, *Chanson d'Antioche*, 30–31.

29. Edgington and Sweetenham, *Chanson d'Antioche*, 28–29. On the historicity of *CJ*, see also Thorp, "*Chanson de Jérusalem* and the Latin Chronicles."

30. Edgington and Sweetenham, *Chanson d'Antioche*, 101, n. 4. On Graindor, see also Edgington and Sweetenham, *Chanson d'Antioche*, 5–8; Cook, *"Chanson d'Antioche,"* 28–30; Sweetenham, "Antioch and Flanders," 133–136; and Kleber, "Graindor de Douai."

31. The cognomen "Grain d'or" has been found among these; see Edgington and Sweetenham, *Chanson d'Antioche*, 7–8.

32. As Edgington and Sweetenham see it, "The First Crusade is recast as a Picard enterprise." Edgington and Sweetenham, *Chanson d'Antioche*, 35.

33. Claassens, "Cycle de la Croisade," 186.

34. See also *CA* ll. 26–27, 100–116, 9447–51; and *CJ* ll. 5005–9.

35. Edgington and Sweetenham, *Chanson d'Antioche*, 35; Sweetenham, "Antioch and Flanders," 137–39. However, as Cook points out, "We are not required to place the Chanson d'Antioche precisely in 1187 or 1190 in order to consider that it probably served a propaganda effort that was nearly continuous, despite obvious ebbs and flows of interest." Cook, "Crusade Propaganda," 159.

36. Cf. Cook: "The poems of the Cycles of the Crusades were copied, sung, and constantly modified over at least three centuries. As long as the crusading idea stayed alive in northern France they constituted an energetic, if unofficial parallel crusading propaganda, available in a form easily digested by a broad audience." Cook, "Crusade Propaganda," 167.

37. Edgington and Sweetenham, *Chanson d'Antioche*, 84–85.

38. The implications of rendering history as chanson in the Old French Crusade Cycle are capably outlined in Edgington and Sweetenham, *Chanson d'Antioche*, 63–84; and Trotter, *Medieval French Literature*, 110–17.

39. *CA* ll. 492–93: "the terrible agonizing battles that made mothers weep with grief for their children."

40. E.g., "Se Dex le me consent, li fils sainte Marie" [C l. 1082: "If God, the son of Holy Mary allows me"]; the Virgin in turn is "Marie li mere au Creator" [*CJ* l. 108: "Mary, the mother of the Creator"].

41. See also *CA* ll. 176–80 and 201–6. The extent to which religion is thought of in familial terms is indicated by the fact that conversion, an important issue in the Old French Crusade Cycle, is referred to as moving from one family to the next. Brohadas, the son of the sultan, wills for Bohemond to convert: "Puis en ferai mon frere quant sa lois iert fausee, / L'une moitiés de Perse li sera delivree" [*CA* ll. 6420–21: "Once his religion has been overthrown I shall make him my brother and he will get half of all Persia"]. Muslims or Christians become the other's "brother" when they cross the line; Datien, who converts to Christianity and betrays Antioch to the Crusaders, must therefore sever his earlier family connections to Islam by killing his wife and his brother (and taking his son into Christianity with him), as in *CA* ll. 7427–38 and 7830–42, respectively. In C, Kerbogha, who has steadfastly chosen the side of the Christians, refuses as yet to convert because it will hurt his mother (ll. 2933–41); nevertheless, he will eventually do so, and it will kill her (ll. 2765–69).

42. See Riley-Smith, "Crusading as an Act of Love."

43. See also CA ll. 492–93 and 769–71; CJ ll. 8720–50 and 9710–42; see furthermore Cook, "*Chanson d'Antioche*," 56–57.

44. See also, e.g., CA ll. 5103–23; and CJ ll. 3833–36.

45. This mirroring expands the tradition of Christian–pagan parallelism of earlier chansons de geste discussed in chapter 1. Characteristic aspects of this parallelism, such as the notion of the "noble Saracen," occur in the Old French Crusade Cycle as well; see, e.g., CA ll. 5778–79. Intriguingly, the Old French Crusade Cycle goes so far as to grant the Muslims their own particular "pardon" for fighting the Christians; see CA ll. 6464–65. Fighting for Islam will furthermore guarantee entry to paradise, even if *manu militari*. Upon the Saracen's death, "Dedens son puig senestre .II. besans metra / Et dedens son puig destre une piere tenra, / Mahoumés en son sain .I. autre li metra. / Tout droit en paradis li paiens ira, / Que Damedeus de glore a Adan coumanda. / Les .II. besans luisans pour ofrande tenra / Et se il l'en desfent, la piere haucera; / Devant enmi le front li paiens l'en ferra / Et de l'autre del sain si k'il le tuera. / U il voelle u non la dedens enterra. / Les .II. besans a Dieu par acorde donra. / Par sifaite maniere trestous vous sauvera" [CA ll. 6628–39: "[He will] have two bezants put into his left hand and a stone into his right; Mohammed will put another stone in his breast. The infidel will go straight to Paradise where God gave Adam his commandments. He should offer the two bezants to the porter to be allowed in. If the porter refuses, he should throw the stone so that it hits the porter on the forehead and follow it with the other one in his breast so that the porter falls down dead. Like it or not, into Paradise he will go. [He will give the two bezants to God in reconciliation.] That is how he will give you all salvation"].

46. The description of the Saracen gods is characteristically vitriolic and includes a jewel-encrusted image of Mohammed animated by a demon; see CA ll. 6594–616.

47. The difference between Christians and pagans is also expressed in terms of obedience, as Christ describes the pagans having disobeyed his orders and taken his land (see, e.g., CA ll. 122–34 and 166–80); they thereby become the "disloyal vassals" of the chanson de geste tradition, and the Crusade becomes a war between loyal vassals and disloyal ones who hold their land illegitimately.

48. On vengeance in the Middle Ages, see Throop, *Crusading as an Act of Vengeance*, 11–41; Throop and Hyams, *Vengeance in the Middle Ages*; and Smail and Gibson, *Vengeance in Medieval Europe*. On Crusade and vengeance, see Riley-Smith, *First Crusade*, 54–57; and Throop, *Crusading as an Act of Vengeance*.

49. See Riley-Smith, "Crusading as an Act of Love," 49. Innocent included references to vengeance in three bulls, *Post miserabile* (1198), *Utinam Dominus* (1208), and *Quia maior* (1213); see Sweetenham, "Antioch and Flanders," 148.

50. See Throop, *Crusading as an Act of Vengeance*, 73–116; Edgington and Sweetenham, *Chanson d'Antioche*, 32–35; Kleber, "Pèlerinage—Vengeance—Conquête"; and Sweetenham, "Antioch and Flanders," 147–50.

51. See also *CA* ll. 84–99, 168–78, 318–74, 3160–72, and 4855–56. On Crusade as vengeance for God, see Riley-Smith, "Crusading as an Act of Love," 36–38.

52. See also, e.g., *CA* ll. 11038–51; Riley-Smith, "Crusading as an Act of Love," 38–42.

53. See, e.g., *CA* ll. 2253–61; and *CJ* ll. 5609–35.

54. See also *CJ* ll. 4834–37.

55. This kin-group vengeance applies in a wider sense also to those dependents who may not have been immediate family. Hugh of Vermandois on the field at Antioch utters his desire to avenge his dependent Eudes: "Ahi, franc chevalier, con vous suel cier tenir! / Mout vous estes penés toustans de moi servir. / . . . / Se ne vous puis vengier, ne doi terre tenir" [*CA* ll. 10491–95: "Alas, noble lord, how dearly I prize you! You have always done the utmost to serve me. . . . If I cannot avenge you now, I do not deserve to hold any lands"].

56. Hugh of Vermandois will echo Soliman's exclamation on *CA* ll. 10491–95, and will notably succeed in exacting his revenge.

57. *CA* ll. 2632–33.

58. See, e.g., *CJ* ll. 8186–93 and 8392–400.

59. This passage has a precedent in the *GF*, although there it served to highlight the debauchery of the Muslim adversary; see my chapter 2.

60. See also *CA* 76–80.

61. See also *CA* ll. 10145–48. This parallels the propaganda of Innocent III for the Fourth Crusade; see Housley, *Fighting for the Cross*, 36 and n. 71.

62. When offered the land, the magnates of the Crusader host, with the exception of Godfrey of Bouillon, all refuse it in favor of their own lands in *CJ* ll. 5010–297; although the passage closely resembles the magnates' refusal to carry the Holy Lance in *CA* ll. 9452–692, it shows Christian territorial expansion in the Middle East described as an inadvertent consequence and not a goal of the Crusade. Baldwin of Boulogne's acquisition of Edessa is furthermore characteristically described in terms of family expansion, as he wins the territory only as a result of his wedding to the daughter of the Old Man of the Mountain; see *CA* ll. 3001–63.

63. This is in turn echoed by Kerbogha in *CA* ll. 9084–86.

64. E.g., *CA* ll. 531, 573, 1584–90, 2290–96, 2263–64, 5649–55, 8593–615; *CJ* ll. 1375–79.

65. See also *CA* ll. 2752–64.

66. *CJ* ll. 8437–818.

67. The Old French Crusade Cycle may also obliquely recognize contemporary circumstances in its repeated usage of the name "Saladin" (Salahadins, Salhadin, Salehadins) in *CA* ll. 559, 566, 1580, 2197, 2206, and 2616; and *CJ* l. 248.

68. For more on Tatikios, an amiable character who asks his uncle the emperor for permission to join the Crusaders, see *CA* ll. 1214–341.

69. On the multiplicity of the Crusaders, see, e.g., *CA* ll. 1–60, 1006–23, 1507–57; or *CJ* ll. 4478–82.

70. On the notably amicable relationship between Baldwin and Tancred, see *CA* ll. 2794–828. The confrontation between Bohemond of Taranto and Raymond of Toulouse over the fate of Antioch, although mentioned in *CA* ll. 7261–322, is virtually ignored after the fall of the citadel, see *CA* Appendix VI ll. 111–46.

71. This includes an uncomplicated enjoyment of cannibalism: see *CA* ll. 4938–5051. On the Tafurs, see also Janet, *Idéologie incarnée*, 142–55, 171–84, and 345–68.

72. E.g., at the Battle of Antioch, where the corps of the princes (*CA* ll. 9739–10008) fights alongside one of clergymen (*CA* ll. 10009–43) and one of the Tafurs, led by their king (*CA* ll. 10044–92). Likewise at the siege of Jerusalem; see *CJ* ll. 5897–940.

CHAPTER 5

1. Gaston Paris, Review of *La Tapisserie de Bayeux*, 410.

2. Rousset, *Origines et caractères*, 111.

3. Ambroise, *History of the Holy War*. On the identity of Ambroise, see Ambroise, *History of the Holy War*, 2:1–2.

4. On the occurrence of chanson de geste commonplaces in the *Estoire*, see Ambroise, *History of the Holy War*, 2:12–23; and Ailes, "Ambroise's *Estoire de la Guerre Sainte.*" On the dating of the work, see Ambroise, *History of the Holy War*, 2:3.

5. The original is taken from Ambroise, *History of the Holy War*, 1:137–38, ll. 8459–98; the translation is from Ambroise, *History of the Holy War*, 2:145–46.

6. See chapter 4.

7. The original is taken from Ambroise, *History of the Holy War*, 1:172, ll. 10635–54; the translation is from Ambroise, *History of the Holy War*, 2:174.

8. See Ambroise, *History of the Holy War*, 2:146, n. 549, and 2:174, n. 677.

9. See Edgington and Sweetenham, *Chanson d'Antioche*, 2–48. As Ambroise does not refer to the events after the siege of Antioch, he was likely unaware of *C* and *CJ*, the other works in the First Old French Crusade Cycle.

10. Smith, *Crusading in the Age of Joinville*, 63–64.

11. Hodgson, *Women, Crusading and the Holy Land*, 30.

12. Shirley, *Song of the Cathar Wars*, 11 and n. 6.

13. See Brett, *Humbert of Romans*, 173. Humbert considered the *Pseudo-Turpin Chronicle* a historical account rather than an epic invention, juxtaposing it with the books of the Maccabees, Walter the Chancellor's *Bella Antiochena*, and Jacques of Vitry's *Historia Transmarina* as another motivating instance of Christianity's fight against the unbeliever. See also Lloyd, *English Society and the Crusades*, 97; Smith, *Crusading in the Age of Joinville*, 91–92; Trotter, "Mythologie arthurienne"; Trotter, *Medieval French Literature*, 24–25; and Jacoby, "Littérature française," 622. On the *Pseudo-Turpin Chronicle*, see also Purkis, "Rewriting the History Books," 147–50.

14. See, e.g., *CA* ll. 1043–61 and ll. 2678–84.

15. Notable here is the figure of the "Saracen princess," such as Orable in the *Prise d'Orange* (mid-twelfth century) or Nubie in the *Prise de Cordres et de Sebille* (thirteenth century); typically, she falls in love with the hero of the poem, converts to Christianity, and marries him, thereby giving him the right to her property. The affection of the "Saracen princess" therefore serves to win her, and her estates, for Christianity. See Kay, *Chansons de Geste in the Age of Romance*, 29–48; and Kinoshita, *Medieval Boundaries*, 46–73.

16. Kay has analyzed the chansons de geste and chivalric romance as both contemporaneous and complementary genres that shed light upon the "political unconscious" of the other; see Kay, *Chansons de Geste in the Age of Romance*. See also Gaunt, "Romance and Other Genres," 48–49.

17. Pearsall, *Arthurian Romance*, 21–22. For the difference between chanson and chivalric romance, see also Auerbach, *Mimesis*, 123–52.

18. Auerbach, *Mimesis*, 136.

19. On the translation of the Provençal, troubadour idea of fin' amors to chivalric and Arthurian romance, see Keen, *Chivalry*, 116. On the difference between troubadour love and chivalric courtly love, see O'Donohue, *Courtly Love Tradition*, 1–16. On courtly love and the clerks of the court, see Kay, "Courts, Clerks, and Courtly Love." Gaunt has highlighted the problematic nature of the courtly love of the romances; see Gaunt, *Gender and Genre*, 71–121.

20. Pearsall, *Arthurian Romance*, 43–48.

21. A very broad notion of medieval romance is outlined in Fuchs, *Romance*.

22. See Bruckner, "Shape of Romance."

23. On the implications of the structure of the romance quest, see Frye, *Secular Scripture*, 35–61.

24. Andreas Capellanus, *Art of Courtly Love*, 100.

25. Fuchs, *Romance*, 44.

26. Andreas Capellanus, *Art of Courtly Love*, 187–88.

27. Nicholson, *Chronicle of the Third Crusade*, 6–10.

28. Nicholson, *Chronicle of the Third Crusade*, 23.

29. Housley, *Fighting for the Cross*, 195–96.

30. See Hodgson, *Women, Crusading and the Holy Land*, 135–39; and Housley, *Fighting for the Cross*, 174–75. As Housley points out, sometimes even marital relations were deemed too much: according to Fulcher of Chartres, when the First Crusaders had been bogged down at the siege of Antioch in 1098, they expelled *all* women, including wives who had accompanied their husbands on the journey, from the camp. See Fulcher of Chartres, *Expedition to Jerusalem*, 95.

31. Housley, *Fighting for the Cross*, 194; *GF* 58.

32. Tyerman, *England and the Crusades*, 61. Housley's more sanguine view of the ordinances is that "swearing, gambling, and whoring were key targets." Housley, *Fighting for the Cross*, 103.

33. Tolan, *Saracens*, 135–69; Housley, *Fighting for the Cross*, 212.

34. See chapters 1 and 2.

35. On the opposition between the ideologies of courtly chivalry and Crusade, see Ashe, "Ideal of Knighthood."

36. Routledge, "Songs," 93–94.

37. The text is taken from Conon de Béthune, *Chansons*, 224–25; the translation is taken from Routledge, "Songs," 104. For more on the topic of the separated heart, see Routledge, "Songs," 104; and Smith, *Crusading in the Age of Joinville*, 86.

38. Marcabru, *Critical Edition*, 2–3.

39. Marcabru, *Critical Edition*, 42–43.

40. Marcabru, *Critical Edition*, 42–43.

41. See also his exhortatory "Pax in nomine Domini"; Marcabru, *Critical Edition*, 438–41. Gaunt has discovered widespread use of irony in the poetry of Marcabru; however, I do not find evidence for it in "A la fontana del vergier" and "Pax in nomine Domini," which Gaunt does not include in his analysis. See Gaunt, *Troubadours and Irony*, 39–79.

42. Guiot of Dijon's "Chanterai por mon courage" adds a certain sensuality to the separation. See Guiot de Dijon et Jocelin, *Chansons*, 1–3; Routledge, "Songs," 104–5.

43. See Jordan, "Representation of the Crusades."

44. Both the original and the translation are taken from Thibaut de Champagne, *Lyrics of Thibaut de Champagne*, 230–31.

45. Thibaut de Champagne, *Lyrics of Thibaut de Champagne*, 230–31.

46. Thibaut de Champagne, *Lyrics of Thibaut de Champagne*, 232–33.

47. As Jordan points out, Thibaut expands on this in another song, "Au Tens Plain de Felonie." See Thibaut de Champagne, *Lyrics of Thibaut de Champagne*, 234–37; and Jordan, "Representation of the Crusades," 33–34. See also Routledge, "Songs," 102; and Housley, *Fighting for the Cross*, 79–80.

48. Only very rarely do we find secular courtly love congruent with Crusade in the chansons de croisade of this time; to the best of my knowledge only Conon of Béthune sees Syria as the place "Ou on conquiert Paradis et honor / Et pris et los et l'amor de s'amie." [ll. 15–16: "where one wins Paradise and honor, and praise and fame and the love of one's lady"]. See Conon de Béthune, *Chansons*, 225. Trotter includes "S'onques nus hom por dure departie" by Hugues of Berzé (ca. 1150–1220) and "A vous amant, plus qu'a nule autre gent" by the castellan of Coucy (fl. ca. 1186–1203) among the poems that make common cause between Crusade and courtly love, but the correlation between holy war and fin' amors is less evident in these. See Trotter, *Medieval French Literature*, 180–82.

49. Mickel and Nelson, *Naissance du Chevalier au Cygne*, xv.

50. The popularity of these episodes resulted in the composition, in the later thirteenth or early fourteenth century, of a sequence of continuations—such as *La Chretienté Corbaran*, *La Prise d'Acre*, *La Mort Godefroi*, and *La Chanson des Rois Baudouin*—that narrated the aftermath of the First Crusade and the history of the Crusader states up to the rise of Saladin, and are close in dating, subject, and style to the Second Old French Crusade Cycle discussed in chapter 7.

51. These, no less than *CA*, *C*, and *CJ*, glorify the heroes of the First Crusade, *in casu* the first ruler of the kingdom of Jerusalem. For their function as popular history, see Mickel, *Enfances Godefroi*, 56–77.

52. Technically there are three, as a composite version exists. See Mickel and Nelson, *Naissance du Chevalier au Cygne*, lxxxxviii–lxxxxix.

53. Mickel and Nelson, *Naissance du Chevalier au Cygne*, lxxxxv.

54. Mickel and Nelson, *Naissance du Chevalier au Cygne*, lxxxxvi–lxxxxviii.

55. Here and below, the original text is taken from Mickel and Nelson, *Naissance du Chevalier au Cygne*, and will be cited parenthetically; the translation is mine.

56. Compare Chrétien de Troyes, *Romans*, 953 and 948–51, respectively.

57. See Chrétien de Troyes, *Romans*, 636–704.

58. Nelson, *Chevalier au Cygne*, xxvi–xxviii.

59. The original is taken from Nelson, *Chevalier au Cygne*; the translation is my own.

60. Gautier de Tournay, *Histore de Gille de Chyn*. Henceforth *GDC*.

61. "The *Histoire de Gilles de Chyn* is usually termed the first historico-biographical romance of O.F. literature." See *GDC* 11. On the life of the historical Gilles of Chin, see *GDC* 5; and Willard, "Gilles de Chin in History," 358–59.

62. *GDC* 142, l. 5545.

63. Petit, "Reminiscences littéraires," 197–204; and *GDC* 11.

64. See *GDC* 127, ll. 4911–20.

65. *GDC* 10.

66. Willard, "Gilles de Chin in History," 361.

67. Willard, "Gilles de Chin in History," 361; and Moyen, "'Tournois grans et pleniers,'" 22.

68. *GDC* 14, ll. 45–54.

69. On the tournaments in which Gilles is said to have fought, see Moyen, "'Tournois grans et pleniers,'" 21–29. On the tournament, see Keen, *Chivalry*, 8–101; and Barber and Barker, *Tournaments*.

70. *GDC* 23–24, ll. 425–88.

71. The original is taken from *GDC*; the translation is my own. All future references to *GDC* are to this edition, and will be cited in the text parenthetically.

72. *GDC* 27–28, ll. 613–50.

73. *GDC* 31–32, ll. 791–834.

74. *GDC* 48, ll. 1540–44.

75. *GDC* 45–51, ll. 1413–663. See also Moyen, "'Tournois grans et pleniers,'" 23.

76. *GDC* 53, ll. 1718–43.

77. *GDC* 55, ll. 1830–39. "The terms offered in the celestial missive recall both epic and lyric simplifications of the crusade indulgence"; Trotter, *Medieval French Literature*, 144. Gilles reiterates his reasons to take the cross to the count of Duras; the repeated use of the first person plural here suggests that Gautier of Tournai thought Gilles' motivation should also move his audience: "Cil est de sez peciez toz quitez / Qui de bon cuer

fait ceste voie. / . . . / Dix done plus c'on ne desert: / Il fu por nous en la crois mis / Et clauficiés et escopis, / Et ferus el cuer d'une lance. / Nous devons bien penre venjance, / De ciax qui ainsi l'ont traitié / Quant il de nous ot teil pitié / Que de son sanc nous racata. / Ne le devons oublïer ja. / Por lui vengier ai la crois prise, / Que Dius au grant jor du juïse, / Quant il venrra le mont jugier, / Nous puist de nos meffais aidier" [ll. 2033–49: "He who makes this journey with good intentions will be delivered of all his sins. . . . God gives more than we deserve: he was put on the cross for us, and nailed and spat upon there, and struck in the heart with a lance. We must take vengeance appropriately upon them who treated him that way, when he had such pity on us that he bought us back with his blood. We must never forget it. I have taken the cross to avenge him, so that God on the great Day of Judgement, when he will come to judge the world, can help us with regard to our misdeeds"].

78. Participation in tournaments was prohibited by ecclesiastical law. See Barber and Barker, *Tournaments*, 139–49.

79. See Trotter, *Medieval French Literature*, 143–44.

80. GDC 62–64, ll. 2123–201.

81. GDC 67, ll. 2323–25.

82. GDC 79–80, ll. 2866–79. Gilles also declines an offer of lands from the prince of Antioch; see GDC 109, ll. 4122–46.

83. GDC 95–96, ll. 3555–78.

84. GDC 96–99, ll. 3589–710.

85. GDC 99–100, ll. 3701–32.

86. Compare, e.g., GDC 105, ll. 3963–68 with CR ll. 1265–68.

87. GDC 75, ll. 2675–82.

88. GDC 76–79, ll. 2736–839. See also Trotter, *Medieval French Literature*, 142–43; Petit, "Reminiscences littéraires," 198–99; and Willard, "Gilles de Chin in History," 361. It is possible that Gautier was also acquainted with other works of the First Old French Crusade Cycle, as his description of Gilles's actions in the principality of Antioch may draw upon the *Chanson d'Antioche*; see Petit, "Reminiscences littéraires," 199.

89. Petit, "Reminiscences littéraires," 202–3; and Willard, "Gilles de Chin in History," 362.

90. Petit, "Reminiscences littéraires," 202; Willard, "Gilles de Chin in History," 361; Lachet, "'À la griffe on reconnaît le lion,'" 82–83.

91. GDC 111–14, ll. 4239–370.

92. GDC 115, ll. 4381–92.

93. GDC 124–25, ll. 4787–828.

CHAPTER 6

1. Riley-Smith, *Short History*, 206–7.

2. See, e.g., Mayer: "And when an Italian, Martoni, visited Cyprus in 1394 he noticed that when the noble ladies went out of doors they wore long black garments which revealed only their eyes. When he asked for an explanation of this custom, he was told that it was a token of mourning for the

lost city of Acre in 1291." Mayer, *Crusades*, 287. See also Schein, *Fideles Crucis*, 112–13.

3. A great many of them did, and Keen has offered us a wealth of data to suggest that, at least in the English sphere, traditions of crusading persisted in various social strata throughout the period. Crusaders were truly willing to fight wherever the opportunity presented itself. Consider in this context the Scrope family, whose members fought and died on all three major crusading fronts in the fourteenth century alone. See Keen, "Chaucer's Knight," 51–52.

4. In 1277–1278, in 1282–1283, and again in 1294–1295. See Prestwich, *Three Edwards*, 10–17.

5. In 1294–1298. Prestwich, *Edward I*, 376–400.

6. In 1296, 1297, and 1306. See Prestwich, *Three Edwards*, 42–43.

7. Riley-Smith, *Short History*, 225–26.

8. Insightful here is Jean of Joinville's *Vie de Saint Louis*. See Joinville and Villehardouin, *Chronicles of the Crusades*, 137–336.

9. Atiya suggests that Philip IV used the Crusade above all as a pretext to fill his own coffers, most notably at the expense of the papacy. See Atiya, *Crusade in the Later Middle Ages*, 48.

10. The reforms of Philip IV involved a number of issues: "the laying of the foundation of absolutism, the modest beginning of the French 'Parlement,' the extension of royal authority in matters of taxation and jurisdiction outside the king's 'demesnes,' the humiliation of the Roman Curia and the establishment of the Papacy at Avignon, the abolition of the Order of the Templars and the confiscation of their property." Atiya, *Crusades in the Later Middle Ages*, 47; see also Strayer, *Reign of Philip the Fair*, 142–236.

11. Housley, *Later Crusades*, 30–33.

12. Riley-Smith, *Short History*, 227.

13. Strayer, *Reign of Philip the Fair*, 250–51.

14. See, e.g., Kilgour, *Decline of Chivalry*.

15. Dembowski, *Jean Froissart*, 123.

16. See Allmand, *Hundred Years War*, 37–90.

17. Paravicini, *Ritterlich-höfische Kultur*, 38–39.

18. Keen, *Chivalry*, 233.

19. Keen, *Chivalry*, 237.

20. Paravicini, *Ritterlich-höfische Kultur*, 40.

21. Keen, *Chivalry*, 121–24.

22. Kaeuper, *Chivalry and Violence*, 30–33; Kaeuper, "Societal Role of Chivalry," 98; and Kennedy, "Knight as Reader."

23. Kennedy, "Knight as Reader," 72–73; see also Jacoby, "Knightly Values," 166; Jacoby, "Littérature française," 627; and Loomis, "Arthurian Influence," 553.

24. Keen, *Chivalry*, 92–93; and Loomis, "Arthurian Influence," 555.

25. See Cline, "Influence of Romances." Cline notes that even though the majority of romance-themed tournaments drew on the Arthurian texts, some found their inspiration in romances such as the *Voeux du Paon* and *Gui de Warewic*. See also Jacoby, "Knightly Values," 167–68; and Loomis,

"Arthurian Influence," 554. On the influence of secular literature on late medieval tournaments and spectacles, see Barber and Barker, *Tournaments*, 107–37.

26. Crawford, *"Templar of Tyre,"* 86–87. See also Jacoby, "Knightly Values," 166–68 and 176–77; and Jacoby, "Littérature française," 629–30. On how Arthur and the knights of the Round Table influenced thought on the tournament in later centuries, see Jefferson, "Tounaments, Heraldry, and the Knights of the Round Table," esp. 80–89.

27. Vale, "Arthur in English Society," 185–90.

28. Cline, "Influence of Romances," 208.

29. The practice of using Arthurian language to describe the requirements of knighthood may even predate the fourteenth century. Elspeth Kennedy has noted that Ramon Llull's late thirteenth-century treatise on chivalry, the *Libre del Orde de Cavallería*, has some verbal echoes from the prose *Lancelot*, especially in its description of the origins of knighthood and of the knight's duty to protect his lord. See Kennedy, "Knight as Reader," 83–87.

30. Geoffroi de Charny, *Book of Chivalry*, 95.

31. Geoffroi de Charny, *Book of Chivalry*, 119.

32. Philippe de Mézières, *Songe du Vieil Pelerin*, 1:85. My translation.

33. Mentioned in Keen, *Chivalry*, 117. See also Kaeuper, *Chivalry and Violence*, 212.

34. For an interesting overview of such instances, see Keen, *Chivalry*, 117.

35. Lalande, *Livre des fais du bon messire Jehan le Maingre*, 27–28. My translation.

36. Lalande, *Livre des fais du bon messire Jehan le Maingre*, 164. My translation.

37. Keen, *Chivalry*, 191.

38. Keen, *Chivalry*, 192–93.

39. Keen, *Chivalry*, 179–99.

40. It is first documented in in a charter dated 8 June 1337; see Feil, "Ältesten St. Georgsritter in Österreich," 221–22.

41. Van D'Elden, *Peter Suchenwirt*, 187–89; and Feil, "Ältesten St. Georgsritter in Österreich," 218 and 232.

42. For its membership, see Feil, "Ältesten St. Georgsritter in Österreich," 222–23.

43. Van D'Elden, *Peter Suchenwirt*, 178; and Feil, "Ältesten St. Georgsritter in Österreich," 218. Murphy notes that Wolfram appears to have coined the word "Tempeleise" himself as a way to denote a Knight Templar; see Murphy, *Gemstone of Paradise*, 52.

44. Keen, *Chivalry*, 117.

45. Modern research on the Baltic presence of the order has suffered from much bias, often fueled by the events of the twentieth century. Accordingly, the order was either seen as bringing the gift of culture and Christianity to an underdeveloped part of northern Europe or as an aggressively expansionist and repressive force, an exponent of the German *Drang nach Osten*. Joshua Prawer, for instance, famously described the Teutonic Order as "the iron fist of German expansion" that "laid the foundations of the future Kingdom of

Prussia and the cornerstone of Imperial Germany." Prawer, *World of the Crusaders*, 119–20. Partisan treatment of the issue, especially in the hands of German and Estonian scholars, has been well illustrated by Juhan Kreem. See Kreem, "Teutonic Order in Livonia." Recent decades, however, have produced some fine scholarship on the order and on the Baltic Crusades in general. Of note are the works of Eric Christiansen and William Urban, which have contributed substantially to the understanding of both the long and brutal wars between the order and the Baltic tribes and the structures of the Ordenstaat itself. See Christiansen, *Northern Crusades*; Urban, *Prussian Crusade*; Urban, *Samogitian Crusade*.

46. Christiansen, *Northern Crusades*, 79.

47. Housley, *Later Crusades*, 324.

48. On this early fighting between Christians and pagans, including the so-called Wendish Crusade of 1147–1185, see Christiansen, *Northern Crusades*, 6–69; Urban, *Baltic Crusade*, 1–164; and Bartlett, *Making of Europe*, 15–18.

49. The union of Lithuania and Poland and the baptism and coronation of Jogailo of Lithuania as Wladyslaw IV turned the tide irreversibly against the order. Its military power was broken at the decisive Battle of Tannenberg (Grünwald) on 15 July 1410. See Christiansen, *Northern Crusades*, 158–60 and 219–23.

50. Housley, *Later Crusades*, 339–41.

51. Urban, *Samogitian Crusade*, 17.

52. Housley, *Later Crusades*, 324.

53. Urban, *Samogitian Crusade*, 18.

54. Housley, *Later Crusades*, 400.

55. Christiansen, *Northern Crusade*, 149. For an extensive and detailed discussion of these "international" participants, see Paravicini, *Preußenreisen des europäischen Adels*.

56. Keen, *Chivalry*, 173.

57. Keen, *Chivalry*, 174.

58. Päsler, *Deutschsprachige Sachliteratur*, 281–82.

59. Helm and Ziesemer, *Literatur des deutschen Ritterordens*, 44–46, 92–94, and 115–16.

60. See Riley-Smith, "Crusading as an Act of Love," 31–50.

61. Peter of Duisburg, *Chronica Terre Prussie*. All further references to Peter's work will be to this edition, and will be cited in the text parenthetically, abbreviated to *CTP*. The translations are my own.

62. Töppen's edition lists all biblical references in II.6–II.8. These are very rich; next to numerous extracts from Maccabees, it also includes citations from Deuteronomy, Judges, Kings, Exodus, and Judith. See *CTP* 38–40.

63. Keen, *Chivalry*, 119–21.

64. Fischer, "*Di Himels Rote*," 95–123.

65. For a slightly different evaluation of the chronicle's goals, see Fischer, "Des tûvils kint," 260–61.

66. Mary Fischer in particular has emphasized this aspect of both Peter's original and Nicolaus's translation: "In the Krônike von Prûzinlant, which

was completed in its original form in 1326, the Order set out to restate the idea of the *militia Christi* and the holy war in order to provide its members with a unifying ethos, to reinforce their vocation and hence to revive the original zeal of the crusading ideal." Fischer,"*Di Himels Rote,*" 15–21, here 21.

67. Töppen, "Einleitung," 9.

68. Strehlke has identified a handful of Jeroschins or cognate place names in the larger sphere of the order's lands, any of which could have been his home. See Strehlke, "Einleitung," 294.

69. In ll. 302–9 of his *Krônike von Prûzinlant*, Nicolaus pleads for inspiration: "Und want ich tummer sinne bin, / meisterlîcher kunste wan, / darzû lutzil dûtschis kan, / ôt alse mich dî larte, / der spune mich ê narte, / dâvon ouch umbesnittin / nâch hovelîchin sittin / mînes mundis lippin sîn" ["And because I am lacking in intellect, and have not mastered these skills, and additionally do not know much German, other than what I learned with my mother's milk, so that my words are not well tailored to courtly conventions"]. This, together with the fact that in l. 15043 Nicolaus uses the word "ozzek" to translate Peter's "propugnaculum" ("forecastle, outer strongpoint") rather than the Middle High German "bercvrît," has led Strehlke to suggest that Polish may have been native to Nicolaus. Helm and Ziesemer, however, write that "ozzek" found its way into the military terminology of the order fairly early on, and that Nicolaus's admission of his own fallibility should probably be understood as a modesty topos, and as such not necessarily indicative of any language background, is supported by Evald Johansson's suggestion that the grandmaster of the order would only have entrusted Nicolaus with such important work as the translation of the order's official chronicle, "wenn er gewusst hätte, das Deutsch seine Muttersprache war und dass er im übrigen die nötigen Voraussetzungen hatte, die Aufgabe auf befriedigende Weise zu lösen." See Strehlke, "Einleitung," 293; Helm and Ziesemer, *Literatur des deutschen Ritterordens*, 152; and Johansson, *Deutschordenschronik des Nicolaus von Jeroschin*, 31. All subsequent references to Nicolaus's work will be to Nicolaus von Jeroschin, *Krônike von Prûzinlant*; in citations the title of the work will be abbreviated to *KVP*. Unless otherwise stated, the translation is taken from Nicolaus von Jeroschin, *Chronicle of Prussia*. Both original text and translation will be cited in the text parenthetically.

70. The evidence is mostly circumstantial. In a humorous aside, Nicolaus comments on the miraculous regrowth of a brother's hair, wishing the same would happen to him: "Ô, wolde sich daz zeichin / ouch ûf mir armin reichin! / Ich wold mîn crullil streichin / unde in lôsim smeichin / dî andiren kalin leichin, / dî des windis sîn gemût, / der in ofte leide tût, / sô er in vorsturzit den hût / vor der werdin vrouwin lût!" [*KVP* ll. 18918–26: "I wish that this miracle would also happen to poor me. I would stroke my curls and mock the other bald men when, as often happens, the wind blows their hats off in front of the ladies!"] This mention of baldness has led Helm and Ziesemer to assume that Nicolaus had already reached middle or even old age at the time he was instructed to translate Peter's work. This may be supported by the fact that Nicolaus's chronicle ends abruptly, suggesting that he may

have died while still working on it. Given that the last datable event mentioned in the text is the reconsecration of the church at Marienburg on 1 May
1344, it is reasonable to assume that he died shortly thereafter. We are completely in the dark as to his exact date of birth, but Helm and Ziesemer note
that Nicolaus seems to be far more versed—both literally and figuratively—
with the events in his chronicle that occurred after 1311, which may suggest
that his active engagement in the affairs of the order commenced around that
time. This thirty-odd years' activity in the order—from about 1311 to about
1344—probably means that he was born somewhere in the later decades of
the thirteenth century. See Helm and Ziesemer, *Literatur des deutschen Ritterordens*, 152–56; and Johansson, *Deutschordenschronik des Nicolaus von
Jeroschin*, 31.

71. Johansson, *Nicolaus von Jeroschin's Adalbert-Übersetzung*, 10.

72. An up-to-date list of manuscripts and fragments of the *KVP* can be
found in Päsler, *Deutschsprachige Sachliteratur*, 279–81. On the variations
between these, see Bartels and Wolf, "Neues zur Überlieferung," 302.

73. On the cult of the Virgin Mary in the newly Christianized Baltic
lands, see Bartlett, *Making of Europe*, 279.

74. *CTP* 94–95. Nicolaus includes the Virgin's diatribe against secular
literature in *KVP* ll. 10432–50.

75. It should be noted that the terms of love and love service Nicolaus
uses in this passage are also very common in the late medieval *Marienmys-
tik*, and that Nicolaus may here have drawn on traditional tropes of Mar-
ian devotion. Wenzel, however, dismisses this: "Bei der Schilderung dieser
Szene knüpft der Chronist jedoch keineswege direkt an die Formen der
Marienidolatrie an, die ihrerseits auf den Minnesang eingewirkt haben, er
stellt vielmehr den späteren Ordensbruder dar als vorbildlichen höfischen
Ritter im Dienst für seine (Minne-)Herrin." I agree that Nicolaus is in all
probability playing here upon the interests of the court rather than on those
of the cloister. Nicolaus aimed to reach as wide an audience of potential
Crusaders as possible; he therefore molded his message to appeal to lay
tastes. Consequently an allusion to chivalric romance is more likely, especially considering the apparently limited effect of Peter's more religiously
and thematically conservative original. See Wenzel, *Höfische Geschichte*,
41.

76. Wenzel, *Höfische Geschichte*, 41; and Fischer, *"Di Himels Rote,"* 137.

77. Fischer, *"Di Himels Rote,"* 137.

78. It must once again be noted that, as was the case with the Sarrazin
episode, most of this romance wording was added by Nicolaus: whereas the
KVP has "mit alsulchim trôste / sî lîblîch zu mir kôste: / 'Ô vil lîber kempfe
mîn," Peter's work has the rather more pithy "ait: tercia die morieris" [*CTP*
74: "she said: on the third day you will die"]. On courtly love for the Virgin
Mary, see also chapter 5.

79. Heng, *Empire of Magic*, 44.

80. The translation here is mine; Fischer has "freeing from their chains
the girls, women and children." Here and passim, her translation does not
render the implications of rank of "juncvrouwin" and "vrouwin."

81. Translation mine; Fischer has "he had taken around 1,300 girls, women and children prisoner and driven them off with him in chains."

82. Translation mine; Fischer has "finally he went to look at the many women and girls who stood pitifully bound before him."

83. Further instances can be found in ll. 7195–99, 8675–79, and 25800–25805. As Hodgson has pointed out, the practice of highlighting the vulnerability of women confronted by the non-Christian adversary was not wholly new: "The abuse of helpless Christians in the East was a common theme even in the earliest calls for crusade, and sometimes the suffering of women was used in order to appeal to the chivalric sensibilities of the nobility in the West." The consistency of Nicolaus's identification of the Christian victims as especially *aristocratic* women, however, is remarkable. See Hodgson, *Women, Crusading and the Holy Land*, 49.

84. Although it should be noted that the wider context does speak of "mulieres . . . cristiane" [*CTP* 176: "Christian women"].

85. Translation mine; Fischer has "Win your heavenly reward and avenge the humiliating chains, and may the degrading looks they cast on pure women and virgins be your spur to vengeance."

86. After the introduction in ll. 1–330, Nicolaus describes the events discussed by Peter in *capita* I.1–5 in ll. 331–1191, followed by those of IV.1–20 in ll. 1192–497, and those of II.1–13 in ll. 1498–3670. For roughly the next twenty thousand lines he moves back and forth between books III and IV: ll. 3671–5732 cover Peter's capita III.1–30; ll. 5733–864 capita IV.21–29; ll. 5865–9238 capita III.31–67; ll. 9239–728 capita IV.29–36; ll. 9729–15362 capita III.68–174; ll. 15363–802 capita IV.37–56; ll. 15803–8025 capita III.175–220; ll. 18026–295 capita IV.57–70; ll. 18296–21345 capita III.221–78; ll. 21346–2161 capita IV.73–88; ll. 22162–5171 capita III.279–338; ll. 25172–613 capita IV.89–125; and ll. 25614–6687 capita III.339–62. The final part, ll. 26688–7738, covers the events in addenda 1–20 to Peter's text and ends with a brief description of the reign of Grandmaster Lothar of Brunswick. While the work does not follow Peter's subdivision, Nicolaus does begin new parts at lines 1498 and 3671, i.e., after the events described in Peter's book I and the contemporaneous events from book IV; and again after the events described in book II.

87. My translation and italics. Fischer's translation ("Now I will set to rhyme, and while I am rhyming sort into the right order, and having put them in the right order, describe, and while I am describing them insert and order into this piece of writing all the popes and emperors there have been since the time that the Order of the German House was founded, on the basis of reliable documents; it is also probably right that I weave into the narrative some history of the entertaining events which happened in the world in their day and also what they themselves are known to have done") does not adequately render the important phrase "durch hovelîchiz sagin." See also *KVP* ll. 282–91: "Nû ist mîn sin darûf gekart, / daz ich daz teil wil mischin / den andren teilen zwischin / inhant der rede ein stucke / vlechtinde in ein lucke, / swâ daz ich dî gelege / gevûclich noch gewege, / sô daz diz und gene mêr / sich irvolgen î gewêr / an der zal der jâre" ["I have decided to insert section four [*sic*] into

the other sections, weaving it in wherever there is a suitable opportunity, so that all this information is presented in strict chronological order"] and *KVP* ll. 5733–738: "Nû sul wir hî vorzuckin, / dî rede lâzin nuckin / und abir her învlichtin / ein teil von den geschichtin, / dî nach der wârheit jên / in andrin landin sîn geschên" ["Here we are going to give the story a rest and weave in some of the events which, so true accounts tell us, were happening in other countries"].

88. Lot, *Lancelot en prose*, 17–28.

89. See Kullman, "Parallelhandlung in Epos und Roman."

90. Frye, *Secular Scripture*, 53.

91. Van D'Elden, *Peter Suchenwirt*, 96.

92. Van D'Elden, *Peter Suchenwirt*, 187–89.

93. Peter Suchenwirt, *Von Herzog Albrechts Ritterschaft*. All subsequent references to Peter's work will be to this edition. Translations are taken from Smith and Urban, "Peter von Suchenwirt." Both original text and translation will be cited in the text parenthetically.

94. Tinsley, "Romance of History," 129.

CHAPTER 7

1. Hippeau, *Chevalier au Cygne et Godefroi de Bouillon*, abbreviated to *CCGB*.

2. Boca, *Romans de Bauduin de Sebourc*, abbreviated to *BS*. All future references to *BS* are to this edition, and will be cited in the text parenthetically; the translations are my own.

3. Cook, *Bâtard de Bouillon*, abbreviated to *BB*. All future references to *BB* are to this edition, and will be cited in the text parenthetically; the translations are my own.

4. The best recent analysis of the Saladin material was made by Crist; see Cook and Crist, *Deuxième Cycle de la Croisade*, 51–182. See also Grillo, "Saladin Material." Abbreviated to *S*.

5. The Cycle "soit à cause de sa date tardive et de sa mauvaise réputation littéraire, soit à cause de sa longueur proprement rebutante, a été rarement etudié." Cook and Crist, *Deuxième Cycle de la Croisade*, 10.

6. There are two extant versions of *S*. One is found in the two manuscripts of the romance *Jehan d'Avesnes*, Arsenal 5208 and BN f.fr. 12572. The *Jehan d'Avesnes* manuscripts are compilations, containing *Jehan d'Avesnes* itself, *La Fille du Comte de Ponthieu*, and the *Saladin*; they are datable to ca. 1468. The second version is included in the *Histoire des Princes de Déols* of Jean of la Gogue; this latter is dated ca. 1482. See Cook and Crist, *Deuxième Cycle de la Croisade*, 61.

7. Claassens, "Status of the 'Deuxième Cycle de la Croisade'"; and Claassens, "Proto-Saladin."

8. Labande, *Étude sur Baudouin de Sébourc*, 63–66.

9. Labande, *Étude sur Baudouin de Sébourc*, 89.

10. Labande, *Étude sur Baudouin de Sébourc*, 115–21.

11. Labande, *Étude sur Baudouin de Sébourc*, 66–69.

12. Labande, *Étude sur Baudouin de Sébourc*, 75.

13. Labande, *Étude sur Baudouin de Sébourc*, 75.

14. The latter, "loin d'avoir eu, comme on le dit, *Baudouin de Sebourg* comme source, avait au contraire tracé le plan de ce poème et de ses suites"; see Duparc-Quioc, *Cycle de la Croisade*, 98.

15. Duparc-Quioc, *Cycle de la Croisade*, 118–40.

16. Duparc-Quioc, *Cycle de la Croisade*, 141.

17. Duparc-Quioc, *Cycle de la Croisade*, 127 and 155.

18. Cook and Crist, *Deuxième Cycle de la Croisade*, 44.

19. Cook and Crist, *Deuxième Cycle de la Croisade*, 45–46.

20. They go even further than Labande: "Par 'atelier' nous entendrions une 'corporation' de gens de lettres (écrivains, jongleurs, ménestrels) qui se connaissent et connaissent leurs œuvres respectives; qui peut-être même se communiqueraient mutuellement des 'bonnes feuilles,' qui se raconteraient des morceaux de leurs 'œuvres en chantier,' qui, tout au moins, pourraient assister à la lecture-récitation des œuvres des membres du 'groupe'; bref, des gens dont chacun serait au courant du travail de ses collègues." Cook and Crist, *Deuxième Cycle de la Croisade*, 93.

21. Cook and Crist, *Deuxième Cycle de la Croisade*, 153. Nevertheless, Cook, earlier in the text, suggests a composition in some form of S prior to that of *BB*, *BS*, and *CCGB*: "Le Saladin était connu et goûté, apparemment, des auteurs de tous les textes conservés, et une version de Saladin a dû précéder leurs poèmes." Cook and Crist, *Deuxième Cycle de la Croisade*, 44.

22. Only Janet F. van der Meulen has questioned the Hainault origins of the texts. She has suggested Bruges as the place of origin of *BS*. Departing from a curious hagiographic episode in *BS*, in which the protagonist's Saracen friend Polibant converts to Christianity and changes his name to become St. Brendan, she associates this and other instances of the text with elements of popular devotion and history in Bruges in the later fourteenth century, concluding that *BS* must be seen as having originated in a Bruges milieu ca. 1360–1370. I am inclined to argue against her view that even though Bruges is referred to habitually, and the count of Flanders himself ends up being one of the heroes of the work, the Flemish depicted in *BS* are seen as being as foreign a people as Cook says they are in *BB*. The author's sympathies lie with the French and against their Flemish enemies; indeed, it is his stated goal to tell a story "ch'est des fais d'outre-mer, et en sievant venra / Jusqu'au biau roy Phylippe qui les Flamens mata" [*BS* 2:263, ll. 436–37: "about the deeds across the sea, and will follow them up to fair King Philip, who killed the Flemish"]. A Hainault origin of *BS* therefore still seems most plausible. See van der Meulen, "Bruges, Brendan et Baudouin de Sebourc"; and *BB* lxi.

23. Geert H. M. Claassens has questioned whether, given Cook's theory of the origin of the works, we can genuinely speak of a second Crusade "cycle" to begin with. Defining a "cycle" as "a coherent collection of stories united by a central theme and brought together in a clear and stable narrative overall structure," he has stressed that the uncertainty of the connections between *BS*, *BB*, *CCGB*, and *S* weaken the case for regarding them as

a "Second Cycle" on a par with an authentic First Cycle. Claassens, "Cycle de la Croisade," 184.

24. Cook, "Crusade Propaganda," 161.

25. Suard, "Épopée française tardive," 454.

26. The later texts burnish their historical credentials with frequent and creative auctoritas commonplaces. See, for instance, BS 1:123, ll. 1–6 and 2:128, ll. 104–11.

27. It is this more than anything else that binds the works of the First Cycle to the fourteenth-century texts: "C'est le fil conducteur de l'idéologie qui relie entre elles les épopées de la croisade. . . . Ces textes incitent au respect envers les grands ancêtres croisés, et appellent directement ou indirectement à l'imitation de leurs gestes." See Cook, "Épopées de la croisade," 101–2.

28. See, e.g., BB ll. 132–37; and BS 2:394, l. 35.

29. For individual benefits, see, e.g., BB ll. 54–58. There is some creativity in the texts with regard to the advantages of fighting in the East, and BS sees the benefits of crusading as transferable. Where it was common knowledge that taking the cross was a way of saving one's own soul, the text makes it the salvation of not one but three souls. See BS 1:9, ll. 277–84.

30. See chapter 5 on the theme of the "Saracen princess."

31. Cook, "Idéologie de croisade," 138.

32. BS, incidentally, is neither the only nor the first work to refer to the historical Baldwin of Rethel or of Bourg, the third ruler of Jerusalem, as Baldwin of Sébourc. It follows a tradition going back to the version of the Continuations of the First Cycle found in ms. fr. 12569, held in the Bibliothèque Nationale. Grillo ascribes the use of "Sébourc" for "Bourg" not to harmless confusion resulting from homonymy but to conscious action. Nicholas of Fontaine, the bishop of Cambrai (1247–1272) and the probable patron of the manuscript, had become related through marriage to the family of Sébourc; consequently he "aurait cherché de la sorte à encourager personellement une habile exploitation des hauts faits légendaires à Jérusalem d'un preux nommé Baudouin de Sebourg. Fils donc de sa nouvelle famille par alliance, que d'autres rédacteurs n'hésiteront pas à identifier au deuxième roi du royaume latin." See Grillo, "Romans de Croisade," 393.

33. Cook and Crist, Deuxième Cycle de la Croisade, 139.

34. He is, for instance, referred to as "Gaufroi, le traïtour frarin" [BS 1:183, l. 217: "Godfrey, the miserable traitor"], a man who "Estoit tant hardis homs et de si haute emprise, / Qu'il n'avoit plus crueus de lui jusques en Pise" [BS 1:4, ll. 116–17: "was such a bold man and had such great power, that there was no man more ferocious between him and Pisa"].

35. This designation sticks throughout Baldwin's journeys. Later on he is called ".j. homme d'aventure, mais je ne sais son non; / Chevalier d'aventure enseïment l'apiell-on" [BS 1:267, ll. 11–12: "a man of adventure, but I do not know his name; everybody calls him the knight of adventure"]; "Chevalier d'aventure ensi l'apeloit-on" [BS 2:211, l. 902: "he is called the knight of adventure"]; while Baldwin refers to himself as ".j. hons sui d'aventure, qui par le païs va" [BS 1:309, l. 137: "I am a man of adventure, who travels throughout the country"].

36. *BS* 2:144, ll. 681–87. As discussed in chapter 5, a similar, though less sturdy animal briefly accompanies Gilles of Chin in *GDC*. On other helpful lions in Crusade sources, see Sweetenham and Patterson, *Canso d'Antioca*, 11–14; and Paul, *To Follow in Their Footsteps*, 86.

37. *BS* 2:145, ll. 700–705.

38. In the more forgiving words of Gerald Herman, "The author of Baudouin de Sebourc delights in portraying his protagonist as an ambivalent figure, midway, as it were, between the worlds of knight and churl, incorporating traits of each yet belonging to neither." Herman, "Fourteenth-Century Anti-Hero," 356.

39. *BS* 1:297, ll. 1068–73.

40. In rather elegant lines, he explains his departure to his wife Blanche by saying: "belle soer, je m'en vois / Vengier le mort de Dieu. Tant que je serai drois, / N'aront païen durée, ore ni autre fois" [*BS* 2:394, ll. 34–36: "Beautiful sister, I want to avenge the death of God. Inasmuch as I am just, the pagans will not get to keep their life, not now and not at any other time"].

41. See chapter 5.

42. This Ernoul is similar to the one avenged by Baldwin of Bauvais in *C*; see my chapter 4.

43. Monique Malfait-Dohet argues that this behavior is common to *all* bastards as represented in the Second Cycle. The Bastard of Bouillon as well as the Bastard of Sébourc, she suggests, are "très sensible aux insultes qui le rejettent dans leur bâtardise, surtout pointilleux quant à la moralité de leur mère," and "se définissent tous deux par l'excès et la démesure qui, s'ils ne sont pas une nouveauté dans le paysage épique, sont ici le reflet d'une hyperbole sociale." See Malfait-Dohet, "Fonction de la bâtardise," 175.

44. Before crossing the Red Sea, Baldwin I of Jerusalem says: "Dist li roys Bauduins: 'Ne sai qu'il m'avenra, / Mais je vaurrai nagier outre mer par dela / Pour savoir le païs, et quel gent il i a. / S'il i a Sarrasins, on les essillera: / . . . / Mais pour savoir que ch'est, li miens corps passera / A privee maisnie tant car on savera / Le deffense du lieu, et quelz gens il i a'" [*BB* ll. 3317–24: "King Baldwin says: 'I do not know what will happen to me, but I want to swim across that sea there, to know the country, and what people live there. If there are Saracens, then we will destroy them . . . but to know what it is, my body will go there with my very own companions, so that we may know the defenses of the place, and what kind of people are there'"].

45. The magical item or act that can only be appropriated by the finest of knights is a mainstay of Arthurian romance especially, and has its ultimate illustration in the Grail, which only the perfect Galahad will find. Other parallels include the Joy of the Court in Chrétien's *Erec* and the "Future Graveyard" in *Le Chevalier de la Charrette*. See Chrétien de Troyes, *Romans*, 255–56 and 553–55, respectively.

46. Malfait-Dohet remarks that, in contrast to their predecessors, a great many epic heroes of the fourteenth century—including the Bastard of Bouillon, a "héros peu sympathique, violent et faible fils d'une Sarrasine non convertie lors de la conception"—appear to abandon "le champ conceptuel pour

rejoindre une réalité socialle individuelle." See Malfait-Dohet, "Héros épique du XIVème siècle," 84.

47. Chrétien de Troyes, *Romans*, 973, ll. 1015–18. The translation is mine.

48. Cook, "Baudouin de Sébourc," 128. This connection between Baldwin and the East, on the one hand, and Yvain and the Arthurian realm, on the other, is expanded upon when the poet adds that the lion "si simple et fu si abatus / Que ne li fesist mal pour le trésor Artus" [*BS* 2:131, ll. 218–19: "was so humble and meek that he would not have hurt him [Baldwin] for all of Arthur's treasure"].

49. On the developing understanding of the East in late medieval Europe and its effect on literature, see Murrin, *Trade and Romance*, esp. 1–107.

50. Kibler, "'Chanson d'aventures.'"

51. Kibler, "'Chanson d'aventures,'" 510. Due to the greater occurrence of romance themes in the later chansons de geste, these were dismissed as decadent for much of the past century and a half. Cook has rightly pointed out, however, that "ce que nous qualifions de décadence fut un jour, un moment, dynamisme"; both he and Suard have advocated approaching the later chansons de geste not as pale shadows of the *Chanson de Roland* but as popular works attentive to contemporary stylistic and thematic taste; see Cook, "'Méchants Romans,'" 69; and Suard, "Épopée française tardive," 449–60. On the late medieval chansons de geste, see also Roussel, "Automne de la chanson de geste"; and Cook, "Unity and Esthetics."

52. Though its deployment in Crusade propaganda was initially hesitant, the association between Crusade and chivalric romance may have begun shortly after the origin of the genre; for instance, see chapter 5 on the *CJ*.

53. *Huon de Bordeaux* notably locates Huon's adventures and amorous exploits among the Saracens on Christianity's eastern frontier; see Burgwinkle, "Utopia and Its Uses," 546–47; and Sunderland, "Genre, Ideology, and Utopia." Similarly, "l'influence du roman sur *Tristan de Nanteuil* se fait particulièrement sentir dans le domaine central des rapports entre chrétiens et Sarrasins"; see Picherit, "Sarrasins dans *Tristan de Nanteuil*," 2:953.

54. Cook, "Arthurian Interlude," 93.

CHAPTER 8

1. Housley, *Later Crusades*, 15–16 and 58. The Hospitaller expedition of 1309–1310, which had included some forces sent by the papacy, was diverted to consolidate the order's hold over Rhodes; the League of 1334 managed to defeat the fleet of the Turkish emir of Karasi but then disintegrated.

2. Contemporary accounts estimate it at between twenty-four and twenty-seven galleys. See Atiya, *Crusade in the Later Middle Ages*, 293.

3. Atiya, *Crusade in the Later Middle Ages*, 301. It was immediately followed by a less successful campaign led by Humbert of Viennois, which only succeeded in fortifying the walls of Smyrna before being disbanded, and has been referred to as "one of the most pathetic crusade ventures of the period." See Housley, *Later Crusades*, 60.

4. In 1349, against the wishes of his father, he had boarded a galley sailing for the West to find the courts and wars of Europe. Atiya, *Crusade in the Later Middle Ages*, 321.

5. Atiya, *Crusade in the Later Middle Ages*, 324–25.

6. Pratt, *Chaucer and War*, 114.

7. Iorga, *Philippe de Mézières*, 124.

8. Atiya, *Crusade in the Later Middle Ages*, 324.

9. For details on the settlement, see Seward, *Hundred Years' War*, 99.

10. Atiya, *Crusade in the Later Middle Ages*, 330.

11. Iorga, *Philippe de Mézières*, 147–53.

12. Atiya, *Crusade in the Later Middle Ages*, 332. The unqualified support of the French monarch was a coup that would not be repeated at the other courts of Europe. In England, Peter was received honorably, but noncommittally, by Edward III, and in the Holy Roman Empire he received the same cordial but wary welcome from Emperor Charles IV. Iorga, *Philippe de Mézières*, 172–201; Luttrell, "English Levantine Crusaders," 146.

13. As to the variety of Crusaders, see Iorga, *Philippe de Mézières*, 278–80; and Luttrell, "English Levantine Crusaders."

14. The fleet has been estimated at 165 ships carrying up to ten thousand men and fourteen hundred horses. In addition to Peter's "own" European Crusaders and Cypriots, the Venetians, Genoans, and Hospitallers all contributed contingents. See Housley, *Later Crusades*, 40; Edbury, "Crusading Policy," 93; and Atiya, *Crusade in the Later Middle Ages*, 342–43.

15. The profit was enormous—up to seventy ships were laden to the brim with plunder, many so heavily that they were forced to jettison some of the cargo into Abukir Bay to avoid foundering. Atiya, *Crusade in the Later Middle Ages*, 366.

16. Iorga, *Philippe de Mézières*, 300–302.

17. Apparently his fame spread as far as Russia. See Bliznyuk, "Crusader of the Later Middle Ages," 52–53.

18. Atiya, *Crusade in the Later Middle Ages*, 373.

19. For an informative study of the events leading up to and including the king's brutal death, see Edbury, "Murder of King Peter I."

20. Hanly, "France," 153–54.

21. Guillaume de Machaut, *Prise d'Alixandre*, 3. All further references to the work, unless otherwise stated, will be to this edition, abbreviated to *PA*. Both the original text and the translation of Machaut's work are taken from this edition, and will be cited in the text parenthetically.

22. *PA* 4.

23. R. Barton Palmer suggests that "it may be that Machaut came to Jean's notice during one of the latter's sojourns in northern France, perhaps his visit to Reims for the coronation of Charles IV in 1322." In the *PA*, however, Machaut himself refers to his service with the king of Bohemia as follows: "je fus ses clers ans plus de .xxx. / si congnui ses meurs et sentente / sonneur son bien sa gentillesse / son hardement et sa largesse / car jestoie ses secretaires / en trestous ses plus gros affaires" [ll. 785–90: "I was his clerk for more than thirty years / And knew well his manner and his beliefs, / His honor, his virtue, his

gentility, / His courage and his generosity, / For I was then his secretary / In all his most important dealings"]. John of Bohemia died at Crécy in 1346, and it is possible that Machaut left his service even before that time. Consequently, unless Machaut is greatly exaggerating the duration of his employment, which is of course a possibility, the above appears to suggest that he entered the king's service far earlier than 1322. See *PA* 4.

24. *PA* 5.

25. *PA* 5.

26. Guillaume de Machaut, *Poésies lyriques*, xlv–xlvi.

27. Palmer, however, argues that "Machaut's association with the duke was perhaps much the same as the poet had enjoyed with Charles of Navarre; he served neither man as he had served the king of Bohemia, in whose household he was a constant and intimate presence." See *PA* 8.

28. *PA* 8. It has furthermore been suggested that Machaut, in addition to the *Dit de la Marguerite*, wrote another short poem, the complainte *Mon cuer, m'amour, ma dame souvereinne* for Peter. See Guillaume de Machaut, *Capture of Alexandria*, 9.

29. Lanoue, "Prise d'Alexandrie," 104.

30. Guillaume de Machaut, *Capture of Alexandria*, 9.

31. Although Machaut wrote the *Prise* rather late in life, it was the first time in his career that he tried his hand at history, and he appears to have approached the subject with some solemnity. See Calin, *Poet at the Fountain*, 204.

32. Calin, *Poet at the Fountain*, 204.

33. Calin, *Poet at the Fountain*, 205.

34. Calin, *Poet at the Fountain*, 204–5.

35. Lanoue, "Prise d'Alexandrie," 99.

36. Existing studies include Lanoue, "Prise d'Alexandrie"; Calin, *Poet at the Fountain*, 203–24; and Delogu, *Theorizing the Ideal Sovereign*, 92–123.

37. "The Prise d'Alexandrie, while it certainly contains some of the formal attributes of medieval chronicles, is essentially an epic designed to be read as useful history for a divided Europe tottering on the brink of modernity." Lanoue, "Prise d'Alexandrie," 108.

38. Lanoue, "Prise d'Alexandrie," 104.

39. Lanoue, "Prise d'Alexandrie," 105. Daisy Delogu, however, contends that Machaut's work, "while it celebrates crusade, also reveals its many shortcomings and limitations," and that Peter's dedication to Crusade is "precisely the characteristic that makes him unfit for ruling and surviving in his time." See Delogu, *Theorizing the Ideal Sovereign*, 122.

40. Calin, *Poet at the Fountain*, 217.

41. Calin, *Poet at the Fountain*, 217.

42. See also Calin, *Poet at the Fountain*, 214–15.

43. In the words of Calin, the *Prise* "to some extent follows the pattern of quest-romance. The protagonist desperately seeks to leave home in search of adventure." See, e.g., the description of Peter's first flight from Cyprus: "si se pensa quil partiroit / de son pais et quil iroit / en france pour honneur acquerre / car aussi y avoit il guerre / et pour

acointier les signeurs / les grans . les moiens . les meneurs / les chevaliers
les escuiers / les bourgois et les saudoiers / et pluseurs autres qui armer /
se vorroient outre la mer" [ll. 513–22: "And he determined that he'd quit
/ His own land and set out / For France in order to pursue honor / Since
war was also being waged there; / And in order to meet with the lords
too, / The great, the small, and those in-between, / The knights, the
squires, / Townspeople and soldiers, / As well as many others who might
be eager / To take up arms across the sea"]. Peter attempts to leave his
homeland and cross the Mediterranean to prove himself in war, to find
honor and possible allies for the struggle that he is even then planning.
His goals invoke those that drive the knights of romance forward—to
leave the security of home for a world of danger, to prove oneself and
to reinforce the values of chivalry and *courtoisie*. See Calin, *Poet at the
Fountain*, 218.

44. Calin, *Poet at the Fountain*, 215. Palmer associates this preponderance
of honor with the particular code of human behavior that underlies the *Prise*:
"for Machaut and Froissart, as for the men whose deeds they recounted, that
system of values of feudal chivalry was directed toward 'the personal honor
of the aristocrat.'" See *PA* 25.

45. Guillaume de Machaut, *Œuvres*, 40–42. The translation is my own.

46. This passage also touches on an important aspect of Machaut's doc-
trine: that the Crusade is not just where adventure and service to God can
be found together but rather is *the best* place on earth to find them. Brémont of la Voulte insists that there is "no destination better for the winning
of honor"; Peter of Lusignan too will insist that nowhere on earth is better
suited to that purpose when attempting to convince his men to stay and protect the newly conquered Alexandria from the encroaching Saracen forces:
"certeinnement je ne doubt mie / que cil ne doient acourir / qui vuelent a honneur venir / car il na en trestout le monde / tant comme il tient a la reonde /
place qui soit si honnourable / ne reputee si notable / comme est ceste place
ou nous sommes / je ne donroie pas .ii. pommes / de cuer . ou lonneur est si
morte / qui dou tenir ne se conforte / et qui seroit a pampelune / a bruges . a
gant . ou a brune / se deveroit il venir ci / et nous y sommes dieu mercy / tele-
ment . que vous en serez / toute vostre vie honnourez" [ll. 3460–76: "Certainly I don't doubt at all / That men eager for honor / Will hurry to our side.
/ For in all the world, / As far as it reaches in its compass, / There's no place so
full of honor, / Or reputed to be so notable / As the place where we are now.
/ I consider not worth two apples / The heart in which honor is so dead / It
does not rejoice in holding out. / And that man who would be at Pamplona,
/ At Bruges, at Ghent, at Bron, / He is bound to make the passage here. / We
are there already, God be thanked, / In such fashion that for it you'll be /
Honored [e]very day of your life"].

CONCLUSION

1. Chaucer, *Riverside Chaucer*, 342, ll. 1019–33.
2. Dimarco, "Historical Basis," 64.

3. On the Knight and the Crusade, see Vander Elst, "'Tu es pélérin en la sainte cité.'"

4. Chaucer, *Riverside Chaucer*, 24, ll. 86–88. On the Crusade of Bishop Despenser, see Housley, "Bishop of Norwich's Crusade"; and Magee, "Sir William Elmham."

5. Chaucer, *Riverside Chaucer*, 169, l. 9.

6. Chaucer, *Riverside Chaucer*, 170, l. 110.

7. Dimarco, "Historical Basis," 60.

8. Kahrl, "Chaucer's *Squire's Tale*," 196. On Prester John, and the longevity of his myth, see Housley, *Fighting for the Cross*, 257–59; and Housley, *Later Crusades*, 310.

9. Chaucer, *Riverside Chaucer*, 174, l. 409.

10. Mandeville, *Book of John Mandeville*, 35. The author here draws on Vincent of Beauvais; see Fyler, "Domesticating the Exotic," 37–38. Machaut refers to the Dry Tree in his *Dit dou Lion*; see my chapter 8.

11. Chaucer, *Riverside Chaucer*, 177, l. 668.

12. Braddy, "Two Chaucer Notes," 176–77.

13. Veszprémy, "Recent Hungarian Historiography," 224.

14. Atiya, *Crusade of Nicopolis*, 33.

15. Atiya, *Crusade in the Later Middle Ages*, 438.

16. Atiya, *Crusade of Nicopolis*, 67.

17. Housley estimates the amount of troops on both sides at around ten to twenty thousand. See Housley, *Later Crusades*, 76.

18. Atiya, *Crusade in the Later Middle Ages*, 445.

19. Atiya, *Crusade in the Later Middle Ages*, 447.

20. Housley, *Later Crusades*, 77.

21. Atiya, *Crusade of Nicopolis*, 98–112.

22. Atiya, *Crusade of Nicopolis*, 116.

23. On the Reconquista, see Housley, *Later Crusades*, 267–321; on the aftermath of the Battle of Tannenberg, and its effect on the German Order, see Housley, *Later Crusades*, 351–75.

24. Tasso, *Liberation of Jerusalem*.

25. Housley, *Later Crusades*, 127–30.

26. See Housley, *Later Crusades*, 204–33 and 140–42, respectively. With regard to the great naval victory at Lepanto, Housley adds: "It is undeniable that the victory boosted Christian morale and destroyed the myth of Ottoman invincibility. According to Cervantes, in *Don Quixote*, the battle 'revealed to all the nations of the world the error under which they had been labouring in believing that the Turks were invincible at sea.'" Housley, *Later Crusades*, 142.

27. It was first published six years later, in 1581; see Tasso, *Liberation of Jerusalem*, xiv.

28. Tasso, *Jerusalem Delivered*, x–xii.

29. The original Italian, here as well as below, is taken from Tasso, *Poesie*; the translation is taken from Tasso, *Liberation of Jerusalem*. For the sake of convenience, I will refer to the characters of the *Gerusalemme Liberata* with their Anglicized names in the pages below. See Tasso, *Poesie* 4; and Tasso, *Liberation of Jerusalem*, 4.

30. Tasso, *Liberation of Jerusalem*, viii–ix. The history of the First Crusade preoccupied Tasso for decades, and provided the material not only for *Gerusalemme Liberata* but also for *Rinaldo* (1562) and *Gerusalemme Conquistata* (1593). See Tasso, *Jerusalem Delivered*, ix.

31. On Tasso's notion of the "heroic poem," see Rhu, *Genesis of Tasso's Narrative Theory*, 99–153.

32. Tasso, *Poesie*, 20–21; and Tasso, *Liberation of Jerusalem*, 13–14.

33. Tasso, *Poesie*, 18; and Tasso, *Liberation of Jerusalem*, 12.

34. Armida is not the only Saracen magician; she is joined by the apostate Ismen: "Ismen, che trar di sotto a i chiusi marmi / Può corpo estinto e far che spiri e senta, / Ismen che al suon de mormoranti carmi / sin ne la reggia sua Pluton spaventa, / e i suoi demon ne gli empi uffici impiega / pur come servi e li discioglie e lega." ["Ismen, that sorcerer whose might / makes marble vaults yield up their corpses, who / can charm new breath into them and new sight; / Ismen whose murmured spells will fright Hell's crew / and Dis himself, whose fiends he conjures still / for cursed tasks, and chains or frees at will"]. Tasso, *Poesie*, 32; and Tasso, *Liberation of Jerusalem*, 22.

35. Tasso, *Poesie*, 531; and Tasso, *Liberation of Jerusalem*, 398. Erminia, who bears an unreciprocated love for Tancredo, becomes a Christian as well.

36. See, e.g., Scott, *Talisman*; on Scott, see Riley-Smith, *Crusades, Christianity, and Islam*, 63–67.

PRIMARY SOURCES

Albert of Aachen. *Historia Ierosolimitana: History of the Journey to Jerusalem.* Trans. and ed. Susan B. Edgington. Oxford: Oxford University Press, 2007.

Allen, S. J., and Emilie Amt, eds. *The Crusades: A Reader.* Toronto: University of Toronto Press, 2003.

Ambroise. *The History of the Holy War: Ambroise's Estoire de la Guerre Sainte.* 2 vols. Trans. Marianne Ailes. Ed. Marianne Ailes and Malcolm Barber. Woodbridge: Boydell Press, 2003.

Andreas Capellanus. *The Art of Courtly Love.* Trans. and ed. John Jay Parry. New York: Columbia University Press, 1960.

Baldric of Bourgueil. *The Historia Ierosolimitana of Baldric of Bourgueil.* Ed. Steven J. Biddlecombe. Woodbridge: Boydell Press, 2014.

Barber, Malcolm, and Keith Bate, trans. and eds. *Letters from the East: Crusaders, Pilgrims and Settlers in the 12th–13th Centuries.* Farnham: Ashgate, 2010.

Bédier, Joseph, ed. *La Chanson de Roland.* Paris: L'édition d'Art H. Piazza, 1960.

Boca, Louis N., ed. *Li Romans de Bauduin de Sebourc, IIIe roy de Jhérusalem: Poème du XIVe siècle publié pour la première fois d'après les manuscrits de la Bibliothèque Nationale.* 2 vols. Valenciennes: B. Henry, 1841.

Burgess, Glyn S., trans. and ed. *The Song of Roland.* London: Penguin, 1990.

Chaucer, Geoffrey. *The Riverside Chaucer.* Ed. Larry D. Benson. Boston: Houghton Mifflin, 1987.

Chrétien de Troyes. *Romans: Suivis des Chansons avec, en appendice, Philomena.* N.p.: Librairie Générale Française, 1994.

Combarieu du Grès, Micheline de, and Gérard Gourian, eds. *La Chanson de Girart de Roussillon.* Paris: Librairie Générale Française, 1993.

Conon de Béthune. *Chansons de Conon de Béthune*. Ed. Axel Wallensköld. Helsingfors: Imprimerie Centrale de Helsingfors, 1891.

Cook, Robert Francis, ed. *Le Bâtard de Bouillon: Chanson de geste*. Geneva: Librairie Droz, 1972.

Crawford, Paul, trans. and ed. *The "Templar of Tyre": Part III of the "Deeds of the Cypriots."* Aldershot: Ashgate 2003.

Duparc-Quioc, Suzanne, ed. *La Chanson d'Antioche*. 2 vols. Paris: Paul Guethner, 1978.

Edgington, Susan B., and Carol Sweetenham, trans. and eds. *The Chanson d'Antioche: An Old French Account of the First Crusade*. Farnham: Ashgate, 2011.

Fulcher of Chartres. *A History of the Expedition to Jerusalem, 1095–1127*. Trans. Francis Rita Ryan. Ed. Harold S. Fink. New York: W. W. Norton, 1973.

Gautier de Tournay. *L'histore de Gille de Chyn by Gautier de Tournay*. Ed. Edwin B. Place. New York: AMS Press, 1970.

Geoffroi de Charny. *The Book of Chivalry of Geoffroi de Charny: Text, Context, and Translation*. Trans. and ed. Richard W. Kaeuper and Elspeth Kennedy. Philadelphia: University of Pennsylvania Press, 1996.

Gower, John. *The Complete Works of John Gower*. 4 vols. Ed. G. C. Macaulay. Oxford: Clarendon Press, 1899–1902.

———. *Mirour de l'Omme*. Trans. and ed. William Burton Wilson and Nancy Wilson Van Baak. East Lansing: Colleagues Press, 1992.

Guibert of Nogent. *Gesta Dei per Francos*. In *Recueil des Historiens des Croisades*, 4:117–263. Paris: Imprimerie Nationale, 1879.

Guillaume de Machaut. *The Capture of Alexandria*. Trans. and ed. Janet Shirley and Peter Edbury. Aldershot: Ashgate, 2001.

———. *Œuvres*. Ed. Prosper Tarbé. Geneva: Slatkine Reprints, 1977.

———. *Poésies lyriques: Édition complète en deux parties, avec introduction, glossaire et fac-similés*. Vol. 1. Ed. Vladimir Chichmaref. Geneva: Slatkine Reprints, 1973.

———. *La Prise d'Alixandre*. Trans. and ed. R. Barton Palmer. New York and London: Routledge, 2002.

Guiot de Dijon et Jocelin. *Les chansons attribuées à Guiot de Dijon et Jocelin*. Ed. Elisabeth Nissen. Paris: Librairie Honoré Champion, 1928.

Hagenmeyer, Heinrich, ed. *Anonymi gesta Francorum et aliorum Hierosolymitanorum: Mit Erläuterungen herausgegeben*. Heidelberg: Carl Winter's, 1890.

Hill, Rosalind, trans. and ed. *Gesta Francorum et aliorum Hierosolimitanorum*. Edinburgh: Thomas Nelson and Sons, 1962.

Hippeau, C., ed. *La Chanson du Chevalier au Cygne et de Godefroid de Bouillon*. Paris: A. Aubry, 1874–1877.

Joinville and Villehardouin. *Chronicles of the Crusades*. Trans. and ed. Caroline Smith. London: Penguin, 2008.

Konrad der Pfaffe. *Priest Konrad's Song of Roland*. Trans. and ed. J. W. Thomas. Columbia, SC: Camden House, 1994.

Lalande, Denis, ed. *Le livre des fais du bon messire Jehan le Maingre, dit Bouciquaut, mareschal de France et gouverneur de Jennes*. Geneva: Librairie Droz, 1985.

Le Person, Marc, ed. *Fierabras: Chanson de geste du XIIe siècle*. Paris: Honoré Champion, 2003.

Mandeville, John, Sir. *The Book of John Mandeville*. Ed. Tamarah Kohanski and C. David Benson. Kalamazoo: Medieval Institute Publications, 2007.

Marcabru. *Marcabru: A Critical Edition*. Ed. Simon Gaunt, Ruth Harvey, and Linda Paterson. Cambridge: D. S. Brewer, 2000.

Mickel, Emanuel J., ed. *The Old French Crusade Cycle*. Vol. *3, Les Enfances Godefroi and Le Retour de Cornumarant*. Tuscaloosa: University of Alabama Press, 1999.

Mickel, Emanuel J., Jr., and Jan A. Nelson, eds. *The Old French Crusade Cycle*. Vol. *1, La Naissance du Chevalier au Cygne*. Tuscaloosa: University of Alabama Press, 1977.

Myers, Geoffrey M., ed. *The Old French Crusade Cycle*. Vol. *5, Les Chétifs*. University: University of Alabama Press, 1981.

Nelson, Jan A., ed. *The Old French Crusade Cycle*. Vol. *2, Le Chevalier au Cygne and La Fin d'Elias*. University: University of Alabama Press, 1985.

Nelson, Jan A., ed. *The Old French Crusade Cycle*. Vol. *4, La Chanson d'Antioche*. Tuscaloosa: University of Alabama Press, 2003.

Nicholson, Helen J., trans. and ed. *The Chronicle of the Third Crusade: The Itinerarium Peregrinorum et Gesta Regis Ricardi*. Aldershot: Ashgate, 1997.

Nicolaus von Jeroschin. *The Chronicle of Prussia by Nicolaus von Jeroschin: A History of the Teutonic Knights in Prussia, 1190–1331*. Trans. and ed. Mary Fischer. Farnham: Ashgate, 2010.

———. *Di Krônike von Prûzinlant*. In *Scriptores rerum Prussicarum: Die Geschichtsquellen der preussischen Vorzeit bis zum Untergange der Ordensherrschaft*, ed. Theodor Hirsch, Max Töppen, and Ernst Strehlke, 1:303–624. Leipzig: S. Hirzel, 1861.

Orderic Vitalis. *The Ecclesiastical History of Orderic Vitalis*. 6 vols. Ed. Marjorie Chibnall. Oxford: Oxford University Press, 1983.

Peter of Duisburg. *Chronica Terre Prussie*. In *Scriptores rerum Prussicarum: Die Geschichtsquellen der preussischen Vorzeit bis zum Untergange der*

Ordensherrschaft, ed. Theodor Hirsch, Max Töppen, and Ernst Strehlke, 1:21–219. Leipzig: S. Hirzel, 1861.

Peter Suchenwirt. *Von Herzog Albrechts Ritterschaft*. In *Scriptores rerum Prussicarum: Die Geschichtsquellen der preussischen Vorzeit bis zum Untergange der Ordensherrschaft*, ed. Theodor Hirsch, Max Töppen, and Ernst Strehlke, 2:161–69. Leipzig: S. Hirzel, 1863.

Peters, Edward, ed. *The First Crusade: The Chronicle of Fulcher of Chartres and Other Source Materials*. Philadelphia: University of Pennsylvania Press, 1998.

Petrus Tudebodus. *Historia de Hierosolymitano itinere*. Trans. and ed. John H. Hill and Laurita L. Hill. Philadelphia: American Philosophical Society, 1974.

Philippe de Mézières. *Le Songe du Vieil Pelerin*. 2 vols. Ed. G. W. Coopland. London: Cambridge University Press, 1969.

Ralph of Caen. *The Gesta Tancredi of Ralph of Caen: A History of the Normans on the First Crusade*. Trans. and ed. Bernard S. Bachrach and David S. Bachrach. Aldershot: Ashgate 2010.

Raymond d'Aguilers. *Historia Francorum qui ceperunt Iherusalem*. Trans. and ed. John Hugh Hill and Laurita L. Hill. Philadelphia: American Philosophical Society, 1968.

Robert of Reims. *The Historia Iherosolimitana of Robert the Monk*. Ed. D. Kempf and M. G. Bull. Woodbridge: Boydell Press, 2013.

———. *Robert the Monk's History of the First Crusade: Historia Iherosolimitana*. Trans. and ed. Carol Sweetenham. Aldershot: Ashgate, 2005.

Scott, Walter, Sir. *The Talisman*. Norwalk, CT: Easton Press, 1976.

Shirley, Janet, trans. and ed. *The Song of the Cathar Wars: A History of the Albigensian Crusade*. Aldershot: Scolar Press, 1996.

Sweetenham, Carol, and Linda M. Patterson, trans. and eds. *The Canso d'Antioca: An Occitan Epic Chronicle of the First Crusade*. Aldershot: Ashgate, 2003.

Tasso, Torquato. *Jerusalem Delivered*. Trans. and ed. Ralph Nash. Detroit: Wayne State University Press, 1987.

———. *The Liberation of Jerusalem*. Trans. Max Wickert. Oxford: Oxford University Press, 2009.

———. *Poesie*. Ed. Francesco Flora. Milan: Riccardo Ricciardi, 1952.

Thibaut de Champagne. *The Lyrics of Thibaut de Champagne*. Trans. and ed. Kathleen J. Brahney. New York: Garland, 1989.

Thorp, Nigel R., ed. *The Old French Crusade Cycle. Vol. 6, La Chanson de Jérusalem*. Tuscaloosa: University of Alabama Press, 1992.

SECONDARY WORKS

Ailes, Marianne. "Ambroise's *Estoire de la Guerre Sainte* and the Development of a Genre." *Reading Medieval Studies* 34 (2008): 1–19.

———. "Faith in *Fierabras*." In *Charlemagne in the North: Proceedings of the Twelfth International Conference of the Société Rencesvals, Edinburgh, 4th to 11th August 1991*, ed. Philip E. Bennett, Anne Elizabeth Cobby, and Graham A. Runnals, 125–33. Edinburgh: Société Rencesvals British Branch, 1993.

Albu, Emily. "Probing the Passions of a Norman on Crusade: The *Gesta Francorum et Aliorum Hierosolimitanorum*." In *Anglo-Norman Studies XVII: Proceedings of the Battle Conference 2004*, ed. John Gillingham, 1–15. Woodbridge: Boydell Press, 2005.

Allmand, Christopher. *The Hundred Years War: England and France at War c. 1300–c. 1450*. Cambridge: Cambridge University Press, 1988.

Asbridge, Thomas. *The First Crusade: A New History*. Oxford: Oxford University Press, 2004.

Ashe, Laura. "The Ideal of Knighthood in English and French Writing, 1100–1230: Crusade, Piety, Chivalry and Patriotism." In *Writing the Early Crusades: Text, Transmission and Memory*, ed. Marcus Bull and Damian Kempf, 155–68. Woodbridge: Boydell Press, 2014.

———. "'A Prayer and a Warcry': The Creation of a Secular Religion in the Song of Roland." *Cambridge Quarterly* 28, no. 4 (1999): 349–67.

Atiya, A. S. *The Crusade in the Later Middle Ages*. London: Methuen, 1938.

———. *The Crusade of Nicopolis*. London: Methuen, 1934.

Auerbach, Erich. *Mimesis*. Princeton: Princeton University Press, 1953.

Barber, Malcolm. *The Crusader States*. New Haven: Yale University Press, 2012.

Barber, Richard, and Juliet Barker. *Tournaments: Jousts, Chivalry and Pageants in the Middle Ages*. New York: Weidenfeld and Nicolson, 1989.

Bartels, Ulrich, and Jürgen Wolf. "Neues zur Überlieferung der 'Kronike von Pruzinlant' des Nikolaus von Jeroschin." *Zeitschrift für deutsches Altertum und deutsche Literatur* 127, no. 3 (1998): 299–306.

Bartlett, Robert. *The Making of Europe: Conquest, Colonization and Cultural Change 950–1350*. Princeton: Princeton University Press, 1993.

Bédier, Joseph. *Les légendes épiques: Recherches sur la formation des chansons de geste*. 4 vols. Paris: Librairie Honoré Champion, 1908–1913.

Bennett, Matthew. "First Crusaders' Images of Muslims: The Influence of Vernacular Poetry?" *Forum for Modern Language Studies* 22, no. 2 (April 1986): 101–22.

Biddlecombe, Steven. "Baldric of Bourgueil and the *Familia Christi*." In

Writing the Early Crusades: Text, Transmission and Memory, ed. Marcus Bull and Damien Kempf, 9–23. Woodbridge: Boydell Press, 2014.

Bliznyuk, Svetlana. "A Crusader of the Later Middle Ages: King Peter I of Cyprus." In *The Crusades and the Military Orders: Expanding the Frontiers of Medieval Latin Christianity*, ed. Zsolt Hunyadi and József Laszlovszky, 51–57. Budapest: Central European University, Department of Medieval Studies, 2001.

Bloch, R. Howard. *Etymologies and Genealogies: A Literary Anthropology of the French Middle Ages*. Chicago: University of Chicago Press, 1983.

Braddy, Haldeen. "Two Chaucer Notes." *Modern Language Notes* 62, no. 3 (March 1947): 173–79.

Bréhier, Louis. *L'église et l'Orient au Moyen Âge: Les croisades*. Paris: Librairie Victor Lecoffre, 1907.

Brett, Edward Tracy. *Humbert of Romans: His Life and Views of Thirteenth-Century Society*. Toronto: Pontifical Institute of Mediaeval Studies, 1984.

Bruckner, Matilda Tomaryn. "The Shape of Romance in Medieval France." In *The Cambridge Companion to Medieval Romance*, ed. Roberta L. Krueger, 13–28. Cambridge: Cambridge University Press, 2000.

Buc, Philippe. *Holy War, Martyrdom, and Terror: Christianity, Violence, and the West, ca. 70 C.E. to the Iraq War*. Philadelphia: University of Pennsylvania Press, 2015.

Bull, Marcus. *Knightly Piety and the Lay Response to the First Crusade: The Limousin and Gascony, c. 970–1130*. Oxford: Clarendon Press, 1993.

———. "Overlapping and Competing Identities in the Frankish First Crusade." In *Le concile de Clermont de 1095 et l'appel à la croisade: Actes du Colloque International de Clermont-Ferrand (23–25 juin 1995) organisé et publié avec le concours du Conseil Régional d'Auvergne*, 195–211. Rome: École française de Rome, 1997.

Bull, Marcus, and Damien Kempf. "Introduction." In *Writing the Early Crusades: Text, Transmission and Memory*, ed. Marcus Bull and Damien Kempf, 1–8. Woodbridge: Boydell Press, 2014.

Burgwinkle, William. "Utopia and Its Uses: Twelfth-Century Romance and History." *Journal of Medieval and Early Modern Studies* 36, no. 3 (Fall 2006): 539–60.

Calin, William. *A Muse for Heroes: Nine Centuries of the Epic in France*. Toronto: University of Toronto Press, 1983.

———. *A Poet at the Fountain: Essays on the Narrative Verse of Guillaume de Machaut*. Lexington: University Press of Kentucky, 1974.

Christiansen, Eric. *The Northern Crusades: The Baltic and the Catholic Frontier 1100–1525*. London: Macmillan, 1980.

Claassens, Geert H. M. "The Cycle de la Croisade: Vernacular Historiography." In *Cyclification: The Development of Narrative Cycles in the Chansons de Geste and the Arthurian Romances*, ed. Bart Besamusca, Willem P. Gerritsen, Corry Hogetoorn, and Orlanda S. H. Lie, 184–88. Amsterdam: North-Holland, 1994.

———. "Some Notes on the Proto-Saladin." In *Aspects de l'épopée romane: Mentalités, idéologies, intertextualités*, ed. Hans van Dijk and Willem Noomen, 131–40. Groningen: Forsten, 1995.

———. "The Status of the 'Deuxième Cycle de la Croisade': A Preliminary Note." *Olifant* 17, no. 3–4 (1992–1993): 119–33.

Cline, Ruth Huff. "The Influence of Romances on Tournaments of the Middle Ages." *Speculum* 20, no. 2 (April 1945): 204–11.

Cohen, Jeffrey J. *Medieval Identity Machines*. Minneapolis: University of Minnesota Press, 2003.

Cook, Robert Francis. "The Arthurian Interlude in the *Bâtard de Bouillon*." In *Conjunctures: Medieval Studies in Honor of Douglas Kelly*, ed. Keith Busby and Norris J. Lacy, 87–95. Amsterdam: Rodopi, 1994.

———. "*Baudouin de Sébourc*: Un poème édifiant?" *Olifant* 14, no. 2 (Summer 1989): 115–35.

———. *Chanson d'Antioche, chanson de geste: Le cycle de la croisade est-il épique?* Amsterdam: John Benjamins, 1980.

———. "Crusade Propaganda in the Epic Cycles of the Crusade." In *Journeys Towards God: Pilgrimage and Crusade*, ed. Barbara N. Sargent-Bauer, 157–75. Kalamazoo: Medieval Institute Publications, 1992.

———. "Les épopées de la croisade." In *Aspects de l'épopée romane: Mentalités, idéologies, intertextualités*, ed. Hans van Dijk and Willem Noomen, 93–110. Groningen: Forsten, 1995.

———. "Idéologie de croisade et thématique courtoise dans les dernières épopées de la croisade." In *Les épopées de la croisade: Premier colloque international (Trèves, 6–11 août 1984)*, ed. Karl-Heinz Bender and Hermann Kleber, 132–38. Stuttgart: Franz Steiner, 1987.

———. "'Méchants romans' et épopée française: Pour une philologie profonde." *L'esprit créateur* 23 (Spring 1983): 64–74.

———. "Unity and Esthetics of the Late Chansons de Geste." *Olifant* 11, no. 2 (Summer 1986): 103–14.

Cook, Robert Francis, and Larry S. Crist. *Le deuxième cycle de la croisade: Deux études sur son développement*. Geneva: Librairie Droz, 1972.

Cowell, Andrew. *The Medieval Warrior Aristocracy: Gifts, Violence, Performance, and the Sacred*. Cambridge: D. S. Brewer, 2007.

Daniel, Norman. *Heroes and Saracens: A Re-Interpretation of the Chansons de Geste*. Edinburgh: Edinburgh University Press, 1984.

Delogu, Daisy. *Theorizing the Ideal Sovereign: The Rise of the French Vernacular Royal Biography*. Toronto: University of Toronto Press, 2008.

Dembowski, Peter F. *Jean Froissart and His Meliador: Context, Craft, and Sense*. Lexington: French Forum, 1983.

Dimarco, Vincent J. "The Historical Basis of Chaucer's Squire's Tale." In *Chaucer's Cultural Geography*, ed. Kathryn L. Lynch, 56–75. New York: Routledge, 2002.

Duparc-Quioc, Suzanne. *Le cycle de la croisade*. Paris: Librairie Ancienne, 1955.

Edbury, Peter W. "The Crusading Policy of King Peter I of Cyprus, 1359–1369." In *The Eastern Mediterranean Lands in the Period of the Crusades*, ed. P. M. Holt, 90–105. Warminster: Aris and Phillips, 1977.

———. "The Murder of King Peter I of Cyprus (1359–1369)." *Journal of Medieval History* 6, no. 2 (1980): 219–33.

Erdmann, Carl. *The Origin of the Idea of Crusade*. Trans. and ed. Marshall W. Baldwin and Walter Goffart. Princeton: Princeton University Press, 1977.

Feil, Josef. "Über die altesten St. Georgsritter in Österreich oder die Gesellschaft der Tempelaise." *Österreichische Blätter für Literatur, Kunst, Geschichte, Geographie, Statistik und Naturkunde* 5 (1848): 217–48.

Fischer, Mary. "Des tûvils kint? The German Order's Perception of Its Enemies as Revealed in the *Krônike von Prûzinlant*." *Archiv für das Studium der Neueren Sprachen und Literaturen* 244:159, no. 2 (2007): 260–75.

———. *"Di Himels Rote": The Idea of Christian Chivalry in the Chronicles of the Teutonic Order*. Göppingen: Kümmerle, 1991.

Flori, Jean. *Chroniqueurs et propagandistes: Introduction critique aux sources de la première croisade*. Geneva: Librairie Droz, 2010.

———. "Guerre sainte et rétributions spirituelles dans la 2e moitié du XIe siècle: Lutte contre l'Islam ou pour la Papauté?" *Revue d'histoire ecclésiastique* 85, no. 3 (July 1990): 617–49.

Frye, Northrop. *The Secular Scripture: A Study of the Structure of Romance*. Cambridge, MA: Harvard University Press, 1976.

Fuchs, Barbara. *Romance*. New York: Routledge, 2004.

Fyler, John M. "Domesticating the Exotic in the Squire's Tale." In *Chaucer's Cultural Geography*, ed. Kathryn L. Lynch, 32–55. New York: Routledge, 2002.

Gabriele, Matthew. *An Empire of Memory: The Legend of Charlemagne, the Franks, and Jerusalem before the First Crusade*. Oxford: Oxford University Press, 2011.

Garrison, Mary. "The Franks as the New Israel? Education for an Identity from Pippin to Charlemagne." In *The Uses of the Past in the Early Middle*

Ages, ed. Yitzhak Hen and Matthew Innes, 114–61. Cambridge: Cambridge University Press, 2000.

Gaunt, Simon. *Retelling the Tale: An Introduction to Medieval French Literature.* London: Duckworth, 2001.

———. "Romance and Other Genres." In *The Cambridge Companion to Medieval Romance*, ed. Roberta L. Krueger, 45–59. Cambridge: Cambridge University Press, 2000.

———. *Troubadours and Irony.* Cambridge: Cambridge University Press, 1983.

Gillingham, John. *Richard I.* New Haven: Yale University Press, 1999.

Grégoire, Henri, and Raoul de Keyser. "La *Chanson de Roland* et Byzance, ou de l'utilité du Grec pour les romanistes." *Byzantion* XIV (1939): 265–315.

Grillo, Peter R. "Romans de croisade, histoires de famille: Recherches sur le personnage de Baudouin de Sebourg." *Romania* 110, no. 3–4 (1989): 383–95.

———. "The Saladin Material in the Continuations of the First Crusade Cycle." In *Aspects de l'épopée romane: Mentalités, idéologies, intertextualités*, ed. Hans van Dijk and Willem Noomen, 159–66. Groningen: Forsten, 1995.

Guard, Timothy. *Chivalry, Kingship and Crusade: The English Experience in the Fourteenth Century.* Woodbridge: Boydell Press, 2013.

Hanly, Michael. "France." In *A Companion to Chaucer*, ed. Peter Brown, 149–66. Oxford: Blackwell, 2000.

Hardman, Phillipa, and Marianne Ailes. "Crusading, Chivalry and the Saracen World in Insular Romance." In *Christianity and Romance in Medieval England*, ed. Rosalind Field, Phillipa Hardman, and Michelle Sweeney, 45–65. Cambridge: D. S. Brewer, 2010.

Helm, Karl, and Walter Ziesemer. *Die Literatur des deutschen Ritterordens.* Gießen: Wilhelm Schmitz, 1951.

Heng, Geraldine. *The Empire of Magic.* New York: Columbia University Press, 2003.

Herman, Gerald. "A Fourteenth-Century Anti-Hero: Baudouin de Sebourc." *Romance Notes* 15, no. 2 (1973): 355–60.

Hodgson, Natasha R. *Women, Crusading and the Holy Land in Historical Narrative.* Woodbridge: Boydell Press, 2007.

Holmes, Urban Tigner, Jr. *A History of Old French Literature, From the Origins to 1300.* New York: Russel and Russel, 1962.

Housley, Norman. "The Bishop of Norwich's Crusade, May 1383." *History Today* 33, no. 5 (1983): 15–20.

———. *Contesting the Crusades*. Malden, MA: Blackwell, 2006.

———. *Fighting for the Cross: Crusading to the Holy Land*. New Haven: Yale University Press, 2008.

———. *The Later Crusades: From Lyons to Alcazar 1274–1580*. Oxford: Oxford University Press, 1992.

Innes, Paul. *Epic*. Abingdon: Routledge, 2013.

Iorga, Niculae. *Philippe de Mézières 1327–1405*. Paris: Librairie Émile Bouillon, 1896.

Janet, Magali. *L'idéologie incarnée: Représentations du corps dans le premier cycle de la croisade (Chanson d'Antioche, Chanson de Jérusalem, Chétifs)*. Paris: Honoré Champion, 2013.

Jacoby, David. "Knightly Values and Class Consciousness in the Crusader States of the Eastern Mediterranean." *Mediterranean Historical Review* 1, no. 2 (1986): 158–86.

———. "La littérature française dans les états latins de la méditerannée orientale à l'époque des croisades: Diffusion et création." In *Essor et fortune de la chanson de geste dans l'Europe et l'Orient latin. Actes du IXe congrès international de la Société Rencesvals pour l'étude des épopées romanes, Padoue-Venise, 29 août–4 septembre 1982*, 2:617–46. Modena: Mucchi, 1984.

Jefferson, Lisa. "Tounaments, Heraldry, and the Knights of the Round Table: A Fifteenth-Century Armorial with Two Accompanying Texts." In *Arthurian Literature XIV*, ed. James P. Carley and Felicity Riddy, 69–157. Cambridge: D. S. Brewer, 1996.

Johansson, Evald. *Die Deutschordenschronik des Nicolaus von Jeroschin*. Lund: C. W. K. Gleerup, 1964.

———. *Studien zu Nicolaus von Jeroschin's Adalbert-Übersetzung*. Lund: C. W. K. Gleerup, 1967.

Jones, Catherine M. *An Introduction to the Chansons de Geste*. Gainesville: University Press of Florida, 2014.

Jordan, William Chester. "The Representation of the Crusades in the Songs attributed to Thibaud, Count Palatine of Champagne." *Journal of Medieval History* 25, no. 1 (1999): 27–34.

Kaeuper, Richard. *Chivalry and Violence in Medieval Europe*. Oxford: Oxford University Press, 1999.

———. *Holy Warriors: The Religious Ideology of Chivalry*. Philadelphia: University of Pennsylvania Press, 2009.

———. "The Societal Role of Chivalry in Romance: Northwestern Europe." In *The Cambridge Companion to Medieval Romance*, ed. Roberta L. Krueger, 97–114. Cambridge: Cambridge University Press, 2000.

Kahrl, Stanley J. "Chaucer's *Squire's Tale* and the Decline of Chivalry." *Chaucer Review* 7, no. 3 (1972): 194–209.

Kangas, Sini. "Inimicus Dei et Sanctae Christianitatis? Saracens and Their Prophet in Twelfth-Century Crusade Propaganda and Western Travesties of Muhammad's Life." In *The Crusades and the Near East*, ed. Conor Kostick, 131–60. London: Routledge, 2011.

Kantorowicz, Ernst Hartwig. *Laudes Regiae*. Berkeley: University of California Press, 1958.

Kay, Sarah. *The Chansons de Geste in the Age of Romance: Political Fictions*. Oxford: Clarendon Press, 1995.

———. "Courts, Clerks, and Courtly Love." In *The Cambridge Companion to Medieval Romance*, ed. Roberta L. Krueger, 81–96. Cambridge: Cambridge University Press, 2000.

Keen, Maurice. "Chaucer's Knight, the English Aristocracy, and the Crusade." In *English Court Culture in the Later Middle Ages: Papers from the Colston Research Society Symposium*, ed. V. J. Scattergood and J. W. Sherbourne, 45–61. London: Duckworth, 1983.

———. *Chivalry*. New Haven: Yale University Press, 1984.

Kempf, Damien. "Towards a Textual Archaeology of the First Crusade." In *Writing the Early Crusades: Text, Transmission and Memory*, ed. Marcus Bull and Damien Kempf, 116–26. Woodbridge: Boydell Press, 2014.

Kennedy, Elspeth. "The Knight as Reader of Arthurian Romance." In *Culture and the King: The Social Implications of the Arthurian Legend, Essays in Honor of Valerie M. Lagorio*, ed. Martin B. Shichtman and James P. Carley, 70–90. Albany: State University of New York Press, 1994.

Kibler, William W. "La 'chanson d'aventures.'" In *Essor et fortune de la chanson de geste dans l'Europe et l'Orient latin. Actes du IXe congrès international de la Société Rencesvals pour l'étude des épopées romanes, Padoue-Venise, 29 août–4 septembre 1982*, 2:509–15. Modena: Mucchi, 1984.

Kilgour, R. L. *The Decline of Chivalry as Shown in the French Literature of the Late Middle Ages*. Cambridge, MA: Harvard University Press, 1937.

Kinoshita, Sharon. "Crusades and Identity." In *The Cambridge History of French Literature*, ed. William Burgwinkle, Nicholas Hammond, and Emma Wilson, 93–101. Cambridge: Cambridge University Press, 2011.

———. *Medieval Boundaries: Rethinking Difference in Old French Literature*. Philadelphia: University of Pennsylvania Press, 2006.

Kleber, Hermann. "Graindor de Douai: Remanieur—auteur—mécène?" In *Les épopées de la croisade*, ed. Karl-Heinz Bender, 66–75. Stuttgart: Franz Steiner, 1987.

———. "Pèlerinage—vengeance—conquête. La conception de la première croisade dans le cycle de Graindor de Douai." In *Au carrefour des routes d'Europe: La chanson de geste*, 2:757–75. Aix-en-Provence: Publications du CUER MA, Université de Provence, 1987.

Kostick, Conor. "A Further Discussion of the Authorship of the *Gesta Francorum*." *Reading Medieval Studies* 35 (2009): 1–14.

Kreem, Juhan. "The Teutonic Order in Livonia: Diverging Historiographic Traditions." In *The Crusades and the Military Orders: Expanding the Frontiers of Medieval Latin Christianity*, ed. Zsolt Hunyadi and József Laszlovszky, 467–79. Budapest: Central European University Department of Medieval Studies, 2001.

Kullman, Dorothea. "Frühe Formen der Parallelhandlung in Epos und Roman: Zu den Voraussetzungen von Chrétiens *Conte du Graal*." In *Erzählstrukturen der Artusliteratur: Forschungsgeschichte und neue Ansätze*, ed. Friedrich Wolfzettel and Peter Ihring, 23–45. Tübingen: Niemeyer, 1999.

Labande, E. R. *Étude sur Baudouin de Sébourc*. Paris: Librairie E. Droz, 1940.

Lachet, Claude. "'À la griffe on reconnâit le lion': Quelques échos du *Chevalier au Lion* dans les romans en vers des XIIIe et XIVe siècles." In *L'œuvre de Chrétien de Troyes dans la littérature française: Reminiscences, resurgences et réécritures. Actes du colloque (23 et 24 mai 1997)*, ed. Claude Lachet, 73–86. Lyon: Université Jean Moulin Lyon 3, 1997.

Lanoue, D. G. "*La Prise d'Alexandrie*: Guillaume de Machaut's Epic." *Nottingham Medieval Studies* 29 (1985): 99–108.

Leverage, Paula. *Reception and Memory: A Cognitive Approach to the Chansons de Geste*. Amsterdam: Rodopi, 2010.

Lloyd, Simon. *English Society and the Crusades 1216–1307*. Oxford: Clarendon Press, 1988.

Loomis, Roger Sherman. "Arthurian Influence on Sport and Spectacle." In *Arthurian Literature in the Middle Ages: A Collaborative History*, ed. Roger Sherman Loomis, 553–63. Oxford: Clarendon Press, 1959.

Lot, Ferdinand. *Étude sur le Lancelot en prose*. Paris: Édouard Champion, 1918.

Luttrell, Anthony. "English Levantine Crusaders, 1363–1367." *Renaissance Studies: Journal of the Society for Renaissance Studies* 2, no. 2 (October 1988): 143–53.

Magee, James. "Sir William Elmham and the Recruitment for Henry Despenser's Crusade of 1383." *Medieval Prosopography* 20 (1999): 181–90.

Maier, Christoph. *Crusade Propaganda and Ideology: Model Sermons for the Preaching of the Cross.* Cambridge: Cambridge University Press, 2000.

Malfait-Dohet, Monique. "La fonction de la bâtardise dans la définition du héros épique du deuxième cycle de la croisade." In *Aspects de l'épopée romane: Mentalités, idéologies, intertextualités,* ed. Hans van Dijk and Willem Noomen, 167–76. Groningen: Forsten, 1995.

———. "Le héros épique du XIVème siècle est-il l'image archaique d'un monde qui s'efface ou le reflet d'un monde nouveau?" In *Nouveaux mondes et mondes nouveaux au Moyen Âge: Actes du colloque du centre d'études médiévales de l'université de Picardie Jules Verne, Amiens, mars 1992,* ed. Danielle Buschinger and Wolfgang Spiewok, 73–85. Greifswald: Reineke, 1994.

Mayer, Hans Eberhard. *The Crusades.* Oxford: Oxford University Press, 1988.

Morris, Colin. "The *Gesta Francorum* as Narrative History." *Reading Medieval Studies* 19 (1993): 55–71.

Moyen, Philippe. "'Tournois grans et pleniers, grant tournoiement et tornoy': La hiérarchie des tournois dans *La Chanson de Gilles de Chin.*" *Cahiers du centre d'histoire médiévale* 2 (2003): 21–29.

Murphy, G. Ronald. *Gemstone of Paradise: The Holy Grail in Wolfram's Parzifal.* Oxford: Oxford University Press, 2006.

Murrin, Michael. *Trade and Romance.* Chicago: University of Chicago Press, 2013.

Naus, James. "The *Historia Iherosolimitana* of Robert the Monk and the Coronation of Louis VI." In *Writing the Early Crusades: Text, Transmission and Memory,* ed. Marcus Bull and Damien Kempf, 105–15. Woodbridge: Boydell Press, 2014.

Ní Chléirigh, Léan. "*Nova Peregrinatio*: The First Crusade as a Pilgrimage in Contemporary Latin Narratives." In *Writing the Early Crusades: Text, Transmission and Memory,* ed. Marcus Bull and Damien Kempf, 63–74. Woodbridge: Boydell Press, 2014.

Nicholson, Helen J. *Love, War, and the Grail: Templars, Hospitallers, and Teutonic Knights in Medieval Epic and Romance 1150–1500.* Leiden: Brill, 2004.

O'Donohue, Bernard. *The Courtly Love Tradition.* Manchester: Manchester University Press, 1982.

Paravicini, Werner. *Die Preußenreisen des europäischen Adels.* 2 vols. Sigmaringen: Thorbecke, 1989.

———. *Die ritterlich-höfische Kultur des Mittelalters.* Munich: R. Oldenbourg, 1994.

Päsler, Ralf G. *Deutschsprachige Sachliteratur im Preußenland bis 1500: Untersuchungen zu ihrer Überlieferung*. Cologne: Bohlau, 2003.

Paris, Alexis-Paulin. *Nouvelles études sur la Chanson d'Antioche*. Paris: L. Techener, 1878.

Paris, Gaston. *Histoire poétique de Charlemagne*. Paris: Librairie A. Franck, 1865.

———. Review of *La Tapisserie de Bayeux: Étude archéologique et critique*, by Albert Marignan. *Romania* 31 (1902): 404–19.

Paul, Nicholas L. *To Follow in Their Footsteps: The Crusades and Family Memory in the High Middle Ages*. Ithaca: Cornell University Press, 2012.

———. "A Warlord's Wisdom: Literacy and Propaganda at the Time of the First Crusade." *Speculum* 85, no. 3 (2010): 534–66.

Pearsall, Derek. *Arthurian Romance: A Short Introduction*. Malden, MA: Blackwell, 2003.

Petit, Aimé. "Les reminiscences littéraires dans les *Gilles de Chin* en vers et en prose." In *Mettre en prose aux XIVe–XVe siècles*, ed. Maria Colombo Timelli, Barbara Ferrari, and Anne Schoysman, 197–213. Turnhout: Brepols, 2010.

Phillips, Jonathan. *The Second Crusade: Extending the Frontiers of Christendom*. New Haven: Yale University Press, 2007.

Picherit, Jean-Louis. "Les Sarrasins dans *Tristan de Nanteuil*." In *Au carrefour des routes d'Europe: La chanson de geste*, 2:941–57. Aix-en-Provence: Publications du CUER MA, Université de Provence, 1987.

Pratt, John H. *Chaucer and War*. Lanham, MD: University Press of America, 2000.

Prawer, Joshua. *Crusader Institutions*. Oxford: Oxford University Press, 1980.

———. *The World of the Crusaders*. New York: Quadrangle Books, 1972.

Prestwich, Michael. *Edward I*. London: Methuen, 1988.

———. *The Three Edwards: War and State in England, 1272–1377*. London: Routledge, 2003.

Purkis, William J. "Rewriting the History Books: The First Crusade and the Past." In *Writing the Early Crusades: Text, Transmission and Memory*, ed. Marcus Bull and Damien Kempf, 140–54. Woodbridge: Boydell Press, 2014.

Queller, Donald E., and Thomas F. Madden. *The Fourth Crusade: The Conquest of Constantinople*. Philadelphia: University of Pennsylvania Press, 1999.

Rhu, Lawrence F. *The Genesis of Tasso's Narrative Theory: English Transla-*

tions of the Early Poetics and a Comparative Study of Their Significance. Detroit: Wayne State University Press, 1993.

Richard, Jean. "L'arrière-plan historique des deux cycles de la croisade." In *Les épopées de la croisade: Premier colloque international (Trèves, 6–11 août 1984)*, ed. Karl-Heinz Bender and Hermann Kleber, 6–16. Stuttgart: Franz Steiner, 1987.

Riley-Smith, Jonathan. *The Crusades: A Short History.* New Haven: Yale University Press, 1987.

———. *The Crusades, Christianity, and Islam.* New York: Columbia University Press, 2008.

———. "Crusading as an Act of Love." In *The Crusades: The Essential Readings*, ed. Thomas F. Madden, 31–50. Oxford: Blackwell, 2002.

———. "Family Traditions and Participation in the Second Crusade." In *The Second Crusade and the Cistercians*, ed. Michael Gervers, 101–8. New York: St. Martin's Press, 1992.

———. *The First Crusade and the Idea of Crusading.* Philadelphia: University of Pennsylvania Press, 1983.

———. *The First Crusaders, 1095–1131.* Cambridge: Cambridge University Press, 1997.

Roussel, Claude. "L'automne de la chanson de geste." *Cahiers de recherches médiévales* 12 (2005): 15–28.

Rousset, Paul. *Les origines et les caractères de la première croisade.* Neuchâtel: Le Baconnière, 1945.

Routledge, Michael. "Songs." In *The Oxford Illustrated History of the Crusades*, ed. Jonathan Riley-Smith, 91–111. Oxford: Oxford University Press, 1995.

Rubenstein, Jay. *Armies of Heaven: The First Crusade and the Quest for Apocalypse.* New York: Basic Books, 2011.

———. "Guibert of Nogent, Albert of Aachen and Fulcher of Chartres: Three Crusade Chronicles Intersect." In *Writing the Early Crusades: Text, Transmission and Memory*, ed. Marcus Bull and Damien Kempf, 24–37. Woodbridge: Boydell Press, 2014.

Runciman, Steven. *A History of the Crusades. Vol. 1, The First Crusade and the Foundation of the Kingdom of Jerusalem.* Cambridge: Cambridge University Press, 1952.

———. *A History of the Crusades. Vol. 2, The Kingdom of Jerusalem and the Frankish East, 1100–1187.* Cambridge: Cambridge University Press, 1952.

Schein, Sylvia. *Fideles Crucis: The Papacy, The West, and the Recovery of the Holy Land 1274–1314.* Oxford: Clarendon Press, 1991.

———. *Gateway to the Heavenly Jerusalem: Crusader Jerusalem and the Catholic West (1099–1187)*. Aldershot: Ashgate, 2005.

Schulze-Busacker, Elizabeth. "L'expression de la foi dans les chansons de geste." In *Charlemagne in the North: Proceedings of the Twelfth International Conference of the Société Rencesvals, Edinburgh, 4th to 11th August 1991*, ed. Philip E. Bennett, Anne Elizabeth Cobby, and Graham A. Runnals, 103–24. Edinburgh: Société Rencesvals British Branch, 1993.

Seward, Desmond. *The Hundred Years' War: The English in France 1337–1453*. Harmondsworth: Penguin, 1999.

Siberry, Elizabeth. "Criticism of Crusading in Fourteenth-Century England." In *Crusade and Settlement: Papers Read at the First Conference of the Society for the Study of the Crusades and the Latin East and Presented to R. C. Smail*, ed. Peter W. Edbury, 127–34. Cardiff: University College Cardiff Press, 1985.

Smail, Daniel Lord, and Kelly Gibson, eds. *Vengeance in Medieval Europe: A Reader*. Toronto: University of Toronto Press, 2009.

Smith, Caroline. *Crusading in the Age of Joinville*. Aldershot: Ashgate, 2006.

Smith, Jerry, and William Urban. "Peter von Suchenwirt." *Lituanus* 31, no. 2 (Summer 1985): 5–26.

Spiegel, Gabrielle. *Romancing the Past: The Rise of Vernacular Prose Historiography in Thirteenth-Century France*. Berkeley: University of California Press, 1993.

Strayer, J. R. *The Reign of Philip the Fair*. Princeton: Princeton University Press, 1980.

Strehlke, Ernst. "Einleitung." In *Scriptores rerum Prussicarum: Die Geschichtsquellen der Preussischen Vorzeit bis zum Untergange der Ordensherrschaft*, ed. Theodor Hirsch, Max Töppen, and Ernst Strehlke, 1:291–302. Leipzig: S. Hirzel, 1861.

Strickland, Debra Higgs. *Saracens, Demons, and Jews: Making Monsters in Medieval Art*. Princeton: Princeton University Press, 2003.

Suard, François. *La chanson de geste*. Paris: Presses Universitaires de France, 1993.

———. "L'épopée française tardive (XIVe–XVe s.)." In *Études de philologie romane et d'histoire littéraire offertes à Jules Horrent à l'occasion de son soixantième anniversaire*, ed. Jean-Marie d'Heur and Nicoletta Cherubini, 449–60. Liège: N.p., 1980.

Sunderland, Luke. "Genre, Ideology, and Utopia in *Huon de Bordeaux*." *Medium Aevum* 81, no. 2 (2012): 289–302.

———. *Old French Narrative Cycles: Heroism Between Ethics and Morality*. Woodbridge: D. S. Brewer, 2010.

Sweetenham, Carol. "Antioch and Flanders: Some Reflections on the Writing of the Chanson d'Antioche." In *Epic and Crusade: Proceedings of the Colloquium of the Société Rencesvals, British Branch, Held at Lucy Cavendish College, Cambridge, 27–28 March 2004*, ed. Philip E. Bennett, Anne E. Cobby, and Janet E. Everson, 131–51. Edinburgh: Société Rencesvals British Branch, 2006.

Thorp, Nigel. "La *Chanson de Jérusalem* and the Latin Chronicles." In *Epic and Crusade: Proceedings of the Colloquium of the Société Rencesvals, British Branch, Held at Lucy Cavendish College, Cambridge, 27–28 March 2004*, ed. Philip E. Bennett, Anne E. Cobby, and Janet E. Everson, 153–71. Edinburgh: Société Rencesvals British Branch, 2006.

Throop, Susanna A. *Crusading as an Act of Vengeance, 1095–1216*. Aldershot: Ashgate, 2011.

———. "Zeal, Anger and Vengeance: The Emotional Rhetoric of Crusading." In *Vengeance in the Middle Ages: Emotion, Religion and Feud*, ed. Susanna A. Throop and Paul R. Hyams, 177–201. Farnham: Ashgate, 2010.

Throop, Susanna A., and Paul R. Hyams, eds. *Vengeance in the Middle Ages: Emotion, Religion, and Feud*. Farnham: Ashgate, 2010.

Tinsley, David F. "The Romance of History in Peter Suchenwirt's *Herzog Albrechts Ritterschaft*." *Medieval Perspectives* 6 (1991): 122–34.

Tolan, John V. *Saracens: Islam in the Medieval European Imagination*. New York: Columbia University Press, 2002.

———. *Sons of Ishmael: Muslims Through European Eyes in the Middle Ages*. Gainesville: University Press of Florida, 2008.

Töppen, Max. "Einleitung." In *Scriptores rerum Prussicarum: Die Geschichtsquellen der Preussischen Vorzeit bis zum Untergange der Ordensherrschaft*, ed. Theodor Hirsch, Max Töppen, and Ernst Strehlke, 1:3–20. Leipzig: S. Hirzel, 1861.

Trotter, David A. *Medieval French Literature and the Crusades (1100–1300)*. Geneva: Librairie Droz, 1988.

———. "La mythologie arthurienne et la prédication de la croisade." In *Pour une mythologie du Moyen Âge*, ed. Laurence Harf-Lancner and Dominique Boutet, 155–77. Paris: École Normale Supérieure de Jeunes Filles, 1988.

Tyerman, Christopher. *England and the Crusades 1095–1588*. Chicago: University of Chicago Press, 1988.

———. *The Invention of the Crusades*. Toronto: University of Toronto Press, 1998.

Urban, William. *The Baltic Crusade*. Chicago: Lithuanian Research and Studies Center, 1994.

————. *The Prussian Crusade*. Lanham, MD: University Press of America, 1980.

————. *The Samogitian Crusade*. Chicago: Lithuanian Research and Studies Center, 1989.

Vale, Juliet. "Arthur in English Society." In *The Arthur of the English*, ed. W. R. J. Barron, 185–96. Cardiff: University of Wales Press, 1999.

Van D'Elden, Stephanie Cain. *Peter Suchenwirt and Heraldic Poetry*. Vienna: Karl M. Halosar, 1976.

Vander Elst, Stefan. "'Tu es pélérin en la sainte cité': Chaucer's Knight and Philippe de Mézières." *Studies in Philology* 106, no. 4 (Fall 2009): 379–401.

van der Meulen, Janet F. "Bruges, Brendan et Baudouin de Sebourc," *Queeste* 3, no. 1 (1996): 1–17.

Verbruggen, J. F. *The Art of Warfare in Western Europe During the Middle Ages from the Eighth Century to 1340*. Trans. Sumner Willard and R. W. Southern. Woodbridge: Boydell Press, 1997.

Veszprémy, László. "Some Remarks on Recent Hungarian Historiography of the Crusade of Nicopolis (1396)." In *The Crusades and the Military Orders: Expanding the Frontiers of Medieval Latin Christianity*, ed. Zsolt Hunyadi and József Laszlovszky, 223–30. Budapest: Central European University, Department of Medieval Studies, 2001.

Wenzel, Horst. *Höfische Geschichte*. Bern: Peter Lang, 1980.

Willard, Charity Cannon. "Gilles de Chin in History, Literature, and Folklore." In *The Medieval Opus: Imitation, Rewriting, and Transmission in the French Tradition. Proceedings of the Symposium held at the Institute for Research in Humanities, October 5–7, 1995, The University of Wisconsin-Madison*, ed. Douglas Kelly, 357–66. Amsterdam: Rodopi, 1996.

Wolf, Kenneth Baxter. "Crusade and Narrative: Bohemond and the *Gesta Francorum*." *Journal of Medieval History* 17 (1991): 207–16.

ACKNOWLEDGMENTS

During the writing of this book I have incurred debts that I will never be able to fully repay. First and foremost, I would like to thank John V. Fleming, William C. Jordan, and Janet M. Martin of Princeton University, who first introduced me to the propaganda of the Crusades in the later Middle Ages, and who helped me develop an extraneous idea into a working hypothesis. I benefited from the kindness and generosity of a great many people as I expanded this hypothesis into the present volume. Abraham Stoll provided sage advice and good company throughout the writing process. Emily Albu, Renate Blumenfeld-Kosinski, Cynthia Caywood, Ann Hutchison, Joseph McGowan, and Derek Pearsall read early versions of the chapters and offered insightful feedback. Thomas Barton, Geert Claassens, Brian Clack, Christopher Davis, Maura Giles-Watson, Michael Hanly, William D. Paden, Fred Robinson, and Sr. Elizabeth Walsh helped me think through historical and philological puzzles. I sincerely thank my *commilitones* in the English Department at the University of San Diego for providing a collegial and productive working environment, and the staff at Copley Library for their help in locating and acquiring sources often long out of print. The indexing was supported by a grant from the College of Arts and Sciences at the University of San Diego, for which I am grateful to Dean Noelle Norton and Perla Myers.

A happy year spent as a fellow at the Pontifical Institute of Mediaeval Studies in Toronto allowed me to access the holdings at the Institute Library, as well as to enjoy the learning of Fred Unwalla and Jonathan Black. I thank the Pontifical Institute for granting me permission to include, in chapter 6, a revised version of my "Chivalry, Crusade, and Romance on the Baltic Frontier," *Mediaeval Studies*

73 (2011): 287–328 (© 2012 by the Pontifical Institute of Mediaeval Studies, Toronto).

At the University of Pennsylvania Press, I would like to thank Jerome E. Singerman, who is as helpful and forgiving an editor as one could wish, as well as Noreen O'Connor-Abel, Tim Roberts, and Hannah Blake. I am furthermore grateful to Helen Nicholson and Luke Sunderland, who reviewed the manuscript and made perceptive and valuable recommendations. Without them this book would not be what it is.

I am, of course, deeply indebted to friends and family members for being their gracious selves in these past years. Among too many to include them all, special mention goes to Padhraig Higgins, Philo Juang, Christoph Machiels, Quinton Mayne, Andrea Nazarian, André and Seza Nazarian, Michael Nazarian, Juliet O'Brien, Michael Onofrio, Kevin Osterloh, Amanda Petersen, Atreyee Phukan, Rima Rantisi, Mark Rowe, John Pedro Schwartz, and Michelle Wright.

I would furthermore like to extend my deepest gratitude to my grandmother, Maria De Keyzer-Dubois; to my sister, Marjan Vander Elst; to my beloved parents and allies, Charles and Agnes Vander Elst-De Keyzer; and to the brilliant Cynthia Nazarian, without whom nothing would ever get done.